UNCONVENTIONAL
WARFARE

THE REDISCOVERING GOVERNMENT SERIES
Center for Public Management

Unconventional Warfare: Rebuilding U.S. Special Operations Forces
Susan L. Marquis

UNCONVENTIONAL
WARFARE

*Rebuilding U.S. Special
Operations Forces*

SUSAN L. MARQUIS

BROOKINGS INSTITUTION PRESS
Washington, D.C.

Library of Congress Cataloging-in-Publication data

Marquis, Susan L. (Susan Lynn), 1960–
    Unconventional warfare : rebuilding U.S. special operations forces
/ Susan L. Marquis.
        p.   cm.
    Includes bibliographical references and index.
    ISBN 0-8157-5476-0 (alk. paper). — ISBN 0-8157-5475-2 (alk.
paper)
    1. Special forces (Military science)—United States.   2. United
States—Politics and government—20th century.   I. Title.
    UA34.S64M37   1997
    356'.16—dc21   96-53963
                                                            CIP

The paper used in this publication meets the minimum requirements of the
American National Standard for Information Sciences—Permanence of Paper
for Printed Library Materials, ANSI Z39.48-1984

Set in Garamond

Composition by Cynthia Stock
Silver Spring, Maryland

Digital printing
Manufactured in the United States of America

For
Chris and Kevin

Foreword

Following every war for the past fifty years, U.S. special operations forces—despite their wartime accomplishments and between-the-war usefulness—have been cut back to the bare bones. Almost completely deactivated after Vietnam, special operations forces found new life in the wake of a relatively small, failed mission—the April 1980 hostage rescue attempt in the Iranian desert. That tragic event triggered a resurgence of political advocacy for rebuilding and reequipping special operations forces, a task that took almost a decade to accomplish. Today those forces comprise U.S. Army Special Forces, U.S. Navy SEALs, U.S. Air Force special operations air crews and Special Tactics Group, U.S. Army Rangers, and civil affairs and psychological operations units. This book is the story of how a community of believers, in and out of the military, marshaled political and bureaucratic resources to fight and win a battle in the corridors of the Pentagon and on Capitol Hill to ensure that the United States had the force it would need to meet the emerging low-intensity conflict threats of the late twentieth century.

Susan Marquis, a Brookings Institution Center for Public Management fellow and a senior civilian official in the Department of Defense, tells this story based on first-person interviews and Department of Defense documents and in the context of ongoing military operations—Urgent Fury, Just Cause, Desert Shield and Desert Storm, and others. She shows how a handful of advocates, some imbued with the tenacity and self-assurance gained in the distinctive organizational culture of special operations, successfully turned the slow, resistant wheels of government to protect the precarious value of a strong U.S. special operations capability. Marquis, relying on her own experience in the arcane process of Pentagon resource allocation, also demonstrates how the work of legislation is only the beginning of the long, equally hard fight for successful implementation of policy.

Unconventional Warfare: Rebuilding U.S. Special Operations Forces is the first volume in the Rediscovering Government series of the Brookings Institution's Center for Public Management. The series, coedited by John J. DiIulio Jr., Douglas Dillon nonresident senior fellow, Center for Public Management, and Donald F. Kettl of the University of Wisconsin at Madison, seeks to promote civic education about the crucial administrative dimensions of public policy. How a policy is implemented is at least as important to citizens as how policies are debated and enacted. The Rediscovering Government series will produce a body of reliable work about what public leadership and management strategies work best, under what conditions, and at what human and financial costs.

Susan Marquis thanks the special operations community for the access they provided throughout her research for this book, especially Lieutenant Colonel (ret.) Jim Crawford, John Partin, General (ret.) Carl Stiner, and General (ret.) Wayne Downing. She also thanks David Chu, Michael Parmentier, and Kathi Webb, who taught her much about intelligent and tenacious opposition. Rear Admiral Ray Smith, Jim Locher, Noel Koch, and Lieutenant General (ret.) Sam Wilson were generous with their time and encouragement. Colonel Corson L. "Corky" Hilton and Rear Admiral Irve "Chuck" LeMoyne, both recently deceased, offered invaluable insights into what it means to be a special operator. Finally, many members of the SEALs, Special Forces, Air Force special operations, and civil affairs and psychological operations units gave demonstrations and tours of their equipment, aircraft, firing ranges, boats, ships, and simulators. The author appreciates their efforts to provide her with as thorough an understanding of U.S. special operations forces as can be had by an outsider.

The author is most grateful for the assistance, enthusiasm, and unflagging support of John DiIulio Jr. and William O'Neill. Donald F. Kettl, Colonel Clint Anker, and Stephen Rosen offered valuable suggestions on the manuscript. Theresa Walker edited the manuscript, Fred Dews and Tara Adams Ragone verified it, Carlotta Ribar proofread it, and Julia Petrakis prepared the index.

The project was supported by the Ford Foundation, and Brookings gratefully acknowledges that support.

The views expressed in this book are solely those of the author and should not be ascribed to the Department of Defense, to organizations whose assistance is acknowledged above, or to the trustees, officers, or staff members of the Brookings Institution.

February 1997   MICHAEL H. ARMACOST
Washington, D.C.   *President*

Contents

Chapter 1   Introduction   1

Chapter 2   A Precarious Value   6
    The U.S. Army's Special Forces / 8
    Underwater Demolition Teams and SEALs / 20
    Air Commandos and the U.S. Air Force / 28
    Into the Abyss: SOF and the Post-Vietnam Era / 33

Chapter 3   Survival of a Precarious Value   44
    Building an Organizational Culture / 44
    Selection, Training, and Assessment: Navy SEALs / 48
    Special Forces: Innovation in the Face of Uncertainty / 52
    Flip Corkin and the Air Commandos / 55
    Maintaining a Distinctive Organization / 57

Chapter 4   Protecting a Precarious Value   60
    Naval Special Warfare: Reconnecting to the Fleet / 65
    Surviving the 1970s / 68
    The Tragedy of Desert One / 69
    Revitalizing Special Operations: First Steps / 73
    Air Force Special Operations and Desert One / 75
    Hopes Rise: The Struggle for Reform / 79
    Congressional Support Grows / 86
    Protecting a Still-Precarious Value / 89

Chapter 5   Urgent Fury   91

Chapter 6   Legislating Change   107
    Building the Case for Reform on Capitol Hill / 107
    Inside the Pentagon / 112
    Going Public / 116
    Heading toward Legislated Reform / 127
    Loss of a General / 132
    Department of Defense: Too Little, Too Late / 134
    Division on the Hill / 140
    Nunn-Cohen Amendment to the 1986 Defense
        Reorganization Act / 144

Chapter 7   The New Bureaucrats   148
    Setting Up Shop / 149
    Washington, D.C., or the Ends of the Earth? / 151
    Who Are Special Operations Forces? / 154
    Special Operations Command Begins Work / 162
    The New Special Operations Bureaucrats / 165

Chapter 8   Malicious Implementation?   170
    Implementation / 173
    Confusion and the Office of the Assistant Secretary
        of Defense / 176
    Secretary Marsh and the First Confirmed ASD (SOLIC) / 179
    Capitol Hill Comes to the Pentagon / 181
    Peacetime Engagement / 184
    A Special Operator's War—Operation Just Cause / 187
    Operation Promote Liberty / 201

Chapter 9   Who's in Charge?   203
    The Fight to Control Resources / 203
    The Department of Defense / 206
    Controlling SOF Resources / 208
    The View from USSOCOM / 214
    Congress Says "Enough!" / 217

Chapter 10   Desert Shield and Desert Storm   227
    SOF Integration with Conventional Forces / 230
    Desert Storm / 236
    The End of the War and Operation Provide Comfort / 244

Chapter 11   Moving Forward   250
        The Collapse of the Berlin Wall and the New World
            Disorder / 250
        Special Operations Forces Today / 255
        Guaranteeing a Future / 256
        A Road Map / 257
        Service Concerns versus Operational Concerns / 258
        The Risks to SOF Organizational Culture / 261
        Protecting a Precarious Value / 263

Notes   271

Index   307

1

Introduction

Fifty-three staff members of the American embassy in Tehran were captured by radical supporters of Imam Ayatollah Khomeni on November 4, 1979. Soon after, the U.S. government started to put together a rescue team. Because the United States did not have a standing joint counterterrorist task force, the rescue team was made from scratch. It took six months of planning and training before the rescue, designated Operation Rice Bowl, was attempted. The U.S. Army's newly created Delta force had the mission of assaulting the American embassy in Tehran and rescuing the hostages. The U.S. Navy provided aircraft carriers to transport troops and tactical aircraft to the Indian Ocean, including its RH-53D Sea Stallion helicopters. These minesweeping helicopters, forced into action because the U.S. Air Force did not have special operations helicopters capable of the mission, would carry the assault force from the Iranian desert into Tehran. True to the ad hoc nature of the rescue operation, the Marine Corps pilots were flying the navy helicopters since there were no navy pilots qualified to perform a mission of this length over land. The U.S. Air Force provided C-130 transport and tanker aircraft and crews. Virtually none of these forces had worked with the others before.

On April 24, 1980, Delta troops and combat control teams (CCTs) loaded on the air force MC-130s to make the low-level flight into a staging area in Iran's remote Das-a-Kafir desert. The staging area, referred to as Desert One, was necessary because navy helicopters did not have the range to reach Tehran and were not air refuelable. All the C-130s eventually landed safely at Desert One, and there they awaited the arrival of the navy helicopters. The helicopters were not so lucky. On the flight to meet Delta, one Sea Stallion was abandoned in the desert after an indicator light warned of a rotor blade problem, and a second helicopter returned to the aircraft carrier with a malfunctioning gyroscope. After the six remaining helicopters arrived as much as eighty minutes late for their rendezvous, crew members declared a third helicopter disabled and out of action

1

when they discovered one of its hydraulic pumps burned out after a leak in the line. The task force was now down to five operational helicopters, one less than rescue team members and task force planners believed was necessary to complete the mission. At the recommendation of mission commanders Colonel Charlie Beckwith and General James Vaught, President Jimmy Carter aborted Operation Rice Bowl.[1]

Aborting the mission did not end the operation. The task force had to get out of Iran and return to the aircraft carrier and to Masirah Island. The final tragedy was quick and overwhelming. One of the C-130s had to leave within minutes because fuel was running dangerously low. The aircraft's crew, however, could not bring its engines up to power until one of the helicopters cleared the sandstorm caused by the C-130's engines. The helicopter, Dash Three, had to go into a hover to move rather than taxi out of the way because it had blown a tire upon landing. Dash Three's pilot became disoriented and flew headlong into the C-130, bursting fuel tanks that quickly engulfed both helicopter and C-130 in flames. Seven men were in the C-130's cockpit. Five were burned to death. Three helicopter crewmen were also killed. Three of the helicopters were within 150 feet of the fire and burning fuel was everywhere. The helicopter commander elected not to attempt to fly any of the aircraft back to the carrier. The helicopter crews, the survivors from the burning C-130, and the other members of the task force scrambled onto the five remaining C-130s and flew out of Iran.[2]

After decades of mistrust and inadequate funding from the military services, including being nearly eliminated from the active force following the Vietnam War, special operations forces (SOF) have risen from the ashes of the failed April 1980 rescue of American hostages in Iran to become one of the most frequently deployed of all U.S. military forces. Special operations forces, including U.S. Army Special Forces, U.S. Navy SEALs, U.S. Air Force special operations aircrews and Special Tactics Group, as well as the U.S. Army Rangers, civil affairs, and psychological operations units, are now adequately funded, better equipped, and well trained. They have not only made significant contributions to recent American combat operations in Panama, Southwest Asia, and Somalia but have also conducted extensive humanitarian and military assistance operations throughout the world. With additional impetus coming from the end of the cold war, U.S. special operations forces are now recognized by American political leaders as an invaluable foreign policy tool. Special operations forces provide a low-visibility method of building relationships with other nations, an ability to respond to a developing crisis before large-scale conventional forces are necessary, and a flexible military force for accomplishing unconventional combat, or "direct action," missions.

What caused this dramatic turnaround? How were the special operations forces successfully rebuilt and supported with adequate funding and unusual autonomy from the military services? Certainly the beginning of the turnaround can be traced to the aftermath of Desert One. Iranian television footage of the burned bodies of U.S. servicemen and their aircraft in the Iranian desert horrified U.S. citizens and encouraged an international perception of U.S. impotence before a handful of Iranian students and a new revolutionary government. A cry went up, particularly in the U.S. Congress, that something had to be done.

It proved to be a long way from congressional outrage to rebuilding a force currently numbering nearly 45,000 active and reserve personnel, an active force approximately the size of the Canadian army and navy combined.[3] But it happened. The story of the building of a strong special operations capability sheds light on how public policy is made and implemented. It illustrates the complex interaction between internal forces within the special operations community and the complicated dance between the executive and legislative branches of the U.S. government. The drama reached its high point when Congress seized the initiative in the fiscal 1987 defense appropriations bill. This legislation mandated the establishment of a new unified command, U.S. Special Operations Command (USSOCOM), and a new assistant secretary of defense, special operations and low-intensity conflict (ASD [SOLIC]). The bill laid a foundation for operational and bureaucratic roles and missions of the rebuilt special operations force and identified forces that would be owned by the new command. The subsequent implementation of this legislation has rebuilt and protected these forces to an extent never imagined by the early "quiet professionals."

While offering insights into how the U.S. government makes its policy, this book also offers a glimpse into the internal workings within the special operations community, particularly the forces that forged their organizational mission and culture. This book examines the effect of the history of special operations forces on an organizational culture that is unique and separate within the U.S. military and examines how this culture is inculcated and reinforced through training and operations. Finally, this book describes the decade-long struggle to rebuild special operations forces, resulting in new SOF organizations with independence that is unique among U.S. military forces. The rebuilding of the special operations forces has provided the United States with a strong special operations capability and protected that capability to the extent that the new SOF organization has nearly become a new military service, filling the void that has always troubled military and civilian commanders faced with the prospect of hostilities.

The history of U.S. special operations forces is marked by extremes of rapid buildup and near-elimination. Military decisionmakers are well aware of the value of a tank, strategic bomber, or aircraft carrier but find it more difficult to measure the value of a Special Forces military training team working with military forces in Peru. Special operations forces have also been destabilized by a conventional military that does not trust what special operators do, does not understand how they do it, and rejects a force that rarely confronts the enemy head on but, instead, conducts most operations in peacetime, under cover, or behind the lines. The American military has traditionally been disdainful of anything considered elite or special. And yet this label is inevitable for a force that has 50 percent to 80 percent attrition in its initial training programs. Conventional military units, of necessity, value conformity and nearly unquestioning following of orders. When faced with the individualistic, rank-unconscious, questioning special operator who frequently has longer hair, occasionally operates in civilian clothes, and is encouraged to "have a bank robber mentality,"[4] the conventional commander—understandably—is often offended and even outraged that this sloppy soldier is allowed in the army.

Not surprisingly, therefore, American special operations forces have experienced a roller coaster of dramatic highs and lows. The roots of contemporary American special operations forces are found in World War II and organizations such as the Office of Strategic Services (OSS), 1st Special Service Force, Scouts and Raiders, and the air commandos. After World War II, special operations forces were almost eliminated; only a few navy frogmen and air commando pilots were left. The buildup of special operations began in the early 1950s, accelerating in response to activities in Southeast Asia and President John F. Kennedy's call for the regeneration of nonconventional military capabilities. But special operations forces were slashed in the years following Vietnam. By the mid-1970s, the navy was considering moving all remaining naval special warfare forces to the reserves, the air force had reduced the proud air commandos, a separate air force during the Vietnam War, to a few squadrons and a handful of aircraft, and the army had slashed Special Forces' funding 95 percent from its high point during the conflict.[5] As late as 1979, army leadership considered inactivating one of the three remaining Special Forces groups, and only 3,600 troops remained assigned to active duty Special

Forces units. After a decade of inactivity interspersed with failures such as the *Mayaguez* incident in 1975, the tragedy in the Iranian desert in 1980 brought the absence of an effective American special operations capability to the attention of the world.

In response, the U.S. Congress and a handful of military and civilian supporters within the Department of Defense began a ten-year crusade to rebuild these forces and provide the United States with a robust and flexible special operations capability—a crusade that demonstrates how major U.S. policy can be made as a result of the intensive efforts of a few well-placed and tireless individuals. The original coalition included a congressman and one of his staffers, a Special Forces colonel, a civilian analyst in the Office of the Secretary of Defense, a handful of high-level U.S. Army officers, and a few special operators working behind the scenes. Within a few years, the coalition expanded to include a senior OSD official, other members of Congress and their staffs, and retired members of the special operations community. The coalition was aided by the strength of the special operations organizational culture, which enabled these forces to survive following World War II and the Vietnam War and provided a core of true believers willing to risk their military careers to rebuild the special operations capability.

To those working for SOF reform, the struggle to rebuild special operations forces appeared to be exactly that: a decade-long conflict that often seemed hopeless. Most members of this coalition received little in tangible benefits for their struggle. They paid the price of years of effort, great frustration, and, in some cases, ruined careers. As a result of their fight, however, today the United States has a flexible and low-visibility force that is able to quickly respond to, and often defuse, many of the crises—humanitarian, civic, political, and even military—of a new and unstable post–cold war world.

2

A Precarious Value

There is a cultural aversion on the part of conventional soldiers, sailors, and airmen to things that smell of smoke and mirrors and feats of derring-do. . . . It's a little too romantic . . . . It's not doing it the hard way. . . . Most of the people who have made their rank as battleship and bomber drivers, tank riders, and so on, just don't see this as the main way to go. Consequently, when it comes to competition for resources, . . . more often than not special [operations] forces radios and all kinds of special equipment will be just below the red line.

Lieutenant General Samuel Wilson, 1994

Special operators fight a different kind of "war" than conventional forces. To put it simply, armies take and hold ground. Air forces conduct strategic bombing operations and engage enemy fighters. Navies operate carrier battle groups in the open ocean, conduct offshore attacks on enemy targets, or strike from boats beneath the sea. The traditions of the conventional units are, in many respects, shared histories. They fought the same wars, confronted the enemy head on, and won battles through the use of overwhelming force.

Special operations forces (SOF), unlike conventional forces, usually work in small teams. They operate covertly behind enemy lines, train indigenous forces, or work with other countries to rebuild nations after war. Special operations forces may be most useful during periods of relative peace or "behind the lines" in major conflicts. This unconventional, often indirect, warfare has long been unappreciated or even disdained by conventional forces. Ian Sutherland, in his history of U.S. Army Special Forces, writes, "Subversion, sabotage, and guerrilla warfare are the weapons of the politically and materially weak. They have been considered by the American, who has not had much requirement to use them, as wholly unworthy methods. . . . The American military leadership, reflecting the attitudes of Americans in general, expects to directly confront an adversary and overwhelm him with unlimited power."[1]

The status of special operations forces within the American military may be described as that of a "precarious value." As described by Philip Selznick in *Leadership in Administration,* precarious values are those goals or missions within an organization that are in conflict with, or in danger of being overwhelmed by, the primary goals or missions of the organization. Precarious values may be at risk because of a lack of interest by the organizational leadership or because they are in conflict with the primary organizational culture, or sense of mission, of the institution.[2] The precariousness of value or capability increases within an organization that has a unifying organizational culture and, therefore, a strong sense of mission.

Standing outside the mainstream of the American military, special operations forces fit well within Selznick's definition of a precarious value. American special operations forces trace their contemporary roots to World War II: U.S. Army Special Forces from the Office of Strategic Services, U.S. Navy SEALs from the frogmen and underwater demolition teams, and U.S. Air Force special operations pilots and aircrews from the 1st Air Commando Group. American special operators, like special operations forces throughout the world, have developed unique operational capabilities and missions that distinguish them from their conventional counterparts. Each group performs missions and meets requirements that more conventionally trained or organized forces can not adequately address. The success of these operations has often required unconventional men and, occasionally, women.[3] The same characteristics that have allowed special operators to succeed in unconventional missions have often led to a distancing, or even disapproval, by conventional forces as conflicts have ended. A former commander of the 75th Ranger Regiment remarked, "There were obviously people who enjoyed the autonomy [of Special Forces]. And enjoyed being different. Of course, we're all concerned with people who are different. We are uncomfortable with it . . . in particular [in] the military because it is so structured and when all of a sudden you have unstructured beings, people are not comfortable with them. . . . We had some people who had tremendous capabilities, tremendous skills, but people didn't want to be around them. . . . These free thinkers. These people who did things in an unconventional manner."[4]

Special operations forces are nearly always commanded by conventional force commanders who are not trained in SOF capabilities and occasionally mistrust the forces. Add to this drawback the enthusiasm of these all-volunteer forces and the result is a significant risk of misuse of these forces. They have been deployed as underequipped infantry, with little mobility or sustainability, and decimated by heavier armed forces in conventional battles.[5] Although regional commanders, such as General Norman Schwarzkopf in the 1990–91 conflict with Iraq, command forces of all military services, these commanders usually have a far better understanding of the capabilities and doctrine of their conventional components than of special operators. The propensity for misuse has further distanced special operators from their conventional colleagues, created a wariness about the employment of special operations forces, and bound special operators together to the extent that many members of these forces feel a closer kinship with special operators across services than with their own parent service.[6]

The critical values of independence, unconventional thinking, and near equality among the members of the small operational teams are often in direct conflict with the values of conventional military forces. To a commander faced with conventional military missions—to "close with and destroy" the enemy, take and hold ground, and inflict tremendous damage in direct conflict with enemy military forces—special operations capabilities may appear irrelevant, insignificant, and even un-American.

Consequently, U.S. special operations forces, distinct from other military units and having little influence with military leaders, have been a precarious value in American military organizations. Since their establishment during World War II special operations forces have been without the protection necessary for the successful survival of a critical precarious value outside of the primary mission and values of the larger organization. Such protection, often in the form of access to the highest level of leadership or from an outside patron, rarely occurs.[7] Nevertheless, by the early 1990s a small, ad hoc coalition of believers in the precarious value of an American special operations capability had succeeded in providing such protection. The fight to rebuild and protect an American special operations capability was long and bitter. To understand this conflict and to appreciate the depth of the commitment of those who fought on both sides of the issue, as well as to identify the precariousness of these forces in the U.S. military, one must first understand their history.

The U.S. Army's Special Forces

The roots of U.S. Army Special Forces can be traced to the Office of Strategic Services, established during World War II through the efforts of

William "Wild Bill" Donovan, who was a Medal of Honor winner in World War I and a close friend of President Roosevelt. Donovan argued that the United States should develop a capability, like the British Special Operations Executive (SOE), to carry out sabotage, espionage, subversion, and propaganda.[8] As a result of Donovan's persuasion, the office of Coordinator of Information (COI) was established by the president in July 1941, with Donovan at its head. The COI became the Office of Strategic Services (OSS) in June 1942, with a mission defined loosely as intelligence gathering and waging unconventional war. The OSS's unconventional warfare mission laid the foundation for today's Special Forces, emphasizing training of foreign indigenous forces and regional orientation of American forces (including strong foreign language and cultural training). The OSS's intelligence-gathering mission was later transferred to the Central Intelligence Agency.

OSS units were tasked to disrupt, by other than conventional military operations, the enemy's ability to fight; or, to use Donovan's somewhat complicated mission statement:

> The coordination and use of all means, including moral and physical, by which the end is attained—other than those of recognized military operations, but including the psychological exploitation of the result of those recognized military actions—which tend to destroy the will of the enemy to achieve victory and to damage his political or economic capacity to do so; which tend to deprive the enemy of the support, assistance or sympathy of his allies or associates or of neutrals, or to prevent his acquisition of such support, assistance, or sympathy; or which tend to create, maintain, or increase the will to victory of our own people and allies and to acquire, maintain, or to increase the support, assistance and sympathy of neutrals.[9]

The OSS operated in every theater but the Pacific in World War II. The European special operations division of the OSS centered on operational groups (OGs) and Jedburgh teams.[10] Nineteen operational groups and seventy-eight Jedburgh teams were infiltrated into Europe during World War II. Each thirty-three-man operational group received training in land navigation, raiding, ambushes, silent killing, demolitions, parachuting, and small arms. British SOE schools provided the groups with additional training in enemy weapons, guerrilla organization and tactics, demolitions, and clandestine communications. OSS operational groups infiltrated enemy-controlled territory in France and Italy. They joined guerrilla groups to train indigenous forces in unconventional warfare skills and assisted in raiding and sabotage operations against the enemy. Jedburgh teams were three-man teams with expertise in unconventional warfare skills and European languages. Forces for the teams were provided by the French, British, Americans, Dutch, and Belgians. Jedburgh teams were airdropped into Europe just before and after the D-Day invasion at Normandy. Their mission was to organize and coordinate resistance against the Germans.

Although the great majority of OSS operations were conducted in Europe, it was the organization's experience in Burma that taught special operators a critical lesson: successful recruitment and training of indigenous forces depends on the full participation of special operations forces in the local culture. The twenty-one-man OSS Detachment 101, led by Captain Carl Eifler, first received training in unconventional warfare skills similar to the European-oriented OGs. After the unit was activated in April 1942, it received regional orientation training for India and Southeast Asia as well as Chinese language lessons. The unit's recruitment record was remarkable. The initial recruits in Burma came from former members of the Burmese army and then members of the Kachin hill tribes. To gain the trust and respect of the indigenous recruits, members of Detachment 101 learned local cultural and religious customs, slept in the tribal villages, and took part in traditional ceremonies. Detachment 101 and associated guerrilla groups carried out successful intelligence gathering and sabotage missions throughout northwestern Burma for the remainder of the war and earned recognition as the prototypical regionally oriented special operators.

The joint U.S.-Canadian 1st Special Service Force is also a part of Special Forces ancestry. (The Special Forces arrowhead insignia is based on that of the First Special Service.) The 1st Special Service Force placed a greater emphasis on direct assaults than did their Special Forces descendants, the Green Berets,[11] but many of the skills learned by this World War II unit are taught to their members today. The 1st Special Service troops were trained in parachute, mountain, amphibious, and Ranger operations (explained later), and operated as small raiding groups in snow-covered regions, including the Aleutians and Italy. Some sources indicate that while the Canadian volunteers were high-quality soldiers, most of the American "volunteers" came from various jails and detention centers.[12] Members of the 1st Special Service Force were generally regarded as the toughest U.S. soldiers in World War II and, perhaps, the most eccentric.[13] This view of special operators as "characters" continues today. The 1st Special Service Force performed exceptional service against the German "Winter Line" in

Italy during the winter of 1943–44, gaining a fearful reputation among German troops, particularly after developing the habit of placing stickers with the group's insignia on the foreheads of Germans whose throats they had slit during night raids.[14] The 1st Special Service Force, however, paid a horrible price for its fearlessness, with as many as 1,400 out of 1,800 men dead and wounded.[15]

At the conclusion of World War II, the Office of Strategic Services and the 1st Special Service Force, as well as U.S. Army Ranger units, were deactivated. The new focus of U.S. military planning was on war with the Soviet Union, and special operations were viewed by military leaders as outdated and inappropriate for this modern conflict—a perspective that arose again after the Vietnam War thirty years later. Although the outbreak of the Korean War led to the reconstitution of some Ranger units, army special operations played only a minor role in the conflict. The limited special operations that did occur—infrequent sabotage, tactical reconnaissance, and the taking of prisoners—were controlled by Covert Clandestine Reconnaissance Activities, Korea (CCRAK). This small Korea-oriented covert organization faded away at the end of the conflict.

Although special operations were largely ignored in the Korean theater, the need for special operations forces in Europe was recognized by U.S. Army leadership, marking the beginning of renewed, and sporadically successful, efforts to rebuild an American special operations capability. At the instigation of Russ Volckmann and Aaron Bank in the army's Office of the Chief of Psychological Warfare, the army approved formation of the Special Forces Group (SFG) and a psychological warfare-special forces training center at Fort Bragg in December 1951. Volckmann had led indigenous guerrilla forces in the Philippines during World War II. Bank had been the leader of an OSS unit made up of German dissidents and defectors and a member of the Jedburgh teams.[16] As designed by Volckmann and Bank, the Special Forces Group would be assigned about 2,500 men, approximately half "Lodge Bill" troops—forces recruited from refugees from Eastern Europe. The group was centered around twelve-man A-Detachments. Ten of the A-Detachments formed a company, and three companies plus a B-Detachment or headquarters unit formed a battalion. Despite several reviews by Special Forces leadership, this structure remains intact today in all Special Forces groups. The Special Forces' mission defined by Volckmann and Bank was "to infiltrate by air, sea, or land deep into enemy-controlled territory and to stay, organize, equip, train, control, and direct indigenous personnel in the conduct of Special Forces operations."[17] The first Special Forces unit—the 10th Special Forces Group

(SFG) (Airborne)—was activated on June 19, 1952, with Colonel Bank as its commander. Besides unconventional warfare and language training, Colonel Bank emphasized team training and field exercises, an emphasis that continues today.

In November 1953, half of the 10th Special Forces Group, nearly 800 men, deployed to Germany in reaction to increasing East-West tension. The half of the unit remaining in the United States formed the nucleus of a second group, the 77th SFG (Abn). In his history of Special Forces, Charles Simpson provides an amusing illustration of the inevitable friction between conventional army values and SOF organizational culture. As part of the post-Korea cutback, the U.S. Army began to economize, consolidating European-based units on fewer German installations. The result was an incongruous pairing of the 10th SFG and the Seventh Army NCO (noncommissioned officer) Academy. The academy placed a premium on the commander of the Seventh Army General Bruce Clarke's traditional value of army spit-and-polish. The contrast between the Seventh Army's necessary insistence on conformity and the more nonconformist approach of the Special Forces was made clear during the first NCO Academy graduation:

> Inside the quadrangle shared by the Academy and Group, the Academy students were lined up in impeccable ranks at rigid attention. The band played and General Clarke, resplendent in his multiple ribbons and four stars, was on the stand. At his side was the Academy Commandant (also the C.O., 10th SFG). As luck would have it, just at that inappropriate time, Sgt. George Yosich of [the] Special Forces arrived outside the *kaserne* [post] with his troops, an A Team with about sixty acting guerrillas, just in from thirty days in the field. Dirty, bearded, dressed in a hodgepodge of uniforms and civilian clothes, loaded with rucksacks, blanket rolls, and every kind of weapon, hungry as bears, they were a far cry from the troops drawn up inside the kaserne. Hearing the martial music from within, Sergeant Yosich, with an old soldier's pride, lined his troops up and marched them in. Around behind the reviewing stand, they performed a smart column left, arriving at the left flank of the parade ground. He then commanded "Halt, left face" and then dismissed them in a flurry of cheers in front of the snack bar. Yosich later recalled it as "just plain beautiful." General Clarke's reaction is not on record.[18]

When the tensions that highlighted a need for special operations forces relaxed, however, the new Special Forces group lost much of its support.

As the Korean War concluded and American military forces were reduced, the 10th's manpower was cut in half by the Department of the Army. This pattern of buildup during a crisis followed by quick and dramatic cuts at the conclusion of a conflict began with World War II and continued until the reorganization in 1986.

Rising tensions in Southeast Asia in the mid- and late 1950s once again increased interest in special operations forces within the Defense Department. In 1956 the army directed members of the 77th SFG to form the 14th Special Forces Operational Detachment (SFOD). The new unit was oriented toward the Far East and soon deployed mobile training teams (MTTs) to Thailand, Taiwan, and Vietnam. The army established new SFODs, again using 77th SFG manpower, and then consolidated all of these units into the 1st Special Forces Group (Airborne). Soon, these new Special Forces units were training forces in South Korea, the Philippines, Laos, and Indonesia, initially without any increase in their reduced manpower. As a result of the increasing commitment of Special Forces in Southeast Asia, by 1960 there were three understrength Special Forces groups of approximately 1,500 men each, the 10th, 77th, and 1st SFGs.[19]

As Kennedy's Flexible Response doctrine and increasing concern for "wars of national liberation" overtook Dwight Eisenhower's Massive Retaliation policy, the president called for dramatic revision of the conduct of military operations. Shortly after the Bay of Pigs fiasco, Kennedy expressed his concern over U.S. inability to conduct military operations short of all-out war. Addressing a joint session of Congress, the president declared, "I am directing the secretary of defense to expand rapidly and substantially, in cooperation with our allies, the orientation of existing forces for the conduct of non-nuclear war, paramilitary operations and sub-limited, or unconventional wars. In addition, our Special Forces and unconventional warfare units will be increased and reoriented."[20] Kennedy refined this theme when he made direct references to the increasing importance of "wars of national liberation" in U.S. foreign policy in his address to the graduating class at West Point in 1962. "This is another type of war, new in its intensity, ancient in its origins—war by guerrillas, subversives, insurgents, assassins; war by ambush instead of by combat; by infiltration, instead of aggression, seeking victory by eroding and exhausting the enemy instead of engaging him . . . It requires in those situations where we must counter it . . . a whole new kind of strategy, a wholly different kind of force, and therefore a new and wholly different kind of military training."[21]

With the hope of forcing the army's attention to unconventional threats,

Kennedy formed the Special Group, Counterinsurgency (SGCI) in early 1962. Senior members of the administration staffed the group, including General Maxwell Taylor as its chairman, Attorney General Robert Kennedy, Undersecretary of State U. Alexis Johnson, Chairman of the Joint Chiefs of Staff General Lyman Lemnitzer, U. S. Information Agency Director Edward R. Murrow, and CIA Director John McCone.[22] Kennedy also attempted to influence the army from below, directing that counterinsurgency training be added to the curricula of military schools at all levels.[23] Despite these efforts, America's military leaders never embraced President Kennedy's call for a new emphasis on unconventional warfare. General William P. Yarborough recalled, "In the early 1960s it was generally accepted in America's high military command and staff circles that there was nothing unique about Ho Chi Minh's war. As far as most of the senior leaders were concerned, the basic training, leadership, organizational principles, tactics, and strategy that had won America's wars in the past would be more than adequate for Indochina. *Both Special Warfare and Special Forces were terms that raised many hackles among the conventional regulars.*"[24]

Despite remaining unconvinced that the conflict in Vietnam demanded a new approach to warfare, the Department of Defense greatly increased the structure of the Special Forces, if not its influence, within the American military, in response to rising hostilities.[25] Although few American military leaders believed that the conflict would be resolved through the patient training of South Vietnamese forces and improved civil-military relations in Vietnam, U.S. Army Special Forces played this role in Vietnam, training Vietnamese Special Forces as early as 1957. The first Special Forces advisers from the 7th SFG arrived in Vietnam in November 1961. Special Forces operated as the U.S. Army Special Forces Provisional (Vietnam) until 1965, when this organization was replaced by the 5th SFG. The primary role of Special Forces was to train South Vietnamese forces, particularly the Vietnamese special operations forces, Luc Luong Dac Biet (LLDB). In 1962 a pilot Village Defense program was initiated that soon evolved into the Civilian Irregular Defense Group (CIDG) program. Units composed of half American Special Forces and half LLDB were assigned to train local defense forces in basic military skills and fortification.

The Special Forces mission in Vietnam often led to complicated and uncomfortable command-and-control arrangements between the Special Forces and the American chain of command in Vietnam and between Special Forces, LLDB, and the local forces being organized for village defense. In the former, Special Forces A-Detachments usually reported directly to the Special Forces group commander, bypassing the regional representative of the U.S. mission in Vietnam.[26] In the latter, the LLDB officially commanded the camps, composed of two to four 120-man companies of indigenous forces, with the Special Forces acting as advisers. In reality, Special Forces advisers were often the effective camp commanders. According to a former Special Forces lieutenant, "[the] LLDB wouldn't go out on operations. We would invite them to come but they wouldn't come. . . . this [combat] was old to them. Not that they were elderly chronologically but they had been fighting for years and years and years, [and] weren't interested in breaking their respective rice bowls."[27]

Special Forces members who served in Vietnam have strong opinions about the LLDB. Some express disdain for these forces, considering them lazy and corrupt. Many others, however, such as the lieutenant just quoted, point out that the LLDB had been fighting a long time. They did not need to get their combat stripes by following eager SF lieutenants and captains. The SF officers were usually "advising" officers ten years or more their senior who had been fighting the Viet Minh and Viet Cong for many years. Furthermore, the rapid expansion of Special Forces in the early and mid-1960s resulted in less time for cultural orientation and development of language skills. Communication was difficult, and for many of the younger Special Forces members, this was their first contact with Asians. Frictions were aggravated by the ethnic conflicts within Vietnam, particularly between the flatland Vietnamese and the Montagnards, resulting in tragedies such as the Montagnard revolts of 1964 and 1965.[28]

This advisory and training mission placed tremendous responsibility on Special Forces junior officers and NCOs. A twenty-five-year-old SF captain commanding an SF detachment would be expected to

lead his fourteen-man detachment, advise a veteran and frequently hardheaded Vietnamese Special Forces detachment, train a 400- to 500-man battalion of . . . Montagnards, be responsible for approximately half a million dollars of equipment and ammunition, pay a monthly payroll of approximately $15,000, supervise intelligence funds, obtain approximately $50,000 worth of supplies each month, conduct operations that kept one-third of his force in the field at all times, and conduct psychological operations, intelligence operations, and civic action projects, while being capable of briefing General Westmoreland who might drop into any CIDG camp with no notice.[29]

Besides the CIDG program, later Special Forces missions in Vietnam included reconnaissance and sabotage missions through Project Delta and reconnaissance-raid teams composed of Special Forces and LLDB assigned to work with specific U.S. Army units on an operation. During the transition to conventional force operations beginning in 1965, Special Forces and LLDB also carried out such duties as road and base security, sweeps in Viet Cong territory, and even conventional infantry missions. As the war progressed and the number of conventional units increased, Special Forces operated largely as intelligence gatherers and trainers, with some continued civic action such as the Field Epidemiological Survey Team (FEST) mission, where Special Forces members studied Southeast Asian diseases.

The Military Assistance Command Vietnam/Studies and Observations Group (MACV/SOG) conducted the most covert, unconventional operations in Vietnam by using Special Forces, SEALs, air force special operators, and some marines. The SOG was activated on January 24, 1964.[30] The eight operational SOG commands—known as "studies groups" for cover—conducted cross-border intelligence and psychological operations missions, capture of prisoners for interrogation, MIA recovery, and various covert reconnaissance, ambush, raid, and mining operations throughout Southeast Asia. MACV/SOG worked closely with the CIA on many operations. Operations were conducted jointly with the Vietnamese Special Exploitation Service, later renamed the Strategic Technical Directorate.[31]

Associated with the Studies and Observations Group were many officers who later gained special operations fame or notoriety: Colonel Donald Blackburn and Colonel John Singlaub among others. At its peak, MACV/SOG had more than two thousand Americans, most of whom were Special Forces, and eight thousand indigenous forces assigned to it. By 1970, however, SOG had lost much of its effectiveness. According to a former SOG member, this was partly because the North Vietnamese had figured out the teams' methods of operation. The United States soon left most SOG operations to the South Vietnamese before inactivating the group in April 1972.[32]

Perhaps the most well-known special operation in Vietnam was the Son Tay Raid, a mission intended to rescue U.S. prisoners of war held at Son Tay Prison in North Vietnam.[33] Planned and directed by the Joint Chiefs of Staff's SACSA organization, headed by then-Brigadier General Donald Blackburn, the raid was led by Colonel Arthur "Bull" Simons. Although masterly in its execution, the mission demonstrated the difficulty of obtaining and interpreting accurate intelligence, for upon arrival, the Raiders discovered that the prisoners had been moved elsewhere.

President Kennedy's failure to change the conventional military's view of counterinsurgency and unconventional warfare was most visible in the army, which committed hundreds of thousands of conventional forces to Vietnam. Organizational values and culture cannot be changed quickly. They are the essence of the organization and must be changed over time, beginning with the most junior members of the organization.[34] The president's efforts to change the army's approach to the conflict in Vietnam suffered from the inability of any president to oversee implementation of his policy direction, as well as the inexperience and lack of expertise of those subordinates he selected to carry out his directives. This was particularly true of the Special Group, Counterinsurgency. Kennedy had viewed special operations forces as a way to avoid getting American combat troops heavily involved in the war, a perspective not shared by most army commanders and subsequent civilian leaders.[35] Furthermore, according to Andrew Krepinevich, the two members of the administration Kennedy most relied on to ensure the development of a true counterinsurgency capability and approach to the conflict, Walt Rostow and Maxwell Taylor, were both unconvinced that such an approach would be successful. As early as 1961, Rostow firmly believed that strategic bombing of North Vietnam would rescue the United States from counterinsurgency operations in South Vietnam. The revision of army doctrine advocated by Taylor, who served as the president's special military representative, chairman of the SGCI, chairman of the Joint Chiefs of Staff, and ambassador to South Vietnam, was to prepare for fighting mid-intensity wars in addition to preparing for a possible nuclear conflict with the Soviet Union.[36]

Recognizing Taylor and Rostow's lack of enthusiasm for special operations and civil-political operations, conventional military leaders seized the opportunity to "conventionalize" the war in the mid-1960s. The role and influence of Special Forces, despite the force's eventual increase to seven Special Forces groups, declined dramatically. With the arrival of large numbers of conventional troops, Special Forces were increasingly marginalized. The tendency for conventional military commanders to misuse Special Forces, particularly as conventional infantry, and weaknesses in the command and control of these units served only to sully their reputation and reinforce suspicions on both sides. Not surprisingly, the independence from the conventional military leadership of the special operations units receiving most of their direction from the CIA, particularly early in the conflict, increased the distance between conventional military commanders and these forces. The emphasis on training Vietnamese forces was lost. In its place was U.S. domination of the war effort and the belief that the war could be won by the application of overwhelming force. Even the enormous scale of special operations involvement in Vietnam was partially a result of the American belief in "more is better" combined with failure to recognize the unique skills of the Vietnamese guerrillas or the "force multiplier" effect of special operations forces employed in small teams. The American lack of appreciation of the experience of a host country that had spent most of the previous thirty years in conflict was demonstrated time and time again in the infantry operations that made up most of the operations after 1965. A former A-Detachment commander describes the type of tragedy that often resulted from the American perspective:

[We worked] with the 5th Marines out of An Hua. We were the flank security and the point security for a battalion in . . . the Arizona territory. And our Montagnards, who were superbly trained, [from] growing up in the area mountains, in field craft, began to signal to us that the [North Vietnamese] were right up at the woodline . . . .[and the Montagnards said] somebody ought to call artillery. Well, we would relay that back to the marine battalion commander and he says, ". . .just keep on moving." . . . Pretty soon our guys [the Montagnards] began to break away from the front . . . and return to the flanks. Of course the battalion commander . . . said, "Hey, get those dimwitted fools back up front." And I said, "It's because they're not dimwitted fools that they don't want to go up front. They want you to call artillery." Well, they didn't [and] the marines came forward . . . they didn't commence firing . . . [until the NVA] began to fire on them. We lost about nine guys up front killed and about fifteen wounded.[37]

Concurrently with the conventionalization of the conflict, control of Special Forces transferred from the CIA's Combined Study Group to the MACV.[38] With the MACV in charge, the focus of the CIDG program shifted from area defense and development to establishing strategically located fighting camps, particularly in areas populated by ethnic minorities other than the Montagnards. This new orientation spread Special Forces thin, resulting in a loss of control, and the replacement of the nation-building mission with a search-and-destroy mission. The light CIDG companies were often misused by their new conventional commanders, who tended to equate these forces with American infantry units. CIDG companies would be sent out in search of the enemy, end up surrounded as a result of their enthusiasm, and then take heavy casualties or be extracted by helicopters.

An egregious example of the misuse of these light companies occurred in 1965. The highway from coastal Qui Nhon to Pleiku, in the II Corps area of operation, was blocked by Viet Cong and North Vietnamese forces. Commanders within the II Corps ordered Special Forces to take several CIDG companies to open the highway. The SF officers protested that road clearing against large forces was beyond the capabilities of the light units and a misuse of forces that were put together to defend their own tribal areas and families. Additionally, the Rhade tribe, making up most of the force, did not get along with the Bhanar who lived in that area of Vietnam. The American conventional commanders told the Special Forces commanders to forget the anthropological argument and to "get on the team." The Rhade companies were deployed to the Bhanar region and were nearly eliminated because of casualties and desertions. The "failure" of these companies fueled conventional prejudices about both indigenous forces and U.S. Special Forces.[39]

The lightly defended CIDG camps became increasingly vulnerable to attack by Viet Cong and North Vietnamese forces. The fixed camps offered appealing targets, especially through ambushes of relieving forces. The victories scored were psychological as much as territorial. After several costly defenses in 1963–65, the Special Forces had created their own mobile strike forces, eventually called Mike forces. The units were composed of Vietnamese civilian irregulars led by Special Forces officers. Unlike the CIDG units, Mike forces usually did not have roots in the areas where they fought. The SF and CIDG troops believed Mike forces were the only reliable reaction to large-scale attacks on CIDG camps. The most well known of the Mike units was a battalion of Nung tribesmen formed in Danang in 1965. After the Nung battalion was inactivated, the Nungs served as bodyguards for the Special Forces in the reorganized and reoriented CIDG program. Although effective, they gained a reputation, deserved or not, as mercenaries, and the Nungs were often in conflict with the South Vietnamese military. In 1965 five mobile strike teams, evolved from the first Mike forces, were established, one for each Special Forces C-Detachment and one for the commanding officer of the 5th SFG in Nha Trang. Starting in the fall of 1966, supplemented Mike forces were used as mobile guerrilla forces in enemy-held areas.

With increasing misuse of the Special Forces and CIDG units, and too rapid expansion of the program, the CIDG program soon lost much of its credibility with the Vietnamese and the American people. Nonetheless, the Special Forces-CIDG program was the primary American activity in Vietnam that was tied to the local people. Its initial goal was improving security to villages through self-help and training programs. It could be argued that "Vietnamization," touted as a startling new idea in 1969, was the basis of the CIDG program from its beginnings.[40]

To this day army Special Forces units are still trying to live down their reputation from Vietnam. The Special Forces' and other special operators' link with the Central Intelligence Agency gave SOF a freedom in Vietnam that alienated the conventional military. Allegations, and the occasional reality, of such excesses as torture and assassination damned army Special Forces in the eyes of an already suspicious military command and the American people. The most highly publicized of these excesses occurred in July 1969 when several members of the 5th Special Forces Group executed a Vietnamese double agent. Some of the men involved reported that the group commander, Colonel Robert Rheault, directed the murder. After an investigation by his staff, General Creighton Abrams relieved Rheault of command. An intense public debate followed, fueled by accusations from the defendants' lawyers and some members of the Special Forces community that Abrams was strongly anti-Special Forces and had made the charges in an attempt to discredit these units. After much public furor, the CIA refused, most likely after White House intervention, to allow its agents to testify, and the army dropped the charges. Although the accusations against Abrams were somewhat discounted, both Abrams and the Special Forces paid a price with their reputations for the ugliness of this incident.[41]

Even when the reported misdeeds were few, they reinforced the impression that special operations forces, in general, were out of control or at least not under the control of U.S. military leadership. Most members of the Special Forces did admirable work, but the dilution of the quality of the force, owing to its rapid increase in size, reduced the ability of Special Forces to recruit selectively. The attrition rate at the U.S. Army's Special Warfare Center fell from a high of nearly 90 percent to a low of 30 percent, despite the school's acceptance in the mid- to late 1960s of untrained recruits directly from the civilian world. This was especially dangerous because special operations forces usually worked in small teams, far removed from the control, direction, and monitoring of more senior commanders. With the end of the Vietnam War, Special Forces faced backlash from political and military leaders. Special Forces groups were cut from seven down to their 1950s structure of three groups.

Underwater Demolition Teams and SEALs

World War II also gave birth to American naval special operations, referred to in the U.S. Navy as special warfare, or SPECWAR. Navy Underwater Demolition Teams (UDTs) and the Scouts and Raiders were both established during the first years of American participation in the war. These were the forerunners of today's SEAL teams, special boat units, and SEAL delivery vehicle units. Like Special Forces, navy special warfare units have a history of boom and bust: rapid buildup during World War II and Vietnam and near elimination following each of these conflicts.

The Scouts and Raiders were established in the opening months of American involvement in World War II to directly support amphibious landings: guiding marines and soldiers ashore. Led by Phil H. Bucklew, a legendary character in SEAL history, they were first employed in Operation Torch in November 1942, the first American invasion of the war. Operation Torch was directed at the North African coast, near Algiers and in French Morocco. The seventeen-man Scouts and Raiders team used a small, wooden-hulled boat, launched from an American ship in the Mediterranean, to enter a heavily guarded Moroccan river. The team's mission was to cut cables anchoring a boom and antishipping net strung across the river, thereby allowing American warships to fight up the river and protect the invading force. On their second attempt and under fire, the team succeeded in its mission, demonstrating the value of small, preinvasion teams.[42]

Bucklew and the Scouts and Raiders participated in European operations throughout 1942. The Scouts and Raiders teamed with the British Combined Operations Pilotage Parties (COPP) in preparation for the Allied landings in Sicily. The Scouts and Raiders and their British counterparts were brought near the coast of Sicily in small British submarines. The teams left the deck of the submarine in small canoes and paddled to shore to conduct reconnaissance of the shore and beach, checking the beach's gradient, and searching for underwater obstructions. The Scouts and Raiders then led the invasion force, including General Patton's Seventh Army, ashore.

In January 1943, while Bucklew's Scouts and Raiders were operating off the North African and European coasts, the chief of naval operations, Admiral Ernest J. King, directed that naval demolition units be established and trained for the mission of clearing manmade beach obstacles in the European theater. The new units were to be led by Draper L. Kauffman. Kauffman had served as a volunteer ambulance driver in support of the French forces who were defending against the Germans in 1940, as a volunteer in the British navy, and as a bomb disposal volunteer in the winter of 1940–41 during the German blitz in England. In May 1941 Kauffman returned to the United States and received his commission in the U.S. Navy. After the Japanese strike at Pearl Harbor, Kauffman was once again responsible for bomb disposal, earning a Navy Cross for his efforts.

In May 1943 Kauffman established the first school for training naval combat demolition units, the direct predecessors of the SEALs. The school was built in Fort Pierce, Florida, near the Scouts and Raiders school established by Phil Bucklew after the Algerian operation. All students were volunteers—the first coming from the U.S. Navy's Seabees—and the training emphasized physical stress to determine if a student would become careless when fatigued, an emphasis that persists in training received by today's SEALs.

Indeed, much of the training for the first naval combat demolition units, including miles of running each day and training with rubber boats in the mud and surf, is still seen in SEAL training today. However, in 1943, surprisingly little emphasis was put on swimming. The earliest concept of operations called for the use of canoes to get ashore in advance of amphibious operations and then demolition work in relatively shallow water. As is done today, most training took place at night. Technical training focused on learning about the safe handling of explosives, placing explosives on the obstacles and wiring the demolitions together to allow simultaneous explosion.

The 11th Naval Combat Demolition Unit was the first demolition unit to see action when it deployed in November 1943 in preparation for the Normandy invasion. The demolition unit was divided into thirteen-man gap-assault teams, one for each of the eight gaps planned for Utah beach and sixteen gaps for Omaha beach. The teams' task was to destroy the barriers emplaced by the Germans close to the water or submerged. Many barriers were made of steel posts driven into the sand and connected with barbed wire and reinforced by mortar and machine-gun emplacements or were "Belgian gates," steel latticework barriers weighing three tons and propped up by heavy steel braces.

On the day of the invasion, Bucklew and his Scouts and Raiders, using rubber boats, conducted reconnaissance and led the troops ashore. The demolition teams were to go ashore after air force and navy bombing and shelling of the German positions, and following a lead force of Sherman tanks. The teams met success on Utah Beach, but disaster struck as elements of the demolition unit approached Omaha. Pilots and naval commanders feared hitting American troops with bombs and naval gunfire. Consequently, most of the air and naval ordnance fell behind the German guns protecting the beach. Making matters worse, the strong current off shore caused many of the gap-assault teams to drift out of position, often making them the first force to reach the shore, without the protection of the tanks. In the chaos, many members of the demolition teams were killed or wounded before they could destroy the barriers. Those teams able to attack the barriers worked throughout the day and by evening had cleared thirteen of the planned sixteen gaps. Naval combat demolition units suffered a casualty rate of 52 percent, with thirty-one men killed and sixty wounded during the initial American invasion on Omaha Beach.

Early U.S. Navy operations in the Pacific indicate that the U.S. Navy leadership had not yet learned the African and European lessons of the importance of beach reconnaissance, pilotage, and obstacle clearance: the mission of the Scouts and Raiders and naval combat demolition units. The U.S. invasion of Tarawa on November 20, 1943, was an amphibious disaster. Amphibious landing ships carrying tanks and supporting marine forces ran aground, drowning many marines and subjecting the remainder to fierce enemy fire. Responding to the tragedy, the navy's amphibious commander in the Pacific, Rear Admiral Richmond Kelly Turner, called for the formation of nine underwater demolition teams (UDTs) and the establishment of an "Experimental and Tactical Underwater Demolition Station."[43]

The navy quickly established a training site for these teams in Hawaii for what it called the 5th Amphibious Force, which would include naval combat demolition unit graduates from Fort Pierce. The first test of the UDTs in the Pacific occurred within four weeks of the formation of the teams in the attack on Kwajalein. There, after abortive attempts to use remote control floating bombs constructed from wooden boats, the UDT members learned that the destruction of underwater obstacles was best accomplished directly by team members. Most important, reconnaissance operations in support of the Kwajalein attack taught the UDTs the effectiveness of swimming to shore, particularly during daylight, rather than relying on the boats used in the European theater.

Following Kwajalein, the navy established the U.S. Naval Combat Demolition Training and Experimental Base on Maui in the Hawaiian islands. The new school revised the Fort Pierce curriculum substantially, especially by a new emphasis on long-distance swimming. Here, the underwater demolition team combat swimmer, referred to in the press as the "naked warrior," was born. The combat swimmer operated "wearing a jock strap, button-fly cotton trunks, sneakers, and a face mask. Strapped to his leg was a hunting knife."[44] Late in the war the swimmers added swim fins. This preference for traveling and fighting light remains with the SEALs today.

The UDTs were active throughout the remainder of the Pacific war, conducting day and night reconnaissance, destroying obstacles to the amphibious landings, and leading the forces ashore. UDTs were employed in the invasions of Saipan, Iwo Jima, and Okinawa. During the July 1944 invasion of Guam, the UDTs worked for three days and nights removing and destroying manmade and natural obstacles. According to a report from a member of UDT 3, "150 obstacles [were] removed using 3,000 pounds Tetrytol. . . . The enemy had placed obstacles in an almost continuous front along the reef. These obstacles were piles of coral rock inside a wire frame made of heavy wire net."[45] After demolishing the obstacles the UDTs then led the conventional forces ashore.

As a result of many operations during the last years of the war, the UDTs developed and refined their tactics. New tactics and methods included conducting daylight reconnaissance under the protection of naval shelling, painting stripes on the swimmers' bodies to aid in estimating the depth of the water, and high-speed methods of reloading the swimmers into rubber boats towed by landing craft. The key role of the UDTs in the Pacific war was kept secret throughout the war at the insistence of Kauffman. Kauffmann believed that the less the Japanese knew about the swimmers, the more effective and safer they would be. His insistence on absolute secrecy was, according to author Orr Kelly, the beginning of the obsession with secrecy that is characteristic of today's SEALs.[46]

If the reconnaissance and shoreline demolition skills of the navy SEALs evolved from the Scouts and Raiders and the UDTs, their commando capability evolved from the combat swimmer corps established within the Office of Strategic Services by Christian Lambertsen, a medical student who developed a closed-circuit, underwater breathing system—the Lambertsen Amphibious Respiratory Unit (LARU). Unlike the navy UDTs, who operated often during the day with the support of naval gunfire and close to the water's surface, the OSS swimmers operated under the water at night and used the LARU. The LARU, unlike an open respiratory system, did not release bubbles and was therefore ideal for stealthy underwater operations. The OSS swimmer's mission was to mine enemy ships and transport and support undercover agents.

The OSS swimmers were never used operationally by the American commanders. Those assigned to work as combat swimmers were quickly subsumed by the demolition teams. The UDTs saw little value in an underwater capability and adopted only the OSS swimmer's swim fins. If the navy was not receptive to the new ideas of the OSS swimmers, the army was even less so. General MacArthur disdained and distrusted the unconventional approach of the OSS and refused to allow its forces to operate in his command.[47] The result was that many of the OSS swimmers were limited to training and research work, where they developed many of the underwater swimming techniques and technology used in later years by the SEALs.

Like the army special operation forces, the navy UDTs were largely disbanded at the conclusion of World War II. Most of the men who remained in the navy joined the surface fleet. Those who remained in the few remaining UDTs had little or no hope of making commander. They formed a core of officers who had little concern for promotions but loved the teams. The UDTs played only a minor role, except for supporting the landing at Inchon, in Korea. They spent much of the 1950s attempting to define their role in a military force that found little value in World War II–style UDT operations. The result was an evolution and expansion of UDT skills to include the development of a commando capability. Army personnel were brought in to teach the UDTs about infiltration onto land and the use of small arms. The goal was to conduct narrowly defined commando raids close to the water's edge. Advances were also made in retrieving commandos through the use of Robert Fulton's Sky Hook harness, in UDTs who trained ship crews to defend against combat swimmers, and in helicopters that dropped swimmers into the water and recovered them again.

In the 1960s the UDTs and naval special warfare were rediscovered as a result of the Kennedy administration's interest in unconventional warfare. The chief of naval operations (CNO) directed the commander of UDT-21, Bill Hamilton, to take charge of the creation of a "SEAL" team on each coast, the new acronym being a contraction of *Sea*, *Air*, and *Land*. The new units shared with the UDTs a hydrographic reconnaissance mission but expanded special warfare capabilities with an emphasis on inland warfare.[48]

The conventional navy was no different from the army in its mistrust of the new units. Orr Kelly writes about the conventional military's suspicion: "[The new SEAL units] would take money and manpower from other parts of the navy. And [they] would run counter to the long traditions of a blue-water navy that had plenty of work to do out on the open seas without getting into messy guerrilla operations or venturing up muddy inland rivers."[49] To some extent, this suspicion remains to this day. Fortunately for the teams, the SEALs had the support of the CNO, Admiral Arleigh Burke, and his successor, Admiral George Anderson. SEAL teams were organized along the UDT model, with one on each coast at Little

Creek, Virginia, and Coronado, California. Initially, each had fifty enlisted men and ten officers with a lieutenant as the commanding officer.

The first SEAL teams were commissioned in January 1962. The new SEAL team commanders quickly developed reputations for impatience with the navy supply system and made many of their rapid innovations—including the introduction of high-altitude, low-opening (HALO) parachutes, new underwater breathing devices, and AR-15 rifles—with convenient off-the-shelf purchases that raised the ire of the navy's more senior officers. The SEAL teams quickly learned to raid other units to salvage equipment they could modify to meet their unconventional needs, a willingness to innovate still evidenced today.

Training for the new teams was adapted from UDT training conducted on Maui during World War II, with additions taken from the army's Special Forces training. Training included underwater, air, and land operations and emphasized physical and mental stress to identify those who would break down on the long and demanding SEAL team missions.

SEALs first deployed operationally in April and May of 1962, when a six-man team was sent to Cuba on a reconnaissance mission. The swimmers successfully completed the mission, going so close to shore that they could see people in their beachside apartments. The swimmers surveyed over two miles of beach before being picked up by a submarine.[50] Further reconnaissance operations were conducted during the October 1962 missile crisis. By early 1962, SEAL Team 1 was preparing for operations in Vietnam. The SEALs, like U.S. Army Special Forces, were extensively involved in Vietnam and, on a percentage basis, were the most decorated units during the war. Of the fourteen members of the navy who received the Medal of Honor, three were from SEAL Team 1. Seven members of the SEAL and UDT units earned the Navy Cross. The members of SEAL Teams 1 and 2 and UDTs 11, 12, and 13 were awarded more than fifty Silver Stars and several hundred Bronze Stars. Despite the number of dangerous operations evidenced by these decorations, not one member of the SEAL or UDT units was left behind, either dead or missing.[51]

Like the Special Forces, the activities of the SEALs in Southeast Asia merit a separate book but will only be covered briefly here.[52] Although their impact at a strategic level was low, the SEALs were successful in accomplishing many missions that were new to a military accustomed to high-intensity conflicts in Europe and Korea. The first SEAL unit arrived in Da Nang in early 1963, before the arrival of U.S. conventional forces in Vietnam. Its mission, under the control of the CIA, was to infiltrate agents into the north in the hopes of organizing resistance movements. The first commandos to be trained were Vietnamese, although later trainees were from the ethnic minorities in the country. The commander of this first SEAL unit was appalled at the arrogance of the initial mission. SEALs who had never fired a shot in battle were training veterans of more than ten years of fighting with the French forces.[53] Although the number of operational successes increased, neither the SEAL commander, "Irish" Flynn, nor the CIA official in charge of the operation, William Colby, believed the operations were having any effect on developing substantial resistance in North Vietnam. By 1964 the CIA had turned over control of the SEAL operations to U.S. military commanders, and the pace of training and operations increased even more rapidly.

In July and August of 1964 U.S. involvement in Vietnam escalated, apparently partially as a result of one of the naval commando raids. Four torpedo boats, intending to drop off South Vietnamese commandos, approached two islands off the central coast of North Vietnam. The commander of the operation, having been warned that the raid was compromised, decided to fire on the targets from the boats. The U.S. torpedo boats, returning south after the incident, came close to the USS *Maddox*, a U.S. destroyer patrolling off the coast and intercepting enemy radio transmissions. Three days later, the North Vietnamese, believing the boats were operationally related to the larger intelligence ships, had three torpedo boats attack the *Maddox*. Following another U.S. torpedo boat attack on two other North Vietnamese installations, the *Maddox* and another destroyer, USS *Turner Joy*, were attacked again by North Vietnamese torpedo boats. This reported series of exchanges became known as the Gulf of Tonkin incident. American leaders quickly claimed the North Vietnamese had attacked the U.S. ships without provocation. On August 5 aircraft from two U.S. carriers conducted a retaliatory attack against North Vietnamese targets, and on August 7 Congress passed the Gulf of Tonkin Resolution.[54]

Units from SEAL Team 1 and UDTs 11 and 12 were extensively involved in the Vietnam conflict from 1965 to 1966. Elements of SEAL Team 2 were deployed to Vietnam beginning in 1967. Most SEAL-UDT operations in Vietnam were essentially small-unit, infantry-like operations in a riverine-jungle-swamp environment. Reconnaissance was limited to tactical operations, and their special operations capabilities were never integrated into the overall war effort. The SEAL teams were supported by the navy's riverine forces or "brown-water navy," particularly the boat support units established in 1964. The boat support units used small boats, including river patrol boats, Mike boats, and Boston whalers, to move

SEAL and UDT patrols into and out of enemy rear areas. Operations were also launched from specially modified submarines—the USS *Perch*, USS *Tunny*, and USS *Grayback*.[55]

Perhaps the most unsung accomplishment of the SEALs in Vietnam is their success at rescuing prisoners of war. While critics have focused attention on the failure of the United States to rescue any Americans from North Vietnamese or Viet Cong prison camps, little attention has been paid to the relative success of the SEALs in rescuing South Vietnamese prisoners of war. More than three hundred South Vietnamese were freed in twenty successful rescue operations conducted by American forces. Of those freed, 152 were rescued by the SEALs. They accounted for 48 percent of the prisoners of war freed during the war.[56]

Many SEALs regard Vietnam as the high point of their history. SEALs like to be where the bullets are flying, and for the individual SEAL or UDT member, life in Vietnam was dangerous and exciting. SEALs and UDT members typically served two tours in Vietnam, usually on a schedule of six months in Vietnam, six months in recovery and training, and then back to Vietnam. With this extensive experience in Vietnam, SEAL and UDT personnel quickly learned the "tricks of the trade" necessary for survival and success in Vietnam. Returning to the United States with the drawdown of troops from Vietnam was for many SEALs disorienting and demoralizing, particularly as the SEALs became increasingly isolated from the fleet and the conventional navy in the early 1970s.[57]

Air Commandos and the U.S. Air Force

Like the SEALs and the Special Forces, air force special operators have a history distinct from that of their parent service. Air force special operators trace their lineage back to the 1st Air Commando Group, which served in Burma during World War II, and the U.S. Army Air Forces special operations squadrons used in covert operations over France in 1943 and 1944.

As the Allies began preparing for the invasion of Normandy, the U.S. Army Air Forces commands in the United Kingdom and North Africa organized a handful of special operations squadrons to provide specialized airlift for covert operations that were supporting conventional ground forces taking part in D-Day.[58] The earliest USAAF special operations combat mission was flown into Europe by the B-17, B-24, and B-25 bombers of the Special Flight Section of the 12th Air Force's 5th Bombardment Group in North Africa. The largest Army Air Forces effort in Europe came from the 801st Bombardment Group, the Carpetbaggers, based in England.

The Carpetbaggers used highly modified, mission-unique, black-painted B-24 bombers to drop supplies, leaflets, and agents behind German lines. The Carpetbaggers dropped the OSS Jedburgh teams, described earlier, into France before and during the Normandy invasion. With an average of less than forty aircraft, these squadrons flew thousands of missions from January 1944 through September 1944. The clandestine missions included parachuting intelligence agents and guerrilla warfare teams deep behind enemy lines; dropping supplies, including weapons and munitions, to French resistance groups; and extracting teams from German-held territory. The special operations pilots were pioneers in developing techniques for low-level night flying and long-range navigation, and they enabled American and British special operations forces and French irregular units to operate with great effectiveness behind German lines.[59]

The 1st Air Commando Group, known originally as Project 9, was created at the direction of U.S. General of the Army Henry H. "Hap" Arnold in response to Winston Churchill's request for U.S. assistance in reopening the Burma Road after the retreat of the British and Chinese in May 1942. The British had attempted to disrupt the Japanese defense by using a special operations force that operated behind Japanese lines with the intent of cutting off the main railway line between Mandalay and Myitkyina and harassing Japanese forces in the Shwebo area of central Burma. The British force, known by the nickname "Chindits" after a mythological half-lion, half-griffin beast that was portrayed in statues guarding Burmese pagodas, had been established by its commander, then-Colonel Orde C. Wingate. Wingate's Chindits had some success, even without the support of a diversionary conventional assault on Japanese front lines and effective air resupply. Although they were eventually forced to retreat in the face of Japanese resistance, Chindit operations were viewed as a success since, "For the first time, British troops had fought a jungle war against the Japanese and had delivered punishment."[60]

Upon returning to India, Wingate was called by Prime Minister Churchill to attend the Quadrant Conference in Quebec, Canada, and brief Allied military leaders on Chindit operations and propose a new plan for the invasion of Burma. Wingate requested support by the U.S. Army Air Forces, initially for light planes to aid in the evacuation of ground casualties. R. D. Van Wagner, in his history of the 1st Air Commando Group, writes of General Arnold's reaction to Churchill's call for help. "In his mind, Arnold saw an opportunity to exploit and expand air power. He became determined to form a new air organization which would be totally dedicated to supporting Wingate's troops on the ground in Burma."[61]

Critical to the success of this new group, an air force organization that had no precedent in the U.S. military, was its new commander. Arnold "hoped to find a man to lead his unique organization who was aggressive, imaginative, and highly organized,"[62] and he did so by selecting two men to be co-commanders. The first was Lieutenant Colonel Philip G. Cochran. Cochran had an unusual and impressive war record as a fighter pilot in Africa, most notably in Tunisia where he was awarded numerous medals, including the Distinguished Flying Cross, for his actions. (Perhaps more notably, Cochran and his exploits had provided the model for the character of Flip Corkin in Milton Caniff's "Terry and the Pirates" comic strip, a fact that today's air commandos relay with much pride.)[63] Cochran's cocommander, Lieutenant Colonel John R. Alison, was noted for his technical abilities and service in Russia and Iraq in support of the U.S. Lend-Lease program, in addition to becoming an ace fighter pilot after downing six Japanese aircraft while serving in the 23rd Fighter Group (previously known as the Flying Tigers).

Cochran and Alison, with the unlimited support of General Arnold, put together Project 9. Its mission was to provide air, transport, and evacuation support for the Chindit operation. The new unit was the first true implementation of what has come to be known as a composite wing. It included P-51A Mustang fighters, C-47 Dakota transport aircraft pulling CG-4A Waco gliders used as troop transports, the UC-64 Noorduyn Norseman transport, and L-1 Vigilant and L-5 Sentinel light planes for medical evacuations. Although a standard USAAF wing had approximately 2,000 men, because all of Project 9's forces were to be air transported, it was limited to just over 500 men. Training for the unit began October 1, 1943, in North Carolina.

Deploying in early November 1943, Project 9 set up shop at airstrips in Lalaghat and Hailakandi, India. The forces were received with some disbelief by the Southeast Asia Command and, eventually, great joy by General Wingate. Colonel Cochran, now sole commander with the full support of his deputy, Colonel Alison, quickly initiated flight training and within a week and a half the unit conducted a joint exercise with the Chindit soldiers, using twenty gliders to airlift and land 400 men. Continuous training with the British force resulted in teamwork so strong that after a fatal accident killing four British and three American men, the Chindit unit commander wrote to Cochran, "Please be assured that we will go with your boys any place, any time, anywhere," thus providing the 1st Air Commandos with its motto.[64]

As confidence in the command grew, its mission expanded, eventually including a combat engineer and a bomber capability. The Quadrant Plan, and General Arnold's guidance, called for the renamed 5318th Provisional Unit (Air) to "facilitate the forward movement of the British Chindit force, facilitate the supply and evacuation of the Chindits, provide a small air covering and striking force, and acquire air experience 'under the conditions expected to be encountered.' "[65]

This purpose was regularly at risk. British and American conventional commanders kept attempting to modify the special operations mission or subsume the 5318th into their own forces. By February 1944, however, General Arnold had made it clear that the sole purpose of Cochran's unit was the support of General Wingate's special force and Operation Thursday.

Wingate's plan for Operation Thursday called for two small columns of Chindits, airborne engineers, and air transportable equipment to be moved by gliders to jungle clearings in Burma. USAAF engineers would prepare landing strips on the day of the initial landing. C-47 transport planes would bring in supporting members of the special force on the following nights. The operations began on March 5, 1944, and the initial day's losses were high. Of the thirty-seven gliders that arrived during the first night of Operation Thursday, thirty-four were severely damaged. Twenty-four men were killed, and thirty-three were injured seriously enough to require evacuation. At the same time, 539 troops and 29,972 pounds of supplies were unloaded in the middle of the Burmese jungle, behind Japanese lines. By the end of the first day an airstrip had been cut into the jungle and overnight the first group of sixty-two C-47s landed at that first airfield.

Operation Thursday continued until March 11. During that week of operations the 5318th Provisional Unit (Air) transported over 2,000 personnel and 104,681 pounds of supplies. Eighty gliders were launched, and the C-47 force, including the 5318th's Troop Carrier Command and RAF flights, conducted 579 sorties, all behind enemy lines. It was the first use of airlifted forces as a primary invasion force.

After the initial operation's conclusion, Colonel Cochran's unit continued to support the Chindits with resupply, close air support, and casualty evacuation. The Allied air forces gained air superiority over Burma. During March and April the Japanese forces lost well over 200 aircraft. Cochran's single squadron of fighters and twelve bombers, renamed once again as the 1st Air Commando Group, accounted for more than 35 percent of the total Japanese aircraft destroyed. The new unit had accomplished its mission with tremendous success. The air commandos and Wingate's special force caused confusion and chaos behind the Japanese lines, destroyed a large portion of the Japanese force, and greatly limited the ability of Japan to resupply the force that remained.

General Arnold, recognizing the success of the 1st Air Commando Group, planned to establish four more air commando groups, each with an associated Troop Carrier Command, now known as a Combat Cargo Group. Two new groups, the 2nd and 3rd Air Commando Groups, were activated and Colonel Alison was in charge of their training. The two other planned groups were never activated because, with the death of General Wingate, the argument for the retaking of Burma lost its strength. Eventually the 2nd Group and its Combat Cargo Group were deployed to India to support the operations of the 1st Group. The 3rd Group was deployed to New Guinea for the assault on Mindanao as part of the invasion of the Philippines. When Allied commanders decided to make the initial landings at Leyte, the 3rd Group was no longer required, and it was integrated into the 5th Air Force as a standard operating unit. Soon after, the 1st and 2nd Groups were also subsumed by conventional air units.

The United States maintained only a small air force special operations capability in the years following World War II. With the onset of the Korean War, air force special operations aircraft supported CIA and army intelligence teams infiltrating North and South Korea, primarily with C-47 and C-119 transport aircraft. Intending to provide greater support to unconventional warfare and counterinsurgency operations, the U.S. Air Force activated three wings, the 580th, 581st, and 582nd air resupply and communication wings. These were mixed wings, including transport and bomber aircraft as well as seaplanes and helicopters. Despite the great potential of these units, only one wing ever saw action in Korea, and all three were inactivated by late 1953.[66]

In the years after Korea, air force special operators, like their army and navy counterparts, were asked to respond to the perceived threat of "wars of liberation" in the third world. In April 1961 the air force established the 4400th Combat Crew Training Squadron (CCTS) at Hurlburt Field, Florida. This squadron is the direct predecessor of today's air force special operations units. CCTS developed techniques for advising and training counterinsurgency forces throughout the third world. Following quickly upon the unit's first operation, training Malayan paratroopers, CCTS soon deployed to Vietnam in Operation Farmgate. Working out of Bien Hoa in South Vietnam, the CCTS deployment soon became the center of all air force counterinsurgency efforts. The 4400th was enlarged to a group in March 1962, and in April it became part of the U.S. Air Force Special Air Warfare Center at Eglin Air Force Base, Florida.

In 1964 air force special operations expanded to Laos and Thailand, where teams trained Laotian and Thai pilots as part of Operation Waterpump. By 1966 air force training teams were deployed to nine countries. This was the peak of air force special operations: force levels rose above 6,000 men and 550 aircraft. During that same year, in an innovation that had begun the year before, airborne gunships, including AC-47s, AC-119s, and AC-130s, joined the force. These special operations gunships performed invaluable service throughout the remainder of the Vietnam War.

During the late 1960s, air commandos often worked quite closely with American and Vietnamese special operations forces. When the air force forced the army to give up the twin-engined Caribou transport planes used to supply the CIDG camps and villages in Vietnam, air force special operations pilots and crews gave the CIDG program their full support. Crews flew at night, in the mountains, and often in bad weather. Air force special operators also supported the 5th Mike force in nighttime airdrops. Air force forward air controllers (FACs) lived in Special Forces camps and flew Bird Dog propeller planes to conduct aerial reconnaissance.[67]

Like the special operations forces in the army and navy, air force special operations lost its sense of purpose and apparent relevance in the post-Vietnam American military. The Special Air Warfare Center had become U.S. Air Force Special Operations Force (USAFSOF) in July 1968, the equivalent of a numbered air force, the largest type of air force operational unit. By 1974, however, air force special operations were in a dramatic decline. In June 1974 USAFSOF was redesignated the 834th Tactical Composite Wing. The following year, the organization was renamed once again, becoming the 1st Special Operations Wing. By 1979 only one air force special operations wing was left, with its squadrons composed of AC-130A Spectre gunships, MC-130E Combat Talons, and CH-3E Jolly Green and UH-1N Huey helicopters.

The extent to which the U.S. Air Force special operations capability had been diminished would be demonstrated to the world in the tragedy in Iran in April 1980. Following this failure, the air force's refusal to support special operations would be critical in the fight to rebuild the U. S. special operations capability.

Into the Abyss: SOF and the Post-Vietnam Era

The withdrawal of American forces from Vietnam and the eventual fall of South Vietnam plunged the American military into a period of darkness, confusion, and frustration. The lessons of Vietnam were not willingly learned. Instead, the focus of both the American public and its military forces was on the single thought, "Never again." "Never again" meant to the military that U.S. forces would never again be sent to war without the "full support" of American public opinion. Lost on the conventional military leadership were many lessons on how low-intensity-conflict wars in general, or counterinsurgency wars in particular, should be fought. Andrew Krepinevich argues that as it entered Vietnam, "The United States Army was neither trained nor organized to fight effectively in an insurgency conflict environment. . . . [It had] a focus on mid-intensity, or conventional, war and a reliance on high volumes of firepower to minimize casualties—in effect, the substitution of material costs at every available opportunity to avoid payment in blood."[68] The U.S. Army's doctrine, referred to by Krepinevich as the "army concept," resulted from a history that was centered on the three successful conventional wars that the army had fought in the first half of the twentieth century. As American involvement in the Vietnam conflict fizzled out, the army did not recognize that the inflexibility of the "concept" ingrained in its organizational culture had an impact on American operations in Vietnam.[69]

Ironically, U.S. involvement in Vietnam was largely the operational highpoint for U.S. special operations forces until the reorganization in the late 1980s. U.S. special operations force structure reached its peak during the late 1960s with seven active Special Forces groups, two active SEAL teams, two UDT teams, and the U.S. Air Force Special Operations Force. Although, as described above, special operations forces were frequently misused and rarely had a significant strategic effect, Vietnam gave American special operators the opportunity to do what they were trained to do at a tactical level, including undertaking unconventional direct action missions and nation building or foreign internal development, which also meant training indigenous forces. Special operators were recognized during Vietnam to an unprecedented extent. They were highly decorated and celebrated in movies and songs.

With recognition, however, came identification. And if the American public wanted to turn its back on the military in an effort to forget the mistakes and excesses of Vietnam, the first to be discarded were the special operators. Special Forces, SEALs, and air commandos were doubly penalized upon withdrawal from Vietnam. Tarred by the experience in Vietnam, the special operations forces fell victim to public opinion and to a conventional military leadership who resented and mistrusted those forces they viewed as having acted "unilaterally" and "unprofessionally." As discussed by a former commander of the 75th Ranger Regiment, "After

Vietnam, special operations forces were cut back to a greater degree than conventional forces. Were these cuts the result of a backlash? . . . I think a lot of it was backlash. You heard people talk about the 'snake-eaters' and 'those cowboys.' . . .Vietnam had a real derogatory effect on the army . . . [on] Special Forces in particular. . . . [Special operations forces] were seen [by the conventional forces] as less than professional. . . . the people who run the services, all of the services, are not special-operations-forces-type people. . . . They come from the conventional world. . . . They didn't want to understand [special operations]."[70]

The penalty was a near-eradication of an American special operations ability during the 1970s. As mentioned earlier, the air 'commandos were almost completely disbanded. Many pilots and air crews either left the air force or moved to conventional aircraft. It was difficult to convince a Strategic Air Command (SAC) or Tactical Air Command (TAC) commander that special operators offered any demonstrable benefit to the air force. Special operations missions supported army, and occasionally navy, ground forces. As the U.S. military turned back toward the Soviet menace, and the air force emphasized World War III and turned its back on the jungle warfare of Vietnam, air force special operations were greeted with an unenthusiastic "so what" by the TAC and SAC commanders.

The fate of naval special warfare was more complicated. The good news for special operators was that the navy created a special warfare specialty (designated 1130) for its officers in 1969 and a special operations specialty (designated 1140) in 1971. SEALs and members of the UDTs had initially been "unrestricted line officers," or "1100s." The 1100 designation meant that an officer had to spend a part of his career with the surface fleet and was expected to successfully complete a "command at sea" to be eligible for the rank of captain. Enlisted personnel in naval special warfare continued to have the traditional navy "ratings," or specialties. These specialties joined the surface warfare, submarine warfare, and air warfare designations.[71] After 1969 officers could spend their entire careers within naval special warfare and no longer required "credentialing" through surface assignments. The good news is, however, also the bad news. Although the creation of the special warfare specialty is frequently offered by SEALs as evidence of the navy's moving ahead of the army and air force in developing special operations forces,[72] on closer examination it seems likely that the navy established the specialty to push the "problem" of special operators aside and farther away from the mainstream navy.

It is true that most naval special operators, particularly the SEALs, had little interest in a career in the conventional navy. Even during the 1960s and Vietnam, the heyday of the SEALs, officers were discouraged from joining special operations units. Those who volunteered to serve with the team were willing to accept the cost to their careers in return for the challenge offered by these highly motivated and demanding units. Rear Admiral Raymond Smith, naval special warfare commander, joined the navy as an enlisted sailor in 1962. His commanders recognized his potential and supported his applying to a preparatory school and then the Naval Academy. Upon graduation in 1967, then-Ensign Smith "went to sea in a ship, because in those days Annapolis graduates were not permitted to become SEALs. [I]t was not considered an appropriate career for an Annapolis man. Appropriate careers were flying an airplane, driving a ship, or being on a submarine. You were permitted to volunteer [for the SEALs] after a year. Which I did."[73]

Most officers who volunteered for the SEALs or UDTs, particularly Naval Academy graduates, had served in surface fleet assignments before entering training. All accepted the fact that their opportunities for promotion would be greatly limited when they chose to leave the surface fleet.

Interviews with SEALs who chose to join special warfare in the 1960s and early 1970s reiterate the question of whether the navy was interested in allowing these officers to pursue their vocation when it established the SPECWAR specialty or whether it was instead only attempting to push aside those who were "depriving" other surface line officers of command opportunities aboard ship. The new specialties allowed officers to spend more time in SPECWAR units, but it also prevented them from serving in those assignments necessary to reach higher command. The primary cost to naval special operators was a severe limit on career potential. The change in career path and potential did not, however, dissuade those who wanted to become a SEAL or join the UDTs. A long-time SEAL officer explained the trade-off between a special warfare specialty and rank, "You could reasonably stay in [for your entire career] and have all your assignments within naval special-warfare-related jobs. . . . Reasonable expectation after a twenty-year career would be to retire as a lieutenant commander. . . . And all of us entered into it knowing that. Just because this is what we wanted to do for a living."[74]

Finding its place in the post–Vietnam world was not easy for the naval special warfare community. Having their own career path allowed the special operators to do what they loved best, but it also increasingly isolated them from the conventional navy, which nearly resulted in the placement of the SEALs in the U.S. Navy Reserve. The SEALs and UDTs found themselves in the ironic situation common to all American special operations forces. As it attempted to learn and act upon the lessons from extensive combat experience in Vietnam, Navy SPECWAR's organizational focus became more and more removed from the concerns of the conventional commanders of the 1970s. Naval special operators had their own warfare specialty and their own insignia.[75] They were able to continue the kind of training they enjoyed. SEAL teams and UDTs took advantage of their senior officers' and NCOs' extensive experience in Vietnam to learn the tricks of the trade. The SEALs focused on land warfare in a riverine-jungle environment, while the UDTs continued to emphasize hydrographic reconnaissance.[76] But the navy, like other military services, was trying to escape Vietnam and return to a more traditional orientation as American security interests aggressively returned to a bipolar strategic view. The navy's interest was in submarines and aircraft carriers, not in small-boat operations in third world jungles: "The navy was under a lot of stress in terms of . . . mission and role. . . . Vietnam was something we wanted to put behind us—anything that even smacked of Vietnam. And we [SEALs] smacked of Vietnam; we were a preeminent force there. We smacked of it and we didn't evolve. We stayed in the Vietnam mentality. That's how we started, and that's what we thought we were. The navy wanted out of that. We became almost irrelevant."[77]

The navy appeared not to know what to do with the SEAL teams, in particular. Identifying amphibious missions for the UDTs to support was difficult enough. Imagining what need there was for riverine operations by the SEALs was nearly impossible. The conventional commanders were thoroughly occupied with their efforts to define their role in the redefined strategic environment.

Funding for naval special warfare in the Department of the Navy program and budget dried up rapidly in the early and mid-1970s. Although training continued at Coronado and Little Creek, training deployments were few. Actual operations were even rarer. One of the few actual SEAL combat operations after the withdrawal from Vietnam demonstrates the confusion in the navy about what SEALs were to do. In 1975 a small Cambodian force stopped the freighter *Mayaguez* and kidnapped its crew.[78] The American response was a task force composed of marine, air force, and navy forces, including air force and navy special operations forces. The president and the Defense Department sent a U.S. carrier task force to rescue the hostages.[79] The task force included several air force special operations aircraft and air crews. Delta platoon from SEAL Team 1 was alerted in Subic Bay but then ordered to stand down. In the first rescue attempt, made without any reconnaissance by special warfare units, Cambodian forces downed three marine helicopters, resulting in heavy casualties. Intelligence and communications were so poor that an air force special operations pilot was forced to use walkie-talkies in combination with his aircraft radio and act as a go-between for the ground forces involved in the assault on Koh Tang Island off the Cambodian coast.[80] The over 200-strong marine force was forced to withdraw from the island where the hostages were believed held. By the time the marines were withdrawn, they suffered fifteen killed, three missing, and most of the helicopters destroyed.[81]

Following this disaster, Delta platoon from SEAL Team 1, commanded by Lieutenant (j.g.) D. T. Coulter, was brought forward by Rear Admiral R. T. Coogan, the carrier task force commander. Coogan informed the lieutenant that the SEALs' mission was to approach the Cambodian island unarmed and waving a white flag. Once they arrived on the island, the SEALs were to retrieve the bodies of the marines and helicopter crew members, as well as the black boxes and coding devices from the helicopters. The admiral planned to drop leaflets to notify the Cambodians that the SEALs were on a humanitarian mission and should not be harmed. The wisdom of this mission was certainly unclear, and one is hard-pressed to conclude that such a mission would have taken advantage of the SEALs' unique capabilities. Apparently reaching the same conclusion, the SEAL platoon commander refused the mission, arguing that the chances of the Cambodians' reading or believing the leaflets were small, and of honoring the U.S. request even less likely. Instead, the lieutenant proposed a true SEAL mission: having the SEALs swim in at night to conduct a strategic reconnaissance and collect the bodies and boxes. Fortunately for Lieutenant (j.g.) Coulter, the admiral had not issued a direct order, and the platoon commander had offered an alternative. The Cambodians returned the missing crew members before the task force officers made a decision about the next step.[82]

As naval special warfare approached its nadir, training was at a bare minimum. Equipment left over from the Vietnam era was at the end of its usefulness. One SEAL who joined the navy in 1975 for the sole purpose of going into special operations recalled: "I can remember being issued an M-16 and cleaning it one day and looking down the barrel and not seeing any rifling. Basically it was a smooth bore weapon. It had so many rounds fired through the barrel that it was absolutely worn out."[83]

Bottom was hit in the mid-1970s when the Department of the Navy considered decommissioning all naval special warfare units or at least placing them in the U.S. Navy Reserve. The marines and some naval commanders believed that the marines could be self-supporting for most traditional amphibious missions and could easily fill in any gaps in their capabilities for hydrographic reconnaissance. The unconventional warfare mission of the SEALs was generally regarded as separate from the mission of the fleet. According to Rear Admiral Irve "Chuck" LeMoyne, who eventually became the highest-ranking SEAL, the effort to remove these units from the active-duty navy was made because the navy wanted money to support its surface fleet and gave little value to naval special warfare. During the course of putting together the navy's "program,". a document describing how resources would be used over the five-year midterm, a vice admiral on the navy staff in Washington proposed a new class of surface combatant ships. A captain who was working for the admiral recognized the paucity of support for the SEALs and proposed inactivation of special warfare to provide additional funding. When then-Lieutenant Commander LeMoyne asked the captain why he had recommended elimination of the SEALs' unique capability, given the relatively small savings, the captain responded that he wanted any and all money he could find.[84]

Following this incident, the chief of naval operations, Admiral Elmo Zumwalt, sent the two fleet commanders messages requesting recommendations for the future of naval special warfare. The fleet commanders recommended either placing all SEALs into the reserves or disestablishing the units. The UDTs, according to the fleet commanders, should remain in the active force because they clearly supported the fleets' amphibious capabilities. Despite the lack of support by the fleet commanders, Admiral Zumwalt provided a stay of execution, directing that the SEALs were to remain in the fleet. The future of the SEAL teams remained as uncertain as the support of the next chief of naval operations.[85]

Like the SEALs and the UDTs, U.S. Army Special Forces were indelibly marked with the war the United States and its military wanted to forget. If the conventional forces had largely ignored Special Forces before Vietnam, the conventional soldiers now distrusted and deplored the units that had gained the "snake-eater" reputation during the war. As the military shifted its focus from Vietnam to direct conflict with the Soviet Union, Special Forces and their unconventional warfare and foreign internal defense skills were no longer held to be useful. The army's cold war concerns and increasingly constrained resources resulted in a force structure that was dominated by heavy forces (mechanized infantry and armor) destined for deployment to Europe in the event of a Central European war.

As a result of Vietnam, foreign assistance programs in general, and military assistance programs in particular, became discredited in Congress. Congress reduced or eliminated military civic action programs, foreign assistance, and diplomatic missions, otherwise known as "foreign internal defense" or "nation-building" missions.[86] These reductions encouraged further slashing of Special Forces units and manpower. The fabled Green Berets faded into the legends of the war.

The decline of Special Forces began even before the American pullout from Vietnam was complete. Special Forces were pulled from Vietnam beginning in 1969, with the 5th Special Forces Group returning to Fort Bragg in March 1971. After the pullout of ground troops from Vietnam, Special Forces manpower was slashed from tens of thousands to approximately 3,600 by the mid-1970s. There was, in addition, an authorized strength of 5,800 in four reserve and National Guard groups spread over the United States.[87] The 3rd, 6th, and 8th SFGs, all augmented in the early to mid-1960s to become special action forces during Vietnam, were all inactivated by 1971. The remaining members of the 8th SFG in Panama became the third battalion of the 7th SFG that was headquartered at Fort Bragg. The 1st SFG in Okinawa was inactivated in 1974, leaving behind a small SF detachment in Korea. Although not quite reaching the low of 1,500 men assigned to Special Forces units in 1957, the 3,600 men remaining in Special Forces were not enough to fill out the three active component groups that remained in the late 1970s.[88]

In a study sponsored by the Army War College, Colonel Corson Hilton writes, "Special Forces [in the 1970s] reflected the lower priority that had been placed on it. Single units were tasked to conduct operations in multiple theaters, with obsolescent equipment, and at marginal manning levels. Command and control was cumbersome and not well understood by the army. Special Forces' doctrine was developed in the 1950s for unconventional warfare and did not address the new and emerging Air-Land Battle concepts."[89]

The quality of Special Forces personnel, like that of the conventional army, declined further during the 1970s. Although Special Forces units were a volunteer force during Vietnam, veterans left the army at the end of the conflict. Recruits during the mid- to late-1970s could be assigned to Special Forces training and assessment immediately upon joining the army. The result was a loss of maturity in Special Forces and a downgrading of requirements for entering and completing the Special Forces qualification course. A-Detachments (teams) consisted primarily of E-3s (privates first class) and E-4s (corporals), often commanded by second lieutenants.[90] This remained true throughout the 1970s. One Special Forces colonel explains, "The Special Forces 'qual course' as it now stands is significantly more rigorous than when I went through [in 1974]. But . . . in defense of the Army, we had a manning problem. We had the hollow Army. People today don't believe what the Army of 1976 was like. That's seared in the brains of all [of us in the military]."[91]

Training also suffered during the 1970s. Although Special Forces still offered its qualification course (Q-course) at Fort Bragg, the opportunities for overseas and regional orientation training were few and far between. Increasingly, menial housekeeping and post details took precedence over training opportunities. The opportunities for joint training were nonexistent. Neither the Special Forces nor the SEALs trained regularly with the few remaining air force special operations units, and virtually never did the Special Forces and SEALs train together. The one exception was the occasional sending of a SEAL officer to the Special Forces and/or Ranger schools.[92]

Still, there were volunteers who wanted an adventure beyond what could be found in the conventional forces, and they valued the camaraderie of small teams. Special Forces provided a challenge and an element of excitement that attracted volunteers no matter what the advice of their peers in conventional units. Like those who had joined Special Forces units in the 1960s, many volunteers took a kind of perverse pride in swimming against the tide. These men joined Special Forces in the 1970s, recognizing that qualifying for Special Forces would not help a career. Officers usually served in command or headquarters positions twice, once in a Special Forces unit and once in a conventional unit, in order to qualify for promotions. Unlike the SEALs, the army did not have a Special Forces branch until 1987, and so all SF officers were assigned to some other branch, such as armor or infantry. Qualified officers in Special Forces rotated between Special Forces and conventional units. If, for example, an SF officer had been the executive officer of an SF battalion, he was then expected to serve a tour as the executive officer of a "real," or conventional, combat unit: "In order to survive you had to bounce back and forth [between conventional and SF units]. But that was good . . . because one of the main things that Special Forces does is train other people . . . and you have some credibility.[93]

As promotions slowed down throughout the army during the 1970s, assignments to the Special Forces were generally regarded by the conventional leadership as something to be tolerated, an assignment to fill in the time between serious conventional assignments.

By 1975 the only remaining Special Forces groups were the 5th, the

7th, and the 10th SFGs. Those units that were forward deployed were nearly inactive. For example, the third battalion of the 7th SFG was deployed in Panama with the primary mission of providing mobile training teams (MTTs) to train Latin American forces. During one eighteen-month period from 1977 to 1978, the battalion sent out only three MTTs. As a result of the army's REFORGER exercise for reinforcing and defending Europe in the case of a Warsaw Pact invasion, and the belief that any future conflict in Europe would be so short (approximately ten days) that partisan operations would be irrelevant, all but one battalion of the 10th SFG was withdrawn from Europe.[94] Perhaps the lowest point for Special Forces came in 1979, when the army's leadership considered placing the 7th SFG in the U.S. Army Reserves, partly because of an aversion to the possibility that the United States could become involved in another Vietnam-type conflict in Central America.[95]

As a result of their relatively high profile during the Vietnam conflict, the special operations forces had lost not only their meager support in the conventional military but also the support of the American public, which was sick of Vietnam and appalled by the excesses attributed to some members of the U.S. special operations forces in CIA-sponsored operations in the late 1960s. And yet, as the leadership of the conventional military pushed the special operations forces aside to reorient the military toward the U.S.-Soviet conflict and a large-scale conventional war in Central Europe, it lost sight of the value of special operations forces in support of the conventional mission. Brigadier General William Kernan used hindsight to comment on the conventional military's dismissal of the applicability of special operations forces to post–Vietnam national security interests: "With the Soviet threat there was probably more need for SOF. . . . [In] combined warfare, or what we now call 'multinational operations,' . . . you're going to need the unique skills that the Special Forces bring in the way of language skills and cultural awareness. [SOF are] . . . expert trainers that you would need to go out and support some of [our] allies. . . . Couple[d] with the deep [reconnaissance] operations, there was probably as much a need post-Vietnam as there was during the Vietnam era, if not more. But we just didn't see the world that way then."[96] Decisionmakers in conventional forces, trying to escape the legacy of Vietnam, cut the forces they most identified with the "bad news" of that conflict. The result was undermanned, underequipped special operations forces that had little effective capability. Military leaders turned away from the tactical and strategic lessons of Vietnam and thus did not recognize the potential value of the flexibility of special operations forces and their unconventional capabilities, especially when applied before a crisis had reached the point of a major military conflict. Lieutenant General Wilson argued, "We may have come retching and vomiting out of Vietnam saying, 'never again,' but the only way it would be never again would be if we attended to the Vietnam-type of problems while they were still in their incipient states."[97]

3

Survival of a Precarious Value

There's no doubt in my mind that when [a Special Forces candidate has] reached me, he's a good bayonet fighter. But how do I make him think at the operational level of war and even focus a little on the strategic level. . . . The training is to see if the young man can think. . . . Now he's got to be able to do that for himself.

Major Greg Phillips, May 1994

The special operations forces (SOF) are a unique community within the U.S. military. Their organizational culture is separate and distinct from the conventional military. Indeed, the strength of this organizational culture has allowed the special operations community to survive the dramatic force cuts and dislocation that have followed World War II and Vietnam, including near-elimination of the special operations forces in the late 1970s. This culture also led members of the SOF community, aided by like-minded members of Congress and the Department of Defense to develop, pass, and implement SOF reform legislation of the 1980s.

Building an Organizational Culture

Theories about organizational culture abound in the scholarly literature. Two in particular resonate with the SOF story. In *Administrative Behavior,* Herbert Simon views organizational culture with a narrow focus on the loyalty of the individual to organizational objectives.[1] Philip Selznick (who also came up with the concept of "precarious values") takes a much broader view of organizational culture in *Leadership in Administration.*[2] He recognizes the role of organizational history and the importance of membership-selection criteria for defining and maintaining a distinct culture. "Organizational character," he says, is the result of a unique organizational history supported by selectivity in recruiting new organizational members and the use of training to inculcate organizational doctrine. The result is the emergence of special capabilities, or "distinctive competence," and special limitations.[3]

James Q. Wilson discusses the costs and benefits of a strong organizational culture. A widely held culture provides a sense of mission. "A sense of mission confers a feeling of special worth on the members, provides a basis for recruiting and socializing new members, and enables the administrators to economize on the use of other incentives." The downside of this strong, unifying culture is the problem of "selective attention," that is, those tasks outside of the culture will be valued less and receive less attention.[4]

Analysis of military organizational culture is not new.[5] In the U.S. Navy there are the black shoe, brown shoe, and "felt" shoe cultures, referring to those whose careers are focused on ships of the line, naval aviation, or submarines. The U.S. Army's combat support and combat service support branches, including the engineers and logistics, have a different perspective on combat operations than the combat arms branches such as infantry and armor. The U.S. Air Force is also divided into distinctive communities, with the three largest being those in the bomber force, "tac air" or fighters, and airlift. Each of these subgroups within the military services has its own traditions, insignia, and unit pride.

Within each of these groups are prestigious units and specialties such as the 82nd Airborne Division, fighter pilots, or even the Marine Corps. Each is defined by particular skills or qualifications and a selectivity beyond the usual military recruiting standards. However, certain units in the military are distinct even from this classification. As argued by Eliot Cohen, even in "a well-run and motivated army . . . some units are more elite than others."[6] Cohen argues that three criteria define elite units: they are perpetually assigned special or unusual missions; they conduct missions that require only a few exceptionally trained and physically capable volunteers; and they gain a reputation for bravery and success.[7] The first two criteria have applied to, and been encouraged by, U.S. special operations forces. The third criterion is a fragile characteristic that ebbs and flows according to the perceived need for, and misuse of, these units.

What, then, is unique about SOF organizational culture? How is SOF culture somehow different from the "unit pride" that is traditional throughout the conventional military? Although unit pride—exhibited through the wearing of berets, special insignia, and so on—is certainly at least as important to the special operations forces as to conventional units, the unique missions of special operations forces require unique training, equipment, tactics, thought, and ultimately, a different type of individual. Special operators do not do what conventional forces do, and they do not think the way conventional forces think. This unconventional approach was apparent in the earliest years of U.S. special operations in World War II. The unique special operations approach to military operations is supported by the SOF selection and assessment process, and developed and maintained by training both within and outside of units.

Special operators conduct operations that are outside the realm and tactics of the conventional battlefield. Military personnel attracted to special operations forces are those who thrive within the looser structure and culture of innovation that characterizes SOF. Most often, they are also attracted to the closeness and trust inherent in a small team. Serving in a special operations unit has rarely, if ever, been "career-enhancing." Careers were made and promotions received for service on navy ships, battalion command, or flying jets. Those who stayed in the special units stayed because that is what they wanted to do, regardless of the effect on their careers.

Operational requirements for special operations forces both attract and result in a set of personal characteristics, an identifiable mindset or way of thinking about things that further distinguishes members of the SOF community from conventional officer and enlisted personnel. John M. Collins, a long-time staff member of the Congressional Research Service, has conducted several studies of U.S. special operations forces and has summarized the unique characteristics found in a successful special operator:

> Innate intelligence, physical strength, agility, stamina, and standard training are not enough. Temperaments also must combine resourcefulness, ingenuity, pragmatism, and patience with self-discipline and dependability to extraordinary degrees. . . . Area orientation is a universal requirement, for psychological warriors as well as those with lethal weapons, whether operations take place on native or foreign soil. Even common tasks call for uncommon skills applied under uncommon circumstances. [For example] . . . any rifle company can conduct conventional raids and ambushes, but it cannot do well indefinitely, [and] while [it is] living off hostile land, safely relieve an enemy convoy of volatile cargo, . . . or accomplish many other special missions.[8]

In interviews with members of the special operations forces, this common set of characteristics was brought up time and time again. Captain Tom McGrath, a former commander of SEAL Team 4, explained the dominant characteristics of himself and other SEALs this way: "Most SEALs, I think, maximize their God-given ability. Quitting is very, very selected against. Our training is spent in the water, cold water, and you can quit anytime. I mean it's absolutely easy to quit, but it is irreversible."[9]

The development and maintenance of a unique SOF culture, part of which is the identification of these common personal characteristics, begins with the selection and assessment process. Training reinforces Selznick's "distinct way of thinking," the element of organizational character that separates special operations forces from the conventional U.S. military. Special operators are selected and trained to "respond in different ways to the same stimuli" because it is vital to how they operate.[10] Rear Admiral Ray Smith, former commander of the Naval Special Warfare Command, explains what the SEALs look for in selecting candidates for SEAL training:

> We want a kid who can think. . . . who can make decisions on his own. . . . Our enlisted are put in incredibly responsible positions. . . . SDVs [SEAL delivery vehicles] are piloted by an E5 [mid-level enlisted grade]. The [U.S.] Army and Marine Corps stand in absolute amazement at things like that. . . . You have to have a young man who has the capacity to think on his own under very stressful conditions.[11]

Although what makes a strong special operator is readily identified by members of the SOF community, identifying these characteristics among prospective trainees has proved to be extremely difficult. This difficulty is addressed through extremely demanding training programs for army, navy, and air force special operators, programs that are designed to identify those who have not only the physical ability but also the mental and emotional strength to become a successful special operator. For this reason, attrition rates in training classes for SEALs and Special Forces run from 50 percent to 70 percent, with a somewhat lower rate for air force special operators, who have strong flying and air crew skills before entering their specialized training. General Wayne Downing, third commander in chief of U.S. Special Operations Command, describes the goals of the selection, assessment, and training phases as follows: "Our assessment and selection programs are designed to get people who do things in an unconventional manner. Who are accustomed to working in scenarios and in situations that are very unstructured. . . . Our people will generally come up with a very novel approach of how to solve problems, and many times people on the conventional side of the armed forces are very uncomfortable because our people do not do things in the traditional ways."[12]

Selection, Training, and Assessment: Navy SEALs

Prospective SEALs, like all members of special operations forces, volunteer. They do not become SEALs, informally known as "frogmen" in reference to the earlier underwater demolition teams, until they successfully complete Basic Underwater Demolition/SEAL (BUD/S) training and have served a probationary period of six to eighteen months in a SEAL unit. For most of those who volunteer, a defining characteristic is that they want to be a SEAL rather than follow the more traditional career paths for outstanding officer and enlisted personnel. When asked, "Why does a Naval Academy graduate want to be a SEAL?" a current SEAL platoon commander, a third-generation Naval Academy graduate, responded, "When I got there [the Academy] I wasn't quite sure what I wanted to do. I think I wanted to be a pilot. But I started rowing crew when I was a freshman. There's a lot of guys that rowed crew that ended up going special warfare. A lot of [the] upper class that I saw got into the mindset of working out hard, taking care of yourself, that kind of camaraderie. In crew it was an eight-man team in the boat, totally relying on each other. That kind of thing [bodes] real well for special warfare.[13]

When asked how his advisers at the Naval Academy reacted to his interest in the SEALs, the lieutenant responded, "I was a mechanical engineer that was over a 3.4 [grade point average] and that automatically puts you in submarines in a lot of people's minds. But I got interested in [SEALs], kept paying attention to it. There was a lot of pressure from senior officers, 'Well, I don't think you should do that with your career— you should go surface, or you should go nuclear-powered submarines.' Without a doubt, the day I got to BUD/S I knew I made the right choice."[14]

Volunteers are assigned to the Naval Special Warfare Center in Coronado, California, where after a seven-week pretraining conditioning course, the "tadpoles" enter BUD/S training, a twenty-five-week course divided into three phases. Unlike nearly all other military training, officers and enlisted personnel train together at BUD/S. Officers maintain leadership roles while adhering to the same mental and physical standards as the enlisted personnel.[15] Special Forces officers and enlisted personnel are now going through selected training together as a result of the lesson learned from the SEALs.

The first phase officially focuses on physical conditioning, but in addition to evaluating and improving the physical capabilities of the prospective SEALs the primary goal of the first phase is to determine if a trainee can think like a SEAL and work with a team. Trainees go through BUD/S as a part of six-man boat crews. They learn to trust and rely on each other. The physical and mental demands of the training rapidly increase as BUD/S instructors attempt to identify who won't quit and who can "maximize innate abilities." Mental games are played by the instructors on students who are forced to their physical limits. One BUD/S graduate remembered, "We'd do a four mile run, come back, and that wasn't fast enough. Grab your paddle this time and do it faster. Go back down. Come back. No, that wasn't fast enough. So now you've run eight miles [and you've got to do it again]. We only ran about 500 yards [the third time]. But in the process of that 500 yards [guys say], 'I quit. I can't make it.'"[16] The instructors had never intended to have the group run a third four-mile run. In reality, they were trying to find out who would quit because of believing they couldn't make it and who would try to see if they could succeed.

The climax of the first phase, and in many respects the defining moment of SEAL training, is the sixth week, better known as Hell Week. During the week the trainees are pushed to their absolute limits. They accomplish things they had not known they were capable of. From Sunday through Friday the trainees are kept on the move twenty-four hours a day. They are deprived of sleep, with a ration of six hours of sleep for the entire week and in reality as little as four. The recruits are running, swimming, climbing, and exercising nonstop. They are in and out of the water throughout the night and are generally cold, wet, and exhausted.

The week has several purposes. The first is to determine how the trainees deal with uncertainty and confusion. The trainees do not know what lies ahead, and they don't know how well they are doing or what it even means to "do well." They are given conflicting and constantly changing orders and are not told when one task is complete or when the next one will begin. Sleep deprivation is considered key in an attempt to determine how the stress will prey on a trainee's mind. A second assessment made during the week is how a trainee functions as part of a team. During the week each boat crew must carry its "rubber duck," a large inflatable boat, wherever the members go. Losing the boat is a team failure.

The stress and physical demands of Hell Week are nearly unimaginable to those who have not been through it. Trainees sometimes complete the week with sprained ankles, bone fractures, or pneumonia. Tales are told of trainees coming out of the water after a cold night swim, completely exhausted and shivering. An instructor approaches the trainee and whispers that if the trainee will just admit he can not continue the training, and that being a SEAL may not be right for him, the instructor will get him some hot coffee, a beer, and let him drive the instructor's car. The offer is a hard one to refuse at three o'clock in the morning on the fourth night without sleep.

Those who refuse to accept the BUD/S instructor's offer, however, are well on their way to proving they have what it takes to be a SEAL. The goal of the training is to determine who will not quit under extreme physical and mental stress, even in the face of seemingly impossible tasks. As might be imagined, attrition is high during Hell Week. Trainees in the first phase wear green helmets, and as they drop out during the week their helmets are lined up along the side of the courtyard at the Naval Special Warfare Center, a reminder both that it is possible to quit and that those who do not quit belong to a special group.

Hell Week is occasionally criticized outside the SEAL community, yet it is generally viewed as a key to SEAL training by those who have made it through. According to the Naval Special Warfare Center, every effort is made to prevent the week from being mere hazing and to prevent trainees from being seriously injured or killed. Medical personnel examine trainees each day. All trainees are provided with four meals a day to maintain the energy required to make it through. Trainees are allowed to declare "training time outs" to get clarification if the direction for the immediate task is unclear and "safety time outs" if there seems to be an immediate danger of injury. In talking with the Naval Special Warfare commander, Admiral Smith, it is clear that each dropout during the week is considered a regrettable loss of a good man. Admiral Smith and the BUD/S trainers work to prepare the students for the trials of Hell Week in the hope of reducing attrition and guaranteeing that those who quit are those who could not be SEALs. The week is in many respects like a SEAL operation gone wrong. Things do not go as planned, and one is asked to do more and endure more than one ever thought possible. A SEAL lieutenant described the mental skills needed to survive the ordeal:

> They always tell you to take it . . . step by step. . . . When an hour is too long, take it a minute at a time. . . . Some guys quit based solely on the fact that they thought the next evolution was a twenty-two-mile run, or they were convinced . . . we were going to . . . row up to La Jolla [from

Coronado]. . . . They [the instructors] have this briefing and safety boats all lined up. You're sitting there going, "OK, we're going to row to La Jolla." And the guys figure . . . there's no way we can do that, I'm out of here. But [in fact] we don't go. . . . It was a game. . . . When I was in Somalia, some of the ops we did over there, . . . night after night. No sleep. Hell Week is a great preparation for that."[17]

The second and third phases of BUD/S are no less demanding than the first. The second phase concentrates on diving operations with the use of open- and closed-circuit scuba gear. During this phase the trainees learn and are tested in "drown-proofing," underwater swimming skills, and scuba or closed-circuit techniques, including free ascents from a diving bell and coping with emergency situations such as damaged equipment. After learning the basic skills in a swimming pool and diving tank the trainees move to the Pacific Ocean, where the focus is on nighttime operations and swimming endurance. The final test of the second phase is a 5.5-mile, open-water swim. Once again, attrition is high during this phase, particularly once the students move into the ocean and meet the reality of very cold water, marine life, and strong currents, discouraging even to champion swimmers.

The third phase of BUD/S focuses on skills related to land warfare, demolition, and weapons. The trainees must now learn to become soldiers, or something resembling Special Forces, as they learn to shoot and conduct small-unit land operations. Perhaps the most difficult aspect of the third phase, besides the physical conditioning, and one which contrasts with more conventional land warfare training, is strict fire control. Conventional soldiers are taught to fight and shoot. SEALs, like the Special Forces, are taught to avoid fighting and shooting in order to remain undercover and complete their special reconnaissance or direct action mission. An eight-man SEAL squad is no match for the larger conventional forces they are working against. SEALs are taught to avoid shooting unless they are directly threatened by the gunfire and, when they must shoot, to fire only as much as is necessary for protection in order to save ammunition for the next situation that might be encountered as they escape.[18]

BUD/S identifies and strengthens those particular characteristics in trainees that make a SEAL a SEAL. What is most important about BUD/S training is what is learned about the potential of the trainees to think like SEALs: to come up with unconventional solutions for difficult problems; to work in a small team with very little outside support; to deal with uncertainty, confusion, and stress; and to never give up. Instructors learn which trainees are able to maintain calm in an atmosphere of chaos. The trainee learns the basic technical skills required in navy special operations and gains physical and mental confidence.

Navy trainees are not SEALs upon completing BUD/S. Instead, they have successfully shown that, having passed through a physical and psychological filter, they are capable of becoming SEALs. BUD/S graduates attend the U.S. Army Airborne School and are then assigned to a SEAL team. Trainees must serve a six- to eighteen-month probationary period, and be evaluated by their peers, to determine whether they fit into the community.[19] If the trainee successfully completes this final training he is presented with his trident device, or "Budweiser," the gaudy—and hard-won—gold badge proudly worn by SEALs.

The SEAL training illustrates how training is used to inculcate key characteristics of the SEAL organizational culture: working with and relying on team members; going beyond imagined physical limits; and never quitting until the mission is complete. Training is also used to develop a bond with the SEAL community, inadvertently lessening the tie with the conventional navy. Once the trainees complete BUD/S they learn other cultural characteristics, including "unconventional" thinking and absolute operational security, in their first SEAL unit.

Special Forces: Innovation in the Face of Uncertainty

The physical and mental demands made upon prospective members of the U.S. Army's Special Forces are in many ways similar to those made on the SEAL trainees. Although SEALs are recognized among special operators as having the most physically demanding training, Special Forces training emphasizes creativity and innovation under physical stress, and leadership and problem solving in the middle of isolation and uncertainty.

Attrition rates are high in Special Forces assessment, selection, and training, just as they are for SEALS. Most attrition occurs during the initial twenty-three-day assessment and selection phase, with its emphasis on physical conditioning. During the selection and assessment phase students take on an obstacle course, complete lengthy runs, carry forty-five pound rucksacks over long distances (ruck marches) in varying terrain, and successfully complete a series of military orienteering exercises. Students must also successfully complete a series of team drills. These are generally excruciatingly mundane tasks—such as using sandbags to move sand from one location to another—which, nonetheless, require ingenuity and teamwork to complete. Students also take tests that measure their educational level and language aptitude.

According to General Downing, one of the trickiest, and often most frustrating aspects of Special Forces training is the uncertainty: students do not know what is required to "successfully complete" any of the drills or exercises. Special Forces trainees are not told how they are doing or even what the standards are. "They just have this task that we have them do either as individuals or in small groups. Then we are subjecting them to increasing amounts of pressure. . . . we give them a lot of stress, they're not getting a lot of sleep, there's a lot of physical activity, and this just starts really preying on [their] minds."[20] Only the instructors know the acceptable range of the "management time" within which the student must complete an exercise. Records are kept of the student's performance in each event, and if he does not complete one of the events within the management time, that fact is highlighted. Highlighting does not necessarily mean passing or failing, although there are certain critical events that the instructors would prefer to be completed successfully. Failure to complete one or even a few events within management time does not necessarily prevent a candidate from moving on to the Special Forces Qualification Course. Special Forces instructors and evaluators evaluate the entire soldier—education, aptitude, motivation, accountability, communications, and his performance in each of the physical events.[21]

Only about 45 percent of the students who begin army Special Forces selection and assessment successfully complete it.[22] Eighty-five percent of those students who do pass selection and assessment subsequently succeed in the Special Forces Qualification Course. Some drop out late in the training, for instance, in the three-day, individual survival exercise in the woods.

The Special Forces Qualification Course is conducted at Fort Bragg. The Q-course is twenty-four to fifty-six weeks long, depending on the specialty of the individual candidate. NCO candidates begin the Q-course with military operational specialty (MOS) training. Officer candidates take the detachment officer course with instruction in Special Forces tactics, techniques, and procedures; mission planning; and, survival, escape, resistance, and evasion (SERE). Officers and NCOs return to the field together to learn or improve land navigation skills. In the land navigation phase of training, candidates learn terrain associations and participate in several exercises in which they must check into a series of control points over the course of two to eighteen kilometers. All candidates receive instruction in basic infantry skills and small unit tactics. This has become increasingly necessary since a combat arms background is no longer a requirement for volunteering for Special Forces. Students are also given an introduction to special operations. They learn skills for operating behind enemy lines and how to set up drop zones for personnel or equipment drops and landing zones for aircraft.[23]

Special Forces training emphasizes planning. Indeed, detailed, pre-mission planning in small units is a distinctive characteristic of special operations. The army captains and their NCO A-Detachment team members take the intelligence data and mission given to them by battalion commanders and instructors and go through a detailed process of mission planning, development, and analysis over the course of five or six days.[24] This leads up to a "brief back" where each NCO on the team stands up before the instructors, declares his mission specialty, such as medic, and tells how he is supporting the A-Detachment's mission.

The culmination of months of training is a final exercise known as Robin Sage. Robin Sage emphasizes the primary mission of army Special Forces—advising and training forces from other countries. Robin Sage is a field exercise that takes place over 7,000 square kilometers in rural North Carolina. One-quarter of the land used is national forest. The rest of the land is in the countryside away from Fort Bragg.[25]

For the Robin Sage exercise, the class of noncommissioned officers (NCOs) and officers work as twelve to sixteen A-Teams. Each team's mission is to assist and train members of a resistance movement in the country of Pineland. Although the roles of guerrilla leaders and forces are usually played by members of the 3rd or 7th Special Forces Groups, the resistance auxiliary are from the community.[26] Over the course of the week, the candidates in their teams must parachute into their area of operation, meet with auxiliary forces and find their way to the guerrilla band, and then assist and train the guerrillas in preparation for a final direct action mission, such as securing a bridge.

Robin Sage combines all that the students have learned about physical conditioning, individual specialties, land navigation, small unit tactics, and mission planning. Robin Sage requires the candidates to work as a team whose members think their way through problems. In the past, the major Special Forces field exercise was also used to haze candidates, in the belief that hazing tested how well the candidates would perform under pressure. In recent years, the hazing has been largely eliminated.[27]

With hazing minimized, pressure instead comes from uncertainty, the challenge of the mission, and the necessity for the student to shift from a learning role to a teaching role. Highly motivated, charged-up, new A-

Team members, particularly when they are working with the resistance hierarchy or chain of command, must learn how to be patient and gain the trust of the guerrilla forces.

Robin Sage marks the end of the Q-course. Candidates who successfully complete the course move on to eighteen to twenty-four weeks of language instruction. Once they complete their language course, they are assigned to an A-Detachment or team. There, they will undergo the same kind of apprenticeship as the SEALs do upon joining a SEAL team. Candidates who graduate from the Q-course possess entry-level Special Forces skills. They have the basic technical and tactical knowledge they need to join an A-Detachment. They are physically fit. They have learned patience and the importance of teaching. Most important, they have learned to think on their own and work within a Special Forces team.

Flip Corkin and the Air Commandos

There are two types of U.S. Air Force special operators, all of whom are referred to as air commandos. The smaller of the two is the Special Tactics Group (STG). The STG works with army Special Forces or SEAL units whenever operations require coordination with air force aircraft. Special Tactics Group members support special operations with combat control, communications, and weather observation skills. Prospective members of the STGs receive training similar to Special Forces. Unlike the Special Forces, all STG candidates go through high-altitude/low-opening (HALO) jump training. STG members are also known for being excellent marksmen. STG personnel include pararescue men whose primary mission is emergency medical treatment. The second type of air force special operators, pilots and aircrew members, enter their training fully qualified in one or more aircraft. Their specialized training develops night and low-level flying skills. The training emphasizes the importance of close coordination with the Special Forces and SEALs that the aircraft are supporting. Special operations pilot and air crew training places tremendous value on detailed planning, exact timing, and strong teamwork.[28]

Until the 1980s, U.S. Air Force special operators did not have the same strong sense of identification that the SEALs or Special Forces had. The air force, unlike the navy and the army, does not have a separate special operations personnel "branch" and, in the air force, what defines a special operator in many respects depends on the aircraft the operator is assigned to fly. In Vietnam, special operations assignments were flown by AC-47s (Puff the Magic Dragon), AC-119 Shadows, AC-110 Stingers, and AC-130

Spectre gunships. All were designated "special operations aircraft" by the U.S. Air Force, but they flew both conventional and special operations missions. According to a special operations gunship pilot, "What made a mission special ops in those days was the guy at the other end that we were doing the support for. If he was a special operator, [he] had no artillery, no nothing, and we were sometimes the only fire support [he] had. They were special ops. If we did it for conventional forces, it was just close air support."[29]

Even today, many air force special operators initially argue that the designation "special operations" is still little more than an aircraft indicator. If a pilot flies an AC-130 gunship, an MC-130 aircraft, or one of the Air Force MH-53 or MH-60 helicopters he is assigned to what is now the 16th Special Operations Wing at Hurlburt Field in Florida. Despite these protestations, however, it becomes clear upon talking with air force special operators that this type of crew is distinct from the rest of the air force. After arguing that the only thing that makes an air force special operator is a crew qualification in an aircraft designated special operations, a longtime air force gunship pilot reconsidered. "Actually, some sort of mindset does develop. As a matter of fact, I don't think it, I know it because I've witnessed it both while I was at crew member level and at the command level. . . . It's centered around your machine. . . and it has a lot to do with association with the customer. [The] customer is generally a SEAL or SF. We do somewhat consider ourselves the same as those guys. . . . We feel a very close camaraderie with them. And certainly . . . the gunship and the Rangers are almost inseparable."[30]

From Vietnam until the summer of 1993 the primary U.S. Air Force special operations unit at Hurlburt Air Field was known as the 1st Special Operations Wing, or the 1st SOW, tracing its ancestry back to the 1st Air Commando Group. The wing patch of the 1st SOW is essentially the same as that worn by Cochran and his men in "Terry and the Pirates," and air force special operators take great pride in their ties to World War II and Vietnam war units. Unfortunately, if recent events are to be a guide, the importance of Air Force special operations history appears to be given little credence by the leadership of the conventional air force.

Upon becoming the chief of staff for the U.S. Air Force in 1992, General Merrill McPeak, a fighter pilot, decided that there could be only one first wing in the air force, and he gave that designation to the 1st Tactical Fighter Wing at Langley Air Force Base. Adding what was perceived by special operators as insult to injury, McPeak did not re-designate the 1st SOW either the 14th Special Ops Wing or the 56th Special Ops Wing, after other special operations units that existed in Southeast Asia. Instead, he renamed the 1st SOW the 16th SOW in "honor" of a long inactivated, and not particularly distinguished, bomber wing.[31] This was especially surprising in that McPeak had recently proclaimed a renewed emphasis on history and heraldry in an attempt to remind the air force of its roots and founding fathers. As might be expected, McPeak's decision was and is not popular with air force special operators.[32]

Maintaining a Distinctive Organization

Special operations forces were developed to solve problems that could not be resolved by a conventional military force. Special operators are selected and trained to take advantage of their independence, courage, teamwork, and refusal to be bound by conventional solutions for unconventional tasks. Since World War II special operations forces have stood slightly to one side of conventional military organizational culture. Because of what they do, they have an organizational culture, with its own values and mission, that is separate from conventional American military culture. Once a special operator has accepted these values and mission, upon leaving the unit, or even the military, he remains a part of the SOF community. Charles Simpson writes in the preface to his book *Inside the Green Berets*, "A term not present in this book is ex-SF. There is no such person, for once in Special Forces, a soldier is always SF, although he may retire or be assigned duty out of the Forces. We are an exceptionally clannish group of men . . . and we have a Special Forces Association numbering thousands of members in over two dozen chapters in the United States and Korea."[33]

While members of other military units, particularly in the Marine Corps, maintain a strong sense of loyalty and identity long after leaving the organization, a distinctive aspect of SOF organizational culture is that it cuts across military service lines. A sense of a common and highly valued organizational bond exists among the active and retired members of the Special Forces, SEALs, U.S. Air Force special operators, Rangers, and also members of the civil affairs and psychological operations (PSYOP) units. A strong belief in the need for special operations forces has extended a sense of community to those who have never served in these units but who have become active supporters of their mission. In the more than forty years since American special operations forces were established, these supporters have included members of the conventional military forces, civilians in the Department of Defense, members of the press and publishing world, and members of Congress and their staffs. Combined, all of these players may be referred to as the SOF community. Less neutrally they have been called the SOF Liberation Front or the SOF Mafia.[34]

SOF organizational culture and, to some extent, support from the broader SOF community have enabled at least a skeleton special operations capability to exist since World War II. Even when the OSS units and air commandos were deactivated, the UDTs continued to exist as a small force, largely through the leadership of team members such as Francis Douglas Fane, who was in charge of the East Coast UDTs.[35] A belief in the critical value of special operations drove Colonel Aaron Bank to fight for and put together the first Special Forces group in the early 1950s. Colonel Bank designed the structure of the group, developed its operational doctrine, and became its first commander. Colonel Bank laid the groundwork for an organization that was called upon during the earliest years of Vietnam. Believing that there was more to combat flying than protecting carriers or high-level bombing, pilots and air crews joined the reactivated air commandos in the early 1960s. They believed in the lessons and mission of Terry and the Pirates and flew their missions tied to the troops on the ground. They joined with Special Forces and SEALs when they turned away from the glamor and promotions of fighters and strategic bombers, flying "low and slow" in impossible weather to offer the only fire and airlift support the special operators had.

The same organizational culture and the same values and belief in the importance of unconventional approaches to warfare, which kept the special operations forces alive during the 1950s and provided the foundation for the buildup of the 1960s, kept special operations going in the 1970s. Once again, after Vietnam, SOF, like the end of a whip, suffered the extremes of the cyclical buildups and cuts typical of American force structure and funding. In the first half of the 1970s there was an approximately 70 percent reduction in the manning of special operations forces and a 95 percent reduction in funding.[36]

A love of their work, the ties between team members, and in some cases a sense of alienation from the conventional forces kept those special operators who remained in the military following Vietnam either in SOF units or involved in SOF issues. Many of those who left the military kept in touch with those operators still on active duty, and in at least one case, an officer who had left played a major role in the push for SOF reform. The strength of this culture allowed a cadre of special operators to survive through the late 1970s when the nearly lost precarious value began its slow recovery. The recovery of SOF was partially due to outside events, particularly the rise of international terrorism. Special operators themselves also assisted in the recovery as they fought to escape the shackles of Vietnam and adapt themselves to the cold war focus of American national security policy. The belief of the special operations community that they offered a capability essential to the support of U.S. security objectives, and their refusal to give up fighting to rebuild that capability, was the foundation of the dramatic reorganization and reforms of the 1980s.

4

Protecting a Precarious Value

*By the late 1970s, we were getting the SEALs written into the CINCs'
[operational plans]. [We were] getting out and doing foreign cross-
unit training, starting to feel more comfortable in areas of the world
other than Southeast Asia . . . . We were not disestablished, not
totally put in the reserves. [We] started to get viable missions in other
areas of the world. . . . And started showing the CINCs the types of
things that SEALs could do.*

Captain Ron Yeaw, February 1994

Even as the nation's special operations capability was reaching its post-
Vietnam nadir in the mid- to late 1970s, signs were appearing that special
operations forces had a few supporters after all. A few officials scattered
throughout the Defense Department and Congress were beginning to recognize the nation's need for the unique capabilities of special operations
forces. In the wilderness of the late 1960s and 1970s, Army Lieutenant
General Sam Wilson was one of the few senior voices upholding the
value of special operations. Wilson had fought in northern Burma during
World War II as a "mustang" junior officer in Merrill's Marauders. During
Vietnam, although only a lieutenant colonel, he was seconded to the
Foreign Service and served as Ambassador Henry Cabot Lodge's deputy
with the rank of minister. While in Vietnam Wilson hosted many high-
level visitors, including Richard Nixon before his election, and, perhaps
most critical to the cause of special operations reform twenty years later,
Representative Dan Daniel from Virginia. Wilson took his charges on helicopter tours of the provinces, emphasizing civic action projects and U.S.
economic aid as much as conventional military activity.

At the end of his time in Vietnam, Wilson returned to the army as a colonel to command the 6th Special Forces Group. He served at the army's Institute for Military Assistance at Fort Bragg, where he wrote the curriculum for the successor to the army's counterinsurgency course. Soon after becoming assistant division commander of the 82nd Airborne Division, Wilson was given the opportunity to become the first U.S. military attaché to the Soviet Union. Despite the advice of his senior commanders and mentors, Wilson accepted the post and served for three years. He returned to the United States to serve first as the deputy to the director of the Central Intelligence Agency and then as director of the Defense Intelligence Agency. Throughout his career, Wilson repeatedly called for maintaining a viable American special operations capability. He believed that conventional military force was rarely the appropriate first response to conflict, particularly outside of Central Europe. Wilson strongly appreciated the political and economic aspects of conflict as well as the value of unconventional forces in a major conventional war. During his last years in the army, Wilson was one of the few senior officers who believed that the critical weakness in American military capabilities was the inability to respond to conflicts other than World War III. His influence can be seen in the late 1970s, as part of a small group within the army's leadership who sought to address that weakness.[1]

Another member of the army leadership who recognized the need for unconventional military capabilities was General Edward Charles "Shy" Meyer. Meyer initiated the moderate support for special operations forces that the army continued into the early 1980s. Meyer was and is an intelligent and strong-willed army officer, generally recognized as one of the army's most capable chiefs of staff. He became chief of staff of the army in 1979. Since his retirement from the army, Meyer's hawk-like face has frequently been seen on television as a member of the defense intelligentsia commenting on world events.

Meyer had encountered unconventional and terrorist threats throughout his more than thirty years in the U.S. Army. As a first lieutenant and captain with airborne forces in Korea, Meyer realized the importance of linking Special Forces with conventional forces and of being cognizant of the cultural environment in which one is fighting. In two tours with the 1st Cavalry Division (Airmobile) in Vietnam, Meyer worked with Special Forces groups and special operations units operating along the border with Cambodia. When U.S. forces went into Cambodia, Meyer assisted in planning operations for the 1st Cavalry, including SOF. During the 1970s, following the highly publicized Israeli operation at Entebbe and the success of German special operations forces at Mogadishu, Meyer developed a more personal appreciation for the terrorist threat when a bomb exploded outside of his office in Heidelberg, Germany. In 1973, when General Creighton Abrams, chief of staff of the army, was focusing solely on army training and war plan development, as well as increasing the armored forces in U.S. Army divisions, for a Central European conflict with the Warsaw Pact, Meyer was arguing that the war being planned for was the one least likely to be fought. According to Meyer, "Even back in 1973, you could see the Third World and the relationship between the haves and the have-nots, between the north and the south. All of that [had] such a tremendous impact on me."[2] Stemming in part from his studies of the Middle East at the army's Command and General Staff College in 1959–60, Meyer had long believed that geopolitical pressures from the Muslim movements in the Middle East were a far more likely concern than events in Central Europe. He also thought the United States could not afford to ignore the rest of the world while focusing on the Soviet threat. By the mid-1970s it was clear to Meyer that the U. S. defense establishment's single-minded emphasis on the Soviets striking through the Fulda Gap was far removed from the actual world security environment.[3]

Upon becoming the assistant deputy chief of staff of operations and plans on the U.S. Army staff in the late 1970s, General Meyer was able to turn his concern into action. Soon after assuming office, Meyer and Robert Kupperman, chief scientist for the Arms Control and Disarmament Agency and responsible for the federal government's studies on terrorism, paid a visit to the army's Special Forces Center at Fort Bragg. The center was commanded at the time by Major General Robert Kingston, who had trained with Britain's Special Air Service (SAS) before becoming the commander of the army's Special Forces and was a long-time SOF advocate. Kingston had received recommendations from Colonel Charlie Beckwith on how to improve the army's unconventional warfare capability. Beckwith, who had trained with the SAS in the early 1960s and would later become the commander of the ground element used in the hostage rescue attempt by U.S. forces in Iran in 1980, had long argued for the development of an elite counterterrorist unit. Meyer, Kupperman, and Kingston agreed at the Fort Bragg meeting to convince the Department of the Army and the army's Training and Doctrine Command (TRADOC) that a counterterrorist capability was essential to the national security interests of the United States.[4]

General Meyer knew there was little interest in the Department of the Army or at TRADOC for rebuilding a special operations capability. "It was necessary for us to try to create a requirement. When we started to lay out the differences between what Ranger forces could do and what they couldn't do, and what light infantry [forces] could do and what they couldn't do. . . . it became clear that there was a void that needed to be filled on the low end of the spectrum of warfare that included not just counterterrorism but a host of other requirements."[5]

Counterterrorism, despite its clandestine nature, became more visible, and public support for it grew in the face of the apparent increase in terrorist attacks in the 1970s. Television coverage of events such as the 1972 Olympics, when Arab terrorists captured and murdered members of the Israeli Olympic team in Munich, made a deep impression on the public. Finally, the lack of a credible counterterrorist capability could, and would eventually, dramatically embarrass the United States. Meyer and Kingston, aided by Kupperman and Beckwith, therefore concentrated on building an army counterterrorist force rather than on rebuilding Special Forces.

The new counterterrorist unit, Special Forces Operational Detachment-Delta (SFOD-D) or simply Delta, was established in late 1977.[6] It went against the grain of the conventional army for the same reasons that Special Forces units were opposed in the 1950s and 1960s. In the aftermath of Vietnam, the army had turned against anything that appeared to be an elite unit. Airborne forces even lost their distinctive maroon beret during the 1970s. Other aspects of the new unit also rankled the conventional army: Delta was modeled after a foreign unit, the British Special Air Service; the creation of a new unit implied that existing units could not get the job done; and the new unit was an additional drain on limited resources, both manpower and fiscal.[7] Meyer envisioned the new counterterrorist organization as working directly for the army's deputy chief of staff for operations, thereby avoiding the obstacles being planted by the U.S. Army's Training and Doctrine Command or Forces Command (FORSCOM). Kingston's direction to Beckwith to draw up a proposed budget and table of organization and equipment for the new unit initiated the effort to put it in place.

The new force was to be unconventional in its orientation toward counterterrorism and in its establishment as an elite unit with unique training. In promoting the new unit, the planners emphasized initiative and flexibility, with men and components being interchangeable. Beckwith believed exceptional physical fitness was vital to the unit's success. He expected each member of the force to become expert in many standard military, as well as unit-unique, skills such as demolitions, parachuting, covert entry, and escape and evasion. The unit's soldiers would also gain expertise with a wide variety of individual weapons.

The force-building strategy pursued by Meyer and friends in the late 1970s was the precursor to the bureaucratic, suprisingly effective, guerrilla warfare practiced by the SOF community and its supporters for most of the 1980s. Kingston pushed the group's counterterrorist concept through TRADOC. When the action reached the Department of the Army staff in the Pentagon, General Meyer feigned surprise, knowing that if he were the one advocating the initiative, the idea would be rejected out of hand.[8] According to General Meyer, TRADOC approved the idea as soon as the head of the Joint Staff's Special Operations Division offered his support. The greatest obstacle remaining within the army was the commander of the XVIII Airborne Corps, General Volney Warner, who "violently opposed" anything at Fort Bragg that would not be under his command (the XVIII Airborne Corps was headquartered there).[9]

The final impetus for the activation of Delta was the rescue of the passengers on a hijacked Lufthansa 737 in Mogadishu, Somalia, by the West German counterterrorist unit, GSG 9, on October 19, 1977. The successful rescue demonstrated to U.S. civilian and military leaders that it was possible to use military force against terrorists. Within a day of the rescue, General Bernard Rogers, the army chief of staff, received a copy of a note from President Carter addressed to Secretary of Defense Harold Brown and National Security Adviser Zbigniew Brzezinski. In the note Carter had written, "Ask [German Prime Minister] Schmidt (or perhaps [Israeli Prime Minister] Begin) for a thorough briefing on handling terrorists. Develop similar U.S. capabilities."[10] Meyer had proposed establishment of Delta to General Rogers more than four months earlier, on June 2, 1977. The incident at Mogadishu and the president's interest were enough to push Rogers to activate the unit. On November 19, 1977, the army's new counterterrorist force was activated at Fort Bragg, with Colonel Beckwith as its first commander.[11]

As expected, the conventional army was suspicious of this interloper. The airborne and Ranger units viewed the new counterterrorist detachment as competition for the army's best talent. Objections were even raised by the 5th Special Forces Group, whose commander argued that the unique capabilities of Delta could be added to the 5th's own capabilities. The commander of the 5th Special Forces Group went so far as to establish his own elite counterterrorist force named Operation Blue Light. Only the direction of General Rogers forced the competing group to disband.

The establishment of Delta was the first indication since Vietnam of the army's interest in a force that was not primarily oriented toward stopping the Soviet threat. Although it was an important first step toward rebuilding the U.S. unconventional capability, the creation of the counterterrorist unit did not establish a joint special operations capability, nor did it signal wholehearted support for special operations forces in general. It was, in fact, General Meyer who, as chief of staff of the army in 1979, considered deactivating the 7th Special Forces Group.[12]

Naval Special Warfare: Reconnecting to the Fleet

Having nearly been consigned to the ash heap, the naval special warfare community, particularly the SEALs, fought in the late 1970s to tie themselves to the fleet and the conventional navy. Only with the support of the fleet commanders would the SEAL teams continue to exist. The underwater demolition teams had maintained that support by holding onto their hydrographic reconnaissance mission in support of amphibious operations. Following Vietnam, the UDTs continued to deploy with amphibious-ready groups in support of this traditional mission. Although large amphibious landings were becoming less likely—marines increasingly tended to approach the shore by helicopter—as long as the U.S. Navy and Marine Corps had amphibious ships there was a need for UDTs.

The SEALs, however, had lost their link with the fleet with the conclusion of the American involvement in Vietnam. Created in 1962 as a result of President John F. Kennedy's call for unconventional and counterinsurgency capabilities, the SEALs had matured with the buildup of American troops in Vietnam. The riverine focus of the SEALs was a direct result of the circumstances of their birth. As the navy turned to focus on World War III and the cold war conflict, the SEALs were left behind.[13]

After Vietnam, the SEALs were still able to deploy for training as a part of "counterpart training." SEAL platoons would go overseas and train with allied nations' counterpart units. They went to the Caribbean and trained with South American forces from Argentina, Brazil, Peru, and Colombia. Some platoons trained with the Dutch, Norwegians, Finns, British, French, and Germans. The special operators enjoyed the training because it was overseas and allowed the SEALs to, as described by a SEAL who participated in the training, "work with their counterparts who fought and acted and were of the same cut."[14] The training kept talented SEALs interested and trained and introduced the SEALs to the fleet commanders and regional commanders in chief (CINCs) whose commands had not been a part of Vietnam and who had, therefore, never worked with SEALs.

Counterpart training, however, was not enough to end the SEALs' isolation from the conventional navy, nor did it convince most of the navy commanders that the SEALs had a major role to play in supporting the fleets. In the mid-1970s crisis loomed when navy headquarters staff recommended placing the SEALs in the naval reserves. Nevertheless, the SEALs pulled themselves out of their post-Vietnam depression and set to work convincing the conventional navy of their value. The effort to define that new mission and sell it to the fleet commanders was led by a group of senior SEAL officers. As described by a SEAL who was a junior officer in the late 1970s, "It appeared to me as though the staff across the street, or [Naval Special Warfare] Group 1, their job in life was to justify our existence. And that was a full time job. . . . I can't say everybody, but at least the UDT and SEAL teams seemed to be struggling for survival."[15]

SEAL officers made their case before the navy's senior commanders, arguing that SEALs could support the fleet in its post-Vietnam scenarios.[16] One of these officers was Captain Ted Grabowsky, who has been called a visionary by many SEALs. He made things happen. Grabowsky was then one of the few members of the naval special warfare community who had spent time in the Pentagon. He knew how the system worked and had countless contacts in Washington. Even upon returning to command an operational unit at Subic Bay in the Philippines, Grabowsky was able to work the system, demonstrating the value of special warfare to the commander of the Seventh Fleet and the commander of the Pacific Command.

Grabowsky and others, including Cathal "Irish" Flynn and George Worthington, who later became two of the SEALs' first flag officers, worked to identify targets and situations in a World War III scenario that were particularly difficult for the conventional forces but could be susceptible to a SEAL operation. These were often third world operations in support of a world war against the Soviet Union and the Warsaw Pact. SEALs reviewed war plans for the unified commands and fleet commands and identified areas where the SEALs could provide support to the fleet's mission. Once they had identified four or five scenarios in which the SEALs could directly support the fleet's war plans in, for example, the Western Pacific region, the SEALs briefed the Seventh Fleet commander and his staff. The focus was on demonstrating to the fleet commander what the SEALs could do to support him. No mention was made of independent or joint operations.

East Coast SEALs were also making every effort to tie themselves to the Second Fleet and Sixth Fleet. The SEALs recognized that they had to ensure that the navy fleet commanders at the operational level understood who the SEALs were and what they could do to support the fleet commander's mission. Captain Ron Yeaw described the East Coast effort:

When we had the cold war . . . the commander of the Sixth Fleet had two major problems: Soviet submarines in the Mediterranean, and Soviet aircraft being launched from bases in the Soviet Union. The SEALs couldn't do much with the submarines but [SEALs] had many contingency plans to go after the Badgers and the long-range bomber aviation that could blow the Sixth Fleet out of the water. . . . [SEALs] had plans and capabilities to interdict those aircraft on the ground. . . . If [the Sixth Fleet commander] bought the capability, which [he] did for good reasons, then he would say, "Yeah, I need SEALs." And if the fleet commanders ever say, "We don't need SEALs anymore," . . . the SEALs [will probably] go away.[17]

Absent from this effort was any attempt to develop counterinsurgency or nation-building capabilities by the SEALs. The emphasis was on direct action and special reconnaissance missions in a major conventional war, particularly war with the Warsaw Pact. The assumption was that all other missions were "lesser included cases," and the recognition was that all other capabilities were irrelevant if the SEALs could not gain the support of the CINCs and the fleet commanders. The SEALs had to reach for high-impact missions previously thought beyond the scope of naval special warfare. It was at the high end of the spectrum of conflict that the SEALs would make or break their future. It was the high end of the spectrum that was important to the fleet and, therefore, mattered to the U.S. Navy.

By the late 1970s and early 1980s, the efforts of SEAL leaders had largely succeeded. The SEALs had proved their importance to the fleet commanders and gained the support of the Second, Sixth, and Seventh fleets but at the cost of some of their unconventional capabilities. The SEALs developed and demonstrated the capability to support the fleet in operations against enemy airfields, patrol bases, ports or ships, and material improvements in the commands were visible at the operational level by the early 1980s.[18] Training expanded from river and jungle environments to include cold weather and desert environments. The UDTs and SEALs were combined in 1983, with the result that SEAL teams now had responsibility for hydrographic reconnaissance in addition to supporting the navy's "maritime strategy" for bringing the war to the Soviet Union, disrupting Soviet operations, and striking at the periphery of Soviet influence. Planned SEAL operations in support of the strategy included sabotage of vulnerable Soviet installations; providing "instantaneous" battle-damage assessment after carrier-based strikes; and marking targets with lasers to guide munitions from carrier-based aircraft.[19] The SEALs had succeeded in proving their value to the fleet. It was this same success that caused the SEALs to view the move for reorganization in the mid-1980s with some caution, and the navy to fight it tooth and nail.

Surviving the 1970s

Despite the progress in naval special warfare and the growth of the army's counterterrorist unit into a viable force, all was not well in U.S. special operations forces at the end of the 1970s. The SOF units had survived the decade after Vietnam, but just barely. The SEALs had traded away many of their unconventional capabilities in order to support the fleet. The navy was spending little on SEAL modernization, particularly in support of SEAL tactical mobility. The three remaining army Special Forces groups had little money for training and support and were rarely called upon by military leaders. The 7th SFG had barely escaped being consigned to the U.S. Army Reserves by one of the few supporters of SOF, General "Shy" Meyer.[20] The army's new counterterrorist force was well funded and well trained but had no mobility since the air force had maintained little of its special operations aircraft and had modernized none of it. The new force could not fulfill its mission until it had support from the air force. Funding remained spotty at best. Although funding for special operations improved slightly in the late 1970s, after reaching a low point in 1975, it constituted only one-tenth of 1 percent of the total defense budget.[21] At this level, training and operational tempo remained low, tactical mobility was severely limited, and there was no significant SOF modernization program in place. As the 1970s came to a close, the future of the American special operations capability looked uncertain at best. The decade had seen a rise in international terrorism, and the United States seemed unable to respond. Operational failures during the 1970s, such as the *Mayaguez* incident, illustrated the frustrations and flaws of a military designed to fight World War III yet incapable of responding to the taunts of third world opponents. The 1980s opened with an event that would reveal this flaw to the world.

The Tragedy of Desert One

The tragedy and failure of the U.S. effort to rescue hostages held in Tehran by supporters of the revolutionary Khomeni government is viewed by most observers as clear evidence of the inadequacy of U.S. special operations capabilities in 1980 and as the event that began the turnaround for SOF.[22] The U.S. government started to put together a rescue team soon after members of the American embassy staff in Tehran were captured by a group of Iranian militants, supporters of Imam Ayatollah Khomeni, on November 4, 1979. Six months of planning and training, reminiscent of the American raid on Son Tay prison in 1970, went by before the rescue was attempted. Because the United States did not have a standing joint counterterrorist task force, the rescue task force was pulled together from scratch and the mission named Operation Rice Bowl (because of later events, the mission became known as Desert One). Members of the newly created Delta force, having just completed training in November 1979, formed the assault team that was assigned the mission of entering the embassy and rescuing the hostages. The remainder of the task force was drawn from the other services. The navy provided the aircraft carriers to transport the troops and tactical aircraft to the Indian Ocean as well as RH-53D mine-sweeping helicopters. Consistent with the ad hoc nature of the formation of the rescue force, the marines provided pilots for the helicopters since the navy had none who were qualified to fly this type of mission over land. The air force provided C-130 transport and tanker aircraft and their crews. Virtually none of these groups had worked with the others before. The mission commander and the chief planner of the operation was General James Vaught, an U.S. Army Ranger who had fought in World War II, Korea, and Vietnam.

The operation began with an attempt to gather intelligence from within Iran. During the 1970s as the Central Intelligence Agency increased its reliance on "national technical means," or intelligence from technical rather than human resources, intelligence sources within Iran virtually disappeared. In preparing for Operation Rice Bowl the CIA relied on an Iranian national, who had contacted the agency to offer his services, and a retired agent who was living in Italy at the time of the embassy seizure. The U.S. Army's counterterrorist force commanders did not fully trust these sources and therefore sent legendary retired Special Forces officer Dick Meadows (a key player in the Son Tay raid) into Iran in the days before the rescue attempt. Meadows was supported by an air force sergeant and two Special Forces sergeants. The final intelligence source was the American embassy's Pakistani cook, who had been allowed by the Iranian militants to leave the embassy and Iran.[23]

On April 24, 1980, the 132-man ground element of the task force flew from Egypt to Masirah Island off the coast of Oman, in C-141 transport aircraft. The force then transferred to MC-130 transport aircraft for the low-level flights into the prepared staging area in the Das-a-Kafir desert in a remote location of Iran. The staging area was necessary because navy helicopters did not have the range to reach Tehran and were not air refuelable. The site was referred to by the task force as Desert One. The lead MC-130 carried the commander of the army's counterterrorist force, Colonel Charlie Beckwith, as well as one squadron of its troops, support troops including a combat control team, drivers for the assault force's trucks, weapons, and support vehicles. The lead aircraft was followed by five C-130s loaded with troops and fuel.[24] At Desert One the assault force was to meet eight RH-53 helicopters, known as Sea Stallions, and the C-130 tankers that would be used for refueling the helicopters.[25]

Eight helicopters lifted off the aircraft carrier *Nimitz*, sixty miles south of the Iranian coast, at just past seven o'clock on the night of April 24. The mine-sweeping helicopters were selected because they had the range to reach Desert One and were often deployed on aircraft carriers. The pilots, equipped with night-vision goggles, conducted low-level flights at about 100 to 200 feet, except when higher altitudes were necessary to clear Iran's coastal mountain ranges, to avoid detection by Iranian air defense radars.[26]

As the lead C-130 approached Desert One, a member of the combat control team switched on the lights that had been hidden in the sand three weeks earlier. Immediately after exiting the aircraft, the road-watch team encountered a tour bus heading through the desert. The team stopped the bus and searched and unloaded the passengers. Minutes later a fuel truck approached the site and refused to stop. The team stopped the truck with a light anti-tank weapon. The passengers of the truck fled to a second vehicle following the truck and escaped. Although none of the passengers or drivers had seen or heard anything that could compromise the mission, nor heard English being spoken, it was an unsettling beginning to a difficult mission.[27]

All five of the C-130s eventually landed safely. The helicopters were not so lucky. The first of the helicopters to drop out was forced to land when a cockpit indicator warned that one of the rotor blades was losing pressure, indicating an impending blade failure. The marine pilot had not been told that the rotors of the navy version of the H-53 were made of a different material from those of the marine's SH-53. The navy's titanium rotor blades had never cracked or failed. The pilot could have continued had he known this information. Soon after this loss—the helicopter was abandoned by its crew—the remaining seven helicopters flew into an unanticipated dust storm so severe that the fine talcum-powderlike dust sifted into the aircraft cockpits and practically eliminated all visibility unless the helicopters flew at 9,000 feet, clearly visible to the Iranian air defense radars. A second helicopter was lost when the aircraft's gyroscope failed. At that point the pilot decided to return to the *Nimitz* even though he was not certain he had enough fuel to get back to the carrier. Because of the dust storm, the six remaining helicopters were more than fifty minutes late for their rendezvous at Desert One. Misfortune remained with the rescue force even after the helicopters were on the ground and had begun loading the assault force. A third helicopter was declared disabled when it was discovered that one of its hydraulic pumps had burned out after a leak in the line. The task force was now down to five operational helicopters, one less than required to complete the mission. The only way all of the assault force could board five helicopters was to leave behind the extra fuel that would be needed the following night in Tehran. Colonel Beckwith and General Vaught recommended to President Carter that the mission be aborted. After consulting with the Joint Chiefs of Staff and Secretary of Defense Harold Brown, and over the objections of National Security Adviser Zbigniew Brzezinski, President Carter agreed to go with his commanders' recommendation.[28]

Aborting the mission did not end the operation. The task force had to get out of Iran and return to the aircraft carrier and to Masirah Island. The hope was to fly as much equipment as possible out of the Iranian desert. Colonel Beckwith and Lieutenant Colonel Ed Seiffert, the helicopter commander, decided to fly out five of the helicopters, leaving the third disabled helicopter behind. Fuel was running low and the aircraft would have to leave quickly in order not to burn up fuel at the loading site and still be able to make it out of Iran.

The complexity of the final disaster is overwhelming. One of the C-130s had to leave within minutes but could not bring its engines up to power until helicopter Dash Three moved out of the way of the sandstorm caused by the C-130's engines. Dash Three could not taxi out of the way because it had blown a tire upon landing. Instead, the helicopter went into a hover to clear the C-130. Dash Three's pilot oriented on the only object available, a seemingly stationary member of the air force control team. When the air force sergeant backed away from the rotor blast, the pilot became disoriented and flew into the C-130. Fuel tanks burst into flame, igniting the helicopter and the C-130. Seven men were in the C-130's cockpit and five were burned to death. Three helicopter crewmen were also killed. Because three of the remaining helicopters were within 150 feet of the fire and burning fuel was everywhere, the helicopter commander decided to remove classified documents from the other two helicopters on the far side of the road from the fire and then abandon all the helicopters. The helicopter crews, the survivors from the burning C-130, and the other members of the task force loaded onto the five remaining C-130s and flew out of Iran.[29]

Within days, the entire world learned of the tragedy at Desert One. Iran showed pictures of the burned and desecrated bodies on television. The causes of the disaster were to be examined at length by the press, the Holloway Commission, and members of the special operations community. General Carl Stiner, as commander in chief of the organization born out of the ashes at Desert One—the U. S. Special Operations Command (USSOCOM)—stated that "the failure revealed serious shortcomings in the ability of the United States to equip, employ, and command special operations forces effectively in complex, high-risk operations." Key problems identified by General Stiner included the ad hoc nature of the task force, unclear command relationships, the lack of dedicated joint forces, and inadequate equipment.[30]

Only weeks after Desert One, the Special Operations Review Group, also known as the Holloway Commission after its chairman, Chief of Naval Operations Admiral James Holloway, was chartered by the Joint Chiefs of Staff to "independently appraise the rescue attempt [and] recommend improvements in planning, organizing, coordinating, directing, and controlling any such operations in the future."[31] The group's focus was on the Department of Defense and military issues. The Special Operations Review Group consisted of six flag and general officers, who represented all four military services. Holloway's deputy was retired Lieutenant General Sam Wilson.

Although the commission was careful to point out that issues and criticism brought out in the report should not be "misinterpreted as an indictment of the able and brave men who planned and executed this operation," the group's conclusions emphasized the uncoordinated character of U.S. special operations. The Holloway report concluded command and control relationships, and coordination in general, were poorly defined. Additional problems occurred because a comprehensive, full-scale training exercise was never conducted. Such an exercise might have helped strengthen weak command and control, pointed out the inadequate number of helicopters taking part in the operation, and made better provisions for poor weather conditions. The group also criticized the lack of an independent review of operational plans and poor intelligence support in both quality and integration.

In the end, the recommendations of the Holloway report were cautious, but the report was the first critical assessment of the U.S. special operations capability conducted outside of SOF. The group's recommendation for the establishment of a Counterterrorist Joint Task Force was implemented over the next three years. Furthermore, many members of the commission later served on the Special Operations Policy Advisory Group, also established at the recommendation of the Holloway Commission, and were important in the battle for SOF reform.

Revitalizing Special Operations: First Steps

One of the first steps toward revitalizing SOF following Desert One was taken by the U.S. Army. In May 1980, a few weeks after the tragedy, General "Shy" Meyer, who was then chief of staff, followed up on his earlier counterterrorist initiative. He recognized that special operations could not be effective without full cooperation and support among the services and other U.S. government agencies. He conceived of a new organization that would reach beyond the army and bring the counterterrorist forces of each of the military services together in a joint permanent task force.[32] Meyer proposed a new combatant command called Strategic Services Command (STRATSERCOM), whose mission would be to counter terrorism in peacetime or in periods of conflict short of war, and to protect the U. S. leadership and command and control centers in a major war with the Soviet Union.

General Meyer received no reaction to his 1980 proposal, and so in August of 1981, he formally proposed STRATSERCOM to the chairman of the Joint Chiefs of Staff as a specified command for special operations forces.[33] Once again, the silence in response was deafening, not only from the services and the Joint Chiefs but also from the SOF community. Support was slim even in "Shy" Meyer's army. "[The army] was not interested in elite forces. As you know [the army] took the maroon beret away from airborne. There was a great dislike for anything elite. Everybody had to be the same."[34] This belief was deep-seated in the other military services as well. All the services "feared STRATSERCOM as a fifth Service, feared it would take away their responsibilities and cut into their resources."[35]

Surprisingly, according to Ted Lunger, a former member of the army's Special Forces and staff member for Representative Dan Daniel on the House Armed Services Committee, even the SOF community was not behind General Meyer's initiative. Lunger claims he and the SOF Liberation Front did all they could to "kill off" the STRATSERCOM proposal. Lunger and the activist members of the SOF community believed that the proposal was a mistaken attempt to expand the army's counterterrorist force (Delta) into a joint SOF command. Lunger argued that STRATSERCOM was motivated by the army's Special Forces groups and air cavalry units looking for missions, and that the concept failed to include the broader low-intensity-conflict missions, particularly psychological operations and civil affairs.[36]

An alternate explanation for the squashing of STRATSERCOM was provided by several officers who were assigned to SOF units during the STRATSERCOM debate. According to these officers, STRATSERCOM was vetoed by the theater unified commanders in chief (CINCs), led by General Bernard Rogers, who was CINC of the European Command during the early to mid-1980s. As imagined by General Meyer and the supporters of STRATSERCOM, the SOF command would conduct special operations in the theater commands, but their chain of command would not be through the theater CINC and his staff. The theater CINCs could not allow operations to take place in their theaters without their "chop," or approval.[37]

The Joint Chiefs of Staff were not ready to make substantial changes in the reorganization of U.S. special operations forces in response to the Desert One tragedy, even when those changes were recommended by their own Joint Staff. In response to a January 1982 memorandum to the Joint Chiefs of Staff from the Office of the Secretary of Defense directing a review of SOF capabilities, the Joint Staff again offered a study that reported that special operations capabilities were inadequate and that reorganization was required. The July 1982 study concluded that SOF "can only respond to assigned missions in a fragmented way" and recommended that the Joint Staff "develop a concept for establishing a joint C2 [command and control] structure to coordinate . . . SOF employment in selected situations at the NCA [National Command Authorities] direction."[38] Upon review of the Joint Staff's recommendation, the Joint Chiefs rejected this alternative and shelved the study.

Recognizing that STRATSERCOM was doomed, General Meyer continued to work to improve the army's special operations capabilities through moderately increased funding and organizational changes. He combined all army SOF, both in and outside of the United States, including Special

Forces, Rangers, civil affairs, and psychological operations units under a new command, 1st SOCOM, located at Fort Bragg. The new command replaced the U.S. Army John F. Kennedy Center for Military Assistance. Furthermore, the army provided Special Forces with more than 1,500 additional spaces, allowing the activation of the 1st Special Forces Group at Fort Lewis and the filling of the undermanned existing SFGs, particularly the 10th. The 1st SFG eventually had one battalion forward-deployed on Okinawa.[39] With these actions, combined with the establishment of the counterterrorist force in the late 1970s, the army stepped far in front of the other services in rebuilding a special operations capability.

Air Force Special Operators and Desert One

The tragedy of Desert One compounded the frustration of U.S. Air Force special operators, who were embarrassed and frustrated even before the tragedy occurred. Because the air force did not have helicopters with the necessary range, task force planners pulled together navy helicopters and Marine Corps pilots.[40] The air force had provided C-130s and C-141 fixed-wing aircraft to the hostage rescue attempt, but their special operations rotary-wing pilots and outdated aircraft were left home.

Major General Hugh Cox was the vice wing and later wing commander of the 1st Special Operations Wing (1st SOW), the commander of the now-disestablished 2nd Air Division (SOF), the first director of operations, and later the deputy commander in chief of U.S. Special Operations Command. In 1992 he published a letter in the *Air Commando Newsletter* summarizing the history of U.S. Air Force Special Operations Force (AFSOF) in the 1980s. When discussing special operations, it is not uncommon for current and retired air force special operators to offer this letter as evidence of the U.S. Air Force's long history of ignoring SOF. That bitterness developed after years of frustration is strongly evident in Cox's letter, but his perspective was shared by many in the SOF community. Cox described his view of the state of air force special operations after Desert One as follows:

> Those of us in the 1st SOW in the early 80's were suffering from a "hangover" due to the failure of Desert One. Morale was low, the wing was overtasked, and SOF personnel were still suffering from a lack of promotions and general higher headquarters indifference. The failure at Desert One and the high-pressure preparations for the planned second hostage rescue attempt had taken its toll. Wing operations were

asking too much from the aircraft maintainers and the downward spiral of mission capability was pervasive.[41]

A long-time gunship pilot gave one explanation for the perceived bias in the air force against special operators after 1980. He thought not only that good officers were facing discrimination because they had been assigned to special operation aircraft but also that the air force was assigning less capable pilots and crews to AFSOF.[42]

Whether the air force demonstrated disdain for the capabilities of those who flew special operations aircraft by promoting them at a lower rate or by using these assignments to dump those who were less than exceptional may be two sides of the same coin. Certainly, all officers interviewed who have been assigned to AFSOF units agreed that those who flew F-15s were more likely to be promoted than those who flew the AC-130s or H-1 and H-3 helicopters that were the bulk of the special operations units.

The frustrations of the air force special operators in the early 1980s were not necessarily because of malice displayed by air force leadership. Clearly, conventional pilots were suspicious of special operations pilots and crews. They were known as "cowboys" during the Vietnam War, and that reputation remained into the 1980s. Nonetheless, it seemed that a good deal of the problem in the early 1980s was that the air force neither understood what special operations were nor knew what to do with AFSOF. During and immediately after Desert One, the 1st Special Operations Wing reported directly to the Tactical Air Command (TAC) headquarters. The following year, Lieutenant General Larry Welch assumed command of the 9th Air Force, a command under TAC, and the 1st SOW began to report to him. Many air commandos believe that this reorganization and increased attention by General Welch was the first positive turning point for AFSOF after the Vietnam War. Promotion rates increased, the operating tempo of the command was brought under control, and morale improved. Part of General Welch's increased attention was probably because of the issuance of post–Desert One analyses that were extremely critical of SOF aviation in general and the air force special operations helicopters in particular. Several studies recommended replacing the H-1s and H-3s by transferring the PAVE LOW helicopters used by the air force Combat Search and Rescue (CSAR) unit to AFSOF.[43] This transfer was made and in the following year was at least partially to blame for yet another reorganization of U. S. Air Force Special Operations Forces. The need for more of these helicopters was to become a continuing issue between the air force and Congress.

In late 1982, Air Force Chief of Staff General Charles Gabriel decided to transfer the AFSOF mission from TAC to the Military Airlift Command (MAC): one of the most traumatic and controversial decisions in the history of air force special operations. It is a decision that is still debated among air force special operators and continues to leave a bitter taste in the mouths of many, including General Cox. TAC is viewed in the air force as a "command of warriors," and the special operators believed themselves to be just that. Members of AFSOF regarded the move to MAC as "a step down" and "an indicator that the [Air Force] leadership viewed them as 'trash haulers' and combat supporters, not leading-edge, point of the spear, warriors."[44]

Part of General Gabriel's decision was the result of the U.S. Air Force view of the world: combat aircraft were either strategic bombers or tactical fighters; all other aircraft were in supporting roles. Special operators worked as tight-knit air crews rather than as pilot-gods in single-seat fighters. Most air force special operations were in support of special operators from other services: transporting Special Forces, SEALs, and Rangers to and from their missions ("infil/exfil" operations), usually at night, often in bad weather, and flying predominantly at low levels. Gunships were more of a puzzle. Although these were clearly offensive aircraft, as opposed to transport, they still supported ground operations through close air support. These were not missions assigned to either fighter pilots or members of the strategic bomber command. In the reorganization in 1982–83 it appears that air force leadership believed that because much of the AFSOF mission was airlift, though under difficult conditions, AFSOF fit under MAC. Even the gunships were modified C-130s, an airlift aircraft for the conventional air force. Even better, because MAC had responsibility for the combat search-and-rescue mission and therefore had helicopters, AFSOF's helicopters would find kindred spirits in the airlift command.

Additional pressure on General Gabriel to reorganize came when the first Reagan administration Defense Guidance, the primary planning document within the Defense Department, issued by Caspar Weinberger, directed the services to "revitalize SOF." The commander in chief of the Military Airlift Command (CINCMAC), General Jim Allen, campaigned for the AFSOF mission, arguing that MAC could better support the special operators and would therefore fix the many problems in the 1st Special Operations Wing.[45] Reorganizing and placing AFSOF within a seemingly more sympathetic command allowed the air force to argue that it was attempting to rectify the problem of inadequate attention to its special operations forces.[46]

Since AFSOF had rarely received the resources or attention it required under TAC, the air force argument seemed to have some merit. The Military Airlift Command, however, was bound and determined to force the round AFSOF peg into MAC's square hole. Some special operators believe that they were caught between TAC's not wanting to pay the bills required from getting SOF "well" and MAC's interest in reclaiming their lost helicopters, since at one point in the transition talks, MAC reportedly refused to accept the gunships and their mission.[47] The MAC representatives also argued that special operations were essentially the same as combat search and rescue. The MAC's Aerospace Rescue and Recovery Service, responsible for rescuing downed air crew members, would therefore assume responsibility for the AFSOF mission. Little heed was paid by MAC commanders to the requirements for night and low altitude flying under any and all weather conditions. To its credit, TAC balked at the loss of visibility for SOF, given congressional and OSD interest in special operations. In the end MAC agreed to establish a new numbered air force, 23rd Air Force, with separate subordinate commands for rescue and special operations.[48] The 2nd Air Division, reporting to the 23rd AF, was activated in March 1983 and had command of all U.S. Air Force special operations forces worldwide. Importantly, this was the first time in the history of AFSOF that there was a single command for all air force special operations, the first move toward protecting this precarious value within the air force.

Although CINCMAC was well respected by special operators and seemed interested in supporting the special operations forces, the integration was an awkward fit. The Military Airlift Command took pride in its egalitarian approach to life, so the insertion of elite units was bound to cause some friction. MAC's mission was viewed as a support role and had always been a notch or two lower in respect and promotions than TAC and the Strategic Air Command. Into this conventional, supporting role came SOF airlift and gunship pilots and air crews who believed they had a unique combat mission. The MAC commanders insisted that any MAC pilot could fly the special operations mission. MAC was determined, as described by General Cox, "to effectively take the 'special' out of special operations."[49] Adding to AFSOF's dilemma was the essential fact that few senior officers in the U.S. Air Force, especially general officers, had any special operations experience. There were no advocates with the clout to fight MAC's effort to subsume the special operators within the conventional airlift mission.[50] Few special operators were added to the staff of the 23rd AF or MAC. Nonvolunteer MAC pilots were assigned the low-level flying Combat Talon mission of the MC-130s—whether or not these pilots wanted to fly 250 feet above the earth or demonstrated any talent in doing so. The Military Air Command filled key positions in the 2nd Air Division, such as the vice commander's job, with officers who had no special operations experience. In late 1984 a MAC colonel was given command of the 1st SOW. When he became a strong advocate for AFSOF, he was replaced with another colonel with a long airlift career. The pattern of filling senior AFSOF positions with officers with little or no experience in special operations continued through the reorganization in 1987 and has, to some degree, continued into the 1990s.[51]

Besides organizational struggles and prejudices within MAC, AFSOF suffered as a result of the basic problem of limited resources. The Military Airlift Command had, by the mid-1980s, staked the future of the command on the C-17.[52] The C-17 is a large transport aircraft intended to replace the workhorse C-141. It is expensive to begin with and has been plagued with cost overruns in the development process. Buying the C-17 did not allow funding for many other programs that were MAC's responsibility, particularly special operations, which were, of course, outside of MAC's primary mission of global airlift. AFSOF was again on the outside. Few of the SOF modernization or acquisition programs promised by MAC leadership in the negotiations for reorganizing air force special operations forces were funded by the command. The Military Airlift Command's ability to fix the problem of air force special operations capability seemed negligible. Funding for improvements had to come from decisions made by the U.S. Air Force leadership in the Pentagon or at the direction of the Office of the Secretary of Defense. With no representation among the senior air force hierarchy, AFSOF remained in a precarious position.

Hopes Rise: The Struggle for Reform

A new administration arrived in Washington in January 1981. The American hostages in Iran were released on inauguration day. Both events inspired talk of improving the U.S. special operations capability and of increased attention to low-intensity conflict. Hope was high in the SOF community because the Republican Party had included "revitalizing SOF" in its party platform, and the new president frequently spoke of an increase in Soviet sponsorship of "wars of national liberation." In reality, there seems to have been little but talk in the early Reagan years. A modest increase occurred in the special operations forces budgets, and a few organizational changes were made that did little to improve the capability of SOF or even to increase the visibility of these forces.

The exception to this observation existed in the office of the principal deputy assistant secretary (International Security Affairs), where Noel Koch (pronounced "Cook"), who, with the strong support and encouragement of Lynn Rylander and Colonel George McGovern, conducted guerrilla operations throughout the Defense Department bureaucracy and on Capitol Hill. These three men were special operations' strongest advocates in the Defense Department and were the executive branch connection that enabled Congress to insert itself into nearly every aspect of American special operations policy during the 1980s. Their struggle for SOF reform took a toll on the lives and careers of both Koch and Rylander.

Noel Koch had joined the army as a high school dropout and served in Vietnam in covert operations. He left the army after six years, returned to school, and eventually received his graduate degree in international relations from Bryn Mawr. He served as a special assistant to presidents Nixon and Ford. In 1980 Koch joined Senator Robert Dole's presidential campaign staff. When Dole dropped out of the race, Koch moved to Ronald Reagan's campaign staff, and as a reward for his support, received a principal deputy's job in the Office of the Secretary of Defense under Caspar Weinberger.[53] Although he had no inherent interest in special operations, other than his experience in working in intelligence in Vietnam, Koch came into the building with a strong interest in counterterrorism.[54] In late 1981 Colonel George McGovern became Koch's military assistant. McGovern was a former commander of the 5th Special Forces Group and an active member of the SOF community. He had a strong network "all over the building, all over the country, all over the world," according to Koch, and was working to get SOF concerns heard by the Defense Department and congressional leadership. Part of McGovern's mission became convincing Koch that rebuilding the nation's special operations capability was a fight worth fighting.[55] Joining McGovern was Lynn Rylander, an analyst in the Office of International Security Affairs, who had among his other responsibilities the job of tracking special operations issues. Rylander had served in the Pentagon for many years and, like McGovern, had an extensive network of contacts throughout the Defense Department. Although he never served in the military, Rylander was a fervent believer in the value of special operations forces and the need to look outside of Central Europe for the most immediate threat to American national security interests.[56]

The combination of trouble in El Salvador, including the killing of Americans in San Salvador soon after Koch entered the Department of Defense, and the efforts of McGovern and Rylander were successful in attracting

Koch's interest to SOF reform. By early 1982 Koch was sponsoring the first briefings to Secretary Weinberger and the Defense Resources Board on special operations and what he and his staff believed was wrong and needed to be fixed.[57] According to Lynn Rylander, the briefings were spurred on by the lingering repercussions from Desert One, which had led initially to the Carter administration's interest in the problem and support for the acquisition of twelve additional Combat Talons in the last Carter defense budget.[58] Weinberger's interest was piqued to the point that Noel Koch's office was soon providing a special operations briefing to the secretary on the average of once every six months.

Noel Koch and George McGovern became close friends, to the point that Koch "trusted George explicitly with everything—to the extent that he could use whatever authority my office had."[59] McGovern died in October 1982, and Koch, after reading McGovern's files and meeting with members of his "network," "just determined . . . that . . . as a memorial to him, I was going to finish the job. We were going to restore these [special operations] capabilities which the military was trying to erase."[60] Rylander took over McGovern's role, working the SOF network and organizing the attacks on foes of special operations within the building. Koch's office quickly became the spearhead for special operations forces and low-intensity conflict in the Office of the Secretary of Defense. Their approach, according to Noel Koch, was that anyone who was not a friend, was an enemy—a perspective held by many throughout the decade-long debate over SOF reform.[61] Initially the team attempted to work with the rest of the Pentagon, especially with the Joint Staff. But after members of the Office of the Joint Chiefs of Staff sat on pertinent memoranda for months at a time, Koch and Rylander began to conduct full-scale guerrilla warfare.

One of the first attempts by Noel Koch, McGovern, and Rylander to work around a bureaucracy that shared few of their beliefs was Koch's creation of his Special Planning Directorate. As a principal deputy assistant secretary, Koch's chain of command ran through the assistant secretary for international security affairs, through the undersecretary of defense for policy, to the deputy secretary and the secretary of defense. As the director for special planning responsible for special operations and low-intensity conflict issues, Koch reported directly to the deputy secretary of defense. Access is influence, and Koch now had direct access to the secretary and deputy secretary of defense.

Koch became fully involved in working to build a U.S. special operations capability. He soon understood that once the SOF's opponents grasped that Koch and Rylander and the other supporters of special operations were not going to let the issue die, they would begin to question the credentials of those who were forcing the issue. As described by Koch, "It wouldn't be fought on the merits. It would be fought on the basis of, 'how many wars has Noel Koch won?' We in the military are the ones that can handle this and these people should be kept in their place."[62]

Koch headed off this argument by putting together the Special Operations Policy Advisory Group (SOPAG), a committee composed of retired flag and general officers, many of whom had special operations experience. Koch chose retired officers in recognition of the reality that they were more likely than those still in the midst of their military careers to take a stand. He chose senior officers with highly respected careers in the conventional military and who had demonstrated some support for the special operations forces. Charter members of SOPAG included Lieutenant General Sam Wilson, Admiral James Holloway, Lieutenant General Leroy Manor, Lieutenant General Jim Ahmann, Major General Richard Secord (later of Iran-contra fame), and Brigadier General Donald Blackburn.[63] Both Blackburn and Wilson, whose career was described earlier, had a long relationship with special operations forces. Blackburn led "Blackburn's Headhunters" on Luzon during World War II, served in Special Forces units during the 1950s and 1960s, and was the director of the Office of the Special Assistant for Counterinsurgency and Special Activities (SACSA) on the Joint Staff during Vietnam.[64]

As SOPAG's chairman, Wilson recommended that the group report to the secretary of defense rather than to Koch. The advocacy group, therefore, flanked the undersecretary of defense and applied pressure from above, providing credibility for the arguments supporting the rebuilding of the SOF. They also worked to derail any attempt by opponents to claim there was a danger in these efforts of leading the country into "another Vietnam."[65] Interestingly, Koch intended to disband the group once SOF reform 'got over the hump.'[66] The SOPAG remained intact into the early Clinton administration although its meetings became few and far between.

A second, and eventually more embittering, end run involved an attempt by Koch and Rylander to have the secretary or deputy secretary issue a special operations policy directive to the military services. According to Koch, in January 1983 he and Rylander were providing an update to the secretary of defense on what the Defense Guidance had directed the services to do in support of SOF and what had actually occurred. During the course of the briefing Secretary Weinberger asked, "Well, what's the problem? Is it that it is not clear what we want? Or they don't understand it?. . . What do we need to do?" Koch replied that leaders in the OSD had to be much more explicit in what they were directing the services to do.[67] With Weinberger's approval, Koch and Rylander worked to put together an OSD policy statement. They integrated into their statement the analysis of a retired Air Force officer, General Vogt, who was leading a study for the OSD on rear area operations in a major European war. By including Vogt's work, Koch and Rylander ended up with a directive classified top secret.

According to Rylander, "the problem with that kind of document [classified top secret] is that nobody can see it, nobody is going to read it, and nobody is going to respond to it."[68] It became immediately clear to Koch and Rylander that "in order to make it stick, what was important was that the world understand and this document would be one the world would never read. Six or seven old men [would be] reading it and that was it, because the classification and distribution would be so tight."[69] Koch and Rylander immediately wrote an unclassified companion to the original directive and sent it out for coordination in August 1983. No one, however, would coordinate and sign off on the new document since it would now have a wide audience, including the SOF community, Congress, and the press, and it would be immediately clear whether or not the services were in compliance with the secretary's direction. Koch and Rylander were stymied at every attempt to push the coordination process. They were avoided in the halls of the Pentagon, and their phone calls were no longer returned.[70]

Frustrated after months of being told their recommended directive was "still in the pipeline," Noel Koch went to see Deputy Secretary of Defense Paul Thayer on a Friday afternoon.[71] Koch told Thayer his story and asked that he sign the memorandum. On October 3, 1983, Thayer signed the policy directive, which stated that U.S. national security required the maintenance of special operations forces and called for the completion of several steps. The memo stated the following:

1. Necessary force structure expansion and enhancements in command and control, personnel policy, training, and equipment will be implemented as rapidly as possible and will be fully implemented not later than the end of Fiscal Year 1990.

2. Collateral activities will be enhanced as necessary to provide fully effective support to the planning and execution of special operations.

3. Each Service will assign SOF and related activities sufficient resource allocation priority and will establish appropriate intensive management mechanisms to ensure that these objectives are met.

4. Resource decisions for current and programmed SOF, once made at the Secretary of Defense level, will not be changed or reduced by OSD or Service staffs unless coordinated by the Principal Deputy Assistant Secretary of Defense (International Security Affairs) and the Assistant Secretary of Defense (Comptroller) and approved by the Secretary of Defense.

By 1 March 1984 each Military Department and Defense Agency will submit a time-phased master plan for achieving these objectives for review by the Principal Deputy Assistant Secretary of Defense (International Security Affairs).[72]

The effect of this memorandum can be argued. Direction does not guarantee implementation, and Koch and Rylander had written a directive without providing the means and oversight to ensure that the services would take the required action. Without support from the secretary of defense and his staff throughout the resource decisionmaking process, nothing could make the services fulfill the vague terms of the directive. Phrases such as "necessary force structure expansion . . . fully effective support . . . sufficient resource allocation priority" were not specific enough to force resource decisions by the services that would build a strong special operations capability for the United States.

Nonetheless, the Thayer memo was important in several respects. First, it signaled that the Office of the Secretary of Defense was paying attention to special operations forces. Second, it clarified that if the secretary of defense made a resource decision on the SOF, changing of that decision by the services would be a clear violation of the secretary's direction. Third, the memorandum required the services to at least go through the exercise of preparing a master plan for the special operations forces. Finally, this memorandum showed that the principal deputy assistant secretary of defense (International Security Affairs), Noel Koch, was going to be involved in any decisions made about special operations forces.

An immediate effect of the Thayer memorandum was the establishment by the Joint Chiefs of the long-embattled Joint Special Operations Agency within the Joint Staff. Attempts to establish such an organization had begun almost a year earlier. In November 1982, General Shy Meyer had tried again, proposing to the OJCS a joint organization for command and control of special operations forces. According to an internal Defense Department chronology, this time the Joint Chiefs of Staff all agreed that a problem existed with special operations forces. They directed the Joint Staff to again evaluate alternative solutions and recommend "how best to organize to provide the CINCs with the best special operations capability."[73]

With the analysis still in progress, General Meyer proposed in early 1983 a revised special operations joint command structure to the JCS, including a Washington-based coordination-liaison element, a joint operational headquarters based on the army's counterterrorist unit, and expansion of the regional commanders in chiefs' (CINCs) special operations planning staffs.[74] The SOF community was, however, still attempting to put an end to the STRATSERCOM concept. They were successful when the JCS study, led by Colonel Link German, was released. German's study recommended establishing a "subunified" special operations command under the unified U.S. Readiness Command. The concept of the Joint Special Operations Agency (JSOA) evolved from this option months before Koch and Rylander succeeded in getting the SOF policy signed by the deputy secretary.[75] Ted Lunger and other JSOA supporters, including Noel Koch and Lynn Rylander in the Office of the Secretary of Defense, believed that the new agency could help raise the visibility of special operations and improve the planning for actual operations.

According to Lunger, the Joint Chiefs of Staff Directorate for Operations (JCS/J-3) wanted to slow down the establishment of the JSOA, and the Chairman of the Joint Chiefs of Staff (CJCS), General John Vessey, kept the recommendation in "his in-box" for nearly a year.[76] Lunger believed that the service chiefs opposed a strong SOF organization because they had "made war a lifelong study and having fought to get to the top, they were loathe to admit that their careers and weapon systems were irrelevant to the real world."[77]

With Thayer's signing of the SOF directive, the Joint Chiefs recognized that they had to respond to the languishing proposal for a JSOA. Approved by the Joint Chiefs of Staff in October 1983, the JSOA was established on January 1, 1984, with Major General Douglas Rice from the Marine Corps as its first director. Eventually, Rice was replaced by Major General Tom Kelly, who, under the tutelage of Lieutenant General Sam Wilson, became an effective proponent of SOF issues.[78]

After more than a year of effort by General Meyer, the Office of the Secretary of Defense, and supporters on Capitol Hill, the reality of the Joint Special Operations Agency was a disappointment. Lynn Rylander believed that the services supported the JSOA option because it "was farthest removed from anything that smacked of a command or command and control arrangement. Very easy to control."[79] In the end, the JSOA turned out to be a weak and largely ineffective organization. Its establishment in 1984 contained, however, elements of victory for SOF advocates. The JSOA was the first military special operations office at the general officer level since the Office of the Special Assistant for Counterinsurgency and Special Activities during the Vietnam War. The agency provided a forum for monitoring special operations issues and was an advocate within the OJCS for the SOF community.

What JSOA's director did not have was authority. And without authority, the JSOA could only lobby and not direct. The Terms of Reference for the Agency, approved by the secretary of defense at Congressman Daniel's urging, directed that the new organization would coordinate, not command. Furthermore, the agency was placed under the Directorate for Operations (J-3) on the Joint Staff, placing another layer of authority between the director of the JSOA and the chairman.[80] Finally, despite the recommendation of the Special Operations Policy Advisory Group (SOPAG) that the director of the new agency be a three-star general or flag officer to have the clout to make it work, the new director was only a two-star officer. According to Neil Koch, Secretary Weinberger backed off on his initial insistence that SOPAG's recommendation be followed and okayed the services' insistence that the director be a two-star officer.[81] The result was an agency without the authority, the visibility, or the seniority to change the direction of service "support" for special operations forces.

Recognizing its lack of authority, the JSOA focused on policy and doctrinal issues. It developed a Defense Department policy on how and why special operations forces would be used.[82] This pattern of establishing a new special operations organization with a vague mandate, uncertain responsibilities, and virtually no authority was to repeat itself in the late 1980s.

Congressional Support Grows

Following the failed rescue operation in Iran, Representative Daniel, a senior member of the House Armed Services Committee and chairman of the Readiness Subcommittee, became a fervent supporter of "SOF revitalization." Daniel, a long-time friend of the now-retired Lieutenant General Sam Wilson, usually relied on Ted Lunger, a member of his staff and a former Special Forces operator, for the details.[83] Lunger had been concerned with special operations even before Desert One finally focused congressional attention on the lack of a coordinated U.S. special operations capability. Daniel and Lunger became the relentless force behind congressional concern for SOF through the mid-1980s.

In 1983, having recently finished work on legislation mandating the establishment of a new unified command for Southwest Asia—the U.S. Central Command—and recognizing that there had been little change in America's special operations capability since 1980, Lunger plunged into the issue of SOF reform. Ted Lunger had maintained many of his special operations contacts over the years, and he became deeply involved in what he and others referred to as the SOF Liberation Front. This decidedly informal coalition of retired SEALs, Special Forces, and air force special operators, who maintained contact with active duty special operators and supporters outside the military, worked behind the scenes attempting to gain support for the SOF community. The "Washington office" of this "SOF Mafia" included Noel Koch, Lynn Rylander, and a few congressional staffers including Ted Lunger.

The coalition believed that something had to be done to build an effective special operations capability in the United States. Members of the coalition knew that acquisition, particularly of aircraft, was essential. They also knew in the early 1980s that the problem of cyclical and largely inadequate funding for SOF had to be addressed. They did not, however, know how to fix the problem.

Eventually, pressure from the various directions for SOF reform in the mid-1980s evolved into a two-pronged approach. The first was to try to resolve the narrow problem of SOF aviation. The second was to raise the priority of the SOF in the resource decisions of the services and the Office of the Secretary of Defense, with an emphasis on solving the "jointness" problem demonstrated in Operation Rice Bowl/Desert One.

By 1983 it was clear that Congress wanted the problem of SOF aviation resolved. Congress recommended that the U.S. Air Force purchase additional PAVE LOW and Combat Talon aircraft. In a response known as Initiative 17, the air force attempted instead to transfer its SOF rotary-wing mission to the army.

At first glance Initiative 17, one of a series of initiatives offered by the chiefs of staff of the air force and the army in 1983, seems to be a reasonable approach to reducing the apparent duplication of the rotary-wing aviation mission by the army and the air force. The intent of Initiative 17, according to a memorandum of understanding signed by the army deputy chief of staff of operations and plans and the air force deputy chief of staff for plans and operations, was "for the Army to assume responsibility for helicopter lift support [to SOF]. The Air Force will continue to provide fixed wing support for SOF forces."[84]

Despite an apparent reasonableness in this rationalizing of roles and missions, Initiative 17 was viewed by many in the SOF community as "an atrociously dumb idea."[85] According to Noel Koch, "The memorandum of understanding basically says the Army is going to take over the mission. . . . [But] if the Air Force divested itself of the [SOF aviation] mission, the Army had no ability to pick up the mission."[86]

Initiative 17 was viewed by SOF supporters as, if not evidence of the military services' malicious intentions for the SOF, then at least evidence of their inability and unwillingness to build an effective special operations capability in the United States.

The army and the air force made public in early 1983 the memorandum of understanding that included Initiative 17. If implemented, Initiative 17's potential impact on SOF aviation would have been dramatic and most likely negative. Noel Koch was told of the memorandum the day before it was to be announced by the air force and army. Koch immediately held a meeting with the staffs of the deputy chiefs of staff, operations and plans, of the air force and army. After confirming that the services intended to transfer the helicopters from the air force to the army, Koch asked whether the generals had consulted the unified CINCs or the commander of the counterterrorist command. According to Koch and Rylander, the generals said, "Yes, and we all agree that this is a great idea."[87] Subsequently, Koch found out that the army and the air force had at the very least consulted neither the commander in chief of U.S. Central Command (CENTCOM), nor the Military Airlift Command, the owner of AFSOF. Both commanders vehemently opposed the initiative.[88]

Immediately upon the services' announcement of Initiative 17, the SOF community and its supporters began fighting it. Koch and Rylander led the debate from within OSD while Ted Lunger and Dan Daniel worked from Capitol Hill.[89] Although supporters of the initiative asked, "Why the fuss about nine helicopters?" SOF advocates believed a great deal was at stake.[90] They argued that the U.S. Army did not have the capability to begin responding to the weaknesses in SOF aviation seen in the Iranian hostage rescue mission, much less deal with the broader SOF mission. Army helicopters were not refuelable in the early and mid-1980s. Army helicopters did not have the avionics necessary to conduct low-level operations at night, nor could they fly in the extreme weather conditions seen, for example, in the Iranian desert. Initiative 17 would be expensive too. There would be a lengthy delay in building a long-range rotary-wing aviation capability in the army. Pilots, crews, and support personnel would have to be trained and doctrine developed for the use of special operations helicopters within the army. The nine Pave Lows that the air force under duress had finally agreed to transfer to the army were not enough to support SOF aviation requirements, and so the army would have to develop a new helicopter, significantly modify one of its existing helicopters, or buy more PAVE LOWs. Finally, the Holloway Commission had argued that Desert One had proved it was better to put a pilot and crew who were trained for special operations aviation missions into a strange aircraft than it was to take a special operations aircraft and provide it with a pilot and crew who were not trained in special operations. The army helicopter pilots and crews were talented and well-trained but had neither the training nor the mindset for long-range infiltration and exfiltration special operations missions. The air force refused to meet congressional requirements and had no intention of using its funds to pay for special operations helicopters.[91]

When a working group composed of representatives from the army and air force recommended a shared rotary-wing mission, with only the short-range mission transferred from the air force to the army, and the long-range mission remaining with the air force, the services rejected the group's report, and Noel Koch went to Defense Secretary Caspar Weinberger. At Koch's request, Weinberger signed a memorandum to the service chiefs of staff urging caution from the military services, and a guarantee that any recommendation they made would not degrade the existing SOF aviation capability. Weinberger also directed that Noel Koch or his staff be included in any discussion of Initiative 17. The air force and army staffs, however, were not eager to accommodate the Office of the Secretary of Defense, and staff members from Koch's office were only able to force themselves into one meeting of the study group. Koch and Rylander were not, however, going to give up easily. Skirmishes over Initiative 17 continued for the next several years.[92]

Protecting a Still-Precarious Value

By the mid-1980s, there were signs that increased support for special operations forces was resulting in some improvement in the U.S. special operations capability. Owing to the recommendations of the Holloway Commission and the work of the small but relentless group of SOF supporters, the Department of Defense had activated the new Joint Special Operations Command (JSOC) with Brigadier General Richard Scholtes as commander. Scholtes was commanding an elite subset of American special operations forces, including SEAL Team 6, Special Forces Operational Detachment-D (Delta), the army's SOF aviation unit Task Force 160, and two battalions from the 75th Ranger Regiment.[93]

The army and navy had activated new units and increased manpower in some of the previously existing units. The air force had provided its special operators with their own wing, and although the air force was not meeting the modernization requirements levied by Congress, the issue at least had the attention of supporters both on Capitol Hill and in the Defense Department. Overall, the special operations budgets within the military services had increased slightly, although in total they were still no more than one-tenth of 1 percent of the total defense budget.[94]

As events in 1983 were to make clear, these improvements were not enough to build the special operations capability the SOF community and its supporters believed essential to support U.S. national security goals. They were changes at the margin. They did not address what turned out to be the core issues of SOF reform: the need for unified command of special operations forces and protection of SOF fiscal and manpower resources. In the mid-1980s, following the invasion of Grenada, the coalition of SOF supporters in Congress, in the Pentagon, and throughout the broader defense community was convinced that, if left on their own, the military services would never protect the precarious value of a strong and flexible special operations capability. The SOF reformers in the mid-1980s believed they had no choice but to resort to stronger measures.

5

Urgent Fury

I was a member of the 1st Ranger Battalion during Operation Urgent Fury. The battalion's mission was to conduct a night combat parachute assault to secure Point Salines Airfield and surrounding terrain so follow-on forces could land at the airfield.

Some Rangers did not have the opportunity to re-rig their rucksacks for the jump, so they took their claymores [mines] and M-60 machine gun ammo and stuffed [them] down the front of their jungle fatigue jackets. . . . With the delays in the jump we ended up conducting a daylight combat assault instead of the night drop we had planned for.

Sergeant First Class Terry Allen, March 1993

Ninety miles north of South America lies Grenada, the southernmost island of the eastern Caribbean. The small island was the site of an American military operation critical to the reform of U.S. special operations forces. Operation Urgent Fury, although ultimately successful in terms of American political-military interests, demonstrated that the declarations of support for SOF revitalization by Secretary of Defense Caspar Weinberger and the military services had not been backed up with effective reform. Of the eight D-Day targets in the American plan, special operations forces—including SEALs, U.S. Army Rangers, and members of the SFOD-D (Delta)—were directly involved in seven of them, the only exception being the marines' taking of Grenville in the northeast. Only the Ranger operations and those of SEAL Team 4, operating in support of the marines in a traditional role as an underwater demolition team (UDT), were fully successful. Efforts by the SEALs to rescue the governor general of Grenada were politically successful, but the SEALs required diversion of a marine company from other operations to reach safety. Three other special operations were tragic failures. Operations in Grenada made it clear that much remained to be done before the American special operations capability could be declared rebuilt and effectively integrated with conventional military forces. The SOF casualties in Urgent Fury were heavy. Many special operators died as a result of poor planning and coordination and gross intelligence failures.

Grenada was a territory of Great Britain until 1974, when independence was granted and Eric Gairy became the new country's first prime minister.[1] Gairy was corrupt and brutal and was overthrown in 1979 by the Marxist New Jewel Movement (Joint Endeavor for Welfare, Education, and Liberation Movement) led by Maurice Bishop. Bishop's movement was popular at first, and Bishop remained popular throughout his time as prime minister, despite the increasingly authoritarian and violent nature of his government. Security forces for Bishop's People's Revolutionary Government were composed of the People's Revolutionary Army (PRA) and People's Revolutionary Militia (PRM). The PRA was to play a major role in the turmoil that led to Urgent Fury.

The United States was uneasy from the start about the establishment of a new Marxist government in the Caribbean, and its concerns increased as Bishop cultivated close ties with the Soviet Union and Cuba. Although the details of Grenada's military buildup were not known before the invasion, it was evident to other Caribbean nations and the American government that Grenada was rapidly becoming second only to Cuba among Caribbean nations in its military capability through arms deliveries from Cuba, the Soviet Union, and Libya.[2] The American government's fears that Grenada was becoming a training center for communist subversives in the Caribbean were strengthened when Bishop's government began construction of an airfield at Port Salines capable of accommodating military aircraft. Grenada's only other airport was Pearls Airfield, and it could handle only small aircraft. To make matters worse, Cuba was providing the funding, the materials, and most of the labor force. The number of Cuban workers, mistakenly believed by the United States to be soldiers doubling as construction crews, increased from 150 in 1979 to 650 in 1983.[3] The government of Grenada explained the new airfield as necessary to increase tourism to the country. There was, however, no evidence of plans to build the new hotels that would be necessary to house the predicted influx of visitors. The U.S. government believed Grenada intended to become a refueling stop for Cuban forces who would be "exporting revolution" throughout Latin America and Africa.

The government of Grenada provided the United States with an opening for reversing apparent Marxist gains in 1983. Even as he gained new commitments from Cuba and the Soviet Union, Bishop was losing support from his own government, most notably from Deputy Prime Minister Bernard Coard. Coard and his followers, eventually including General Hudson Austin, Bishop's minister of defense, interior, and construction and the commander of the PRA, called for a more hard-line revolutionary stance from Bishop, rejecting the prime minister's attempts at moderation with the United States.[4] On October 14, 1983, Maurice Bishop was overthrown by Coard and most Central Committee members, and placed under house arrest.

Most Grenadines were outraged by the coup, and many demonstrated in the streets of St. George's in protest of Bishop's arrest. On the morning of October 19, it appeared that Bishop might win the struggle when he was rescued from his house arrest by a cheering mob. For unknown reasons, Bishop did not order the arrest of Coard and his supporters but instead moved with his supporters through St. George's and to Fort Rupert at one end of St. George's harbor. Coard still had control of the PRA since most of the army's leaders had participated in the coup d'état. At one o'clock in the afternoon on October 19, the army responded to Coard's direction and attacked Fort Rupert. After a bloody battle, Bishop and his supporters surrendered. Bishop and seven others who had remained loyal to him were executed by a machine gun squad of four men.[5]

Coard and his supporters had won the battle over Bishop, but they recognized that they had to quickly establish order or they would be inviting intervention. A radio broadcast that evening announced the military was in charge and General Austin would head the new Revolutionary Military Council. Austin declared martial law and put in place a twenty-four-hour curfew.

There were more than six hundred American students in Grenada at the time of Bernard Coard's overthrow of Maurice Bishop. The safety of these students, who were attending St. George's Medical School, was the initial impetus for American involvement in the crisis in Grenada. As early as October 17, National Security Adviser Robert McFarlane briefed President Ronald Reagan on the need for evacuation plans in case the American students were threatened. The focus of American planning remained on evacuating American nationals until October 20, when the Department of State received a message from the prime minister of Barbados, Tom Adams, urging the United States to take action, in cooperation with other Caribbean nations, not only to protect foreign citizens but to overthrow the Revolutionary Military Council. On October 21 this request was made verbally not only from Barbados but also from members of the Organization of Eastern Caribbean States (OECS) and Jamaica.[6]

With the support of many of the Caribbean nations, Washington shifted its planning from evacuation of American students to full-scale invasion of Grenada. Vice President George Bush met with the Special Situation Group in the White House and directed an amphibious task force en route to Lebanon, including the amphibious assault ship USS *Guam* and the 22nd Marine Amphibious Unit with 1,900 marines, to divert to Grenada. Bishop's execution presented President Reagan with not only the need to rescue the American students but also the opportunity to defeat militarily a communist dictatorship in the backyard of the United States and establish a democratic government. The Reagan administration remembered the severe damage suffered by President Carter as a result of the Iranian hostage crisis and also saw the possibility of regaining American confidence in its military after the backlash from the Vietnam War. Thursday, October 20, Reagan was briefed by his national security adviser on the draft National Security Decision Directive (NSDD) that would direct the invasion, and he initialed it the next day.[7]

On that day, Friday, October 21, planning began for the largest American military operation since Vietnam. Unfortunately for the planners, the American intelligence community had virtually no information on Grenada, and D-Day for the operation was set for October 25. Planners had no maps other than black and white copies of an out-of-date British tourist map that provided neither grid coordinates nor terrain information. The Central Intelligence Agency had no agents in Grenada. There were no recent aerial photographs of the island. And the military had no knowledge of where the American students to be rescued were located. Adding to the confusion during the four days of planning, General Vessey, the chairman of the Joint Chiefs of Staff, alerted the Atlantic Command (LANTCOM) to plan and direct the operation. Atlantic Command was primarily a naval command oriented toward NATO and European operations. Atlantic Command usually paid little attention to the Caribbean since this was primarily the responsibility of U.S. Forces Caribbean Command located in Key West, Florida.

To add to Atlantic Command's difficulty, the operation being considered was largely a ground operation. Vice Admiral Joseph Metcalf, commander of the Joint Task Force (TF 120) formed for the invasion, ultimately had to command a joint force that included forces from the air force, marines, Rangers, Special Forces, SEALs, army aviation, and the 82nd Airborne Division. There was great pressure from all the military services to be included. No one wanted to be left out. The forces included were alerted by LANTCOM on October 21 and quickly sent representatives to Norfolk. Unfortunately, the Military Airlift Command representative was unable to arrive until after the planning conference and so was never able to meet with the army representatives. The logistics chief for the Joint Chiefs of Staff was not notified until two days after planning began because of security concerns.[8] The same concerns greatly limited what each organization was told and reduced the effectiveness of planning operations. For example, the members of the Ranger units who participated in the operation were never told of the 82nd Airborne's mission to relieve the Rangers. As a result, the Rangers were overloaded with supplies in fear of leaving something critical behind. At the same time as planning staffs were meeting in Norfolk, the units alerted began their own planning. The result was confusion to the extent that through Sunday, October 23, the marines, Rangers, and 82nd Airborne were all planning to take the same objectives, Port Salines and Pearl airfields.[9]

Planners called for special operations forces because of the necessary speed and surprise of the operation and the possibility of hostages being seized by the Revolutionary Military Council or PRA. For that reason, at the same time General Vessey notified the Atlantic Command, Military Airlift Command, and Readiness Command, he contacted Brigadier General Richard Scholtes, the commander of the new Joint Special Operations Command. General Scholtes commanded most special operations forces participating in Urgent Fury, including his JSOC units plus airlift and gunship support from the air force's 1st Special Operations Wing and air force combat control teams.[10] Elements of SEAL Team 4 supported the 22nd Marine Amphibious Unit. In his book, Mark Adkin is critical of the decision to use both SEAL Team 6 and Delta, and of the missions they were assigned. Adkin believes the decision to use these particular forces was simply the result of these units' wanting to show what they could do rather than a military need for their specialized capabilities.[11] The author of the definitive history of the SEALs, Orr Kelly, agrees with Adkin's assessment of the SEAL attempt to capture the radio transmitter at Beausejour.[12] These elite forces were at tremendous risk and suffered heavy casualties in pursuit of targets that were not critical to the success of the total operation.

H-hour for the invasion was scheduled for 2:00 a.m. on Tuesday, October 25. All objectives, including rescuing American medical students and Governor General Paul Scoon, were to be secured by the invading force by dawn. The first phase was to be carried out by Joint Task Force 123 (JTF123) commanded by General Scholtes and including nearly all special operations forces and Task Force 124 with the 22nd Marine Amphibious Unit, and elements of SEAL Team 4. The marines were responsible for roughly the northern half of the island, while the special operators were responsible for the southern half. In the south, the Rangers, supported by U.S. Air Force special operations forces aviation and an element of SEAL Team 6, were to take Point Salines Airfield, rescue the students at the True Blue campus adjacent to the airfield, and then move on to Camp Calivgny, thought by the Americans to be the center of Cuban military activity on the island. Other SEALs and Delta, supported by Task Force 160 helicopters, were to take targets near St. George's and be out of Grenada by dawn or soon after. In the north, the marines were to first take Pearls Airfield and then Grenville. Phase Two would begin early on D-Day, just after dawn, when elements of the 82nd Airborne Division (under Task Force 121) would arrive to take over from the special operators, begin mopping up and then assume peacekeeping duties until units from the Caribbean peacekeeping forces arrived in Grenada.[13]

In fact, the SEALs opened up Urgent Fury on October 23. Accounts of this still-classified mission differ, but Kelly's is most authoritative. The plan called for a mixed group of twelve SEALs and four air force combat control team members to parachute from two MC-130E Combat Talon aircraft on the night of October 23-24. Once in the water, they would meet with a boat launched from the destroyer *Clifton Sprague* and climb into two Boston Whalers dropped from the aircraft. The SEALs and combat controllers would then head for Point Salines to conduct reconnaissance and, because there were no maps of the airfield or surrounding area available to the military forces, plant radar beacons to guide the aircraft carrying the Ranger assault force. Of particular concern to the SEALs were any obstacles on the runway that would force the Rangers to parachute into the airfield rather than air landing.

The failure of the mission was dramatic and tragic. Although the SEALs had planned to make their jump at last light, they were forced because of delays to jump at night. That made it virtually impossible for them to judge their distance from the water as they were releasing their parachutes. The sea was rough, with twenty-five-knot winds, enough to cancel a peacetime jump and make an operational jump questionable. Finally, although the recommended maximum weight for a SEAL making a water jump was sixty pounds, these SEALs were loaded with weights ranging from 100 to 400 pounds.[14] There had been no time before the operation to conduct a "dip test" to determine the buoyancy of the fully loaded SEALs.[15] After the SEALs jumped from the aircraft and into the night, four SEALs never surfaced. There are two theories about what happened, according to Orr Kelly. The first is that the men were so heavily loaded with weapons and gear that their life jackets did not provide enough buoyancy to keep them afloat or bring them back up to the surface quickly enough. Lack of buoyancy would have been aggravated by the SEALs' releasing their parachutes too early and plunging more deeply than expected into the ocean or being injured upon hitting the water. The second theory is that the men released their parachutes too late and became tangled in the shroud lines and drowned.[16] Subsequently, as is usual in the SEAL community, a great deal of debate took place about whether SEAL Team 6 had to jump as part of its mission or whether another SEAL team deployed to Puerto Rico might have been able to make the approach by ship.

The survivors loaded into their Boston Whaler and headed for shore to conduct their mission. For reasons not stated in the public record the SEALs and combat controllers cut their engine but were then unable to restart it because the engine had flooded out in the rough waters. They drifted back out to sea and were picked up by the USS *Clifton Sprague*.

General Scholtes, believing the reconnaissance and beacon emplacement mission of the SEALs and combat controllers was critical to the success of the Rangers' assault on Port Salines, recommended to Admiral Metcalf that Urgent Fury be delayed twenty-four hours to allow the special operators to try again. Neither Washington, D.C., nor Admiral Metcalf was willing to take the risk of losing tactical surprise, and therefore they agreed only to shifting H-hour from 2:00 a.m. on October 25 to 5:00 a.m., leaving only minutes before daylight for the invasion to begin.[17] The SEALs and combat controllers set out once again on the night of October 24 and ran into a Grenadian patrol boat. They killed the engine and lay low until the patrol boat passed. Unfortunately, the engine flooded out again, so the reconnaissance mission was again unsuccessful. The team drifted for eleven hours before being picked up by the *Sprague*.[18] The Rangers and the air force pilots would have no reconnaissance information about the airfield before their attack and no beacons to guide their approach.

In the early morning hours of October 25, more than a hundred SEALs, members of Delta Force, and Rangers from C Company of the 1st Battalion were preparing to secure three targets in and near St. George's, supported by nine UH-60 Blackhawk helicopters and crews from the army's 160th Aviation Battalion (Task Force 160), or the "Night Stalkers." According to plan, the targets—the radio transmitter at Beausejour, Government House, where Governor General Sir Paul Scoon would be found, and Richmond Hill Prison—were to be seized by the raiders before dawn.

Little resistance was expected, and the special operators were to take their objectives and be out of Grenada before the main invasion began.

As happened in nearly all aspects of the Grenada operation, the pressure of short warning time, inadequate training, and poor intelligence caused delays and surprises in the operation that resulted in tragedy and death. All three special operations relied on the support of Task Force 160, located at Fort Campbell, Kentucky. The unit was not alerted of its October 25 "exercise" until late afternoon on October 23. All of Monday was spent preparing the UH-60s, which did not have the range to fly directly from Fort Bragg to Grenada, for loading onto the C-5 Galaxy aircraft that would transport them first to Pope Air Force Base, North Carolina, to pick up the army and navy special operators, or to Barbados for unloading, and then conclude with the forty-five-minute flight to Grenada. Task Force 160 had, however, never been able to practice loading the Blackhawks onto the C-5s with the air force crews, resulting in hours of delay as the helicopters were loaded, unloaded, and loaded again. The C-5s did not leave Fort Campbell until 11:00 p.m. on October 24, only six hours before they were scheduled to be over Grenada.

The C-5s landed in Barbados at 3:30 a.m. and had only forty-five minutes before they were to be in the air and flying toward Grenada. Given that the helicopters had to be unloaded, reassembled, and prepared for their flight, the task was impossible. Nonetheless, through tremendous effort the Blackhawks and their "precious cargo" of SEALs, Special Forces, and Rangers were in the air and flying over Grenada at some time after 6:00 a.m. Their delayed arrival time meant, however, that they were arriving in the early morning light, after the bulk of the invasion had begun. There was to be no surprise.

The first Blackhawk carried a team of eight SEALs, led by Lieutenant Donald Erskine, whose mission was to secure the radio transmitter at Beausejour. Mark Adkin is highly critical of this mission, arguing that this was a long-range transmitter used by the Bishop government to transmit throughout the Caribbean.[19] The Radio Free Grenada transmitter used to transmit to the country itself was located elsewhere on the island. Orr Kelly takes Adkin's criticism another step when he argues that securing the transmitter was neither essential nor appropriate for the specialized skills of SEAL Team 6.[20]

Appropriate or not, Erskine and his men quickly captured the PRA guards and seized the transmitter. Evaluating the surrounding terrain, Erskine determined that attack by Grenadian forces was most likely along the road running next to the station. He and his men set up defenses on the road just south and north of the transmitter and soon had captured a PRA soldier and ambushed a truckload of militia, killing five. Hearing of the seizure of the station, PRA leaders at Fort Frederick counterattacked with several armored personnel carriers and infantry. The eight SEALs were vastly outnumbered and did as they were taught, seeking safety in the water. Fighting their way to the shore, two of the SEALs were wounded. Erskine was hit several times, and the injury to his elbow was so severe that he almost lost his arm. After making their way along the shore, the SEALs swam for several hours nearly two miles out to sea, where they were rescued by helicopters from the destroyer USS *Caron*. Remarkably, not one of the SEALs was killed. Subsequent air attacks on the transmitter failed to destroy it.

At the same time as Erskine's team was attempting to secure the transmitter, the most politically sensitive of the three special operations missions, the protecting of Paul Scoon, was under way. Grenada was a member of the British Commonwealth, and Scoon was England's representative to Grenada: the one credible government representative on the island. Besides concerns over his safety, the United States needed Scoon to formalize his request for assistance by signing a letter, drafted by the Department of State, requesting American intervention. The rescue of Scoon was a mission that fit most closely with the SEAL team's hostage rescue specialty.[21] The team of approximately twenty-two men was led by Lieutenant John Koenig. They arrived near Government House just before 6:15 a.m. but were delayed when the pilot could not initially find the house hidden beneath the jungle foliage. As they circled, they began taking small arms fire from forces outside of Scoon's compound. This plus the unexpected steepness of the ground covered with trees made a landing by the helicopters impossible, so the SEALs fast-roped into the compound. Ground fire forced the helicopters to leave after discharging the SEALs, taking with them three State Department representatives, the SEALs' second-in-command, and the team's radio for communicating with the *Guam* and Admiral Metcalf.[22]

Despite the bullets overhead, Koenig and his team captured the policemen on guard, made their way into Government House, and quickly moved Paul Scoon, his wife, and nine staff members into the center of the house, where they would be safest. It soon became clear that the PRA knew the Americans were inside as one or more armored personnel carriers and two groups of infantry surrounded Government House, clearly outgunning the lightly armed SEALs. As told by Orr Kelly, at this point the incident occurred that led to one of the myths of Urgent Fury: that an

officer, upon finding his unit surrounded, used his credit card to telephone the United States to request assistance. In fact, the telephones at
Government House still worked, and Lieutenant Bill Davis used the phones
to call the airfield at Port Salines, already controlled by the Americans. He
asked for gunships to drive back the PRA troops.[23] Because the gunships
were already fully tasked at Point Salines, they did not arrive until nearly
four hours later but then continued their protection throughout the day.
The SEALs, supported by the gunships, were able to keep the governor
general, his family, and staff secure, but they could not break away because evacuation by helicopter was impossible. Because Paul Scoon was
protected, the operation was politically successful. Nonetheless, the loss
of surprise meant the small and lightly armed SEAL unit could not escape
until the following morning when a marine company arrived. The marines' support diverted forces from the rest of the operation and did nothing to increase the confidence of conventional commanders in special
operations forces. Paul Scoon was eventually taken to Point Salines, where
he signed, and backdated to October 24, a copy of the State Department
letter held by Brigadier Rudy Lewis, commander of the Barbados Defense
Force.[24]

The remaining six Blackhawks carried a mixed team of Rangers and
Special Forces from Delta who had the mission of taking Richmond Hill
Prison and releasing any political prisoners held there.[25] It is unclear why
the special operators were given this mission since there was no strategic
value to the prison and its seizure would have no effect on the outcome
of D-Day. Furthermore, the American planners had no idea who was
inside the prison or if anyone needed protection. Mark Adkin believes
that Richmond Hill Prison was simply a case of the highly trained Delta
team's wanting to have a role in the only show in town.[26] The meager
intelligence available suggested that the prison would be lightly guarded,
particularly if the operation went as planned and the American forces
arrived before dawn. The assault force expected the operation to be a
simple matter of two helicopters landing on either side of the prison to
provide a defensive perimeter and the other Blackhawks hovering within
the prison walls while their troops fast-roped in and released everyone
who could be found. There was no real intelligence, no detailed plan,
and no rehearsal—all critical elements to conducting successful special
operations.

Tragically, little of what was assumed in the plan occurred. The delays
in the arrival of the Blackhawks in Barbados meant that the special operators were attempting their assault after the Rangers and marines had be-

gun the main invasion. The Blackhawks were sent in unescorted. They were relying on surprise and their ability to get close to the prison. Unfortunately, a company of Grenadian infantry armed with automatic rifles and two ZPU-4 antiaircraft machine guns met the assault force. Additionally, contrary to the information given to the SOF planners, the prison was on a ridge with walls extending twenty feet up from the steep cliff and surrounded by jungle. There were to be no helicopter landings adjacent to the prison.

The special operations force was hit immediately as it rose over the ridge. Bullets ripped through the Blackhawks, wounding many of the Special Forces and Rangers as well as the pilot and door gunner of the fourth helicopter. The helicopters headed out to sea and re-formed to make a second attack, exemplifying the motto of the 160th Aviation Battalion—"Night Stalkers don't quit." As they made their second attempt, the force was devastated by the next major intelligence failure. Three hundred yards across the ravine from Richmond Hill Prison was Fort Frederick, the PRA headquarters. Captain Keith Lucas, the already wounded pilot of the fourth Blackhawk, was hit again and killed by fire from Fort Frederick. His copilot's head was grazed, but he maintained control of the helicopter and turned it back toward Point Salines until it was hit again and slammed into the crest of a hill, breaking in two. Even as the aircraft burst into flames, many of the men ran, or were pulled out, to safety. Reports of this operation are unclear, but it seems that perhaps as many as three men besides Lucas were killed.

Nine men on board one of the other Blackhawks were let down to secure the area and aid the injured. Those who survived the crash waited more than three hours before they were evacuated by navy rescue helicopters, partly because of navy rules about army helicopters landing on their ships and partly because of incompatible communications equipment between the services.

Of these three special operations, only one had any success. The operations were undertaken at great cost to the special operations forces with estimates of four killed and twenty to thirty wounded.

The mission accomplished by the special operations forces who experienced the least delay and complication began on the night of October 24. Elements of SEAL Team 4 had deployed with the 22nd Marine Amphibious Unit in transit to the Mediterranean and Lebanon. When the MAU was diverted to Grenada and given the mission of securing Pearls Airfield and the nearby town of Grenville on the northeast coast of Grenada, the SEALs were given a classic UDT-type mission of conducting reconnaissance in advance of the marine assault. From the landing ship USS *Fort Snelling*, two groups of SEALs boarded two Sea Fox raiding boats, each crewed by three members of Special Boat Unit Twenty, and headed through rough seas ten miles to the coast. By midnight, the teams were ashore. One group headed inland to conduct reconnaissance of Pearls, and the other left to evaluate the shore. At 4:00 a.m. the group on the shore sent the signal "Walking Track Shoes" to the ship, which meant that tracked amphibious vehicles would find landing extremely hazardous and other landing craft would find it impossible.[27] The marines would have to make their assault by helicopter. The airport team reported that the PRA's antiaircraft defenses were such that the helicopters would have to land at a site adjacent to the airport and not at the airport itself. Admiral Metcalf and his staff did not receive the SEALs' message until 4:00 a.m. H-hour was set for 5:00 a.m., and the first flight of helicopters left twenty minutes late. Nonetheless, the marines met only light opposition at the airfield and quickly secured the airfield with no casualties. The situation was even better at Grenville, where the cautious marines were warmly welcomed by the town's citizens.

The largest operation undertaken by the special operations forces in Grenada was the assault of Point Salines Airfield by the Rangers. Two battalions of Rangers were to take part in Urgent Fury. They would conduct a classic Ranger mission of securing an airfield, in this case at Point Salines, and then they would protect the American medical students at the True Blue campus. The 1st Battalion/75th Rangers, commanded by Lieutenant Colonel Wesley Taylor, gave over its C Company to support the assault on Richmond Hill Prison but kept its other two companies at nearly full strength, for a total of 350 soldiers. Lieutenant Colonel Ralph Hagler's 2nd Battalion/75th Rangers was forced to fight with fewer than 250 of its 700 men and was at the added disadvantage of originally being assigned the mission of securing Pearls Airfield and not receiving the reassignment to follow Taylor's battalion into Point Salines until late Sunday, October 23. Aside from C Company of the 1st Battalion, the Rangers were limited to fighting at 40 percent of their normal strength by a shortage of air force crews trained for night operations with the MC-130 and C-130 transport aircraft.[28]

The Ranger commanders were notified of the invasion of Grenada on the evening of October 21. As with the rest of the American force, they had no maps other than the British tourist map and no intelligence on enemy locations, strength, or intentions. The eventual plan, once Hagler received his new mission, was for Taylor's 1st Battalion to move in first, led by the pathfinders of Alpha Company. The pathfinders would make a free-fall parachute jump from an MC-130 into Point Salines at about 3:30 a.m. to conduct reconnaissance of the airfield and mark the landing zone or drop zone with lights if possible. The remainder of A Company would follow ninety minutes later, carried by two MC-130 Combat Talons from the 8th Special Operations Squadron. They would jump into Port Salines to secure the runway and clear it of obstacles. All the aircraft would be guided by beacons emplaced by the SEALs and combat control team members. Alpha Company would be followed thirty minutes later by five C-130s carrying the remainder of the 1st Battalion and then, two minutes later, by five more C-130s with the 2nd Battalion. Only the pathfinders were to jump in, with the remaining Rangers conducting an assault landing and unloading several gun jeeps. The Rangers would secure the airfield and go to the students' rescue.

The entire operation would be supported by AC-130 Spectre gunships from the 16th Special Operations Squadron. The Spectre has a reconnaissance capability and a powerful strike capability since it is armed with either a 105-mm M-102 cannon or a 76.2-mm Gatling gun, a 40-mm gun, and two 20-mm Vulcan cannons. Special operations forces sing the praises of the AC-130s and their crews because of their ability to provide a high volume of precise air-to-ground fire under difficult conditions.

The first complication for the Rangers occurred the evening before when in the midst of briefing his battalion, Lieutenant Colonel Taylor realized that the Rangers' flight schedules were different from those of the 1st Special Operations Wing, and the Rangers were scheduled to load the first MC-130 two hours earlier than he expected. In the rush to load, it became clear that the aircraft did not have hatch antennas attached and there was no time to fix the situation. Taylor would be largely unable to communicate with his troops in flight.

Once in the air, the Rangers were jammed into the aircraft shoulder-to-shoulder for the long flight. Despite the tension, many slept. Soon after taking off, Taylor was told that aerial photographs showed that the runway was blocked with obstacles that had been in place for several days. At 12:30 a.m. the Rangers were told of the tragedy of the reconnaissance mission of the SEALs and combat controllers. The Rangers would have to rely entirely on their own pathfinders for reconnaissance. Taylor decided that all of A Company would have to jump into the airfield, and the men in the lead MC-130s began rigging their parachutes.

The pathfinders jumped at 3:30 a.m. For unknown reasons, either the parachutes or the altimeters of two jumpers failed, and both men were killed when they hit the ground. The pathfinders found heavy vehicles and spikes for puncturing aircraft tires littering the runway. It seemed impossible for the pathfinders to clear the runway in time for the remaining troops' arrival thirty minutes later, so at 4:00 a.m., an hour before the assault was to begin, Taylor decided that all of the Rangers would have to jump. Because of the problem with the hatch antennae, those in the fifth, sixth, and seventh aircraft received Taylor's order only twenty minutes before they were scheduled to arrive over the airfield. The situation was probably less chaotic in the fifth aircraft since Taylor's executive officer, Major John Nix, predicted Taylor's decision and ordered the troops on his plane to rig for jumping. Nix's initiative was for naught. Soon after Nix's order, the loadmaster announced the Rangers would be landing and they all de-rigged. But shortly after the troops had struggled out of their equipment, the loadmaster shouted, "Only thirty minutes fuel left. Rangers are fighting. Jump in twenty minutes."[29] The fifth, sixth, and seventh planes were in chaos as the Rangers scrambled to get their parachutes back on. They had to stuff claymore mines and other equipment inside their uniforms since there was no time to pack their rucksacks correctly.

Confusion continued. Fifteen minutes before H-hour, the lead MC-130 reported to General Scholtes that his navigational equipment had failed and he could not switch positions with the second MC-130 because of a rainstorm. Scholtes pushed H-hour back to 5:30 a.m. and told the MC-130s carrying the remainder of A Company to abort their run. Taylor regrouped the aircraft so that his aircraft would jump first, ahead of A Company and their clearance mission. At this time Taylor also learned of the chaos on the fifth, sixth, and seventh aircraft and had to direct them to circle until they were ready to jump.

At 5:31 a.m., Taylor's aircraft descended to 500 feet. A PRA searchlight locked onto the plane, but the first group of forty-two Rangers jumped anyway. Fortunately, the Cuban construction workers had been ordered by one of the few active duty Cuban officers on the island not to shoot except in self-defense. There was only sporadic shooting, and none of the parachuting Rangers were hit. The first C-130 drew the fire of the antiaircraft guns defending the airfield, and the two pilots following Taylor's plane aborted their runs until two AC-130s were able to soften up the defenses. In the meantime, Taylor and his men worked to begin clearing the airstrip of obstacles, at one point using a hot-wired bulldozer to flatten the spikes. At 5:52 a.m., one of the two MC-130s carrying the rest of A Company made its drop. By 7:10 a.m., all of the Rangers were safely on the airfield except for those needed to drive the jeeps off the aircraft once they were able to land.

Given the chaos of the hours before they jumped, the remainder of the Rangers' operation went smoothly. Two platoons headed for Calliste, a housing area for Cubans just north of the east end of the runway. Two companies of Rangers secured the construction camps. The remaining Rangers either secured the west end of the runway or went to rescue the students at the True Blue campus. Although there was some firing between the Rangers and the PRA guard at the gate of the campus, by 7:45 a.m. the students were protected, with no casualties and no hostages taken. Despite the Rangers' success, there was yet another surprise as the students at the True Blue campus began asking about the safety of those at the Grand Anse campus. None of the American military forces had been told of the other campus or the number of students housed there, on the west side of the island. The Grand Anse students, and most of the other Americans, were reached by the Rangers and marines the next day.

By 11:00 a.m. on October 25, the runway was clear and the C-130s landed with the Rangers' gun jeeps. The Rangers controlled the airfield and successfully defeated a desperate assault by three PRA armored personnel carriers later that day. At 2:00 p.m., the lead element of the 82nd Airborne Division arrived to take over from the Rangers and begin mopping-up operations. The 82nd was later criticized for the slowness of its move to secure the southern half of the island.[30] General Hudson Austin was arrested on October 30 after sitting with other coup leaders in his house for five days. Bernard Coard was arrested on October 29 after he attempted to escape to South America. More than 660 American citizens and 82 foreigners were ultimately evacuated from Grenada. The number of special operators killed or wounded has remained classified, although Mark Adkin estimated that 19 American servicemen died, more than half of them killed accidentally. One hundred and fifty-two Americans were wounded, including approximately 20 to 30 special operators in the Richmond Hill Prison and Beausejour transmitter operations.[31]

In 1986 testimony by General Scholtes about the misuse of the special operations forces, intelligence failures, poor command, control, and communications, and equipment failures during Urgent Fury would be crucial in the battle for SOF reform. The operation in Grenada demonstrated the compromising effect on special operations when basic SOF operating tenets—intelligence, planning, practice, and secrecy—were not adhered to. The consequence of this relaxation of doctrine in Urgent Fury was the loss of life in the missions that were only tangentially related to the success of the American invasion, with the possible exception of securing the governor general. That, however, diverted other American forces from their primary combat mission.

As in Operation Rice Bowl/Desert One, a critical weakness of American special operations was tactical mobility. The failure of SEAL Team 6 to reach Point Salines for reconnaissance and beacon emplacement and the need to break down and load the Blackhawks needed by the Rangers, Delta, and SEALs onto conventional air force transport aircraft proved that there is little value in the special operations forces if they cannot get to their targets. SOF airlift did not have the legs, the firepower, or the nighttime operating capability to support American special operations in Grenada.

Finally, even with the establishment of the Joint Special Operations Command, there was little or no integration of the units of special operations forces with one another or with the conventional commanders and units. Communication failures throughout the American force only amplified the command and control chaos that resulted from a lack of joint planning and training including special operations and conventional forces.

6

Legislating Change

I have discovered in critical areas of the Pentagon, on the subject of special operations force revitalization, that when they [officials there] say no, they mean no; when they say maybe, they mean no; and when they say yes, they mean no, and if they meant anything but no, they wouldn't be there.

Noel Koch, March 1984

By 1984 advocates for the special operations forces were becoming convinced that significant reform would not result from bureaucratic guerrilla tactics confined to the Pentagon. Those agitating for change could embarrass Defense Department leadership, but they could not control Defense Department resources. The reformers began to think that reform would not come from the inside, but it could be directed from the outside. In the early months of 1984 the campaign for SOF reform extended to Capitol Hill. A few members of Congress quickly became involved in the smallest details of Defense Department special-operations-related policy, organization, and resource allocation. Congress stayed deeply involved for the next five years, resulting in a frequent blurring of distinctions between SOF advocates in the military, in the executive branch, and in the legislature.

Building the Case for Reform on Capitol Hill

Supporters of special operations forces developed closer ties with Congress during the early 1980s. Most of this activity was on the House side, and most of the House activity was centered on the Readiness Subcommittee of the House Armed Services Committee, chaired by Representative Dan Daniel. Congress had tested the waters of SOF reform since Desert One, largely through monitoring SOF issues with hearings and occasional legislative language on the procurement of Pave Low helicopters.

107

Representative Daniel, the legislative leader of SOF reform on Capitol Hill until his death in 1988, had first expressed congressional interest through personal contacts and legislative language, in the hope that the military services would make much-needed changes on their own. By 1984 Daniel was becoming convinced the services would never support special operations forces. Although there were clear pockets of support for SOF, particularly under the leadership of General Edward C. "Shy" Meyer in the U.S. Army, and for SEAL operations in support of the fleet in the U.S. Navy, the conventional military at best had bigger fish to fry during the Reagan defense buildup. At worst the military would actively subvert any efforts at SOF reform.

A telling blow to SOF reform within the Pentagon was the struggle over the establishment of the Joint Special Operations Agency within the Joint Staff, described in chapter 4. Daniel saw that the Joint Chiefs of Staff refused to establish the organization until he pressured Defense Secretary Caspar Weinberger to take direct, immediate action. Thus Daniel became convinced that supporters of SOF in the Defense Department needed the impetus of congressional legislation to make the reforms happen. With "expressions of interest" no longer adequate, Representative Daniel and Ted Lunger worked with other SOF supporters, including Noel Koch and Lynn Rylander, to first build interest and then outrage among other members of Congress and their staffs.

For the most part Representative Daniel was leading the charge for the House side. Although there was initial interest in special operations in the Senate during 1984, the Senate would not become actively involved in SOF reform until late 1985. In the early 1980s Dan Daniel was one of the most senior members of the House Armed Services Committee. He could count on the support of the other senior, conservative committee members, including Representative Mel Price, Sonny Montgomery, and Bill Nichols. Advocates of SOF reform also made efforts to gain supporters on the other relevant House committees, including the House Appropriations Committee (HAC), where Koch and Rylander had contacts among the staff.[1] Increasingly, however, relationships such as these supported the activities of Daniel's subcommittee.[2]

The SOF community and its supporters had learned a lesson from the Thayer memo in 1983. To have an impact, the issues had to be made public. Those who hoped the problem of special operations reform would go away could ignore classified directives but had to respond to public challenges. With this lesson in mind, the SOF community began an unusually public attack on the military services. Surprisingly, this public attack was often conducted by senior officials in the Department of Defense, particularly Noel Koch, his staff, and retired military officers.

One of the opening moves of the public campaign for SOF reform brought the issue of the weakness in U.S. special operations to the Senate's attention. On April 3, 1984, Senator Strom Thurmond, who had been a member of a civil affairs unit during World War II, declared, "It is imperative . . . the Congress support the administration's plans for revitalization of our Special Operations Forces." He asked that the Senate unanimously consent to the reading of one of Noel Koch's speeches into the *Congressional Record*.[3] "The administration's plans" referred to by Thurmond were of course those represented by Koch. Koch had given the speech in question on the occasion of the first anniversary of the Military Airlift Command's 23rd Air Force, the home at the time for U.S. Air Force special operations forces (AFSOF).

Koch, in the coldest cold war rhetoric, made the case for special operations forces:

Now . . . the world is really divided in two: countries that are communist and countries that aren't. . . . By happenstance, we have a major share of the responsibility for the free half, and that half is still the larger . . . but it is smaller than it was before Potsdam, and it is getting smaller still every year. . . . If our strategy is to prevent the world from going up in smoke, we are succeeding. . . . If our responsibility is to prevent the world from going down the tube, we are not succeeding. We are not preventing an expansionist power from getting its way in the world, and enslaving nations as it goes . . . [but] the point simply is that we need the means to fight today's war where and how it's being fought.[4]

The answer was clear to Noel Koch. The means to "fight today's war" were special operations forces.

After providing historical quotes demonstrating the disdain conventional military leaders have had for SOF, Koch identified supporters of rebuilt American special operations forces, including National Security Adviser Robert McFarlane, the secretary and deputy secretary of defense, many retired senior military officers, and even the regional, unified commanders in chief.

The Pentagon appeared to be taking action, continued Koch; most notably in the establishment of the Joint Special Operations Agency. The U.S. Army established 1st Special Operations Command (SOCOM) and reactivated a Special Forces group. The Combat Talons were in the budget of the U.S. Air Force. But, warned Koch, and here the tone of his speech changed dramatically, "If anyone is more than hopeful—if anyone thinks we're making real progress and that we're on a roll, they are kidding themselves."[5]

The rest of Koch's speech states the deeply held belief of the SOF community that the conventional services were actively resisting any attempts to rebuild an American special operations capability. Deconstructing the services' claims of support for special operations forces, Koch continued, "1st SOCOM is nice, but we already see the Army nibbling away at it. Fortunately, they are not especially deft and they nibble with a meat ax, so it's easy to track." The 10th Special Forces Group had been activated, but it was "hollow," undermanned and underequipped. Indications were that the U.S. Air Force intended to reduce the buy of Combat Talons or at least stretch out the procurement schedule. Koch then brought into the open the resistance from many high-level military leaders. "My all time favorite example of resistance came from the 3-star on the Joint Staff who sent a handwritten threat to one of his Colonels working on a special operations initiative. 'If you keep on with this,' the note said, 'your next billet will be in a Dempsey Dumpster.' "[6]

Koch argued that this was not simply "a normal institutionalized resistance to something new," since the required capability was not new at all but had existed off and on since World War II and could be traced back to the Revolutionary War. The resistance of the conventional military, warned Koch, was real, although it seldom came into the open. Putting this conflict into the public forum would lead to its resolution.

As hoped, congressional interest increased, and Koch and Rylander joined Daniel and Lunger in encouraging and directing congressional efforts. Still there were few active SOF active advocates, and Daniel's Readiness Subcommittee remained the locus for congressional action on SOF issues throughout 1984 and 1985. Chairman Daniel formed a Special Operations Panel of the committee, chaired by Representative Earl Hutto. The panel initiated a new set of hearings in the late summer and fall of 1984, following up on hearings held by the Readiness Subcommittee earlier in the year and House Appropriations Committee hearings in April 1984. Most members of the Readiness Subcommittee and the Special Operations Panel had little knowledge or understanding of the SOF issue in 1984, although Hutto became a strong supporter of special operations reform. As described by Lynn Rylander, "The members had no idea what we were talking about other than 'sounds like a good thing to do.' . . . They had no background, so Ted [Lunger] essentially was educating them at the same time that he was rolling the hearings along."[7]

On September 6, 1984, Noel Koch testified before the Special Operations Panel on the progress made in SOF revitalization. Once again, Koch directly attacked the military services. He opened gently enough, describing the progress that had been made: the activation of a new Special Forces Group and SEAL team; the procurement of twelve MC-130 Combat Talons; the continuing maturation of the U.S. Army's 1st SOCOM and the 23rd Air Force; and the beginning of a reversal of the decline of funding for special operations forces that occurred throughout most of the 1970s.[8] He continued to list the Defense Department's accomplishments including the Thayer memo, an OSD decision to increase the number of Combat Talons being procured by the air force, and the creation of the Special Operations Policy Advisory Group (SOPAG).

But even this listing of "victories" was two-edged. Koch provided a graph seeming to demonstrate the Defense Department's success in increasing spending on special operations. And yet the graph only emphasized the meagerness of support from the department, particularly given the dramatic increase in the defense budget since 1979. According to Koch's figures and testimony, funding for special operations had remained at one-tenth of 1 percent (0.001) of the total Defense Department budget since 1975. Despite claims by the Office of the Secretary of Defense and the military services, there had been no relative improvement in the status of SOF under the Reagan administration. The failure of special operations during Urgent Fury demonstrated the high costs of inadequate training and poor tactical mobility. The increase in the number of Combat Talon MC-130 aircraft by the Defense Resources Board from twelve to twenty-one was only because the air force refused to follow the advice of SOPAG or its own special operations units. The Joint Special Operations Agency (JSOA), as was known to all the members of the Special Operations Panel, was finally established only after the intervention of Representative Daniel and then Secretary Weinberger.

Few of these accomplishments, with the exception of the new army initiatives and the establishment of the new SEAL team, were the result of the military services taking the initiative and rebuilding SOF. Instead, argued Koch, the services remained locked on the perceived Soviet threat in Central Europe, allocating their resources to building conventional and strategic forces while fighting most efforts to improve the nation's special operations capabilities. Even in the U.S. Army, the momentum for reform had slowed down greatly with the retirement of General Shy Meyer and the ascension of General John Wickham to the position of chief of staff.

In the remainder of his testimony, Koch introduced the concept that joined with counterterrorism to become the second pillar of the argument for SOF revitalization: low-intensity conflict. With Grenada fresh in everybody's mind and Central America occupying much of U.S. foreign—if not defense—policy, it was becoming increasingly clear to special operations advocates that the United States was going to be involved in wars that were significantly lower on the scale of conflict than a major conventional war in Europe.

For this type of conflict, Koch argued, "A different strategy-making process must be employed, and it will not rely on traditional military thinking. . . It will rely on calculations of the national interest which become self-defining in a conventional war; it will rely on closer assessments of the adversary's objectives and his willingness to pay the price for achieving them; it will rely on the political, social and economic circumstances obtained in the environment in which the conflict takes place."[9] Low-intensity conflict (LIC) requires a different type of military advice, including a large political and economic component, and nonconventional forces to support the interests of the United States. For that reason, Koch argued that increased interaction between civilians and military was required by this less-than-conventional conflict in order to develop an effective military and political strategy and doctrine. Koch finally called for the JSOA to establish this relationship in order to guide Defense Department development of policy and doctrine for the use of special operations forces.

To some extent, the combining of counterterrorism and low-intensity conflict by Koch and Rylander within special operations was simply a case of linking the "hottest tickets in town" in the early to mid-1980s, not military grand strategy. In fact, Rylander and Koch's early perception of low-intensity conflict was as a largely political and economic struggle with only the most minimal use of guerrilla forces. Rylander and Koch did not, for example, consider Urgent Fury low-intensity conflict. Nonetheless, as they pursued SOF reform, both men began to believe that the United States was as unprepared to respond to low-intensity conflict as it was to counter terrorism. Special operations forces did have a role to play in low-intensity conflict, particularly in training indigenous forces and in civil affairs operations. Koch and Rylander had made a linkage that still pertains today.[10]

Inside the Pentagon

As mentioned in chapter 4, the U.S. Air Force and U.S. Army's Initiative 17 to put all SOF rotary-wing aviation capability under the army, or at least divide the mission between short-range and long-range infiltration/

exfiltration, continued long after its introduction to the secretary of defense in 1984. And Noel Koch and Lynn Rylander kept fighting the initiative vigorously and tenaciously.[11] Although Koch believed these supporters were lying to themselves about the cost and ease of implementation of Initiative 17, he did not feel that the U.S. Army was being malevolent. It was simply a case of the army's pursuing a new mission and not realizing its implications.[12]

The debate over Initiative 17 came to symbolize the conflict over SOF reform. In its wake innumerable briefings to the secretary and deputy secretary of defense took place, and countless memos circulated among the U.S. Air Force, the U.S. Army, and the Office of the Secretary of Defense. Noel Koch's operations within the Department of Defense were indeed theatrical and also effective—even if they were somewhat outside of the department's standard operating procedures. Colonel George McGovern, followed by Rylander and Koch, had developed an extensive network of allies throughout the military services and Joint Staff. Memos often arrived in Koch's office before they reached the addressee in the services. Reports from confidential meetings kept Koch's office informed of air force plans in particular.

A key factor in the dynamics of the conflict was that Koch would not go away. Most political appointees stay in the Defense Department for less than two years. When Koch began making noise in 1983 and 1984, the services believed the noise would stop when, having received his Defense Department credential, he left the building. But Koch stayed. Partially motivated by his belief that he should carry on the work of the late Colonel McGovern, Koch had a sense of mission that was shared by Lynn Rylander and then by U.S. Air Force Major Tim Davidson, who joined the Office of Special Planning in 1985. These men were going to campaign until the problem was fixed. Their tenacity eventually forced military and civilian leaders in the Department of Defense to recognize that while the services' approach to "revitalizing SOF" was not necessarily malicious, it was poorly thought out and unlikely to provide the capability recommended by the Holloway committee and special operations forces. It also eventually led to Koch's ouster in 1986 from the Department of Defense.

In this bureaucratic contest for influencing military and civilian leadership, Koch and Rylander had an inventory of psychological operations tactics designed to create maximum impact with minimal resources. The most infamous and dramatic of the Koch and Rylander operations is known as Koch's "30-foot rope trick" (although the rope was actually 33 feet long). The army was scheduled to brief the secretary of defense in a secretary's performance review (SPR) on Initiative 17 in the spring of 1985. The problem with the navy helicopters at Desert One had demonstrated the critical need for long-range air-refuelable helicopters to support special operations. The U.S. Air Force had transferred its nine PAVE LOW helicopters from its combat search-and-rescue (CSAR) unit but did not intend to transfer these helicopters and their sophisticated avionics to the army as part of Initiative 17. In order to pick up the SOF rotary-wing mission from the air force, the army would have to develop its own long-range capability. The army's plan called for modifying its CH-47 helicopters for in-flight refueling to extend their range. Such refueling required a cumbersome 32-foot refueling boom on the army helicopter to receive fuel from a C-130's 81-foot-long hose with a 27-inch receptacle.[13] Certainly that would be a difficult connection, made even more complicated in the dark and inclement weather typical of special operations.

In preparation for the briefing, Koch asked Rylander to purchase a 33-foot piece of nylon rope from a local hardware store. Rylander, displaying his flair for the dramatic, tied a hangman's noose into the rope. Next, Koch and Rylander cut a 27-inch circle from a grocery basket.

During the performance review, the unsuspecting army briefer presented the army's plan for in-air refueling of army helicopters in support of the infil/exfil mission. The presenter made it clear that the subject matter was too technical for the civilians in the room. Therefore, they should simply trust the military on the soundness of the plan. As the briefer finished his talk, Koch stood up and called, "Wait!" He pulled the rope out of a paper bag and handed the army officer the hangman's noose. Koch then began stringing the rope across the conference table and past the service chiefs of staff and the deputy secretary. By the time the rope was fully extended, Koch was standing several yards outside of the conference room and inside the deputy secretary's office. Holding up the 27-inch circle he encouraged the briefer to work the rope inside the circle in imitation of the fuel line and its target on the helicopter and asked, "Do you really think this is going to work?"[14]

On May 16, Deputy Secretary William Taft sent a memorandum to the air force and army chiefs of staff stating that he would again defer a decision on the mission transfer in anticipation of a test, scheduled for July 1985, to determine if in-flight refueling of the army's helicopters would work.[15]

Despite the increasing frustration on Capitol Hill and among the SOF community, life continued to improve somewhat in segments of U.S. special operations forces. In 1985, the U.S. Army once again increased its special operations force structure, activating another Special Forces group, a third Ranger battalion, and a Ranger regimental headquarters—the 75th Ranger Regiment. In the U.S. Navy, SEAL Team 3 was activated in the same year.

Much less progress was realized in the U.S. Air Force. The air force still had in its five-year resource program the planned procurement of twenty-one Combat Talons, but a pattern was developing wherein air force leadership stretched out or delayed the program, and actual fielding of these systems was in doubt. In fact, in a damning memorandum obtained by Koch and Rylander, Lieutenant General David Nichols, the air force deputy chief of staff for operations, wrote to Lieutenant General Fred Mahaffey, the army operations deputy, and assured him that the SOF aviation procurement "would not have been programmatically realized" by the air force and so the army should not attempt to replicate it as part of Initiative 17.[16]

U.S. Air Force special operators argue that the air force was in a more difficult position than the other services in the push for reform. It was relatively easy for the army and navy to rapidly increase their special operations assets since most of these assets were in force structure. One long-time special operator commented, "It seemed to be a favorite sport for the other services to blame the air force for the [SOF reform] legislation. . . . it was all too easy for the army, for example, to say, 'Well, special operations now includes Rangers,' and then simply increase the number of people in special operations by 1,800 people. It's easier to build organization and structure than it is to build airplanes."[17]

There are fundamental differences in the way the army and the air force build their forces. U.S. Air Force special operations, as is true for air force conventional capabilities, are "system dependent." The army puts together units of soldiers and then equips them. The air force, however, procures and fields systems (usually aircraft) and then mans them. Aircraft, particularly aircraft capable of special operations, are expensive and require years to procure. Without the procurement of new aircraft, designating more personnel as special operators has little effect on the capability of air force special operations forces. The same can be said for navy conventional forces and ships, but the capabilities of the SEALs reside in manpower and training.

The reliance of the army and navy on manpower for their special operations capabilities was, however, the very reason for the SOF community's unease about the state of SOF in those services. Although it was immediately apparent that the air force was not improving SOF because it was not procuring or modernizing SOF aviation, it was also true that apparent army and navy "revitalization" of the Special Forces and SEALs was fragile support indeed. Units can be disbanded even more easily than they can be created. Although the army and navy could respond quickly to OSD and congressional calls for improving SOF, and even to their own current recognition of special operations as an important capability, once congressional attention was diverted or the fleet commanders were no longer convinced of the need for SEALs, funding could be cut, units could be disbanded, and Special Forces and U.S. naval special warfare units would once again face the decline of the 1950s and 1970s.

Going Public

The campaign for reform by supporters of special operations forces started to pick up steam in the final months of 1984, becoming increasingly high profile through 1986. Statements by Noel Koch, Representative Dan Daniel, and Senator William Cohen were appearing in newspapers, while Defense Department officials and those members of Congress and congressional staffers who had long been pushing for SOF reform escalated their attacks from speeches and statements before government audiences to appearances and interviews before the public. As advocates forced their campaign farther and farther outside the system, their new, high-profile approach included for-attribution interviews in papers such as the *Washington Post* and appearances on shows such as ABC's "Nightline." The most persistent, influential, and controversial aspect of this public campaign appeared in the *Armed Forces Journal International (AFJ)* from February 1985 through April 1986.

Armed Forces Journal, a monthly magazine covering defense issues, is widely read in the broader defense community, including government officials, members of Congress and their staffs, and retired and active duty military. *AFJ*'s editor and owner until 1993 was Benjamin F. Schemmer, a man who has had a substantial impact on the definition and frequently the resolution of defense issues.[18]

Schemmer has been a long-time supporter of a strong U.S. special operations capability. Schemmer was appalled by the attempt of U.S. forces to rescue U.S. prisoners of war at the Son Tay prison camp in November 1970. American prisoners held in the camp had managed to send a message that they were there. The United States then took six months to put together a task force, agree upon a plan, and conduct a rescue operation. Although the operation itself, led by Colonel Arthur

"Bull" Simons, proceeded without a hitch, the rescuers arrived first in the wrong installation and then in the correct, but empty, prison camp. The Vietnamese and their prisoners had moved days earlier.[19]

The tragedy at Desert One rekindled Schemmer's anger. Schemmer believed Desert One demonstrated that the United States had learned nothing from Son Tay ten years earlier and, if anything, the United States had lost ground and was not "organized as a nation to conduct special operations." The United States was spending approximately $250 billion dollars a year in 1980 on its defense and yet could not rescue its hostages in Iran because of one, figuratively speaking, broken helicopter. Schemmer believed the Holloway Commission, although it had done a reasonably good job of identifying the problem, offered no real solutions because it failed to address the root cause of the American failure—the lack of a joint special operations command and control organization.

More evidence of the weaknesses in the American special operations forces piled up in the early 1980s, including the embarrassment of Urgent Fury in Grenada and the inability of the United States to free American hostages held by terrorists in Lebanon. Schemmer published a few articles on special operations during this period, notably an editorial calling for the awarding of military commendations to those involved in Desert One, and two articles on the Iranian operation.

Schemmer, like others advocating SOF reform in the early and mid-1980s, became more and more frustrated with the apparent reluctance of the Office of the Secretary of Defense, the Joint Chiefs of Staff, or, in particular, the air force to fix the problem. His frustration reached the boiling point in the fall of 1984. According to Schemmer, a three-star air force general responsible for deploying Air Force Special Operations Forces (AFSOF) testified in a classified session before Representative Earl Hutto's Special Operations Panel. During the course of his testimony, the general stunned panel members with repeated references to Special Forces Operational Detachment-D (Delta) as "trained assassins" and "trigger happy." The general expressed his concern that Delta might "freelance" a coup d'etat in a nation friendly to the United States. Schemmer obtained a transcript of the hearing, outraged that such a senior military official would express such ignorance of, and disdain for, special operations forces. After he had warned the Air Force Chief of Staff General Charles Gabriel of his general's indiscretion, and received a note of apology and thanks from the errant officer, Schemmer decided enough was enough. It was time to throw his magazine's support behind SOF reform that was long overdue and, as he believed demonstrated by the general's testimony, unlikely to occur if left to the military services. Beginning in 1985, Schemmer and his staff conducted a campaign to highlight inadequacies in the U.S. special operations capabilities and the military services' (particularly the air force) inability or unwillingness to develop these capabilities.[20] Schemmer and the *Armed Forces Journal*, aided by leaks and letters from others outraged by the same issues, sought to keep special operations reform alive among the higher-profile and bigger-dollar defense issues.

Evidence of a deliberate, and in the end effective, campaign can be gained by reviewing issues of *Armed Forces Journal*. From February 1985 through April 1986 more than forty-five articles or letters on U.S. special operations forces were printed in *AFJ*. Sixteen articles or letters appeared in August through December 1985. During a similar period in 1983 the only articles on SOF appearing in *AFJ* were a review of Charlie Beckwith's book, *Delta Force,* and three letters commenting on the review.[21] The 1985 SOF articles were not merely passing mentions of SOF. From August through December 1985, six articles were a full page or more in length, with one article more than four pages long.[22]

The first element of Schemmer's strategy was to make sure that the defense community did not forget SOF. At least one letter or article on SOF appeared each month during this period except in April 1985. Second, the campaign laid out the principal special operations issues, especially the need for joint command and control of SOF and the inadequacy of SOF airlift, including a debate on Initiative 17. Although most articles supported the general concerns of the SOF community, alternative perspectives were occasionally presented in articles and letters usually written by conventional military officers.[23] It was not uncommon for articles on larger defense issues, such as discussion of the overall defense budget, to also highlight issues such as funding for special operations.

A third element of Schemmer's strategy was simply letting Defense Department decisionmakers know that readers were paying attention and that the *Journal* had its sources. *AFJ* is known for its excellent sources in the Defense Department and on Capitol Hill.[24]

AFJ's finger was most often pointed at the air force and its failure to modernize SOF airlift.[25] May 1985 saw the printing of a debate between Noel Koch and Colonel Alan L. Gropman, the deputy director of air force planning integration on the air staff. The topic was the air force's role in low-intensity conflict drawn from a March symposium held at the Air War College at Maxwell Air Force Base. The inset printed with the two articles describes the meeting at Maxwell: "Much of the debate sounded like a fight between the Air Force's 'fighter Mafia' and the nation's special operations experts." The editor's note recounted many of the criticisms of the U.S. special operations capability offered at the symposium and expressed regrets that "unfortunately, there were very few senior officers present from the Air Staff in Washington to hear how many of their officers (and others) questioned the Air Force's ability and commitment to cope with low-intensity conflict."[26]

Koch's article was drawn nearly verbatim from his speech at the symposium. It was a scathing indictment of the air force's failure to meet its airlift obligation. Included in the article is a photograph of the memorandum, mentioned earlier, from Lieutenant General David Nichols to Lieutenant General Fred Mahaffey. In the memo, Nichols made it clear that the air force had no intention of meeting the requirement of its own master plan to support SOF airlift: "The working group appears to be making the transfer [of the helicopters] too hard. The real question is how the Army can best replace the current AF-dedicated SOF aircraft. The Army should not be tied to meeting an AF SOF Master Plan that would not have been programmatically realized. . . .We need to move out on this initiative—the responsibility for rotary-wing SOF should be transferred to the Army while our current Chiefs are still in office."[27]

Colonel Gropman's counterarticle resulted from an air force request that a "responsible" officer be given equal time to reply. He wrote, "Mr. Koch's speech is flawed with historical inaccuracies which must be corrected now." In response to the accusation that the air force was reluctant to support special operations, Gropman turned to cold war priorities: "This President and his Secretary of Defense . . . have . . . delineated specific priorities that place low intensity conflict, however important, *below* being ready to (a) deter the Soviet Union from attacking the United States and its allies with nuclear weapons, and (b) deter and, if necessary, defeat the Soviet Union in a conventional conflict that could be fought globally."

Therefore, explains Gropman, "The Air Force . . . recognizes the dangers of being ill-prepared to confront adversaries at the lower end of the conflict spectrum. But national decisions made in the past dictate that the bulk of the defense budget goes to preparations for the higher-intensity conflicts, in order to deter them because they most threaten the vital interests of the United States of America."[28]

Gropman's restatement of cold war priorities did little to address the SOF issues that were on the table. SOF's supporters argued that the air force had clearly stated SOF requirements in its own master plan, was not living up to them, and seem uninterested in considering how to meet them.

Although many *AFJ* articles of the period successfully got the SOF message out and kept pressure on the Department of Defense, four stand out in notoriety and influence. The opening article in the campaign was the March 1985 interview of Noel Koch by Deborah G. Meyer and Schemmer. The introduction to the article makes the point that the Koch interview is unusual since "Koch purposely kept . . . 'a low profile,'as [had] most other key personnel involved in special operations and counterterrorist activities," and it does not mention the close cooperation of Koch's office and *AFJ*. Koch stresses that SOF advocates had no choice but to go public: "As long as we keep our efforts to restore special operations forces compartmented and quiet, they don't go anywhere. Silence was a benefit to those who were not particularly receptive to enhancing special operations forces."[29]

Overall, Koch seems somewhat moderate in the interview. He frequently refuses to "name names" or point fingers directly, although the criticism of the air force is evident to all. Koch speaks favorably of the navy's efforts to support the SEALs and is supportive of the army too. He claims to be an educator, not an unconstructive critic. "Our best interests lie in trying to educate people and to change their views on what we're trying to do, rather than to put them in a corner where they have no choice but to fight."[30]

Asked about his recent bureaucratic victory in getting the deputy secretary of defense to sign a memorandum to the chairman of the Joint Chiefs indefinitely delaying implementation of Initiative 17, Koch refused (ironically, given his deeply personal conflict with the Pentagon) to describe the argument over SOF reform as an "us versus them" conflict. Instead he responded: "It's not a question of winning or losing the battle. . . . When you create [a] win-lose relationship, you're going to end up with . . . not much progress."[31]

The purpose of the March 1985 *AFJ* interview was to bring the major issues of SOF reform to the attention of an informed public, the readers of *Armed Forces Journal*. Koch, therefore, made many of the same points in this interview that he had made in earlier speeches and testimony. He was most critical of the air force and its failure to support airlift. Koch also stressed the need for the services to develop an understanding of what SOF should be doing. Koch argued that the military services, assisted by civilian policymakers from the Defense Department and other agencies, must develop a whole new strategy for the use of military force that "puts the force option in context. When you get that," Koch argues, "special operations—which is very much a force option—becomes self-justifying."

Koch also emphasized the need for equal career opportunities for special operations forces, a goal he had stated since 1983.[32]

The SOF community, not surprisingly, responded with thanks and congratulations in the May 1985 issue of *Armed Forces Journal*. Letter writers included the commandant of the U.S. Air Force Special Operations School, who joined Noel Koch in questioning why so little had been done by the air force to address low-intensity conflict. Major General Richard Secord (later of Iran-contra notoriety) commended Koch for "performing a great service to the country." He warned that if we "don't wake up to the great threat of 'low-intensity conflict' . . . we will surely pay a devastating price." A third letter refers to the SOF community's regard for Koch as "a staunch ally and . . . the force behind the DoD effort to revitalize this potent element of our national security."[33] Finally, a retired army lieutenant colonel responds: "Until the paid military establishment harkens to the Noel Kochs of this world, we are going to be witness to the drama of the changing political configuration of the whole world with the largest weapon employed being a 60mm mortar, while we in the U.S., waiting in bloated preparedness for the 'real war,' will not have fired a shot."[34]

Clearly the Koch interview signaled the intent of the SOF community to bring the issue into the public view. *Armed Forces Journal* would keep it there for the next year, with regular articles and letters on the subject. Having defined the issues, the magazine's next major and influential article was signed by Representative Daniel. Daniel's article was the most radical call for SOF reform to be offered publicly up to that point by a senior and influential government official. Representative Daniel did not actually write the article. It was, instead, the product of a collaboration between Ted Lunger and Lynn Rylander. Although it is not unusual for members of Congress to rely on their staffs to ghostwrite articles and columns, it is somewhat unusual for such efforts to be the result of a joint project between a Hill staffer and a professional within the organization that is being criticized. In fact, Lunger and Rylander collaborated to ghostwrite or provide outlines for a total of six *AFJ* articles on SOF reform; articles that were split between support for radical reorganization and support for the status quo.[35]

Daniel wanted to create controversy over SOF reform in order to capture the defense community's attention and let the Defense Department know that radical options were under discussion. He therefore sponsored the first article by Lunger and Rylander and accepted the responsibility of authorship. Entitled "U.S. Special Operations: The Case for a Sixth Service," Daniel argues that while special operations forces are organizationally a part of the U.S. Army, U.S. Air Force, and U.S. Navy, "SOF [has] never been [a] truly institutional part of those Services."[36] Daniel's arguments are similar to those brought up earlier: special operations run counter to the conventional view of how wars are fought; training and equipment for SOF are distinct from that required for conventional soldiers, sailors, and airmen; secrecy is essential and elitism is unavoidable; and SOF is often most effective during peacetime. Essentially, SOF has never "fit in" with the conventional forces because "[SOF] operations do not square with the core imperatives of the individual Services and are, in fact, so different that there is little basis for understanding. Their specialized support requirements cannot be conveniently pigeonholed within the system. They are viewed as secretive, elitist, and worst of all, a political time bomb."[37]

Daniel writes that this is not a transient problem. "The reluctance to accept SOF as a legitimate military capability" has persisted since the establishment of the first American special operations units in World War II. Because of this reluctance, the existing "system" will always hold SOF "to be peripheral to the interests, missions, goals, and traditions that [officials] view as essential"— deterring nuclear conflict and major conventional war in Europe.[38]

Thus, argues Daniel, the system that does not work cannot be fixed without a radical revamping—the establishment of a sixth military service.[39] This sixth service would provide U.S. special operations forces with

— a unifying, intellectual core or philosophy;
— a professional home;
— a budget that does not compete directly with F-16s and M1A1 tanks;
— continuity as opposed to the extreme ups and downs of the previous fifty years;
— an acquisition system oriented toward SOF's unique mission;
— a high level advocate; and
— a direct link to the National Command Authorities.[40]

Daniel's article was essentially an attack on the military services' control over special operations forces. He believed the conventional military would never understand special operations and therefore would never adequately support or correctly utilize SOF. The only solution, argued Daniel, was to free SOF from its conventional masters and provide special operators with control over their future.

In October, however, two *AFJ* articles were printed in response to Daniel's proposal and jointly entitled, "Two Cases against a Sixth Service . . . for Special Ops."[41] Both articles countered the Daniel article, calling for SOF reform but also for maintenance of the status quo organization. Both articles were also written or strongly influenced by Ted Lunger and Lynn Rylander although they were attributed to J. Michael Kelly, a former member of the 11th Special Forces Group and, at the time, deputy assistant secretary of the air force (manpower, reserve affairs, and installations), and Noel Koch.[42]

It is difficult to interpret Kelly's article. He was actually a supporter of SOF and was only offering up some of the more reasonable arguments from those who opposed Daniel's extreme solution. Kelly emphasized the role of SOF in supporting conventional military operations, particularly the Rangers as an assault force and the SEAL hydrographic reconnaissance mission. He argued that "while lumping these units together as a separate SOF Service wouldn't necessarily deny their use in conventional military operations, it certainly would degrade their capability to perform them."[43] He also argued that SOF placed into a new service would not be inclusive of all the military units required to perform the SOF mission, for example, conventional air force and navy units that carry out reprisals against terrorists; and conventional engineering and medical units to support the nation-building mission. A third problem suggested by Kelly is that SOF can only address the military portion of the special operations mission. A sixth service would still not include coordination of activities and direction by the U.S. Information Agency, State Department, Agency for International Development, or the Central Intelligence Agency. "Establishment of a sixth military Service would do absolutely nothing to bring order out of the chaos that presently exists."[44] Kelly also said that establishment of a separate service would reduce the promotion opportunities for special operators. Finally, Kelly states that what special operators do is not distinctly different from what conventional forces do. Therefore, argued Kelly, the solution is in "restructur[ing] incentives and command relations along British or Israeli lines rather than in creating a sixth military Service."[45] In the British and Israeli military, according to Kelly, SOF is well supported and considered a prerequisite for promotion to high command.

Noel Koch provided a counter to Daniel that was distinct from Michael Kelly's. Koch's article assumed the voice of reason and moderation, compared with Daniel's attack mode, and revealed some of his very real doubts at the time about a separate service. Koch's moderation may have also been an attempt to attenuate his growing reputation for extremism within the Defense Department. Koch opens with recognition of "legitimate concerns about the existence and employment of Special Operations Forces," but he also argues that the defense community has a tendency to construe "instances of individual and institutional bias as symptoms of insurmountable organic impediments."[46]

Koch declared that there was hope for the future of special operations forces without the creation of a sixth service. The value of special operations forces had been slow in revealing itself, the backlash from Vietnam still existed and resulted in a mistrust of SOF that was only beginning to be turned around; and "The full dimensions of the threat of low-intensity conflict, . . . of the social, economic, and political dimensions of these phenomena are only now achieving widespread appreciation. The U.S. military is coming to share this appreciation; and as it does so, the legitimate role of SOF has become increasingly . . . accepted,"[47] particularly by the commanders in chief of the unified commands. As the CINCs begin to appreciate SOF, SOF gains an advocate with clout for special operations. Finally, the president and the secretary of defense had become strong supporters of SOF, an arguable but necessary assertion by Koch, and so SOF had two of the strongest advocates in the nation. Koch questioned Daniel's assumption that a sixth service would result in increased career opportunities for SOF personnel. Yes, the SOF budget had been inconsistent, but, says Koch, so had the conventional military budget. A sixth service would not solve SOF's budgetary woes.

Koch ended his essay with recommendations for the continued revitalization of SOF. He divided his efforts into two categories: institutionalizing the reforms and "advancing the effort by persuasion, education, increasing the visibility of the SOF concept, and creating a public presumption that SOF must and will be restored." He, of course, was already putting this advice into practice. Koch recommended continued "fencing" of funds for SOF (as was done by Congress for PAVE LOW helicopters), annual reports on SOF support, congressional committees on low-intensity conflict, and increased language training. The most interesting recommendations were for the elevation of the director of the Joint Special Operations Agency to a three-star position to provide the needed influence in the Defense Department, and the forward deployment of Special Forces groups into their designated areas of operations. This last recommendation would result in increased familiarity of the CINCs with special operations capabilities and, it was hoped, the CINCs' advocacy for the support of these capabilities.

In January 1986 *Armed Forces Journal* printed the final major article in its campaign to bring SOF to the attention of the concerned public and force important SOF reforms. In 1985 Ted Lunger had recognized that SOF reform would not be possible without support from the Senate, and he approached Chris Mellon, a member of Senator William S. Cohen's staff, to gain support for legislation being considered by Representative Daniel. Senator Cohen and Chris Mellon already had some interest in SOF reform as a result of conversations with several former special operators. Cohen's and Mellon's attention was captured further with the October 1985 release of the Senate Armed Services Committee staff report, "Defense Reorganization: The Need for Change."[48] The study director, Jim Locher, and his staff (including former 5th Special Forces Group member Ken Johnson) conducted historical analyses of American military operations dating back to the American Revolution and including Vietnam, Desert One, and Grenada. Although the report did not focus on SOF, the authors agreed that the special operations capability of the United States was minimal and had received very little support over the years, especially since Vietnam. American military forces since the Civil War were not designed to conduct unconventional or low-intensity operations, and the capability required to accomplish these missions was neither understood nor supported.[49]

Because of the broad scope of the reorganization study and concern about the possible distraction of the controversial SOF issue, Locher decided to limit the study to identifying gross problems in special operations forces and not make recommendations for fixing the problem. The results of the research by the staff of the Senate Armed Services Committee had a significant influence on Senator Cohen and Senator Sam Nunn.[50] Senator Cohen's article, "A Defense Special Operations Agency: Fix for an SOF Capability That Is Most Assuredly Broken," tied SOF reform in with the committee report's broader findings and the major defense reorganization legislation that it recommended. This legislation, with some modification, eventually became known as the "Goldwater-Nichols" Department of Defense Reorganization Act of 1986. Both Senator Cohen and Jim Locher believed significant SOF reform was in keeping with the intent of this groundbreaking legislation. In his *AFJ* article, Cohen referred to the study's comments on the need for reform. The study said the services traditionally

— did not have the capabilities to respond to low-intensity threats;
— tended to focus strategy and resources on high-intensity conflict;

— needed to coordinate their activities to avoid unnecessary duplication; and

— needed innovative thinking and new approaches in their response to low-intensity threats.[51]

Cohen also compared the articles by Daniel and Koch. He summarized Daniel's position as the need for stronger advocacy and Koch's as the need for joint command and control. "In order to be effective," wrote Cohen, "we need a solution that can address both problems. 'Effective proponency' is important. So is forward deployment. But the critical ingredient is preparation. Currently, we are not prepared to fight the most likely wars of the present or the future."[52]

Cohen described four likely and possible situations to which the United States was currently unable to respond because of its inadequate special operations capability. One was "a short-term, time-sensitive response to crisis" such as the *Mayaguez* rescue attempt and Operation Urgent Fury in Grenada. The second crisis was one, such as the Son Tay raid or the American attempt to rescue its hostages held in Iran, that could be deliberately planned and require precise interaction between highly trained and specialized forces. The third crisis described was low-intensity conflict requiring protracted effort rather than a high-intensity response. Finally, a crisis could occur during a major conflict with the Soviet Union and the Warsaw Pact. Special operations forces would cooperate largely through operations behind enemy lines and in support operations such as working with refugees. Cohen wrote, "Common to all the situations we confront is the need to have sufficient numbers of well-equipped and trained SOF, and an in-place joint SOF command and control that can be readily integrated into a large military or civilian effort. Today we have neither."[53]

The solution "lies somewhere between the strengthening of the JSOA and the creation of a sixth Service." Such a solution must be consistent with the defense reorganization effort of Congress. Cohen proposed that a Defense Special Operations Agency (DSOA), composed of an agency staff and a subordinate joint command and supported by major commands within the participating services, might be the answer. The DSOA's mission would be to "prepare for and conduct joint special operations." Special operations policy formulation, long called for by Noel Koch, would be the responsibility of the office of an assistant secretary of defense for special operations. This office would be the means through which civilian control of special operations would be exercised. Finally, Cohen addressed control of SOF resources by recommending that "it might also be appropriate to have a separate line for SOF within the defense budget. . . . funding and manpower levels should be set by the Secretary . . . In those cases in which certain aspects of SOF are inherently joint (for example, communications and airlift), they would be included in DSOA's budget rather than the Services."[54]

Cohen's article made it clear to the broad defense community that the Senate had joined the House of Representatives in expressing its deep frustration at the failure of the Department of Defense to resolve the problems tragically demonstrated in the Iranian hostage rescue attempt and in Grenada. Congress did not believe the services recognized the likelihood and danger of American involvement in conflicts other than a major European war. Importantly, Senator Cohen's article explicitly warned the Defense Department of what would happen if it did not move quickly and dramatically to fix the problem. "The foregoing proposal, along with legislation forming in Representative Daniel's Subcommittee, may be viewed as too radical by those who believe that the desired goals can be achieved by more modest and evolutionary change. Perhaps. But I am convinced we can no longer temporize on the need to establish a clearer organizational focus for special operations and a clear line for their command and control. As a Member of the Senate Armed Services Committee and the Senate Select Committee on Intelligence, I intend to . . . see that the necessary changes are made."[55] The congressional message was clear: we are watching and a solution will be found.

It is unlikely that SOF reform would have occurred without the support of Ben Schemmer and *Armed Forces Journal*. Clearly, in 1985 and early 1986 Schemmer openly threw the full weight of his magazine's influence behind the reformers. It is also clear that the series of articles, particularly the ones by Lunger and Rylander and the piece by Senator Cohen, had significant influence. As Senator Cohen stated in his January 1986 article, "The recent series of articles on special operations in *Armed Forces Journal* (March, May, August, October 1985) has helped to make this point [that no progress has been made in SOF reform]."[56]

Heading toward Legislated Reform

Perhaps surprisingly to SOF advocates, the military services and the Joint Chiefs of Staff seemed to take little notice of the drama being played out in the pages of the *Armed Forces Journal* and on Capitol Hill. In keeping with the guerrilla tactics adopted by SOF reformers within the

Defense Department, Ted Lunger believed the basic purpose of the *AFJ* articles was to "enrage the chiefs." He was, of course, referring to the Joint Chiefs of Staff. In a 1989 interview, Lynn Rylander describes the articles, including Cohen's, as stalking horses. "Stalking horse[s] to get interest generated. And I think they also put down a marker because they had been asking repeatedly what, DoD, are you going to do about this problem?"[57]

During 1985 and early 1986, articles in the press, particularly in *Armed Forces Journal*, and actions on Capitol Hill made it clear that if the Defense Department did not solve the problem, Congress would—most likely with the radical reform that had few supporters among the military services. Most conventional military leaders, however, seemed to regard the push for SOF reform and the threat of legislated policy as irritations. At the time they didn't recognize that a crusade was under way. Momentum toward legislated reform increased geometrically during 1985 and 1986, and the services and the Joint Staff did little to brake the speeding train.

For most of 1985, debate focused on Initiative 17 and continued on and on and on. In the spring of 1985, at the request of Secretary Weinberger, the army developed an estimate of the cost to transfer the rotary-wing SOF aviation mission from the air force to the army. The army estimated the cost at $1.3 billion.[58] As mentioned earlier, Deputy Secretary of Defense Taft announced in a May 16, 1985, memorandum to the air force and army chiefs of staff that he would defer a decision until after July 1985 tests on modification to the army's CH-47 helicopters to permit in-flight and aerial refueling. Taft deferred his decision until September 4, 1985, because the in-flight refueling test had ambiguous results.[59] Taft's Solomonic decision was announced in a Program Decision Memorandum signed by Assistant Secretary of Defense David Chu: the army and air force would both have a role in future rotary-wing SOF missions. The army would slowly assume more responsibility, first improving its short-range capabilities with modified MH-60 Nighthawk helicopters and the procurement of fifteen MH-47E Chinook helicopters by fiscal 1991. Taft directed the air force to procure ten "enhanced" PAVE LOW helicopters, twenty-one MC-130H Combat Talons, twelve AC-130 Spectre gunships, and to retrofit two existing helicopters.[60]

Despite increased support with unit activations and reorganization in the army and navy, neither service gave the impression that its support for SOF could be maintained over the long term. The new Special Forces group was consistently undermanned during 1985 and 1986, and army special operations units were not combat ready. The army was aware of the low readiness of its units and concerned about congressional reaction if this deficiency were made public. After being briefed on the typically low scores received by army SOF units in a readiness exercise the weekend before a Secretary's Performance Review briefing with Caspar Weinberger in November 1985, the army vice chief of staff responded with remarkable vigor, force-feeding the units with supplies over the weekend until they achieved the army's highest readiness rating.[61]

Stories such as these drove Congress, especially Senators William Cohen and Sam Nunn, Representative Daniel, and their staffs, to become more and more involved in encouraging, warning, and directing the Defense Department to take action. During 1985 Congress made its concern clear in three pieces of legislation. In early May 1985, the House Armed Services Committee recommended deferring the MC-130H Combat Talon procurement because of "cost instability with the program." The committee also nearly tripled funding for upgrading existing HH-53 helicopters.[62] In late May, Senator Sam Nunn expressed dismay that "our special operations forces . . . are probably the most likely to be used in today's environment of any forces we have in the military and yet several years later after the Iranian hostage problem we still do not have the airlift problems of those special operations forces worked out." In order "to get the attention of the Secretary of Defense and services," Nunn, supported by Senator Goldwater, introduced an amendment to the fiscal 1986 Defense Authorization Act that would withhold funds for procurement of the MC-130E and the MH-53 helicopter modifications until the Secretary of Defense: "(1) submits, in consultation with the chairman of the Joint Chiefs, . . . a plan for meeting the immediate airlift requirements of the joint special operations command and a second plan for meeting, by 1991, the airlift requirements of the joint special operations command and the special operations forces of unified Commanders in Chief; and (2) certifies that the plans . . . are funded in the fiscal year 1987 5-year defense plan."[63] Nunn's amendment became law with passage of Public Law 99-145 on November 8, 1985.

Within a week of Deputy Secretary Taft's June 20 announcement that he would determine the fate of Initiative 17 at the close of the summer program review, Representative Dan Daniel offered an amendment to the fiscal 1986 Defense Authorization bill. Daniel's amendment was passed as a nonbinding "sense of the Congress," declaring that SOF reform should be one of the highest defense priorities. According to the amendment, the Office of the Secretary of Defense should "increase its management supervision . . . to a level sufficient for direct, continuous, and intensive control of all aspects of the special operations mission area"; and the unified commanders in chief must have available the special operations assets they require. Supporters of the amendment believed it provided justification for a reorganization of SOF into a truly joint special operations agency or even a single service.[64]

Congressional attention to the problems of special operations forces continued into 1986. In his remarks on the Senate Armed Services Committee staff study on defense organization, Senator Nunn reminded his listeners of the "disaster of Desert One" and the "many failures of coordination and communication" that occurred during the invasion of Grenada.[65] Senator Cohen's proposal for a Defense Special Operations Agency appeared in the January 1986 *Armed Forces Journal*. In the same month the House and Senate appropriations conferees directed in their report on the fiscal 1986 Continuing Resolution that the Defense Department give Congress by March 1, 1986, a report on "the feasibility of creating a single command structure for special operations." The report was to include options other than a command subordinate to the Joint Chiefs of Staff.[66]

Believing the Defense Department was still not paying attention, Senators Nunn and Goldwater wrote in a January 29, 1986, letter to Secretary of Defense Weinberger: "It is discouraging to note that today we have exactly the same number of MC-130 Combat Talon aircraft (14) and AC-130A/H gunships (10/10) as we had at the time of Desert One, and two fewer HH-53 Pave Low helicopters than we had in May 1980 (7 today compared with 9 in 1980)."[67]

Weinberger responded with a January 31, 1986, memorandum to the Joint Chiefs of Staff, military departments, and his own staff reaffirming the Defense Department's goal of revitalizing SOF. Weinberger also directed the military departments to submit an interim report by March 31 on how they would meet the requirements of the fiscal 1987–91 plan, with revised SOF master plans due on July 31.

By early 1986 the Defense Department was making progress on SOF revitalization. Following Weinberger's memorandum, the fiscal 1987 President's Budget presented to Congress in February 1985 called for a total defense budget of $311.6 billion. The special operations forces portion of the budget was a 284 percent increase over the $441 million in fiscal 1981, increasing SOF's allocation to just over 0.005 of the defense budget.[68] At the same time, there was little evidence of improved U.S. Air Force special operations capability. In his testimony before Congress on February 6, 1986, USAF Chief of Staff General Charles Gabriel reported that air force special operations forces were "slightly less" ready than they were in 1981.[69]

In March 1986 the Defense Department still owed Congress a report on SOF aviation and Initiative 17. In late 1985 Noel Koch and his office wrote their version of the draft report. Not surprisingly, Koch's report agreed with the congressional assessment of chaos and disrepair in American special operations aviation units. According to David Chu, the director (later to become assistant secretary of defense) for program analysis and evaluation, the report also recognized that the Defense Department could not afford the congressionally mandated SOF aviation program and therefore offered up a somewhat smaller procurement plan.[70] Also, not surprisingly, the paper was rejected by all who were asked to comment, particularly David Chu. Chu argued that the Defense Department could not offer a program that was below the congressional mandate. Chu's office, therefore, wrote its own report. According to a report in *Armed Forces Journal*, the draft of the classified report offered two alternatives to Congress. The first alternative (implementation of Initiative 17) allowed the army to assume the rotary-wing aviation mission but cost significantly more than the second alternative: keeping the mission with the air force.[71] Both options met the congressional requirement, but neither offered the improved capability sought by the SOF community. On April 1, 1986, Deputy Secretary of Defense Taft sent the following letter to Senator Barry Goldwater and Representative Les Aspin:

> Pursuant to the provisions of Section 152 of the Fiscal Year 1986 Department of Defense Authorization Act, I am pleased to submit a plan, which has been completed in consultation with the Chairman of the Joint Chiefs, that meets the immediate airlift requirements of the Joint Special Operations Command and meets the airlift requirements of the special operations forces of the unified commanders in chief. This plan is funded in the FY 1987 Five-Year Defense Plan.[72]

However, although the funds did appear in the fiscal 1987 Five Year Defense Plan (FYDP), funding soon dropped and the subsequent fiscal 1987 President's Budget submission did not contain sufficient funding for the special operations force structure described in the April 1, 1986, report.[73] In the five years the fight for SOF reform had been going on in the Pentagon, funding had increased from $441 million in fiscal 1982 to $1.7 billion in fiscal 1987. Although a dramatic increase, the total budgeted for all special operations requirements still could not provide the force and modernization SOF advocates argued were critical to the nation's defense capability. The fiscal 1987 SOF budget was, in the words of Noel Koch, "still $100 million less than the Army lost on just one unworkable weapons system."[74]

By the spring of 1986, the battle over special operations reform had two factions within the Office of the Secretary of Defense: the first led by Noel Koch's office and the second by Donald Latham, the assistant secretary for command, control, communications, and intelligence (C³I), and David Chu. The internal conflict would continue for the next several years.

Loss of a General

Noel Koch's resignation from the Department of Defense was effective May 30, 1986. Whether he jumped or was pushed is unclear, although it is likely he was encouraged to leave. According to Lynn Rylander, it was a little bit of both: "Noel was a superb guerrilla fighter, and he fought for what he believed in. . . . I don't think Noel would ever admit that he in essence got fired but that is what happened. . . . I think he was at the point where he just couldn't take it anymore. . . . In May of 1986, another briefing [took place], and in essence what [Koch] said to Will Taft [Deputy Secretary of Defense William H. Taft was] either, 'you're lying,' or 'you're being lied to.' And that was the end of Noel Koch. But everything he said, all the arguments Noel made were true."[75]

When Koch talked about his departure from the Pentagon, he said: "I left, I had just had it! . . . I resigned effective May 30. The secretary called and asked me not to—asked me to withdraw my resignation. So I thought about it a couple of days, but said no, and told him why in a long letter. . . . [It had become] impossible to be loyal anymore."[76]

Koch spent a few more months as a consultant for the Office of the Secretary of Defense and then left the Pentagon, but he continued to fight for special operations. He published several more articles on SOF and testified before Congress. In the summer of 1986, Koch wrote a letter to Senator William Cohen. In it he argued that Congress had to take action because the military services and the Defense Department would not resolve the issues of SOF reform on their own. Koch's letter was critical in the tidal wave of congressional direction during the fall of 1986. In his letter, Koch revealed many of the causes of his frustration with the Defense Department. He began by saying, "The management of Special Operations Forces . . . must be corrected by legislation, because it will not be corrected otherwise."

Koch then listed many of the Pentagon's failings: an initiative to transfer the rotary-wing SOF aviation mission from the U.S. Air Force to the U.S. Army at a projected price tag of one billion dollars; the failure of the air force to bring even one new MC-130 Combat Talon on line even after the air force was directed to procure twelve in 1979; and the costliness in terms of lives lost in Grenada. These failings were not, however, what created the sense of mission and rage in Noel Koch. That came from events in 1983, especially the disaster that occurred on October 23, 1983, when the Marine Battalion Landing Team building in Beirut was blown up, and 241 marines were killed.

In his letter to Cohen, Koch described how he had briefed the secretary of defense early in 1983 on the inadequacy of U.S. political-level command and control in relation to terrorism and how terrorism was changing—moving away from hostage-barricade incidents and toward assassinations and large bombs. He told how even after the secretary had directed him to devise a plan of action and brief the chiefs of the Joint Staff, he was stalled and put off for months by the Joint Staff and service staffs, during which time the U.S. Embassy in Beirut was blown up. Subsequently Koch went with a group to bring the bodies home and report on the disaster. That report "was swept under the rug" because it was seen as having "a special operations association" and "reflecting adversely" on people who outranked the special operators who wrote the report. Koch's outrage increased as he finished his story:

> In August the answer came back. It was indeed critical that I brief the Chiefs, but there was one slight problem. Since the briefing in April, there had been personnel changes, and we had a new Director of the Joint Staff and two new OPSDEPS, and it would first be necessary to brief them. . . . August passed, as did September. On October 23, the Marine Battalion Landing Team building in Beirut was blown up, along with 241 Marines. . . . I never met with the Joint Chiefs. . . . I attempted to clear the air with the Director of the Joint Staff after the fact, so that we might have our disagreements over SOF but do what needed to be done with regard to terrorism. I asked him how it could be possible that in the greater part of a year, no time could be found on the Chief's agenda to discuss the subject. I vividly remember his response in the aftermath of 241 deaths. He said, "Well you know, terrorism is an easy thing to ignore."[77]

Koch ended his letter to Cohen angrily, "Today in the effort to defeat SOF legislation, I am watching the same predominating selfish interests at work, and I have no doubt their success can only lead somewhere, sometime, to some other replay of Beirut, October 23."[78]

Koch's expressed views became more and more extreme once he left the Pentagon. Eventually, as described by Lieutenant General Samuel Wilson, Koch pushed himself out of the debate: "[Koch] is a brash, ego-driven kind of fellow. He wound up . . . rendering himself essentially persona non grata to people whose influence and help he needed. . . . When we went back a second time to testify, I guess it was last summer [1987], to Senator Kennedy's subcommittee, Noel Koch, Shy Meyer, and I testified. Noel Koch's testimony in this instance, was very extremist . . . critical of current efforts. In the long run, I think it probably hurt more than it helped.[79]

Without Noel Koch, and the critical support from McGovern, Rylander, and, later, Tim Davidson, to push the fight within the Pentagon, the cause of SOF reform might not have been successful. Although McGovern, Rylander, and Davidson had an extensive and vital network at the working level, Koch had had access to the secretary and deputy secretary of defense, visibility on Capitol Hill, and the political clout to protect himself from retribution for most of his tenure in the building.[80]

Department of Defense: Too Little, Too Late

Time was running short for opponents of substantial SOF reform. Beginning in May 1986 the House and the Senate began to take action that could only lead to a dramatic reorganization of U.S. special operations forces. Whether this reorganization would be undertaken by the Defense Department or dictated through law was the question. For the Defense Department to maintain some control over the ultimate structure of its special operations forces, it would have to react quickly and with full recognition that marginal changes would no longer suffice.

On May 15, 1986, Senator Cohen introduced a bill cosponsored by Senator Sam Nunn. The initial goal of the bill was "to have the threat of forcing legislation in order to try to get the Department [of Defense] to work on these problems and develop a proposal on [its]own which would satisfy Congressional concern." Both Senators Nunn and Cohen were "very reluctant to make these changes in terms of special operations forces and low-intensity conflict mandatory, enacted in law."[81] In his bill, Cohen listed the reasons why Congress should get involved in SOF reform:

— The threat to the United States and its allies from unconventional warfare, including terrorism, is rising;

— Since the conclusion of the Korean conflict, the use of force by the United States had been primarily in response to guerrilla insurgencies and terrorist attacks. This will continue to be the most likely use of force in the foreseeable future;

— The capabilities needed to respond to unconventional warfare are not those traditionally fostered by the Armed Forces of the United States and the planning and preparation emphasis within the Defense Department has been overwhelming[ly] on fighting a large-scale war;

— The Department of Defense has not given sufficient attention to the tactics, doctrines, and strategies associated with those combat missions most likely to be required of the Armed Forces of the United States in the future;

— Problems of command and control repeatedly beset [the] military of the United States engaged in counterterrorist and counterinsurgency operations, as was evident during the *Mayaguez* incident, the Iranian hostage rescue mission; and the Grenada operation.[82]

Cohen offered a solution to the command and control problems: the establishment of a unified military command for special operations. This command would have responsibility for coordinating the planning of special operations; joint training of SOF units; operational control of special operations forces when they were not otherwise assigned to other commands; and, enhancement of promotional opportunities for members of SOF. Cohen also called for the establishment of an assistant secretary of defense for special operations and low-intensity conflict. The new unified command and assistant-secretary-level reporting were designed to generally improve the effectiveness of SOF and enhance civilian oversight of special operations. A coordinating Board for Low-Intensity Conflict within the National Security Council would work to improve coordination of special operations across government agencies. Finally, the bill recommended, as a "sense of the Congress," that the president establish the position of deputy assistant to the president for national security affairs for low-intensity conflict.[83]

Cohen's May 1986 bill was written largely by his legislative assistant, Chris Mellon, who relied heavily on the ideas of Jim Locher, a member of the Senate Armed Services Committee staff.[84] The bill was unusual in several ways. It went into far more detail than was usual for defense legislation. Congress had never designated a unified command through law, and the 1986 Goldwater-Nichols Defense Reorganization bill had deliberately shied away from having Congress specify assistant secretaries of defense.[85] In a 1988 interview, Mellon said that in early 1986 the SOF issue was relatively unknown to him and other Senate staffers. When he wrote the May bill, Mellon knew nothing of the earlier Stragtegic Services (STRATSERCOM) proposal and had never paid attention to Noel Koch. Mellon was, however, influenced by the history of special operations forces, particularly as described by Andrew Krepinevich in *The Army and Vietnam* and in Jim Locher's 1985 Senate staff study that was the foundation for the Goldwater-Nichols defense organization act.[86]

Jim Locher's perceptions of what would give SOF reorganization the best chance for success are seen in Cohen's May 1986 bill. Locher had begun to focus on the deficiencies of American special operations capability during his research and writing of Goldwater-Nichols: "We started looking at all the operational failures and deficiencies of the U.S. military establishment and one of the things that we noticed was this very excessive focus on conventional warfare . . .But the world [was] turning more toward unconventional warfare, some form of low-intensity conflict. . . . We became concerned that the Department was really neglecting a growing mission area . . . and also neglecting special operations forces which we thought were of increasing utility."[87]

The Goldwater-Nichols bill could not deal with every issue in the Department of Defense. It could do no more than identify problems with the U.S. special operations capability. It did, however, have an influence on the May 1986 Cohen bill. Goldwater-Nichols put some stakes in the ground that stayed in place during the drafting of Cohen's 1986 bill. For example, although Cohen in his January 1986 *AFJ* article had called for the Defense Special Operations Agency, by May 1986 he was acceding to Locher's position that such an agency would be inconsistent with the Goldwater-Nichols reforms. Locher felt that an agency, with a civilian director, would be isolated from the traditional military command structure. He argued that the Senate Armed Services Committee was "not prepared to accept another civilian in the chain of command."[88] The push for an assistant secretary position in the Defense Department also came from Jim Locher, who had at one time worked in the Office of the Secretary of Defense's Program Analysis and Evaluation office. Although hesitant to have Congress specify another assistant secretary, which was also somewhat contrary to the spirit of Goldwater-Nichols, Locher knew that it would be crucial to SOF reform for SOF to have some access to the decisionmaking process for defense resources. This assistant secretary of defense could join the select few who held seats on the Defense Resources Board, the primary decisionmaking body in the Pentagon in regard to resources.[89]

The services' reaction to Senator Cohen's bill was immediate. First off the mark was the U.S. Army. On May 16, Major General William Moore, director for operations, readiness, and mobilization, sent a handwritten memo to Lieutenant General Carl Vuono, the army's deputy chief of staff for operations and plans: "This bill now poses greater threat to JCS management of the SOF C2 [command and control] improvement than the [House Armed Services Committee] action, since the Cohen Bill has a higher degree of reasonableness! Nevertheless, it is likewise founded on misperception and a belief that [low-intensity conflict] should be elevated to a special position in our national foreign and security policy consideration. National willingness to engage more directly and fully in LIC (that is, increased involvement in areas of the world with forces—military, etc.) requires a decision greater than merely the formation of certain organizations and offices."[90]

After Senator Cohen's bill was offered in May 1986, Senators Cohen and Nunn asked the chairman of the Senate Armed Services Committee, Senator Barry Goldwater, to assign Locher the task of heading the Senate's SOF reorganization effort. At the same time, the House of Representatives, where legislation was also pending, turned up the heat. Ironically, while Senator Cohen and the SASC staff had moved away from Cohen's proposal for the Defense Special Operations Agency and toward a plan for a unified command and assistant secretary, a structure that somewhat resembled a military service, on the House side Dan Daniel and Ted Lunger were changing from an emphasis on a "sixth service" to a proposal for a National Special Operations Agency.[91]

Secretary of Defense Weinberger sent a letter to Representative Daniel on June 26 in an attempt to forestall the Daniel bill. In this letter, Weinberger described the review of special operations forces conducted by the Joint Staff, including its latest recommendation. According to Weinberger, the Joint Chiefs of Staff agreed that reorganization of "the Joint SOF structure" was warranted, primarily to better integrate SOF into the conventional war strategy, improve command and control, and establish greater advocacy for SOF in the programming and budgeting process. Weinberger said that as part of the SOF review, the Joint Staff evaluated six alternatives:

— preservation of the existing structure (status quo);
— a Joint Staff Directorate for SOF;
— a separate SOF Command/Task Force;
— a subordinate unified command of REDCOM [the four-star unified Readiness Command];
— a Defense Special Operations Agency; or
— expansion of the Joint Special Operations Command.

In concluding the review, the Joint Chiefs of Staff recommended the establishment of a Special Operations Forces Command, which would be commanded by a three-star general or flag officer. This unusual command, neither unified nor specified, nor at the four-star level, was to have "advocacy responsibility in the Defense Resources Board for SOF funding programs." The SOFC would have "full responsibility for training, readiness, doctrine, and SOF-related professional military education." Weinberger concluded by stating that special operations forces would thus have greater visibility since "advocacy is enhanced in the DRB [resource allocation] process by the SOFC commander's participation like that of any CINC. . . . A separate DRB issue book for SOF will be established to focus better on special operations funding requirements."[92]

Army Chief of Staff General John Wickham and Secretary of the Army John Marsh also offered their comments on the legislation for the National Special Operations Agency in a letter to Representative Daniel. After noting the U.S. Army's many improvements in its special operations forces, Wickham and Marsh concurred that "while such improvement already has occurred, more improvements can be made." They then summarized the Defense Department's alternative of creating a Joint Chiefs of Staff Special Operations Forces Command (SOFC). Finally, in their letter Wickham and Marsh listed the concerns they believed Daniel should address, including some of the omissions in the legislation:

— First, there is a chain of command issue with the creation of a civilian command authority in the person of the Director, NSOA [National Special Operations Agency]. Only the President and Secretary of Defense are National Command Authorities.

— Second, Defense legislation and directives require the commanders in chief [CINCs] to prepare operational plans and the JCS [Joint Chiefs of

Staff] to evaluate them as well as to allocate resources to fulfill them based on worldwide military factors and on Secretarial decisions. The draft legislation would bypass this [step]. . . .

— Third, the draft legislation would, in effect, create a fifth service by assigning to NSOA [National Special Operations Agency] all SOF funding resources and SOF forces, except those assigned to the CINCs.

— Fourth, the draft legislation, by establishing a separate SOF funding category under NSOA, effectively cuts out the Service departments from managing SOF personnel and from research and development of SOF matériel.[93]

Perhaps not surprisingly given the depths of their concern and frustration, Representative Daniel and Ted Lunger did not disagree with the concerns expressed by Wickham and Marsh. However, they regarded the omissions not as deficits of the legislation but as strengths. According to Daniel and Lunger, the Joint Staff's proposal for a Special Operations Forces Command was a clear case of too little, too late. Most critical to Representative Daniel was getting U.S. special operations forces out from under the control of the conventional services and providing them with their own checkbook. Daniel and Lunger believed that only through controlling their own resources could SOF avoid the dramatic cycles of rising and falling service support.[94] Although the proposal for the Special Operations Forces Command appeared to succeed in separating SOF from the services, it failed to provide the high-level advocacy required to win resource battles and did not provide this checkbook.

The Joint Staff's offer to have the SOFC participate in the Defense Resources Board process like any other CINC was of uncertain value. At the time of the legislation, the only permanent DRB members were the secretary and deputy secretary, the under secretaries, selected assistant secretaries, and the director of program analysis and evaluation. The comptroller for the Department of Defense also participated on occasion in DRB sessions. The unified CINCs were only invited to attend a limited number of DRB sessions, generally not decision meetings. And the SOFC commander would not be "like any other CINC" since he alone among the participating commanders would wear only three stars instead of four: a critical difference in influence. Even a Defense Department "defender" of the proposal, Lynn Rylander in the Office of the Secretary of Defense, saw little chance for congressional acceptance of the command, "once they

[JCS] came up with the idea, our office worked with them very closely to package it. You know, I tried to put the best light on it, but it was—well, it just didn't answer the mail." Rylander did not believe that anyone at the working level in the Pentagon believed the Special Operations Forces Command as presented by the Joint Staff had the slightest chance of being accepted on Capitol Hill.[95]

On June 26, 1986, Dan Daniel presented his NSOA bill (known as the Daniel bill) to the House of Representatives. The National Special Operations Agency would indeed be an entity separate from the military services, headed by a civilian with a military deputy and having its own appropriation in the defense budget. The discussions over the next few months were two-tracked: meetings between Capitol Hill and Defense Department staffs and hearings before the congressional committees. The primary participants at the staff level from the Defense Department were U.S. Navy Captain William DeBobes from the Joint Staff and Lynn Rylander from the Office of the Secretary of Defense, with the addition of Larry Ropka, also from the OSD. The staffs of the Senate Armed Services and House Armed Services Committees included Locher, Mellon, Johnson, and Lunger.

The staff discussions were characterized by hostility and inflexibility on both sides. Captain DeBobes and his approach to the negotiations have often been cited as one of the reasons legislation was ultimately passed.[96] Chris Mellon characterized DeBobes as "rigidly inflexible." He would not budge from the JCS offer. At the same time, the congressional staff members became increasingly frustrated and hardened their own positions. There was great resistance to Daniel's NSOA and, on the Defense Department side, to the new unified command proposal. Less was said about the proposed position for an assistant secretary since that position did not appear to have any impact on the services.

Division on the Hill

In a memorandum to Richard Armitage, the assistant secretary of defense for international security affairs (and Rylander's boss), Rylander argued that there was room for Defense Department negotiation with Capitol Hill. Critical to congressional concerns were a four-star commander for the SOFC, assignment of SOF-related intelligence support to the command, upgrading of the special operations commanders (SOCs) assigned to the theater CINCs, and adequacy of SOF resources. The congressional staff seemed to believe that a separate Major Force Program, similar to that provided for the reserves, strategic, and general purpose forces, was the best guarantee of visibility for SOF resources. According to Rylander's memo, Jim Locher viewed the fundamental question as, How important is SOF to the Department of Defense? When a member of the delegation from the Defense Department responded that SOF had progressed "7,000 percent," Locher declared that the issue was not how far the department had progressed but how far remained, "7,000 percent worth of progress is pretty small if you have to go 70,000 percent to solve the problem."[97]

Rylander concludes his memorandum with encouragement and a warning: "The Senate Armed Services Committee remains anxious to work with DoD in deriving a common position and, at the staff level, would like to avoid a legislated solution (preferring a Sense of the Congress Resolution). That predisposition notwithstanding, [SASC does] not see much common ground yet. . . .If DoD does not take serious, fundamental steps with regard to command structure, resources, and management, I believe the Senate will proceed with legislation (they don't seem to trust DoD to fix SOF and keep it fixed)."[98]

With the Cohen-Nunn bill and the Daniel bill, there was a clear division on Capitol Hill about what legislated reform and reorganization should look like. The frustration and fury of Daniel and Lunger were evident in their attempt to sever nearly all ties between special operations forces and the conventional military. The Senate side, particularly Senator Cohen, Jim Locher, and Chris Mellon, were just as determined to resolve the problem, but they were more moderate in their approach and still willing to let the Defense Department provide and implement the solution. They just had to be convinced that the Defense Department solution was for the long term and would meet the SASC requirement for a senior advocate in the resource arena and for truly joint command and control.

Jim Locher partially attributes the differences between the House Armed Services and Senate Armed Services positions to differences in familiarity with the Goldwater-Nichols Defense Organization study and legislation: "The people on the House side [working the SOF legislation] had not been involved in Goldwater-Nichols. And so I was able to take the organizational ideas that we had in Goldwater-Nichols and apply them to the special operations arena. We were convinced that as long as we left special operations in with the conventional military [SOF] would always suffer. . . . The conventional military was very uncomfortable with SOF. So the idea was that we needed to move [SOF] out of the services, give [the forces] a home, . . . a powerful advocate, . . . control over their budget. Give [SOF] the authority to acquire the highly specialized equipment . . .

needed. So it was my idea that [SOF] ought to be a unified command rather than a defense agency. The military was much more comfortable with the idea of a military command. . . . But because we were going to take this out of the military departments, we needed a civilian to oversee it and we also needed the civilian who could work these issues [to be] close to the Secretary of Defense."[99]

On the House side, there was less knowledge of and concern for Goldwater-Nichols. Instead, the paramount interest was in providing SOF with autonomy and control over its resources. For this reason, Daniel and Lunger moved toward an independent defense agency and argued for the special operations forces checkbook, which became known as Major Force Program 11.[100]

The Defense Department never fully exploited this division on Capitol Hill. Instead, the department, without making significant modifications, worked throughout the summer to sell the concept of the Special Operations Forces Command. The inability to guarantee the long-term life of their recommended reforms resulted in the department's loss of the last opportunity it had to reorganize SOF without legislation. In late July and early August senior Defense Department officials met with representatives and their staffers and testified before the congressional committees. Testifying before Daniel's Subcommittee on Readiness of the House Armed Services Committee, Chairman of the Joint Chiefs of Staff Admiral William Crowe and Assistant Secretary of Defense for International Security Affairs Richard Armitage made presentations and provided responses that were largely unsatisfactory to the subcommittee members.

In his testimony, Admiral Crowe criticized the Cohen-Nunn bill. Crowe declared that he "could see no organizational structure that could cut special operations forces off from Service resource and logistics support without being prohibitively expensive." Crowe expressed the traditional wariness of the conventional military for SOF and elite forces in general. He argued that he was "wary of philosophies holding that one community is more elite than another."[101] Crowe and Armitage guaranteed that they would personally act as proponents for special operations forces. When asked how that proponency would be transferred once both men left their positions, Admiral Crowe responded that creating the SOFC would provide a commander as proponent. Admiral Crowe argued that the size and breadth of the new command determined the rank of its commander and that a commander with a strong personality could fight in the budget arena with the four-star unified commanders. Crowe agreed that the SOF budget needed more attention but also claimed, "There are some awfully tough tradeoffs . . . we cannot fully fund SOF with the other DoD concerns getting the leftovers."

Representative John Kasich asked Armitage if there was a middle ground between the Defense Department's plan for the Special Operations Forces Command and Dan Daniel's proposal for the National Special Operations Agency. Even given the explicit opportunity to make a deal, Assistant Secretary Armitage did not seem to understand what was at stake. The Defense Department was about to lose the opportunity to avoid a legislatively directed reorganization of special operations forces. Armitage replied to Kasich's inquiry that SOF airlift was the biggest issue, and that although funding was not in the defense budget, the issue would be addressed by the Defense Resources Board.[102] This was not the definitive statement of support for SOF that Congress was looking for.

By mid-August, it was apparent to all that Congress was going to act on SOF reorganization. Although Dan Daniel and his colleagues on the House Armed Services Committee, supported and pushed by Ted Lunger, were bound and determined to direct reorganization of special operations forces by law, the decision to legislate, rather than recommend, change was not final on the Senate side. Senators Cohen and Nunn were not satisfied with the Defense Department SOFC proposal. They believed a three-star commander was not a strong enough proponent for SOF issues. Although they believed that Admiral Crowe and Assistant Secretary Armitage were committed to advocacy for SOF, they felt the Defense Department proposal was too dependent on personality, with no contingency plan for transferring proponency when these two officials left their positions.[103] Nonetheless, the senators were leaning toward a nonbinding sense of the Congress resolution, particularly if the Department of Defense offered a four-star command instead of one headed by a three-star general or flag officer.

The senators' position changed dramatically after the August 1986 testimony before the Senate Armed Services Committee by Major General Richard Scholtes, recently retired commander of the Joint Special Operations Command during Urgent Fury in Grenada. At the time of the hearing, Jim Locher had rewritten the bill offered by Senators Cohen and Nunn in May. According to Locher, "When we started the hearing that morning, Senator Cohen announced that the provision that would be offered as an amendment to the Defense Authorization Bill was going to be a Sense of the Congress provision. We had drafted it that way. . . .It was a Sense of the Congress that the Department of Defense should take the following actions."[104]

Admiral Crowe was the first to testify in the open SASC session on

August 5, followed by Assistant Secretary Armitage, then by Professor Richard Shultz, who was a member of the Special Operations Policy Advisory Group, and finally by General Scholtes.[105] When it became clear that much of the testimony from Scholtes was classified, the committee adjourned for a closed, classified executive session. General Scholtes spoke largely on how special operations forces had been "misemployed" in Grenada. His testimony was so alarming to Senator Cohen that Cohen arranged for a private meeting later in the day with Scholtes, Nunn, and Senators Warner and Exon. In this private session, General Scholtes was even more frank about the misuse of SOF, the complete failure of conventional commanders to understand and appreciate the capabilities of these forces, and the command and control disasters of the Grenada operation.

The Scholtes testimony was the final turning point in the decision to direct the reorganization of special operations forces through the law. Senator Cohen left the discussions and declared, "By God, we're going to have this in the law."[106] Jim Locher was sent back to rewrite the nonbinding provision into law, with the assistance of the lawyers on the Senate Armed Services Committee. Containing many of the provisions of the original Cohen-Nunn bill, the revised legislation was passed by the Senate on August 6, the day following the testimony of Crowe, Armitage, Shultz, and Scholtes. The House of Representatives passed the Daniel bill days later.

Nunn-Cohen Amendment to the 1986 Defense Reorganization Act

The differences between the Senate and House legislation were profound. When the House and Senate Armed Services Committees entered into the conference committee, the Senate would not accept the Daniel bill, viewing it as incompatible with the Goldwater-Nichols legislation:

> [The] Goldwater-Nichols Act strengthened the unified combatant commanders, strengthened the organization of the Joint Chiefs of Staff, made the Chairman of the JCS the principal military adviser to the President, and in general sought to more effectively integrate the forces of the different services. The Agency proposal ran in the opposite direction of these reforms, undermining the authority of the President's new military adviser and the commanders of the unified commands.[107]

The preliminary conference committee meeting, including Locher, Lunger, Mellon, Ken Johnson, and Bill Cowan, was tense and somewhat acrimonious. Ted Lunger believed strongly in the cause he was championing and had written legislation that he felt offered the only solution to the lack of support and misuse of SOF. The Senate staffers were equally convinced that the Daniel bill ran counter to Goldwater-Nichols and would never be accepted by the senators who were working for the reorganization of special operations forces.

In September, recognizing that an outside voice might assist in the resolution of the conflict, Representative Daniel asked Lieutenant General Wilson to act as a consultant for the House Armed Services Committee and join the conference negotiations. Wilson was retired from the army and had become a professor of political science at Hampden-Sydney College in Virginia. He had testified before the House and Senate and worked informally with the congressional staffers throughout the summer. He agreed to serve as a consultant for twenty-nine days.

The discussions opened with the staffers first delineating ten mission areas that combined the Senate's broader concern for special operations and low-intensity conflict with the House's narrower focus on special operations.[108] As the talks continued, it appeared that Ted Lunger would not negotiate Daniel's proposed reorganization. Eventually, however, after much discussion and occasional calming intervention by Sam Wilson, an agreement was reached. The reorganization of special operations forces would follow the Senate's proposed structure. The legislation would, however, also contain the measure that was most critical to Daniel and Lunger: special operations forces would have their own checkbook. A new major force program would be created, MFP-11, and SOF would be a separate appropriation. Special operations forces would receive fiscal guidance from the secretary of defense, similar to that received by the military services and defense agencies, and then make their resource decisions within "total obligation authority." SOF's resource decisions could be altered only by the secretary of defense or congressional action. Special operations forces would have nearly complete fiscal autonomy from the military services.

The legislation negotiated by the conference committee was written by Jim Locher.[109] On October 14, 1986, the fiscal 1987 National Defense Authorization Act, containing the legislation from the conference report, was passed by the Senate and the House of Representatives. On November 14, 1986, Public Law 99-661, known as the Nunn-Cohen amendment, was passed.[110]

The Nunn-Cohen legislation, and subsequent amendments, had three main elements. The first was the establishment of the U.S. Special Operations Command (USSOCOM) and the Office of the Assistant Secretary of Defense, Special Operations and Low-Intensity Conflict. According to the Nunn-Cohen amendment, USSOCOM would be commanded by a four-star general or admiral and "unless otherwise directed by the Secretary of Defense, all active and reserve special operations forces of the armed forces stationed in the United States" were assigned to the new commander (referred to as USCINCSOC). This amendment also directed that one of the eleven assistant secretaries of defense allowed by law would be the assistant secretary of defense, special operations and low-intensity conflict, ASD (SOLIC), with the principal duty of "the overall supervision (including oversight of policy and resources) of special operations activities and low intensity conflict activities of the Department of Defense."[111]

The Nunn-Cohen amendment also formalized, for the first time in law, the elements of special operations. According to the legislation, special operations activities included each of the following: "Direct action, strategic reconnaissance, unconventional warfare, foreign internal defense, civil affairs, psychological operations, counterterrorism, humanitarian assistance, theater search and rescue, [and] such other activities as may be specified by the President or the Secretary of Defense."

Finally, the Nunn-Cohen amendment greatly increased the visibility of special operations funding and SOF's control over its resources. The amendment created a new Department of Defense major funding category—Major Force Program 11—requiring the Department of Defense to report all special operations funding separate from general service funding. The initial legislation required that "the Assistant Secretary of Defense for Special Operations and Low-Intensity Conflict, with the advice and assistance of the commander of the special operations command, shall provide overall supervision of the preparation and justification of the program recommendations and budget proposals to be included in such major force program category." Furthermore, congressionally approved budgets could only be revised by the secretary of defense after consultation with USCINCSOC.

The special-operations-related legislation of 1986, and follow-on legislation passed in 1987 and 1988, was unusual in its specificity.[112] Its direction was at a level of detail rare in defense legislation and usually shied away from by Congress.[113] The legislation provided direction on the responsibilities of USCINCSOC and ASD (SOLIC), on who would control the fiscal and manpower resources, on promotions of SOF officers, and on the grades of the special operations commanders for some of the regional unified commands.

Nonetheless, all things can be neither foreseen nor legislated, and the establishment of this new near-service has, not surprisingly, been difficult. In part, that difficulty arose because special operators, having won a substantial victory, had to struggle to move beyond their organizational culture, a culture centered on small-team operations and secrecy. In securing the 1986 legislation, they had alienated a great many people in the Defense Department. They would have to learn how to operate within the Pentagon bureaucracy, making trade-offs and gathering support, in addition to preparing for operations around the world. No longer was the mission of U.S. special operations forces purely operational. The new special operations organization now had a bureaucratic mission that could allow U.S. special operations forces to grow and thrive.

7

The New Bureaucrats

*We're . . . overly protective of information. That's very understand-
able when you understand that these guys [special operators] are out
[in the field] by themselves. If they are compromised, . . . nobody else
can come help them. . . . Many times you don't share the information as freely on the staff as you should."*

Colonel Corson L. Hilton, October 1993

Passage of legislation reorganizing special operations forces was a stunning victory for its advocates. But legislation guaranteed neither implementation nor the rebuilding and protection of the U.S. special operations
capability. After years of debate, coalition building, negotiations, and out-
and-out conflict, Public Law 99-661 could not be implemented without
the cooperation of the Defense Department. Many factors were working
against successful implementation. Despite specificity unusual for legislation, numerous exploitable ambiguities remained in the law, particularly
given that those responsible for implementing the law had fought its
passage.

The legislation was complicated. It required sweeping changes in the
organization and management of special operations forces. The legislation directed fundamental exceptions for SOF in Defense Department
resource allocation and management. Implementation would eventually
require the support of high-level Defense Department decisionmakers
and the military and civilian bureaucrats who had to carry out the dictates
of the law and defense policy—the same Defense Department officials
upon whom Congress had forced SOF reorganization. Debate was frequent and seemingly without end during the first four years after the bill
became law. The SOF community, the Office of the Secretary of Defense,

the military services, and Congress argued over where the new organizations were to be located, which forces were to be identified as special
operations forces, and what the respective responsibilities of the new
organizations should be. Most critical to the survival and success of the
new special operations organizations was the debate over who would
control and manage SOF fiscal and manpower resources.

The authors and proponents of the 1986 special operations legislation
intended to give SOF the autonomy and status to control its future. Congress hoped to do so by establishing permanent organizations with direct
access to the highest levels of the Defense Department, particularly the
secretary of defense and the chairman of the Joint Chiefs of Staff. The
commander of U.S. special operations forces was meant to have an independent checkbook.[1] Secretary of Defense Caspar Weinberger was responsible for selecting and nominating the new assistant secretary of defense
(special operations and low-intensity conflict) as well as putting together
an initial staff. The most immediate task was establishing the new unified
special operations command and identifying which forces would be assigned to it. This fundamental responsibility fell to the chairman of the
Joint Chiefs of Staff and the Joint Staff.

Setting Up Shop

The Joint Staff appeared to have a straightforward task. Congress had
directed that, "the President, through the Secretary of Defense, shall establish . . . a unified combatant command for special operations forces."[2]
The law called for a four-star, "warfighting" command. Or did it? In 1986
there were five unified combatant commands: European Command
(EUCOM), Pacific Command (PACOM), Atlantic Command (LANTCOM),
Southern Command (SOUTHCOM), and Central Command (CENTCOM).
Each one was a regional warfighting command responsible for a specific
geographic area. A few four-star commands were known as specified
commands, that is, single-service commands such as Forces Command or
Strategic Air Command that supplied ground forces or strategic nuclear
forces (other than submarines), respectively, to the unified commanders.[3]
The U.S. Special Operations Command (USSOCOM) was to be neither a
true regional unified command nor a specified command. In fact, it had
many of the characteristics of a military service. The commander in chief
of U.S. Special Operations Command (CINCSOC) was responsible for selection and training of special operations forces and acquisition and de-

velopment of equipment peculiar to special operations, as well as allocating resources to support these responsibilities. In nearly all cases the SOF operational "mission shall be conducted under the command of the commander of the unified combatant command in whose geographic area the activity or mission is to be conducted."[4] The exceptional cases came under CINCSOC's operational mission of conducting limited special operations at the direction of the president or secretary of defense. The uniqueness of the command was to cause continuing confusion for the members of the command and the rest of the Department of Defense.

It is not easy to set up any new four-star command, and USSOCOM's unique characteristics made it even more difficult. Four-star unified commands have staffs of four hundred to a thousand people, depending on the command's responsibilities, with functional areas including planning, resources, manpower, intelligence, and operations. Unified commands require extensive communications capabilities, including connections to the National Command Authority, the Joint Chiefs of Staff, intelligence networks, and the command's components. Unified commands require access to military runways to allow the commander easy access to Washington, components, and other commanders. The infrastructure for these high-level commands is extensive and complex and cannot be acquired quickly. Congress, however, had legislated that USSOCOM had to be established within 180 days of the law's passage, giving the Defense Department a deadline of April 16, 1987.

The Defense Department seemed to get off the mark quickly, at least with regard to USSOCOM. On October 31, 1986, within two weeks of the conference report containing the legislation, Deputy Secretary William Taft established a joint Special Operations Reorganization Working Group (SORWG), initially to be cochaired by the assistant secretary of defense for international security affairs and the director, Joint Staff. The first task of the working group was to submit to the secretary of defense within two weeks "a list of options for an implementation plan that identifies specific tasks and milestones and assigns responsibilities to appropriate DoD components."[5] Taft's memo stated that upon appointment, the commander, USSOCOM, and the assistant secretary of defense, special operations and low-intensity conflict, would become cochairs. All work by the SORWG "must provide for implementation within 180 days." Finally, Deputy Secretary Taft emphasized that the administration and Congress were in agreement, declaring "SOF reorganization is an integral part of the revitalization effort undertaken by this administration and reflects the view shared by the Department of Defense and Congress that change is necessary."[6]

Washington, D.C., or the Ends of the Earth?

Over the next several months, papers were written and conferences were held under the sponsorship of the working group and Major General Tom Kelly's Joint Special Operations Agency within the Joint Staff.[7] The first issue to be faced by the working group members and the Joint Staff was where the command would be located. The two obvious options were Washington, D.C., or elsewhere. Although Congress clearly expected the command to be established in the Washington, D.C., area,[8] a sizable group in the Department of Defense believed, for both benign and nefarious reasons, that the new command should be set up anywhere but Washington.

As it turned out, opportunity was offered to members of the latter group by General James Lindsay, who had assumed command of the United States Readiness Command (REDCOM) just as the SOF reorganization legislation was being passed in Congress. Lindsay was a long-experienced soldier, described later by Chairman of the Joint Chiefs of Staff Admiral William Crowe as "one of our most highly decorated combat leaders, a jumping general with a long list of mending bones to prove it."[9] Lindsay had spent most of his U.S. Army career as a commander or member of operational units, including nine different assignments, culminating in command, in the 82nd Airborne Division. Lindsay had also served as a Special Forces A-Team leader as part of the 77th Special Forces Group. Before his REDCOM assignment, General Lindsay commanded the XVIII Airborne Corps. He was fond of large cigars, generally well liked by his forces, and had a reputation for being a superb politician although he had little Washington experience.

Within weeks of assuming command on November 3, General Lindsay began a REDCOM staff meeting by first describing his mission priorities for the command and then presenting to his directors the special operations amendment to the Department of Defense Reorganization Act. Lindsay laid out the ongoing debate about the location of the new command and argued against setting it up in Washington for fear "the commander would become embroiled in the Pentagon bureaucracy and lose sight of the mission to prepare SOF to carry out assigned missions."[10] To the shock of all his staff, General Lindsay then proposed combining REDCOM and the new special operations command into one command (tentatively named USSTRICOM) with responsibility for preparing both unconventional and conventional forces "to carry out assigned missions."[11]

Lindsay initially viewed the mission of the new Special Operations Command as analogous to REDCOM's mission for conventional forces. REDCOM had as its primary mission the preparation of conventional forces to support unified, regional commands. Included in this responsibility was deployment planning, joint training of assigned forces, contingency planning for those areas not assigned to the unified regional commanders, and the defense of the continental United States.[12] Lindsay believed the new Special Operations Command had a similar mission, although limited to special operations forces, and could therefore operate as a "subunified" command within REDCOM. Lost in Lindsay's recommendation was recognition of the broad service-like responsibilities that constituted most of the legislation and had never before been given to a unified or a specified commander.

By the time he met with JCS Chairman Admiral Crowe, Lieutenant General John Moellering (the chairman's military assistant), and Major General Tom Kelly on December 8 to discuss his proposal, General Lindsay agreed that REDCOM's regional missions could be transferred to other commands, but he still made a strong pitch for the combined command. Although Admiral Crowe agreed with Lindsay's argument that there was "critical linkage" between the operations of conventional and unconventional forces, neither he nor General Moellering believed that Congress would accept the combined command.[13] First, the legislation called for a separate, unified, four-star command, not a two- or three-star component of REDCOM. Second, REDCOM was located in Tampa, Florida, and had a reputation as a desirable "terminal assignment," facilitating easy retirement in Florida at the end of a military career. Approximately 80,000 military retirees lived in the Tampa area, and REDCOM was generally viewed as a sleepy and unappreciated command by the defense community.[14] Selling this idea to Congress was going to be tough.

The members of the working group, including representatives from the military service staffs, were caught up in the location debate. The Department of the Army recommended Fort Bragg, North Carolina. It was at Fort Bragg, after all, that the Joint Special Operations Command was located, as were the U.S. Army's 1st Special Operations Command and two Special Forces groups. Some members of the Joint Staff recommended Fort Belvoir in Virginia, just outside of Washington. This would meet congressional concerns. The Office of Strategic Plans and Policy on the Joint Staff was pushing for anywhere *outside* of the Washington area. The U.S. Navy supported Fort Bragg or Fort Belvoir. The final option was locating the command at MacDill Air Force Base in Tampa, Florida, as part of Lindsay's proposed assumption of the SOF mission by U.S. REDCOM.

Before presenting the REDCOM option to the Joint Chiefs of Staff, the working group decided to discuss the location of the new command with retired Lieutenant General Sam Wilson, since he had been a consultant to the conference committee and maintained a good relationship with many on Capitol Hill. On December 23, Major General Tom Kelly, director of the Joint Special Operations Agency, and one of his colonels flew in a helicopter to Wilson's farm in southwest Virginia, just outside of Hampden-Sydney. They landed in one of Wilson's fields, and the group went to Wilson's cabin for a half day of discussion. According to Wilson, Kelly had been sent by the chairman to get a sense from Wilson as to whether or not MacDill Air Force Base would be an acceptable location for USSOCOM, and whether the command should be tied into REDCOM. Wilson describes the essence of his response as follows: "You can't keep all your USREDCOM staffers and simply put special operations and Special Forces patches on them. . . . The Special Operations Command can't be seen as just USREDCOM with the signs painted over. It has to rise up out of the ashes of a completely disestablished USREDCOM."[15] Taking Wilson's advice to heart, Kelly flew back to Washington. Over the next several weeks Wilson acted as an intermediary between the Joint Staff and Capitol Hill, convincing the lawmakers that locating the command at MacDill could be made to work, and keeping Kelly informed about congressional reaction.[16]

It quickly became clear from Kelly's discussions with Wilson, Wilson's discussions with Congress, and the chairman's own discussions with Senators Nunn and Cohen and Representative Dan Daniel that Lindsay's idea of combining REDCOM and the new Special Operations Command into U.S. Strike Command (USSTRICOM) was completely unacceptable.[17] On January 9, 1987, after meeting separately with Kelly, Army Chief of Staff General Wickham, and JCS Chairman Admiral Crowe, Lindsay gave a briefing to the Joint Chiefs of Staff in the "tank."[18] The topic was USREDCOM/USSOCOM amalgamation.

Reporting back to his staff at REDCOM on the day following the tank session, Lindsay said it had quickly become clear in the meeting with the chiefs, particularly after Major General Kelly's briefing of the alternatives, that there was only one real alternative in the minds of Lindsay's audience. Despite Lindsay's warning that "the worst possible solution was to divorce SOF from conventional forces," most of those in attendance recognized that although Congress would not allow Lindsay's STRICOM, forming the new command on the foundation of USREDCOM would save time and money.[19] It might also be noted, and later was, by critics in Congress and in the SOF community, that for some the REDCOM option had the additional "benefit" of placing the new command well out of the Washington area, far away from its congressional protectors.

At the January 9 meeting, the Joint Chiefs directed the Joint Staff to identify the steps necessary to "establish USSOC using USREDCOM Facilities and Sources."[20] The next day, General Lindsay met with his REDCOM staff and remarked, "Even without an explicit decision on the demise of USREDCOM, the Service Chiefs had sounded the death knell of the Command."[21] The final decision was made on January 23, following Admiral Crowe's meeting with Senator Cohen that morning. Cohen had explicitly told Crowe that "the new command had to be pure SOF and the new command would have a 'blank check.'"[22] The importance of this decision to the implementation of the SOF legislation should not be underestimated. According to Kelly, "The 23rd was really the key briefing of the whole year . . . because it was at that . . . session that the Chiefs agreed to form the Special Operations Command at Tampa. . . . That was when they agreed that the baby would be born. Subsequently, all we were doing was deciding on what color hair it was going to have, where the crib would be put, and that type of thing."[23]

Word of the decision quickly reached the streets, and many SOF supporters were not happy. The Special Operations Policy Advisory Group was especially vociferous. Members wrote a stinging letter to the secretary of defense in protest.[24] Later, location of the command in Tampa was offered as evidence of the Defense Department's "malicious implementation" of the legislation. Several Representatives declared that the Defense Department intended to locate USSOCOM "as far away from the rest of the United States government as is possible without setting sail out to sea."[25] In March 1987 Admiral Crowe formally recommended to Secretary of Defense Weinberger that the new special operations command be established on the bones of REDCOM, and the secretary accepted his recommendation soon after.[26] Most of USREDCOM's mission was transferred to a new specified command, formed out of a U.S. Army major command, Forces Command.

Who Are Special Operations Forces?

After it was decided that the new command would be located in Tampa, the next issue was to determine which forces made up the command. Congress had not identified the specific forces it regarded as special operations forces. The legislation stated: "(1) Subject to paragraph (2), for the purposes of this section special operations forces are those forces of the armed forces that (A) are identified as core forces or as augmenting forces in the Joint Chiefs of Staff Joint Strategic Capabilities Plan. . . . (B) are described in the Terms of Reference and Conceptual Operations Plan for the Joint Special Operations Command. . . . (C) are designated as special operations forces by the Secretary of Defense." In paragraph two Congress had allowed the secretary of defense even more flexibility in identifying forces as SOF: "(2) The Secretary of Defense, after consulting with the Chairman of the Joint Chiefs of Staff and the commander of the special operations command, may direct that any force included within the description in paragraph (1)(A) or (1)(B) shall not be considered as a special operations force for the purpose of this section."[27]

During JSOA-sponsored conferences in January and February it quickly became clear that the military services were not willing to turn over all forces generally accepted as SOF to the new command. The assignment of four sets of forces—U. S. Navy Special Warfare (NAVSPECWAR) units, U.S. Army Civil Affairs (CA) and Psychological Operations (PSYOP) forces, and the Joint Special Operations Command (JSOC)—was hotly debated throughout most of 1987. During the JSOA conference the U.S. Air Force elected to provide its special operations forces, at the time under the command of the Military Airlift Command, to USSOCOM, although there was to be some dispute over whether MAC would continue to have some control.[28] None of the Marine Corps special operations units, such as the Force Recon units, were assigned to the command. The navy intended to assign only its Naval Special Warfare Center and special mission unit to USSOCOM. The SEALs, special boat units, and SEAL delivery vehicle units would remain assigned to the fleet through the two U.S. Naval Special Warfare Groups. The U.S. Army, however, opted for including all of its SOF, including the Special Forces groups, special operations aviation units, the 75th Ranger Regiment and all civil affairs and psychological operations units. In February, Under Secretary of Defense for Policy Fred Ikle joined Marine Corps protests against the assignment of PSYOP forces to USSOCOM. Ikle argued that the reassignment of PSYOP would reverse earlier decisions made by Secretary Weinberger without substantive analysis.[29] Finally, the military service and Joint Staff representatives came to an agreement that JSOC should be part of USSOCOM. The JSOC commander, however, argued that the command should continue to report directly to the National Command Authorities without the additional layer of supervision from a four-star command.

On March 24 JCS Chairman Admiral Crowe, recommended to Secretary of Defense Weinberger that all SOF active and reserve components in the United States be assigned to the new special operations command except for U.S. Naval Special Warfare Groups 1 and 2. Despite objections from the under secretary of defense and the Marine Corps, Crowe argued that civil affairs and psychological operations forces would be better supported under the new command.[30] Significantly, Crowe recommended that all of the military service special operations schools be assigned to the command and not to their respective service training and doctrine commands. This would allow the commander of USSOCOM to influence the training and doctrine of all special operations forces, even those forces such as the SEALs that were not assigned to the command.

Weinberger did not accept Admiral Crowe's recommendation in full. The secretary made two major exceptions. Reflecting the uncertainty among the OSD staff and some ambivalence from General Lindsay,[31] the secretary determined that "Army and Air Force CA [Civil Affairs] and PSYOP [psychological operations] units should remain as presently assigned" until a review directed by the Secretary of Defense was completed. Finally, the secretary directed that the "assignment of JSOC remains contingent upon USSOCOM becoming fully operational. USCINCSOC will inform CJCS when he is prepared to accept assignment of JSOC."[32]

The debate over the assignment of forces, particularly the SEALs, continued for nearly a year. The issue of civil affairs and psychological operations unit assignment was resolved most quickly. Those opposed to assigning PSYOP units to USSOCOM, including Ikle, argued that these units supported both conventional and unconventional warfare and that assignment to USSOCOM would shift the focus of these units toward unconventional warfare. Retired Army General Richard Stilwell, who was serving in the Office of the Secretary of Defense as the deputy under secretary for policy, argued that PSYOP and CA were "national assets" and as such should be controlled by the National Command Authorities and located in Washington.[33] Those who supported the assignment of these forces to USSOCOM believed that neither force had received sufficient attention from conventional commanders in the past and had only shown improvement since being assigned to the U.S. Army's 1st Special Operations Command (1st SOCOM). Like other special operations forces, PSYOP and CA offered an "unconventional" response to conflict and as such could only benefit from USSOCOM's mentoring.

In late May an attempt at compromise was offered in the form of an unsigned memorandum written by Lynn Rylander's Special Planning Office in International Security Affairs. The memo recommended the assignment of PSYOP and CA units to USSOCOM, but as the "Joint Strategic Services Command" headed by a two-star commander. The memorandum also contained a recommendation for the establishment of a PSYOP-CA directorate on the USSOCOM staff. These recommendations were essentially a compromise between OSD proponents (for example, the under secretary of defense for policy), who advocated complete separation of PSYOP-CA from special operations, and those who were convinced that its inclusion in the new unified command was critical.

The OSD solution was not, however, the right answer according to those who practiced psychological operations. The commander of the 4th Psychological Operations Group (Airborne) in 1987, Colonel William Depalo argued, "While this compromise may be acceptable within OSD, it fails to acknowledge the unique ongoing relationship between 1st SOCOM and PSYOP forces and cannot insure the continued enhancement of PSYOP capabilities nor provide SOF-dedicated PSYOP support. Since over 70 percent of Active Component PSYOP missions and activities are SOF-related, this latter point takes on extreme importance."[34]

Colonel Depalo then recommended that the PSYOP directorate be established on the USSOCOM staff with a brigadier general at its head. Depalo also recommended that "each Service component of the USSOCOM include a PSYOP section within the operations element of its staff, headed by a fully qualified 0-5 [lieutenant colonel]."[35]

Eventually three positions on the assignment of civil affairs and psychological operations forces coalesced. The first was that PSYOP and CA forces should remain separate from USSOCOM.[36] The other two positions agreed that these forces should be assigned to USSOCOM but differed on whether or not these forces should remain under USSOCOM's army component, 1st SOCOM, or be a separate "subunified command" reporting directly to CINCSOC.[37]

The assignment of PSYOP and CA forces remained an unresolved issue throughout the spring and summer of 1987. Assistant Secretary of Defense (International Security Affairs) Richard Armitage recommended the Joint Strategic Service Command alternative to the secretary.[38] Admiral Crowe wrote to Secretary Weinberger, reemphasizing his support for the recommendation of the Joint Chiefs of Staff that psychological operations and civil affairs forces be assigned to the U.S. Special Operations Command. Crowe argued, "While the missions of PSYOP and CA forces are broader than special operations, these forces should benefit from the resource advocacy that General Lindsay will provide as a unified commander. The assignment of these forces to USSOCOM will provide greater visibility and access to higher levels of representation in the resource arena. Additionally the close relationship that PSYOP and CA forces have with special operations forces in area orientation and language training should foster mutual benefits."[39]

At the same time Admiral Crowe was offering his support in Washington, USSOCOM staff worked to persuade General Richard Stilwell that PSYOP forces benefited from assignment to 1st SOCOM. General Stilwell paid a visit to Fort Bragg, North Carolina, to see and meet with members of 1st SOCOM and the 4th Psychological Operations Group. In the words of the 1st SOCOM commander, Stilwell was "still philosophically unconvinced that SOF and PSYOP should be in the same unit," but he would agree to include PSYOP in USSOCOM for a trial period, "primarily because there is no alternative in the near term."[40]

One of the last efforts to push for assignment of PSYOP and CA forces to USSOCOM came from General Lindsay in a June 25 letter to Deputy Secretary of Defense William Taft requesting the deputy secretary's support. In his letter, Lindsay stressed his strong support for Admiral Crowe's recommendation and countered any ambivalence he had indicated during the spring. Lindsay argued that USSOCOM was "the only organization that can provide 'total' support, to include PSYOP/CA personnel programs, resourcing under Program 11, and four-star advocacy. . . . The special operations community has the resources, climate, and support for PSYOP/CA to grow into a one-of-a-kind force multiplier. USSOCOM stands ready to assume the responsibility for PSYOP/CA."[41]

Simultaneous with the debate over the PSYOP/CA force was a reevaluation of the secretary of defense's original March decision to keep the SEALs attached to the fleet. During the initial discussions over implementing the SOF reform legislation, the navy had agreed to assign its Special Warfare Center and special mission unit to USSOCOM. The navy also agreed to establish a Naval Special Warfare Command as a component of USSOCOM, but it would not include combat forces since the SEALs, special boat units, and SEAL delivery vehicle units were to stay within the navy. Navy leadership argued that the SEALs had a "unique" relationship with the fleet commanders and, therefore, the Naval Special Warfare Groups should be assigned to the naval components of the Pacific Command (USPACOM) and the Atlantic Command (LANTCOM).[42] Many SEALs believe that the navy had finally recognized the value of the SEALs, particularly given that the underwater demolition teams had become SEAL teams in 1983, in supporting the fleet in the early 1980s, and had begun to invest in both manpower and new support systems for these units. The navy was not about to give up these rediscovered units to a new command.

The issue of the assignment of navy forces reemerged in General Lindsay's first quarterly report to the secretary of defense as the new commander of U. S. Special Operations Command. In his report, General Lindsay wrote

> We urge that the special operations forces of all services be assigned to USSOCOM. Specifically, while Army and Air Force SOF units are assigned through their component command structures, Navy SEALs remain assigned to their respective fleet commands. By assigning the Special Warfare Groups to the Navy Special Warfare Command, USSOC will have the ability to develop joint doctrine, tactics, techniques and procedures and enhance the research, development, and acquisition of special operations matériel, supplies, and services for all SOF forces. SOF support to the fleet would be improved by such an arrangement.[43]

Perhaps surprisingly, given his decision only a few months earlier, Weinberger responded favorably to Lindsay's recommendation. "I agree with your suggestion that Naval Special Warfare Groups be assigned to USSOCOM's Naval Special Warfare Command, and look forward to discussing the issue with you at the October Defense Resources Board sessions."[44] Weinberger's response reopened the issue of SEAL assignment and began a new exchange of memos and issue papers.

First off the mark was the Joint Staff. The Director of the Joint Staff, Vice Admiral P. F. Carter, "reminded" Secretary Weinberger of the Joint Chiefs of Staff position. Raising the specter of "military judgment," the admiral indicated that the quality of the chiefs' analysis was such that there was no need to readdress the issue of the assignment of the SEALs:

> (2) The stated JCS position on retention of operational Naval Special Warfare forces under the operational command (OPCOM) of USCINCPAC and USCINCLANT, as opposed to assigning them under the OPCOM of USCINCSOC, was based on JCS consideration of the Joint Explanatory Statement of the governing legislation and the stated positions of the Secretary of the Navy, the Chief of Naval Operations, and USCINCPAC. . . .

> (4) The present policy regarding the assignment of SEALs to OPCOM of USCINCSOC was arrived at after careful and conscious addressal by the Joint Chiefs of Staff. Unless directed otherwise, there is no further review of this decision currently scheduled.[45]

Weinberger, however, decided that military judgment was, at least in this case, fallible. He followed through on his promise to General Lindsay and scheduled the issue for discussion during the Defense Resources Board sessions in the fall.

The positions of the players in the debate are not surprising. General Lindsay, as CINCSOC, believed he was to command all U.S. special operations forces. The SEALs and the other Naval Special Warfare units, were clearly such forces. Their "unique tie to the fleet" was not that unusual; most special operations forces had as a large part of their mission support of conventional forces. Furthermore, when they were not performing the mission formally associated with the underwater demolition teams, the SEALs had a direct action, special operations mission. They, the special boat units, and the SEAL delivery vehicle units regularly trained for such missions. Lindsay argued that assignment of these forces to USSOCOM would meet the requirements of the legislation by enhancing command, control, interoperability, doctrine, training, resource management, and acquisition. According to a JCS issue paper prepared in response to the request by Richard Armitage, the U.S. Army and three of the unified or specified commands, USCINCENT, CINCFOR, and USCINCSPACE, supported General Lindsay's position.[46]

Opposing the assignment of Naval Special Warfare units to USSOCOM were the U.S. Navy, including many of the SEALs, and the commanders of U.S. Pacific Command and U.S. Atlantic Command (both unified commands with primarily maritime areas of responsibility). According to the Joint Staff paper, both commanders believed "the current assignment of NSW [Naval Special Warfare] forces optimizes their training, readiness, and responsiveness through continued integration with the other naval forces with which they regularly deploy in peace and with which they will fight in war." The Military Airlift Command also supported the navy's position while the commander in chief of the U.S. European Command expressed support but offered a caveat regarding the ability of Naval Special Warfare forces to support both navy fleet and unified theater command requirements. The U.S. Air Force recognized the validity of both arguments but did not express a position.[47]

Finally, the two issues, the assignment of psychological operations and civil affairs forces and the assignment of Naval Special Warfare units, moved toward resolution in late September 1987. After months of tortuous arguments, issue papers, and memos, Secretary of Defense Weinberger made his decision on PSYOP and CA forces in a few minutes during a meeting with the the Joint Chiefs of Staff. At this same meeting, Weinberger also declared that enough was enough, he was ready to make a decision on the assignment of Naval Special Warfare forces and would not tolerate much more delay. Excerpts from a memorandum for the record summarizing this meeting provide a glimpse into the Defense Department's decisionmaking process, especially since it is written in the usual Defense Department jargon. (The meeting had been preceded earlier that day by a secretary of defense's performance review (SPR) on special operations forces.)

1. On Tuesday, 29 September 1987, Gen. Lindsay flew to Washington, D.C. to attend the SOF SPR and Brief SECDEF [Secretary of Defense Weinberger]. . . .

3. At 1000 hours, the SPR convened in the SECDEF's Conference Room. . . . Just as the presentation began, SECDEF interrupted to ask whether the PSYOP/CA and SEAL issues would be addressed in the SPR. He noted that these issues had been dragging on for a long time, didn't understand why they remained undecided, and he suggested that they be decided right then as a part of the SPR. After the choking subsided, Gen. [Robert] Herres [vice chairman of the Joint Chiefs of Staff] reminded SECDEF that the PSYOP/CA issue was on the Tank Agenda for that afternoon, and the SEAL issue was scheduled for 6 October. He urged the SECDEF not to make a decision until the Joint Chiefs had had their day in court. SECDEF responded that he would hold a "very fair trial," but he wanted to do it today. They agreed to wait till the afternoon Tank session.[48]

Secretary Weinberger's decision came later that day at the tank session with the chairman of the Joint Chiefs of Staff present:

8. General Lindsay presented the briefing. . . . The SECDEF decided to assign PSYOP and Civil Affairs forces to USSOCOM without any restrictions on how they should be organized. . . .

9. Once the PSYOP/CA issue was resolved, the SEAL issue was presented. . . . General Lindsay presented his alternative proposal for [Naval Special Warfare] force structure. The follow-on discussion boiled down to the SECDEF and General Lindsay on one side, and the Chairman and ADM [Carlisle] Trost [chief of naval operations] on the other. Everyone else was conspicuously silent. SECDEF asked the $64.00 ques-

tion: What were the benefits and drawbacks of reassigning the SEALs? CNO [Trost] insisted that no benefits would accrue and we would only be fixing something that wasn't broken. General Lindsay raised the problems of joint interoperability, but the CNO denied them. Finally, the chairman recommended to SECDEF that he make no decision, but let the JCS continue to study the matter. SECDEF responded that he would defer a decision for today, but he intended to make one in the future and he asked the Chairman to send him a paper on the issue.[49]

Who would command the SEALs was eventually resolved in October 1987 when Secretary of Defense Weinberger, after evaluating additional papers prepared by the Joint Staff, decided that all Naval Special Warfare forces would be assigned to the Naval Special Warfare Command, the navy component of USSOCOM. Weinberger's decision infuriated many in the navy hierarchy, particularly Chief of Naval Operations Admiral Trost. Rear Admiral Ray Smith, a lifelong SEAL and former Naval Special Warfare commander, commented on the final decision, "It was unbelievable. We fought so long to stay alive, and the navy had finally recognized that, 'hey, these are great guys; they do a lot of things.' And then, of course, the transfer took place and we wound up moving out of the navy. At that point [it] just enraged the navy hierarchy. . . . Something was taking [SEALs] away and putting [them] somewhere else. It was a major fight between Mr. Weinberger and the navy leadership. But Mr. Weinberger prevailed, as he should have."[50]

Special Operations Command Begins Work

The U.S. Special Operations Command (USSOCOM) was formally activated, in accordance with the legislation, by the Department of Defense on April 16, 1987. USSOCOM's first commander was to be USREDCOM's last. General James Lindsay was first approached about the position as he was being told that his current command was going away. During their January 9 meeting, Admiral Crowe told Lindsay there was little hope for a combined USREDCOM and USSOCOM, and then asked if Lindsay wanted to take the new command and shape it according to his own design or stay with USREDCOM and risk presiding over the dissolution of the command. General Lindsay replied that though he disagreed with the dissolution of USREDCOM, he would accept the new command and take on the SOF mission.[51] General Lindsay was not nominated by the president for several months, a delay that was to draw the wrath of Congress but was somewhat unavoidable.[52] In fact, the new commander could not be nominated until the president approved the disestablishment of USREDCOM and the establishment of USSOCOM. The president could not give his approval until an implementation plan for both actions existed.

As late as six weeks before the legislated USSOCOM activation date, the implementation plan was not yet complete. On March 6, partially because of pressure from the Special Operations Policy Advisory Group, General Robert Herres, the vice chairman of the Joint Chiefs of Staff, transferred the responsibility of establishing USSOCOM on REDCOM's bones from the Joint Special Operations Agency to General Lindsay and his staff.[53]

On April 13, 1987, three days before the congressional deadline for establishing the new command, and following a last-minute debate over the wisdom of the plan to distribute REDCOM's responsibilities, President Ronald Reagan formally directed the establishment of "a unified U.S. Special Operations command (USSOC)," as well as the deactivation of U.S. Readiness Command and the formation of a new specified Forces Command.[54] Forces Command and the new Transportation Command, approved on April 18, were to receive the bulk of REDCOM's missions and responsibilities.[55]

On April 16, USSOCOM was activated and James Lindsay assumed command. Lindsay had been approved by the Senate as commander in chief, U.S. Special Operations Command, without the holding of confirmation hearings. Although the activation of USSOCOM was the first significant step in implementing the SOF legislation, many critical issues remained unresolved. Besides the problem of force assignment discussed above, two important issues had to be addressed: USSOCOM's relationship with its component commands and the size of the command's headquarters.

The component commands included the U.S. Army's 1st SOCOM, the U.S. Navy's Special Warfare Command, the U.S. Air Force's 23rd Air Force, and the Joint Special Operations Command. The easiest visible transition was 1st SOCOM, which the U.S. Army intended to transform into a "major command" within the army, renamed U.S. Army Special Operations Command (USASOC) and reporting to General Lindsay. The U.S. Navy's Special Warfare Command in April 1987 contained only the Special Warfare Center and no forces other than the naval component of the Joint Special Operations Command. JSOC was to report directly to General Lindsay. The U.S. Air Force was the most complicated, since the 23rd Air Force included search-and-rescue units and the air force's executive airline services besides special operations forces. Eventually an effort by the air force to maintain some control over the 23rd Air Force through Military Airlift Command was squashed after review by Colonel Edwin Wasinger, the USREDCOM Staff Judge Advocate, who made it clear that "a dual hatted SOC [Special Operations Command] component would be in violation of the Congressional intent behind the legislation."[56]

The size of USSOCOM was also much debated. As mentioned earlier, unified command staffs ranged from 400 to 1,000 personnel. USREDCOM had been staffed at just over 400, while USCENTCOM eventually reached more than 800 people. Also of concern was the number of general officer billets or positions in the new command. When USSOCOM was activated, it had positions for an initial staff of 250 people including four general or flag officer slots. This initial figure was believed by General Lindsay to be "somewhat arbitrary" and was much criticized by supporters of SOF reorganization. Lindsay and others, however, believed that the 250 figure was only a starting point and not of great concern since the command was scheduled to increase to 590 spaces by fiscal 1989.[57] In fact, Congress was not willing to wait for the Defense Department increases in the size of the command and in November 1987 directed that the total number of military and civilian employees permanently assigned to USSOCOM on September 30, 1988, "may not be less than 450." Of those, "the number of civilian employees shall be 111 unless otherwise directed by the commander of the command or the Secretary of Defense."[58]

At Secretary Weinberger's direction, the Washington office of the U.S. Special Operations Command was set up in the Pentagon effective June 1, 1987. Its first director was Brigadier General Wayne Downing, who was later to become USSOCOM's third commander in chief. The Joint Special Operations Agency was disestablished on August 1. Its functions were assumed by USSOCOM, the assistant secretary for defense (special operations and low-intensity conflict), or spread throughout the Joint Staff, which maintained its Special Operations Division. The formal activation ceremony for USSOCOM was held on June 1, 1987. Speakers at the ceremony included Deputy Secretary of Defense William Taft and Admiral Crowe. Taft's speech was cowritten by Lynn Rylander and reflected Rylander's and Noel Koch's belief that the true danger in the international security environment was Soviet-sponsored "wars of national liberation." Taft warned, "The enemies you must face are skilled at preying on economic and political inability, therefore, we cannot meet this threat with military assets alone. We must call upon the entire spectrum of tools we have from military operations to civic action to psychological warfare."[59]

Taft also spoke of the unique outlook of special operations in general and USSOCOM in particular:

We have in this country too often looked upon war and politics as two entirely discrete events. The Special Operations Command will not think in those terms. You recognize that the political dimension of conflict is as important—in some cases more important—than our ability to bear only military assets. No challenge will be greater than that of pulling together . . . the political and military dimensions of special operations.[60]

In his remarks, Admiral Crowe, not surprisingly, spoke of the value of special operations forces and the increasing efforts by the Soviet Union to work through "client states." Most importantly to USSOCOM, Admiral Crowe recognized SOF's precarious position within the American military when he gave the command three "taskings":

Above and beyond building the military skills and the procedures which go with your work, I see three tasks which are vital for you to perform, and [that only] you can perform. First, to break down the wall that has more or less come between special operations forces and the other parts of our military, the wall that some people will build higher. Secondly, to educate the rest of the military, to spread a recognition and an understanding of what you do, why you do it, and how important it is that you do it. Lastly, to integrate your efforts into the full spectrum of our military capability.[61]

Following the activation ceremony, General Lindsay had these taskings distributed throughout his command. He and his successors took Admiral Crowe's taskings to heart, making them central to the mission of USSOCOM as the commanders in chief worked to put together an organization that would eventually approach a fifth military service.[62] Each commander recognized the necessity of integrating the new SOF organizations into the larger national security bureaucracy of the United States. The formation of USSOCOM and its staffing with special operators who had little or no experience in high-level staff organizations again highlights the issues of organizational culture addressed earlier in this book.

The New Special Operations Bureaucrats

With the reorganization of U.S. special operations forces, an organizational culture that values independent operational capability most of all and has little history of high-level staff work was thrust into greater bureaucratic responsibility: running a service-like organization. James Wilson's warning about danger arising from a strong organizational culture and sense of mission, the problem of selective attention, is vividly illustrated with the reorganization of SOF.[63] As described above, the culture of special operations emphasizes small-unit military operations that are conducted by individuals who do not think like conventional military personnel. Strict operational security is emphasized. Because special operators have long been excluded from high-level military bureaucracies, in the mid-1980s they had generally spent little or no time working on higher-level military staffs and have had little inclination to develop the skills of an effective staff officer.

Since 1987, special operators have been charged with running a near-military service. This is accomplished largely through the U.S. Special Operations Command, although the Office of the Assistant Secretary of Defense, Special Operations and Low-Intensity Conflict (OASD [SOLIC]), plays an important role in the Pentagon bureaucracy and on Capitol Hill. Like a military service, the U.S. Special Operations Command is required to develop operational doctrine and train its assigned forces. Like a military service, USSOCOM must provide forces in support of the unified regional commanders in chief (CINCs). Like a military service, USSOCOM and OASD (SOLIC) must advise the secretary of defense—in this case, on special operations and policy on low-intensity conflict. Most importantly, like a military service, USSOCOM must manage its resources by developing and directing an acquisition capability and preparing a resource program and budget. The OASD (SOLIC), along with the rest of the Office of the Secretary of Defense staff, must evaluate the USSOCOM program and budget and defend the final product on Capitol Hill. Unlike a military service, USSOCOM's manpower comes from the U.S. Army, the U.S. Air Force, and the U.S. Navy, although USSOCOM does include these personnel costs in its program. Unlike the military services, USSOCOM must rely on other military services to provide most general support, such as military construction, health care, family services, housing, and equipment that is not SOF-unique, including uniforms and 2.5 ton trucks.

The transition from a community that has always focused on operational concerns to one bearing these enormous bureaucratic responsibilities was difficult. The special operations community's values—the ability to face great physical adversity in uncertain circumstances; the importance of technical skills such as reconnaissance, foreign language ability, and demolitions; small-unit leadership; and the maintenance of the strictest operational security—have not translated easily into cross-service administration of training programs, resource management, and coordination within the Department of Defense through "working the building" (that is, the Pentagon).

Examples of the conflict between the values within SOF organizational culture and the needs of an effective bureaucracy occur at the staff level and at the most senior levels. In the day-to-day functioning of the staff, growing pains abound. Running a new "service" requires special operators to act in ways foreign to their upbringing. Colonel Corson L. "Corky" Hilton's comments on the opening page of this chapter underscore how core values within SOF, in this case operational security, were sometimes at odds with the requirements of good staff work.[64]

For most special operations officers, an assignment to USSOCOM as a lieutenant colonel or colonel (or their navy equivalents) is their first staff assignment at a higher-level headquarters, although this has been somewhat less true as the command reaches its ten-year anniversary. Years of being on the outside means that only a very few have served at the component level or higher, with only a handful of officers having spent time in the Pentagon.[65] This is particularly true among navy and air force special operators. The average SOF officer, like many military officers in combat arms branches of the conventional military, does not want to serve on a staff. Like conventional officers, however, it is important to teach SOF officers that staff time is vital to their careers and to the continued growth and well-being of special operations forces as an organization. Today the professional development of the SOF officer includes the broadening experience of staff assignments that has long been the norm on the conventional side. Sooner or later the special operator must leave a SEAL team or the cockpit of a Talon. The officer might return to operational command, but now he or she must also learn the broader training, intelligence, operations, and management systems in order to make these systems work in the future.[66] Since the reorganization, a special operations officer is now expected to spend time in USSOCOM or the Pentagon as a major or lieutenant colonel, similar to an army officer in the infantry branch serving on the army staff or the Joint Staff. Unlike the conventional forces, many senior special operations officers, at least in the early years of the command, have not had this experience and are somewhat at a loss when they assume senior positions in the component commands or at the Special Operations Command. This lack of senior staff experience may partially explain why many of USSOCOM's senior leaders have little experience in Special Forces A-teams, SEAL teams, or flying special operations gunships or helicopters. Instead many come with Ranger, 82nd Airborne Division, or strategic lift backgrounds.

However, there are strengths that the special operations community brings to its new bureaucracy. The first is a great passion for what special operators do. Special operators, particularly more senior officers, joined the community because they believed in what special operations could offer the U.S. defense effort and because they enjoyed the work—not because members of the community had any likelihood of becoming general officers or the next chief of staff. Many were "counseled" not to go into special operations forces, "You're too good an officer to throw away your career on something like that."[67] Or, having spent time in special operations, they were advised to return to the conventional forces and command "real" units. The new special operations bureaucrats, even if they do not always know the correct way to work a memorandum through the Defense Department bureaucracy, will fight hard to get what they believe is important to special operations forces.

A second strength of the new SOF bureaucrats is that to a much greater extent than the conventional forces, special operations have always had an element of jointness. In Vietnam, air force special operations pilots supported both SEALs and Special Forces with infiltration/exfiltration and close air support. SEALs and Special Forces frequently worked together on joint operations. These relationships continued into the 1970s and early 1980s. As mentioned earlier, U.S. Navy, U.S. Air Force, and U.S. Army special operators have often felt a stronger identification with one another than with their parent services. This identification grew stronger as SOF was increasingly marginalized in the 1970s. A common saying among special operators is, "We were 'joint' before 'joint' was cool."[68]

The final strength special operators bring to their new bureaucratic role is tremendous confidence. SOF training, as described above, is designed to teach SOF personnel that they can accomplish whatever is required. The new SOF bureaucrats are rarely cowed by their lack of higher staff experience. Their approach, occasionally similar to the metaphorical bull in a china shop, is to evaluate the bureaucratic terrain and then charge in and get the job done. The first year of USSOCOM's existence was to some extent exactly what General Wilson feared. On April 16, 1987, the signs at the door of each office were changed from Readiness Command to Special Operations Command while much of the staff remained the same.[69] As General Lindsay selected his senior staff, particularly Deputy Commander in Chief Major General Hugh Cox, Readiness Command faded away. The most visible sign of Readiness Command today is found among the civilian employees of the command. USSOCOM's original 111 civilian slots were filled almost entirely with REDCOM holdovers until the command began to realize that perhaps there were civilian experts that could be brought in to assist in the assumption of the responsibilities directed by Congress.

After approximately eighteen months, most of the command's leadership and operationally oriented staff positions were held by special operators or military officers with some experience in special operations. The presence of special operators allowed USSOCOM to take on many of the organizational culture characteristics discussed above, the same characteristics that had allowed SOF to survive for nearly fifty years. The cost of this transition was the time it took to teach the operators the bureaucratic skills necessary to run this near-military service, or at least to learn to trust the specialists that were needed to enable USSOCOM to gain control of the fiscal and manpower resources that were key to SOF's ultimate survival.

8

Malicious Implementation?

After three years of hearings and effort leading to the passage of the special operations legislation, . . . there continue to be elements within the Department of Defense who will resort to almost any ploy to keep the legislation from being implemented. . . . The only possible reason for this bureaucratic foot-dragging is to simultaneously stack the new organizations and attempt to neuter them.

Representatives Earl Hutto, Dan Daniel, and John R. Kasich, March 1987

Despite some progress in implementing the special operations legislation, Congress was not satisfied. In fact, supporters of the special operations reorganization were frustrated, angry, and rapidly losing patience over what they viewed as unnecessary and even "malicious" delay by the Department of Defense in implementing the legislation. In early March 1987, both sides of Capitol Hill responded angrily to Secretary Caspar Weinberger's February 20 progress report to Congress.[1] Senator William Cohen charged that the report was "a contravention of the law." He criticized the Defense Department's decision to leave the U.S. Navy's SEAL teams out of the new command structure and the failure of the department to nominate the new assistant secretary of defense or the commander in chief for the U.S. Special Operations Command (USSOCOM). Representative Dan Daniel called the delay in making the nomination for the assistant secretary "totally unacceptable."[2] Daniel expanded his comments in the March 11 letter cosigned by Representatives Earl Hutto and John Kasich and quoted at the opening of this chapter. The letter expresses a great deal of anger and frustration, although the representatives attempted to avoid directly blaming Caspar Weinberger, and should be quoted at length:

We are writing to express our personal dismay at the contents of the 20 February Special Operations Forces (SOF) Reorganization Report. . . .

There are numerous statements made in the text of the report which were obviously phrased to mislead you (so that you would sign the report) as well as designed to mislead the Congressional recipients.

Examples of how the report, by omission, creates a less-than-truthful impression:

— Potential selectees for the Assistant Secretary's post have been carefully screened so as to force you to choose between either people who know nothing about special operations, or who were publicly opposed to the legislation, or ideally, both.

— A false issue has been raised, that of a totally specious requirement to "create" a [new] twelfth assistant secretary position, in order to delay, harass, canalize, and frustrate implementation. In this manner, DoD elements hostile to implementation remain in control for so long as is humanly possible, especially with regard to hiring personnel and staffing the new organization.

— Similarly the one unified command [USSOCOM] with the daily necessity to coordinate with other agencies outside DoD in order to be successful is proposed to be located as far away from the rest of the U.S. Government as is possible without setting sail out to sea.

— The staff for the new assistant secretary is proposed to be isolated in rental space, leaving the world's largest office building [the Pentagon] free to accommodate banks, drugstores and thousands of square feet of similarly non-critical functions.

— That staff will be absurdly small in relation to both its duties as well as comparable billets supporting other assistant secretaries.

— Hearings have already commenced on the DoD authorization for Fiscal Year 1988. Major Force Program Eleven [the new funding category explicitly identifying SOF resources], mandated in the law, is conspicuous in its absence. Thus, the one mechanism designed to uncover fiscal deceit and trickery, and to expose it to both you and the Congress, is missing.

We could provide numerous other examples. But, rather than waste your and our time—let us just summarize, Mr. Secretary. Beneath you, and largely invisible to your review, elements of the DoD are doing everything possible to frustrate SOF revitalization, for whatever purpose. Neither you, the President, the American people, nor the Congress benefit from this obstructionism. The only possible beneficiaries are our principal adversaries and their presumably unwilling allies. . . .

We are disheartened and dismayed. We invite your attention to this matter on an urgent basis, and we pledge our personal participation in the process through hearings, additional legislation, or whatever remedies are necessary to ensure the success of the SOF revitalization you and we are agreed is critical.[3]

Clearly the authors of this letter understood how the Pentagon works. They were fully aware that if the bureaucracy did not cooperate, legislation alone would not create the new SOF organizations capable of building and maintaining a strong and interoperable special operations capability. Upon receipt of this letter Secretary Weinberger was made aware that the supporters of special operations forces were not going to let the issue go. Members of Congress continued to have eyes and ears throughout the Defense Department, and they were going to watch all that the department did in the course of implementing the legislation.

The representatives' letter received extensive publicity, thereby making "malicious implementation" a public matter. Articles included "Delay on Guerrilla Command Irks Hill" in the *Washington Post* and "3 Key Representatives Assail Delays on Special Forces" in the *Baltimore Sun*. On March 26 the Senate Armed Services Committee followed up on the House letter with a list of seventeen questions for Assistant Secretary of Defense Richard Armitage and, Major General Tom Kelly, director of the Joint Special Operations Agency. The Senate's questions were somewhat more well-mannered than those from the House but contained unusually detailed requests for information. The Senate Armed Services Committee list included questions on the specific components that would be assigned to the command, the initial authorization of a staff of 250 for USSOCOM, the changes in funding in fiscal 1988 and fiscal 1989 if the fiscal 1987 supplemental SOF airlift request were not approved, and the number of general/flag officers in special operations assignments. Certainly in the spring of

1987 the Senate was just as suspicious as the House was of Defense Department intentions.

Even with the activation of the command, the Senate's suspicions were not completely allayed. On May 19, Senators William Cohen and Edward Kennedy expressed the continuing anger of Congress in a letter to Caspar Weinberger that accused the Defense Department of being deliberately uncooperative. Expressing their concern over the apparent delay in implementing the legislation, the senators reiterated many of the points made by their House colleagues: the lack of a nomination for the position of assistant secretary of defense, special operations and low-intensity conflict; that SEAL forces had not yet been assigned to a new unified Special Operations Command; and that the Special Operations Command would be located in Florida rather than in Washington, despite the "sensitive political-military nature of its mission." The Senate too questioned the Defense Department's spirit of cooperation in providing the appropriate budget authority for a new commander, and senators quoted statements from General Edward Meyer, General Sam Wilson, and Noel Koch on the resistance of the Defense Department to the "changes that have been mandated by law." Indeed, they wrote, Noel Koch had said, "The Department of Defense has done everything possible to circumvent the will of Congress as represented in the legislation and to subvert the legislation itself." In their concluding remarks, the senators pointed out that the Defense Department would pay penalties as long as it did not meet congressional expectations: "In sum, we are disturbed by the pace and directions of the Defense Department's response to its mandate from Congress. Consequently . . . we have decided to place a hold on *all* statutory nominations before the Senate Armed Services committee until the nomination for the new Assistant Secretary of Defense for Special Operations and Low-Intensity Conflict has been approved." The senators repeated their hope that nomination for an appropriate candidate would soon be received.[4]

The House and Senate letters are surprising in their openly stated suspicion of the Department of Defense's efforts to carry out the special operations reorganization legislation. The tone of the letters was not altogether unexpected given the SOF advocates' frequently voiced low opinion of the Defense Department's track record with SOF.

Implementation

Many of Congress's frustrations over the early implementation of the legislation were alleviated in the first year following the initial SOF legislation. By the spring of 1988 USSOCOM had been activated by the Department of Defense; General Lindsay had been nominated and approved as commander in chief of the U.S. Special Operations Command (CINCSOC); and the SEALs, civil affairs, and psychological operations forces had all been assigned to the new command. The command was also gradually replacing U.S. Readiness Command (USREDCOM) military personnel with special operators and functional experts. Although these changes took nearly a year to complete, clear progress was being made in establishing USSOCOM.

Despite congressional frustration, some of the delay in implementing the legislation was simply because of the great complexity of what Congress had asked the Defense Department to do. Implementing big policy can be more complicated than making it. As representatives had pointed out, funds in Major Force Program 11, the SOF funding category, had not yet been identified by the time of the House hearing on the Defense Department authorization for fiscal 1988 in March of 1987. It is also true that the Defense Department program and budget process for fiscal 1988 to fiscal 1992, the process that eventually created the Defense Department section of the president's fiscal 1988 budget, was nearly complete by the time new follow-on SOF legislation was passed in late 1987. The budget had already been developed and was being finalized for turnover to the Office of Management and Budget in December or early January 1988. The president's budget usually goes to Capitol Hill in late January or February. There was no time to create a new major funding category before that time. The best the Hill could hope for was identification of Major Force Program 11 funding in the fiscal 1989 budget, which would be developed during the summer and fall of 1988. Although there still might be delays, the accusations were premature and unrealistic on the part of Representatives Daniel, Kasich, and Hutto in March of 1987.

A second complaint of the representatives, locating the command in Florida, in the long run turned out to be much less of a disaster than was originally envisioned by special operations supporters. In fact, building USSOCOM on the bones of USREDCOM saved taxpayers, according to some estimates, $60 million dollars and up to two years in the time it took to activate the new command. Some of the most activist members of the SOF community agreed in retrospect that being located in Tampa has not put the command at a great disadvantage. One U.S. Air Force colonel who has been a long and active member of the "SOF Mafia" commented several years later, "Actually, as much as I disagreed with the idea of using REDCOM as the start point for the command, it did have the effect of getting us started sooner. Because . . . at the rate we were going we would have churned for years trying to figure out how to [set up the command]. . . . So it worked out okay."[5]

This was particularly true after recommendations from Congress and the Office of the Secretary of Defense (OSD) to establish a Washington, D.C., office for USSOCOM were accepted by Secretary Weinberger, thereby providing members of the command a home away from home and Defense Department staff a USSOCOM point of contact in the Pentagon. Lynn Rylander in the Office of the Secretary of Defense described this reevaluation by the SOF community: "The location of the command in Tampa . . . was viewed initially as malicious on the part of the Chiefs [of Staff]. . . . Although in retrospect, it probably was a good idea. . . . The down side is the amount of TDY [travel money and time] that you have to spend, and everybody else has to spend, to get our job done. But the fact that you have a Washington Office has very much ameliorated their concern. I don't think it is an issue anymore."[6]

If many congressional concerns about establishing USSOCOM were resolved during 1987, the same cannot be said for Defense Department efforts to create the new Office of the Assistant Secretary of Defense, Special Operations and Low-Intensity Conflict. In all of the discussion of the assignment of forces to USSOCOM, location of the command, and the nomination of its commander, there was little mention of the OASD (SOLIC).

The decision to locate USSOCOM in Tampa, building on top of REDCOM, enabled USSOCOM to stand up within six months of the conference report that laid out the legislation. The command had its basic infrastructure already in place, including a headquarters building, communications systems, an airfield, and even a staff. As described by an early member of the USSOCOM staff, "Basically, what they did was [take] REDCOM as a boiler plate and . . . take down signs on the offices and put up other signs. The overall structure didn't change all that much immediately."[7] Once the command was activated, General Lindsay was able to tackle issues such as the assignment of forces to USSOCOM and defining his role as CINCSOC. The Office of the ASD (SOLIC) (or simply SOLIC) did not have a confirmed assistant secretary for the first eighteen months of its existence and, therefore, had no leadership, sense of mission, or influence on SOF issues.

The SOF reorganization legislation did not set a deadline for SOLIC's establishment, as it had for the establishment of USSOCOM. Nominating an assistant secretary and establishing the Office of Assistant Secretary, Special Operations and Low-Intensity Conflict, were subject to delay over and over again. Although all delays were not deliberate, and some were inevitable, the seeming unwillingness of the Defense Department, especially the secretary of defense and some of his staff, fueled the SOF community's accusation of "malicious implementation."[8]

Confusion and the Office of the Assistant Secretary of Defense

The first issue for the Office of the Assistant Secretary of Defense, Special Operations and Low-Intensity Conflict, was the selection and nomination of the new assistant secretary. The Office of the Secretary of Defense quickly seized upon the ambiguity in the 1986 legislation over whether the new assistant secretary would be a new assistant secretary position besides the eleven assistant secretaries authorized within the Defense Department by Congress. All authorized positions were already filled in early 1987, and so in his February 20 progress report to Congress, Secretary Weinberger stated that "until authorization for this new position is obtained, the direction and development of this new DoD entity [SOLIC] will be under the cognizance and direction of the Principal Deputy Assistant Secretary of Defense (International Security Affairs)."[9] This solution was, however, far from adequate in the eyes of Congress and only succeeded in increasing its ire.

By March 1987 newspapers reported that senior Defense Department officials had interviewed several candidates for the position of ASD (SOLIC) and were leaning toward nominating Lieutenant General Edward L. Tixier, commander of U.S. forces in Japan. According to news reports, the SOF community opposed the possible appointment of Tixier because he did not have experience in special operations or low-intensity conflict and was, instead, viewed as being a candidate because of his friendship with Richard Armitage.[10] According to the *Washington Post*, SOF's congressional supporters were pushing the nomination of William V. Cowan, a legislative assistant for Senator Warren Rudman and a retired marine, with experience in counterinsurgency during Vietnam.[11]

Criticism was also being heard from the Special Operations Policy Advisory Group. According to an article appearing on March 12 in the *Baltimore Sun,* a draft memorandum from the group to Secretary Weinberger was circulating in the Pentagon. This memorandum was highly critical of the Defense Department's implementation of the legislation, describing the reorganization effort as "mired in bureaucratic inertia." The SOPAG memorandum was especially critical of the time it was taking to nominate the new assistant secretary, suggesting that it "appear[ed] to be a way of delaying the establishment of a [staff] for several months."[12]

The Defense Department was also criticized by the SOF community and its supporters about its early decisions on the size and makeup of the SOLIC staff and where the office would be located. In his February 20 report to Congress, Secretary Weinberger said that the Defense Department had made several small steps toward establishing the SOLIC office. Unfortunately, many of these steps signaled to SOF supporters that Assistant Secretary of Defense Richard Armitage was gaining control of the new organization. Suspicion was high not only because Armitage had actively fought the passage of the legislation but also because Armitage's office would lose the most when SOLIC was established under its own assistant secretary, losses that would include Lynn Rylander's Special Planning Office as well as staff who worked in humanitarian affairs and peacekeeping operations.

One of Assistant Secretary Armitage's first steps was to appoint Lawrence Ropka Jr., his principal deputy assistant secretary, as interim head of the new office. Ropka had replaced Noel Koch in August 1986 but could not have held convictions more different from his predecessor's. According to Lynn Rylander, whose office reported to Ropka, within a month of the legislation being passed, Ropka held a staff meeting and said, "If you favor implementing this legislation, you're being disloyal to the Pentagon." It was, said Rylander, "just the kind of malicious implementation that Congress feared."[13]

The interim SOLIC office was formed from pieces of the Joint Special Operations Agency on the Joint Staff, the Special Planning Office established by Noel Koch under Richard Armitage and International Security Affairs (ISA), and a few members of the Office of the Assistant Secretary for Command, Control, Communications, and Intelligence. The limiting of the initial SOLIC staff by Armitage and Ropka to thirty-nine people was seen by SOF supporters as further evidence of their limited support for the office. Offices headed by assistant secretaries usually run from approximately 120 to 700 people within OSD. Citing space limitation in the Pentagon, OSD leadership decided to house the SOLIC staff in a building outside of the Pentagon, further angering SOF supporters, especially those on Capital Hill, as noted in the letters by the House and the Senate. Lynn Rylander was appalled by the potential move outside the Pentagon: "They were going to put us in a building—it is called the paper clip building [and] it is just across [highway] 395 from here . . . but it was on the first floor of the building, with floor-to-ceiling windows. . . . Makes a lot of sense for people dealing with matters like CT [counterterrorism]!"[14]

The OSD's handling of the new SOLIC organization infuriated Capitol Hill. By May 1987, the SOF supporters in the Senate were angry enough to delay all confirmations of Reagan administration high-level appointees until a nominee for the new assistant secretary was received by the Senate.

The furor increased when on June 9 the White House announced that Kenneth S. Bergquist was its nominee to be the first ASD (SOLIC). In their letter to Secretary Weinberger, Representatives Daniel, Kasich, and Hutto had warned of potential nominees for the new position that might have been selected for knowing "nothing about special operations, or who were publicly opposed to the legislation, or ideally, both."[15] Senators Cohen and Kennedy indicated that any nomination sent to the Senate for confirmation should be of "appropriate background and experience."[16] When he was nominated, Bergquist was a Justice Department lawyer. He had been the assistant secretary of the army for readiness. According to an article in the *Army Times*, "Bergquist . . . may have trouble getting Senate confirmation for the special operations post because he has stated in the past that he did not favor the reorganization creating the assistant secretary's job."[17]

The *Army Times* understated the difficulty that Bergquist's nomination would give the administration. Apparently the Senate Armed Services Committee had copies of letters to Deputy Secretary William Taft, written after Bergquist's interview, reporting that Bergquist had never supported the reorganization legislation.[18] Members of the Senate Armed Services Committee and staff quickly informed the White House that they were not going to hold confirmation hearings for Ken Bergquist and were "bound and determined that they weren't going to confirm him."[19] Eventually, hearings were held in late 1987, but with no intention of moving on Bergquist's confirmation. The president did not resubmit his nomination for the next congressional session.

By late 1987, few people had been assigned to SOLIC other than those in the Office of Special Planning. The organization was allowed to drift under Larry Ropka and was in real danger of fading away. The impression on Capitol Hill was that those who opposed the law in the Office of the Secretary of Defense were delighted with the delay. This assessment was shared by those outside of Congress as well. In the summer of 1988, General Edward C. "Shy" Meyer commented: "I and some of the others who went over to testify [before Congress] a year and a bit ago—in April 1987—were lied to by the Administration, by Armitage and others when they said they would nominate a guy who would be approved, and so on.

Well, they took a guy they could never get through Congress. In my view they did that purely and simply in order to prevent it [confirmation of a new assistant secretary] from happening."[20]

A Congress that had lost all patience seized upon Senate Armed Services Committee staffer Jim Locher's proposal for getting around the impasse over the ASD (SOLIC) nomination during the House and Senate conference committee on the National Defense Authorization Act in November 1987. The resulting conference report required, among other provisions, that until the ASD (SOLIC) "is filled for the first time by a [civilian], . . . the Secretary of the Army shall carry out the duties and responsibilities of that office."[21] The secretary of the army at the time of the report was John O. Marsh Jr.

Asked why he chose the secretary of the army, Jim Locher responded, "He had served for so long in the Reagan Administration. . . . He's one of the most senior civilians in the Department. . . . We knew that Secretary Marsh had some interest in the SOF capabilities in the Army and we designated the Secretary of the Army because that would put a lot of pressure on OSD. The Navy and the Air Force weren't going to like it either. And so what we were attempting to do was . . . put a powerful guy in charge, have him report to the committee every month on what he had done, and try to get the Department moving on nominating an Assistant Secretary of Defense."[22]

Congress had, however, chosen a reluctant savior for SOLIC. Before the conference report was approved, members of Congress had approached Secretary Marsh to ask if he would accept the responsibility. The secretary's first response was no. Representative Dan Daniel then asked Sam Wilson, who was teaching at Hampden-Sydney College, to approach John Marsh. Marsh, like Daniel and Wilson, was from an old Virginia family. General Wilson, who had known March since about 1945, said he had "about a 50-50 chance" of talking Marsh into accepting the job. Wilson pressed March, saying the office "was never going to get off the ground" if Marsh "didn't take it on." So Marsh reluctantly agreed.[23]

Secretary Marsh and the First Confirmed ASD (SOLIC)

As it turned out, the instincts of Jim Locher and other congressional supporters of special operations reorganization were good. Secretary Marsh used his position as secretary of the army, his prestige, and his personal connections to provide SOLIC with an organizational base from which to operate. Special Operations and Low-Intensity Conflict was moved out from under Larry Ropka and became a separate organization reporting through the under secretary of defense for policy to the secretary and deputy secretary of defense. Marsh soon found office space for SOLIC in the Pentagon and gained Secretary of Defense Frank Carlucci's approval for renovation. By February 1988 Secretary Marsh was moving to guarantee SOLIC's participation in the Defense Department resource decision process, particularly the program review scheduled to begin in late spring. The new organization's charter was approved, as required by the same legislation that put him in place, soon after Marsh's arrival.

Congress did not believe that the appointment of Secretary Marsh resolved the SOLIC issue, but SOF supporters hoped that John Marsh, a former representative, could work with members of Congress and calm the waters enough to allow SOLIC to begin to get itself established. Congress required Marsh to report each month on progress made in implementing the legislation. Marsh was to some extent able to use this reporting requirement as a cudgel, or at least a prod, to get approval from Secretary Carlucci of the basic steps needed to get SOLIC going.

Perhaps the most important accomplishment of John Marsh as acting assistant secretary was his encouraging the administration to make a serious nomination for the position of ASD (SOLIC). Secretary Carlucci was not especially interested in special operations issues, but he was interested in nominating Ambassador Robert Oakley. When Ambassador Oakley turned down the offer, Secretary Marsh asked Secretary Carlucci to meet with the Special Operations Policy Advisory Group, which was still meeting on a regular basis. As Sam Wilson remarked, "If you have someone with the stature of a Jack Marsh, you can bring a Secretary of Defense in and say, 'You've got to sit and talk with these people.' Carlucci didn't particularly care who we were . . . but Jack Marsh said, 'Do it,' so he came down."[24]

With Sam Wilson acting as spokesman, the Special Operations Policy Advisory Group made its case to the secretary of defense: "We're in real trouble in the Washington area. So much of what occurs in special operations and low-intensity conflict can be so overwhelmingly political and socioeconomic in its character and its implications that it automatically becomes a subject . . . of interagency, interdepartmental concern. . . . So we've got to have someone with clout who will have influence with NSC [National Security Council], CIA, . . . and especially State [Department]."[25]

Soon after leaving the meeting, Secretary Carlucci took the advice of Marsh and the special advisory group and called a friend of his at the White House. The White House reacted quickly, making the nomination within days of receiving Carlucci's phone call.

The importance of John O. Marsh's tenure as acting assistant secretary should not be underestimated. Sam Wilson praised Secretary Marsh in July 1988, saying, "Without his hand at the helm, without the clout of the Secretary of the Army . . . we would not have gotten some of the things done that we have been able to achieve.[26]

Ambassador Charles Whitehouse, the man eventually nominated for assistant secretary of defense, special operations and low-intensity conflict, was not quite the hard charger looked for by the Special Operations Policy Advisory Group, but he was a man with long and respectable government experience. Because of his diplomatic experience, Ambassador Whitehouse had a good knowledge of low-intensity conflict issues, particularly those in the political and economic arena. He had much less knowledge of defense issues in general, and the Defense Department in particular, but he had the advantage of being a good friend of Secretary Carlucci. By the time of his confirmation, the SOF reorganization legislation had been modified once again so that ASD (SOLIC) reported directly to the secretary and deputy secretary of defense, rather than through an under secretary.[27] Access is everything and access to the secretary, formal and informal, gave Ambassador Whitehouse clout.

Charles Whitehouse was, however, also working at a disadvantage. By the time he became the first confirmed ASD (SOLIC) in the summer of 1988, the Reagan presidency was winding down. Soon after the election of George Bush as president in November 1988, Ambassador Whitehouse moved into a role focusing more on caretaking. With a new president would come a new ASD (SOLIC). Whitehouse could only work to push those issues that had already arisen during the previous year, especially program and budget issues. The last few months of the administration did not allow large issues such as the relationship between the U.S. Special Operations Command and the office of the assistant secretary, and their respective responsibilities, to be addressed. Nor was a short-time political appointee, no matter how well respected, in any position to question decisions made by General Lindsay as the USSOCOM commander in chief.

Capitol Hill Comes to the Pentagon

With the assumption of the presidency by George Bush came the need for a new ASD (SOLIC) although, once again, there was no apparent rush to fill the position. Philosophically, the Bush administration was not attuned to special operations or low-intensity conflict. It was very much captured by the old thinking of the cold war, not surprising given the great speed of the changes that occurred during the late 1980s and resulted in the fall of the Berlin Wall and the collapse of the Soviet Union. Secretary of Defense Dick Cheney was a cautious and conservative thinker concerning the end of the cold war, again, perhaps not an unreasonable position for the man responsible for the nation's defense. He regularly urged caution about overestimating the decline of the Soviet threat to American national security interests. This was not an administration ready to make dramatic changes in the forty-year focus of American defense policy.

George Bush's first nominee for the position of secretary of defense was Senator John Tower, a long-time member of the Senate Armed Services Committee. Jim Locher had worked for John Tower as a member of the SASC staff and continued as the committee's senior foreign policy adviser when the chairmanship was assumed by the Democrats. During the transition period before George Bush's inauguration, Tower met with Jim Locher and told him he would like Locher to come to the Defense Department at an unspecified senior position.

At this point, Jim Locher was already considering the possibility of becoming the second confirmed ASD (SOLIC). Although he had not been a special operations or low-intensity conflict expert when he wrote the final version of the original SOF reorganization legislation, he had been forced to spend increasing time on special operations as a result of congressional monitoring of the Defense Department's implementation of the law. As a result of his work on Goldwater-Nichols and the SOF legislation, Jim Locher knew more about defense organization and management than nearly anybody else. He had a strong background in foreign policy from his time on the SASC, and he had worked in the Pentagon, in Program Analysis and Evaluation in the Office of the Secretary of Defense, for nearly a decade before going to Capitol Hill.

John Tower's nomination to be secretary of defense was defeated in the Senate. President Bush quickly nominated Representative Dick Cheney in his place. After Cheney's confirmation, two influential Republicans wrote on Jim Locher's behalf for the ASD (SOLIC) position. The first was Senator William Cohen. The second, and more influential, was Secretary of the Treasury Nicholas Brady. Brady had served on the Senate Armed Services Committee and knew of Locher's work on Goldwater-Nichols. In a handwritten note, Brady recommended to Dick Cheney that he consider Jim Locher for the ASD (SOLIC) position.

Jim Locher heard nothing from Cheney's transition team until one Friday at 4:30 p.m. when a member of Cheney's staff asked Locher to come to the Pentagon Monday morning for an interview. After his interview, Locher was told by the primary "headhunter" on the team that Locher was the leading candidate for the job. A few weeks later, Locher met with Dick Cheney. The secretary was quite open about his concern over Jim Locher's strong ties to Capitol Hill and the powerful Senate Armed Services Committee. As Locher tells it, "When Secretary Cheney interviewed me for this job [he] said, 'You have more political power than anybody else I've interviewed and I want your assurance that if I make a decision on an issue you won't run to Senator Nunn and have him tell me otherwise.' And I agreed to that. And for the most part we are very loyal here in the Department. . . . the fact that I was from the Hill and had such strong connections to both sides of the aisle in the Armed Services Committees . . . produced a little bit of worry . . . as to how loyal was I going to be."[28]

Cheney asked Locher to take the position of assistant secretary of defense, special operations and low-intensity conflict, during this meeting. Soon after, as is common with most appointees who require confirmation by the Senate, Locher was in the Pentagon as a sort of shadow assistant secretary until his confirmation in October 1989. Jim Locher, because of the depth of his knowledge of the SOF reorganization legislation, assumed office and immediately tried to forge SOLIC into the influential organization he had imagined as he wrote the law. Jim Locher's battles included administrative struggles over increasing the size of his staff to accommodate SOLIC's legislated responsibilities, and working to gain responsibility for those areas such as humanitarian affairs, counterdrug policy, and psychological operations that had been intended to come under the assistant secretary's purview but had been retained by other offices in the Office of the Secretary of Defense.

Locher's most difficult challenges were to establish the relationship between USSOCOM and OASD (SOLIC) and to capture the attention of the secretary and deputy secretary of defense and direct it toward low-intensity conflict. USSOCOM and SOLIC had faced together the continued hostility toward SOF reorganization and worked closely together during the first years of their existence. SOLIC was USSOCOM's best contact in the Pentagon, and it tried to keep the command informed most of the time. But because the command was up and running nearly a year earlier than OASD (SOLIC), and because many in the command were military operators with little experience in the operations of the Pentagon bureaucracy, relationships between the two were deeply strained by Jim Locher's attempt to implement his interpretation of the legislation he had written. The central issue quickly became defining the "oversight" that was the primary duty allocated to the assistant secretary in the 1986 legislation. Many of Locher's ideas were seen by the command as an attack on the authority and responsibility that USSOCOM had been forced to accept and deal with during the previous eighteen months. It would take nearly four and one-half years for relations between USSOCOM and OASD (SOLIC) to become largely amicable and cooperative. The issue of the power relationship between the two has never been fully resolved.

Peacetime Engagement

When Jim Locher came into office, the special operations side of special operations, low-intensity conflict, had received much greater emphasis than the low-intensity conflict side of the house.[29] Unless, he argued, the U.S. government as a whole developed a comprehensive policy toward low-intensity conflict, the nation would be poorly equipped to address the instability in the international security environment, and the resultant threat to American interests, arising from the collapse of the Soviet Union.

Locher was not alone in his concern. Others long involved in the push for SOF reform, especially members of the Special Operations Policy Advisory Group, saw the difficulty the Defense Department, and the executive branch as a whole, was having shifting its attention away from cold war threats. General Meyer had long tried to get the Defense Department to prepare for the most likely conflicts, those at the lower end of the spectrum, including guerrilla wars and terrorism, and along with the reorganization of special operations forces, Meyer argued for a "concept of employment" for SOF. This concept would be part of a larger national policy for low-intensity conflict, encompassing the definition of low-intensity conflict and possible American responses including nonmilitary, political-economic approaches and the use of special operations forces.

The SOPAG had pushed for such a policy during the Reagan administration and believed that Secretary of State George Shultz and Central Intelligence Agency Director William Webster would be supportive if the Defense Department took the lead. The SOPAG had been, however, initially frustrated in its efforts within the Defense Department by Assistant Secretary Richard Armitage. The group's hope was that a change in administration would allow a change in national security focus.

The original intent of many SOF supporters on Capitol Hill, particularly on the Senate side, was a nearly equal emphasis on low-intensity conflict and special operations. Thus the original legislation recommended the formation of an interagency Low-Intensity Conflict Board within the executive branch and the appointment of a special adviser to the president for low-intensity conflict. Both of these recommendations fell to the wayside during the struggles over the establishment of USSOCOM and OASD (SOLIC).

The shift in emphasis toward special operations and away from low-intensity conflict was furthered by USSOCOM's quick start-up in comparison to SOLIC. The responsibility for low-intensity conflict fell to the assistant secretary's office. USSOCOM was responsible for special operations forces. Although these forces would be essential to an American response to low-intensity conflict, they were not the only response needed. The delay in getting SOLIC on its feet put the command in the lead and forced an unintended emphasis on special operations alone.

After taking office, Jim Locher and his staff worked to rectify this imbalance. In July 1991 they sponsored a conference on peacetime engagement. Attendees included representatives from the Office of the Secretary of Defense, the Joint Staff, the military services, the unified four-star commands, doctrinal and educational institutions of the military departments, the U.S. Information Agency (USIA), and the U.S. Agency for International Development (USAID). SOLIC coined the phrase "peacetime engagement" to "designate national security policy for the arena outside of global or major regional war," a term broader than low-intensity conflict that also emphasized the peacetime employment of national security assets. The conference signaled that Locher and his staff were making a legitimate effort to be the assistant secretary of defense, special operations and low-intensity conflict, not just the assistant secretary of defense for USSOCOM.

Using the input from the conference participants, the SOLIC staff wrote a paper, *Peacetime Engagement,* proposing policy guidelines for the U.S. response to potential conflicts, responses ranging from "diplomatic initiatives and humanitarian assistance to shows of force and contingency operations."[30] SOLIC's paper described and evaluated the changing international security environment and proposed a new "security policy for a multipolar world." According to the paper, the primary differences between this new policy and America's cold war approach were an emphasis on selectivity in response, the building of ad hoc coalitions rather than reliance on standing alliances such as NATO, and a continued reliance on forward presence of U.S. military forces but reduced in numbers and duration. In *Peacetime Engagement,* SOLIC provided an illustration of how this new policy might be applied. For example, said the authors, in a country important to the United States threatened with "an ethnically motivated civil war," American diplomacy would first be put to work. "Our country team [within the U.S. embassy], as the overseas representative of all USG [U.S. government] agencies at work in the host nation, would support this diplomatic effort." The U.S. Agency for International Development programs and the International Military Education and Training program would be working together to support negotiations.

If, however, "these efforts were to no avail and hostilities seemed imminent, pre-crisis activities would begin. That might mean stepped-up preparation for a noncombatant evacuation operation (NEO)." Intelligence gathering might also be necessary to support both diplomacy and NEO preparations. Finally, said the authors, "After the civil war had burned itself out or been brought to a negotiated end, USAID and DoD would then work to establish the country's institutions."[31]

SOLIC's *Peacetime Engagement* proposed a national security policy that emphasized early interagency responses to potential crises. The United States faced crises that did not need to escalate to major regional shooting wars. Using diplomacy, humanitarian assistance, and nation-building efforts, SOLIC argued that many crises could be avoided or at least contained to the benefit of the host nation and American national security interests. If military forces were necessary, they could often be used in support of these nonmilitary responses and would most likely be a component of U.S. special operations forces.

Some members of the Defense Department were generally receptive to Jim Locher and SOLIC's proposal when the draft paper was circulated. The OSD offices such as Force Management and Personnel and Program Analysis and Evaluation welcomed the initiatives even if they only pointed out where further study was needed.[32] Notably, the chairman of the Joint Chiefs of Staff, General Colin Powell, became one of the strongest supporters of "peacetime engagement." Other offices in the department, especially the Office of the Under Secretary of Defense (Policy), thoroughly rejected what they perceived as special operators attempting to become the Defense Department's State Department. Jim Locher described the difficulty of making a significant change in Defense Department policy during the Bush administration: "The Bush Administration was not attuned to either SO or LIC. It was very much captured by the old thinking of the Cold War. . . . They did not embrace the LIC mission."[33]

Ultimately, the department as a whole was not ready to leap into heretofore uncharted territory, and the argument by the Office of the Under

Secretary of Defense (Policy) against SOLIC's initiative won out. According to Assistant Secretary Locher:

> [Peacetime engagement] was embraced by General [Colin] Powell and by essentially all of the regional CINCs, by the army, by the Marine Corps, but [Under Secretary of Defense] Paul Wolfowitz was dead set against it. Gen. Powell put [Peacetime Engagement] into the National Military Strategy document and he and Wolfowitz had a knock-'em-down, drag-'em-out and Powell was forced to delete it.[34]

Even now, as evidenced by recent participation in conflicts in Somalia, Haiti, and Bosnia, the U.S. government struggles to develop and implement a coherent post–cold war policy for low-intensity conflict and peacetime engagement. Before the fall of the Berlin Wall, the Office of the Assistant Secretary of Defense, Special Operations and Low-Intensity Conflict, recognized the need for a policy that would cut across federal agency lines. SOLIC must continue to push on this front and work with other defense and national security decisionmakers to consider and develop a logic for the employment of national security assets.

A Special Operator's War—Operation Just Cause

In December 1989 the new special operations organization was combat tested for the first time. Just before midnight on December 19, four SEALs slipped into the waters of the Panama Canal with the mission of attaching two C-4 satchel charges to the hull of the *Presidente Porras*. They worked to sink the armed sixty-five-foot Panamanian naval patrol boat, thus eliminating one of Manuel Noriega's avenues of escape. As they attached the charges, a firefight broke out on shore, and some of the shells exploded dangerously near the swimmers. Using an oxygen rebreathing system that enabled them to remain submerged without surface bubbles, the SEALs began to make their way back to rendezvous with Special Boat Unit 26. It quickly became clear that exploding shells were not the greatest danger the team faced. As described by one of the SEALs, Chris Dye, "A freighter, making its way up the canal, forced us to dive to almost 50 feet to avoid the suction from the propellers. That exposed us to a different kind of threat since pure oxygen can be toxic below a depth of 20 feet. . . . our emphasis on the highest possible physical fitness standards was about to pay off."[35]

The SEALs returned to the surface and swam back to the awaiting boats. Four hours after they had begun their mission, the SEALs returned to Rodman Naval Air Station. As they returned to the base, they heard explosions as the preset timers on the charges reached 1:00 A.M. The *Presidente Porras* sank into the waters of Balboa harbor.

The SEAL operation opened up Operation Just Cause. After several years of increasing tension and conflict with military strongman Manuel Noriega, the U.S. invasion of Panama was intended to "create an environment safe for Americans there, ensure the integrity of the Panama Canal, provide a stable environment for the freely elected [Guillermo] Endara government, and bring [Manuel] Noriega to justice."[36] Just Cause was in many respects a special operations conflict. It was also an initial test of SOF reorganization, particularly joint command and control of special operations forces. Of the 27,000 U.S. troops deployed from seventeen different bases in the United States and Panama, nearly 4,500 were SOF. According to General Carl Stiner, the task force commander for the operation, "Operation *Just Cause* demonstrated the utility of special operations forces as key players across the spectrum of conflict—and demonstrated the ability of special operations forces to work closely with conventional forces to speed the end of conflict—while reducing casualties on both sides."[37] Special Forces, SEALs, special boat units, U.S. Air Force air crews and combat controllers, Rangers, psychological operations and civil affairs units all deployed to Panama.

The United States has been deeply involved in Panama since it became an independent nation in 1903.[38] In fact, it is likely that if the United States had not intervened, Panama could not have declared independence. Less than two weeks after the new government was formed, it signed the Panama Canal treaty with the United States, permitting the Americans to build the canal and maintain control of the zone, surrounding it in perpetuity. The canal was completed and opened on August 15, 1914.

American military forces actually entered Panama before the treaty was signed in 1903 to protect the railroad during the Panamanian conflict with Colombia. In 1915 the U.S. Army established a headquarters in Panama— the Panama Canal Department—and in 1916 moved the command to the red-tile-roofed facility at Quarry Heights that is the headquarters for U.S. Southern Command today. In 1963 the U.S. Southern Command (SOUTHCOM) was established as a unified command including forces from the U.S. Army, U.S. Navy, and U.S. Air Force. From 1975 until Operation Just Cause, the number of American troops in Panama averaged about 10,000.[39]

Arnulfo Arias, fascist and populist, became president of Panama in 1940.

He remained president until 1968, when he was overthrown by members of the Panamanian military. One of the coup leaders in 1968 was Colonel Omar Torrijos, commander of the Guardia Nacional, assisted by then-captain Manuel Noriega. Torrijos led the military junta until he was killed in an airplane crash in 1981.

Noriega quickly consolidated power following Torrijos's death. In 1982 Noriega promoted himself to brigadier as the new commander of the Guardia. Nicolas Ardito Barletta, sponsored by Noriega and his ally Lieutenant Colonel Roberto Diaz Herrara, became president in May 1982. Despite a clearly fraudulent election, the Reagan administration believed Noriega was valuable in its fight against the communist government in Nicaragua and accepted the results.[40]

Over the next several years, Noriega strengthened his nearly absolute control of Panama and, consequently, the power of the renamed Panamanian Defense Forces (PDF). Owing to instability in Central America and growing American attention to drug trafficking from Latin America, the Reagan administration chose to ignore reports of brutality and corruption in the PDF, much of it traced back to Noriega. Congress was the first to withdraw its support from the Panamanian government in the mid-1980s. By late 1987, even the Reagan administration began to pull back from Noriega following his brutal suppression of demonstrators protesting Noriega's tie to the murder of Panamanian national hero Hugo Spadafora. Following protests by the American government, Noriega declared a state of emergency, revoked civil liberties guaranteed by the Panamanian constitution, and began a program of deliberate harassment by the PDF of American military personnel.

On June 6, 1987, General Frederick Woerner assumed command of USSOUTHCOM. Woerner had spent much of his career in Latin America, serving in Colombia, Guatemala, Uruguay, and Panama. He spoke Spanish fluently and had devoted much of his education to studying Latin American issues. Woerner spent much of the next two years struggling to respond to the crisis in Panama.

Noriega's harassment of Americans in Panama increased dramatically from 1987 to 1989. From early 1988 through the end of February 1989 more than one thousand incidents were reported. The incidents quickly escalated in severity. In February 1988 the PDF arrested thirty-three Americans for wearing their uniforms in public, a right allowed by the Panama Canal Treaty. In June, a PDF officer assaulted an American soldier and his wife at gunpoint, forced the soldier into the trunk of his car, and raped the soldier's wife. In February 1989 a U.S. Navy civilian employee was detained and beaten, and in March 1989, six American school buses loaded with children were detained for several hours while PDF members waved automatic weapons at the children. Besides harassment, there were several small attacks on U.S. facilities in the Panama Canal Zone.[41]

General Woerner was faced with a situation that had not been previously imagined by any of SOUTHCOM's contingency plans: Panamanian Defense Forces as the enemy. Despite declarations by President Reagan that there would be no use of force by the United States in Panama, in November 1987, Woerner directed his director of operations and plans, Brigadier General Marc Cisneros, to revise SOUTHCOM's contingency plans to include the reality of the new situation in Panama. The eventual package of combat and postconflict plans was referred to as Prayer Book, with the actual combat plans known as Blue Spoon. For most of the next two years there would be a tug-of-war between SOUTHCOM, especially the command's army component, and the XVIII Airborne Corps over the plans themselves and control over a likely combat operation. Woerner's plans called for a slow buildup of units from the 7th Infantry Division (Light), the 193rd Infantry Brigade located in Panama, the Marine Expeditionary Unit, and the 82nd Airborne Division. The planners included special operations, consulting periodically with General James Lindsay and the new Special Operations Command. One of the most controversial elements of the plan offered by SOUTHCOM was its willingness to look beyond combat operations to stability and civil affairs operations required once the fighting was over. SOUTHCOM was unable to provide the specifics of these operations, but General Woerner firmly believed that only a comprehensive approach to the conflict would provide lasting stability in Panama.

By early 1988, the United States had given up on Manuel Noriega. In February, two Florida grand juries indicted Noriega on drug trafficking charges. In March, U.S. Army Military Police units were sent to Panama to further secure U.S. installations, and on April 8, 1988, President Reagan invoked formal sanctions against the Panamanian government.

Although the Reagan administration put Panama aside during the 1988 presidential election, General Woerner continued his crusade for a comprehensive Latin American policy and in February 1989 publicly criticized American policy in Panama, infuriating the new president, George Bush. Unfortunately for Woerner, the Bush administration had decided to wait until after the May 1989 national elections in Panama before taking action.

Not surprisingly, the elections were disastrous. Despite desperate and blatant attempts by Noriega and the PDF to fix the election, opposition presidential candidate Guillermo Endara was elected, along with his vice presidential running mates, Ricardo Arias Calderon and Guillermo "Billy" Ford. At an opposition rally following the election, PDF riot forces shot and killed Ford's bodyguard in full view of international television cameras. Reacting to reports by a congressional delegation led by Senator John McCain, President Bush recalled the American ambassador and ordered 1,800 more soldiers and marines to Panama, where they began a series of intimidation games with the PDF as part of Operation Nimrod Dancer. Bush's support of his commander, General Woerner, declined further. In mid-July, Woerner was told by Army Chief of Staff Carl Vuono that it would be best to resign.

Woerner was replaced by General Maxwell Thurman. Thurman's previous combat command had been years earlier as the divisional artillery commander for the 82nd Airborne Division. General Thurman had built his reputation from his service as the director of program analysis and evaluation on the army staff, the commander of the U.S. Army's Recruiting Command (where he came up with the slogan, "Be All You Can Be"), the deputy chief of staff for personnel, and the vice chief of staff of the army. After serving as vice chief of staff, Thurman had defied convention and, rather than retiring, continued his military service as commander of the U.S. Army's Training and Doctrine Command at Fort Monroe, Virginia. He was planning to retire in the fall of 1989 when he was asked to accept the U.S. Southern Command by General Carl Vuono.

General Thurman did not regard himself as a "warfighter" and had no expectation of running any war in Panama. At his change of command ceremony at Fort Monroe in August 1989, Thurman approached his old friend Lieutenant General Carl Stiner, who had become the commander of the XVIII Airborne Corps the previous October. Thurman told Stiner that only he could successfully command the operation in Panama. As told by General Stiner, Thurman declared, "I'm going to hold you responsible for putting together the plan and all the fighting. You do it the way you think it needs to be done."[42]

Thurman's order resolved the two-year-old conflict between SOUTHCOM and the XVIII Airborne Corps over whose plan would be followed and who would command the operation. For the first time, and as a result of the Goldwater-Nichols reorganization, Stiner was given command over all conventional and special operations forces that would take part in the operation. The decision allowed special operations forces to be fully integrated into the planning itself and created the unity of command that had been missing from Grenada.

In many ways, few officers would have been more capable of commanding the operation in Panama. General Stiner was one of the very few senior officers in the U.S. Army who had extensive experience in commanding both conventional and special operations organizations. This knowledge encouraged and allowed him to work closely with special operations forces in thoroughly integrating them into the planning and execution of Just Cause. Stiner was viewed by many in the military as a soldier's soldier. With his Tennessee drawl he could quickly shift from charming gentleman to a combat commander with language to match. Stiner would later become the second commander of USSOCOM and play a major role in the maturation of SOF.

As part of the planning process, forces participating in the American operation in Panama were divided into several task forces subordinate to Joint Task Force South commanded by Lieutenant General Stiner. Task forces included Task Force Semper Fi, composed of marines, some of whom were already deployed to Panama; Task Force Bayonet, including the 193rd Infantry Brigade already in Panama; Task Force Atlantic, from the 7th Infantry Division (Light), and Task Force Aviation, made up tactical aviation units, largely from the 7th and 82nd divisions. The remainder of the 82nd Airborne Division and the 7th Infantry Division reported directly to Stiner as the Joint Task Force commander.

Special operations forces made up a separate but equal task force, Joint Special Operations Task Force, commanded by Major General Wayne Downing. Downing's forces included the 75th Ranger Regiment; the 7th Special Forces Group that had one battalion already deployed in Panama; SEAL Teams 2 and 4, Special Boat Unit 26 and Naval Special Warfare Unit 8 already deployed in Panama, and the navy special mission unit; and members of Special Forces Operational Detachment-D, or Delta Force. The 4th Psychological Operations Group and the 96th Civil Affairs Battalion reported directly to JTF-South and Stiner rather than to Major General Downing.[43]

Carl Stiner and his staff reworked the Prayer Book plans, developing operations that could be executed with only a few hours' warning, fourteen to sixteen hours' warning, and, the preferred option, a full deployment with forty-eight hours of warning. Stiner's plan emphasized quick and overwhelming force directed at decapitating Noriega's PDF. Particular attention, as a result of the chaos of Urgent Fury, was given to detailed scheduling of all operations and task force-wide command, control, and communications. In approving Stiner's plan, General Thurman set the ground rules: the operation would be a failure if the wives or children of any of the American military were killed when they were on an American installation in Panama or if any part of the Panama Canal system were destroyed or disabled.[44]

Rehearsals for the invasion following the reworked plans began soon after Stiner took charge. "Freedom of movement" exercises, which closely followed portions of the actual plan, enabled forces in Panama to rehearse and become fully familiar with the terrain surrounding routes they would take as part of the operation. To maintain operational security, the forces participating in the rehearsals were not told of their true intent until a few hours before the actual assault began.[45]

In December 1989, only days before the U.S. invasion, an unusually large exercise was conducted at Hurlburt Field in Florida. Special operations forces and conventional forces, including AC-130 gunships flown back from Panama, combined to jump into and attack targets in the surrounding area at night. Days after the completion of the exercise, the aircrews were called back to duty and deployed to Panama.[46]

As Stiner and his staff worked to finalize and gain approval for their plan, Manuel Noriega did his best to ensure that an American invasion was inevitable. In September 1988, four months after overturning the election results, Noriega installed Francisco Rodriguez as president. The Rodriguez government was not recognized by the United States. In October the PDF's chief of security informed SOUTHCOM that he was going to instigate a coup. General Thurman believed that the coup attempt was poorly planned, and the motivations of its leaders were suspect. The coup collapsed quickly, but it provided useful information on Noriega's response to hostility when he called upon the men of the Machos del Monte, or the 7th Infantry Brigade, and Battalion 2000, Noriega's most elite and loyal troops, to rescue him after his arrest by the coup leaders. The blocking of both of these units from reinforcing Noriega became missions critical to the success of Just Cause.

Events moved quickly in the weeks following the coup. On December 15 Manuel Noriega made his defiance of the United States official when he announced to his national assembly that a state of war existed between Panama and the United States. The following day, an off-duty marine lieutenant was shot and killed by PDF soldiers after he drove through a PDF roadblock. An American navy lieutenant and his wife who witnessed the shooting were detained thirty minutes later by the same troops. The officer was beaten and his wife threatened with sexual assault. Noriega had managed to trigger the invasion at the moment when all planning was complete and troops were fresh from extensive briefings and exercises.

The following day, President Bush declared "enough" and set Stiner's full deployment plan in motion, with an H-hour of 1:00 A.M. on December 20.

Not long after the SEALs entered the canal near Balboa harbor to block Noriega's potential escape, aircraft filled the sky between the United States and Panama. It was one minute past midnight on December 20. Later that morning, 185 fixed-wing and 173 rotary-wing aircraft operated by pilots wearing night vision goggles would fill an area in the sky 140 by 45 kilometers wide. Conducting the assaults at night increased the possibility of tactical surprise and reduced the effectiveness of any PDF air defense weapons. One of the aircraft, a modified C-130, held the Joint Task Force South battle staff in the Airborne Command and Control Center. The assault units were tied together via the Secure Enroute Communications System (SECOMPS), and all elements were using Tactical Satellite Communications (TACSAT) with aircraft hatch-mount antennas. Furthermore, dedicated communications liaison officers were assigned to many units to assist with command and control. As a result, the assault units could receive real-time intelligence from ground elements and situation updates from in-country units. The incoming aircraft were also able to report the delays they had suffered upon leaving Fort Bragg because of a severe ice storm that hit the post earlier that evening.[47]

One critical piece of information passed through the communications network thirty minutes before the simultaneous assault on twenty-seven targets was to begin. General Stiner had been notified that operational security had failed in the final minutes before the operation. Panamanian radio was announcing that the invasion was expected at 1:00 A.M. Not long before 12:30 A.M., Stiner, hoping to maintain some element of surprise, moved H-hour to 12:45 for those units already in Panama.

The changing of H-hour greatly increased the already intense pressure on Major Kevin Higgins and A Company from the 3rd Battalion of the 7th Special Forces Group. Higgins and his twenty-two Special Forces team members and one Air Force combat controller had the mission of securing the bridge across the Pacora River in order to prevent members of the powerful Battalion 2000 from crossing and coming to Noriega's rescue in Panama City once the invasion began. As they readied to load the two MH-60 helicopters and one UH-60 Blackhawk, the special operators and their helicopters were fired upon by a group of Panamanians on the other side of the airfield fence. While waiting for base security forces to put an end to the attack, Higgins received the message that H-hour was now at 12:45, and a convoy of Panamanian vehicles was heading from the direction of Battalion 2000's home at Fort Cimarron toward the bridge.

The news caused great concern because it looked as though the PDF convoy would arrive at the bridge just at H-hour. Estimated flight time was twenty-five minutes, and Higgins received the message at 12:30 A.M. The Special Forces team quickly loaded the helicopters and were told by their commander to expect a hot landing zone. The pilots, aware of the dangers of deviating from the flight plan because of the crowded skies, changed their route nonetheless and arrived over the bridge just as headlights from eight vehicles could be seen coming down the road. The team members leaped from the helicopters and scrambled up a small hill, firing into the lead vehicle with AT-4 and LAW antiarmor weapons. Although none of the rockets ignited the vehicles, the explosion of the munitions caused the convoy to stop several times. Moving to cover, the combat controller called in an AC-130 Spectre gunship, which riddled the convoy with its 40mm Bofors and 20mm Vulcan cannons. Three trucks pulled away, and the rest were destroyed. As the PDF soldiers fled from the vehicles, they fired on the American positions, and the AC-130 continued to put down suppressive fire as well as report on the PDF's movements. Higgins and his team had held the bridge and blocked the PDF unit. They continued to hold the bridge throughout the night with support from the AC-130 crew until they were relieved at 6:00 A.M. by a forty-five-man quick-reaction force from A Company.

Besides having to disable the patrol boat, the SEALs were given several other missions as part of Just Cause. Members of the SEAL special mission unit worked with Delta Force personnel in an attempt to track down Manuel Noriega. An element of SEAL Team 2 raided several islands that were believed to be home to PDF units, but they were abandoned by the time the SEALs arrived. The most controversial SEAL mission, and perhaps the most controversial of any of the special operations in Just Cause, was SEAL Team 4's denying use of Paitilla airfield by disabling the parked aircraft to block the runway and prevent Noriega's escape.[48]

The number of PDF soldiers at the airfield was uncertain but expected to be between twenty and forty men. The SEALs, using small boats and swimming, approached their target from the water. During the course of the operation, the SEALs were detected by the opposing force and were ambushed as they approached the buildings at the far end of the runway. In the ensuing fight four SEALs were killed and eight wounded, the heaviest losses a SEAL unit had ever taken during a single operation.

After the Paitilla airfield operation, the SEAL community made its criticisms of the operation well known. All aspects of the operation were criticized, but the loudest complaint was that this was not a SEAL mission.

To some extent, this criticism is irrelevant. The SEALs had accepted the mission and had trained several months in preparation. The actual operation entailed only relatively minor changes to their established plan. The advantage of using SEALs was that they could approach from the water undetected. One disadvantage is that, because of the anticipated resistance, the SEALs worked in a much larger unit, three platoons, than most SEAL operations. More important, because they approached from the sea they were forced to proceed up nearly three-quarters of a mile of runway with little cover. SEALs are trained to operate in small teams, using cover to mask their approach and escape. Whether it was an appropriate mission or not, brave men died in accomplishing it. Their deaths might not have been necessary if a larger force, perhaps the Rangers or a conventional brigade, had conducted the raid. The Paitilla airfield operation again underscores the dependence of SOF on accurate intelligence and the difficulty of obtaining the necessary information.[49]

The three battalions of the 75th Ranger Regiment were given the classic Ranger mission of assaulting and securing three major airfields in Panama. They had been rehearsing at mock-ups built in Florida for the three weeks before the invasion. First Battalion (1/75th) and C Company of the 3rd Battalion (C/3/75th), designated Task Force Red Tango, were to parachute into Torrijos-Tocumen airfields on the far side of the Pan American Highway from Panama City. There were two airfields at Torrijos-Tocumen. The civilian airfield was Torrijos International Airport, while its twin, Tocumen airfield, was the home of the PDF's 2nd Infantry Company. The Rangers were to jump into Torrijos-Tocumen and secure it before the 82nd Airborne Division's airborne assault scheduled for forty-five minutes later. The assault was scheduled to allow for the passengers from the last commercial flight of the day into Torrijos International Airport, a Brazilian aircraft, to pick up their baggage and leave the terminal.

At 6 P.M. on December 19, the troops of Task Force Red Tango lifted off from Hunter Army Airfield, outside of Savannah, Georgia. Seven hours later, an AC-130, and two AH-6 Little Bird helicopters from the 160th Special Operations Aviation Regiment (the Night Stalkers), destroyed PDF air defense and machine gun positions and the control tower, then opened fire on the barracks of the PDF's 2nd Infantry Company. Three minutes later, the C-141 and C-130 transport aircraft carrying the Rangers arrived over the airfield and four companies of Rangers jumped out from 500 feet. The Rangers, receiving sporadic fire while parachuting, immediately ran into a firefight. Although the Rangers quickly eliminated PDF resistance, an American medic was killed by Panamanian fire, the only U.S. fatality during the Rangers' assault on Torrijos-Tocumen.

Tocumen airfield was secured quickly, but Torrijos airport was to take slightly longer. It was up to C Company from the 3rd Battalion to clear and seize the main terminal. Fortunately, members of the 96th Civil Affairs battalion, who had excellent Spanish language skills and good knowledge of Panamanian culture, jumped in with the Rangers. These special operators were able to convince a group of firemen who were attempting to escape to surrender without a fight. Once U.S. forces were in the terminal, pockets of PDF soldiers were discovered and captured.

As they moved through the terminal, the Rangers and civil affairs team members were surprised to find a mob of several hundred civilians terrified by the shooting and the fires that were beginning to erupt throughout the building. Some of the Rangers gathered up the passengers and escorted them outside. Inside, the remaining Rangers discovered nine PDF soldiers holding twenty passengers hostage in the baggage room. The civil affairs team negotiated with the PDF soldiers and after two and a half hours convinced them to release the hostages with no casualties on either side.

At 2:40 A.M., the 82nd Airborne Division forces jumped in. Both airfields were declared fully secure at 6:00 A.M. No civilians had been injured in the action, thirteen members of the PDF were killed and thirty-four captured, while the Rangers lost one man, had five wounded in the fighting, and nineteen jump injuries.

A and B Companies of 3rd Battalion and two companies from 2nd Battalion were met by small arms and air defense fire when they jumped into Rio Hato airfield west of Panama City. Rio Hato was a large installation with three barrack areas and a 10,000-foot airstrip. It was the home of two of the PDF's best units, the 6th and 7th Infantry Companies. The 7th Infantry Company was of particular concern. Members referred to themselves as the Machos de Monte, or Mountain Men. The 7th had been one of the two units to come to Noriega's aid during the October coup attempt. The Rangers faced the additional complication of Rio Hato being the home to hundreds of teenage NCO recruits and the noncombatant staff of a dispensary.

Because of the size of the base and the opposing force, Stiner's planners elected to use two F-117 Stealth fighter bombers to each drop a 2,000 pound bomb 200 yards from the barracks in the hopes of stunning the soldiers inside without destroying the barracks and killing the soldiers. At 1:00 A.M. the F-117s dropped their bombs. The pilots had strict orders not to destroy the barracks and did not have a fixed aiming point. Instead, they had to measure the distance from their "non-target." The PDF soldiers had been warned of the impending attack on Rio Hato and were already manning their weapons as the bombs were dropped.

Despite their forewarning, the men of the 6th and 7th were pummeled by the AC-130s, AH-6s, and AH-64 attack helicopters that covered the area with devastating fire for ninety seconds. Although eleven of the thirteen Ranger transport aircraft were hit by ground fire, all but one Ranger were able to jump. The jump was made more treacherous since the terrain surrounding the airfield was rough and studded with utility poles and trees. Many of the Rangers were hung up, including Colonel William Kernan, the commander of the 75th Ranger Regiment. The Rangers met PDF resistance throughout the airfield, and even as the PDF soldiers retreated they ambushed pursuing Rangers. Because of the strength of the PDF resistance, Colonel Kernan delayed the arrival of follow-on units until enemy resistance was suppressed, but by morning the airfield was secure. The Rangers killed 34 PDF soldiers and captured between 250 and 362 prisoners.[50]

A rarely discussed use of special operations forces in Panama was the assignment of loudspeaker teams from the 4th Psychological Operations Group to conventional units. The loudspeaker teams were used to reduce resistance from the PDF, later in the operation offering "money for weapons," and to assist in controlling the civilian crowds. As an example of these operations, a PSYOP team supported the 1st Battalion, 508th Infantry securing Fort Amador, an installation shared by American and PDF soldiers. Concerned about operational security, the Joint Task Force commanders had not evacuated American dependents before the attack. To avoid injuring American dependents, and in recognition of the rules of engagement for Just Cause that required minimizing enemy casualties and physical damage, the infantry battalion called upon the loudspeaker teams. The infantry soldiers first sealed off the PDF area within Fort Amador and ensured that the American dependents were safe. Soon after dawn, the American forces moved to secure the PDF area, attempting to persuade the PDF to surrender through the loudspeaker teams. Eventually, the PDF soldiers were warned that "resistance was hopeless in the face of overwhelming firepower." The warning was followed by a series of "demonstrations" with the American unit firing its weapons, escalating from small arms to 105mm howitzer rounds. When once again the loudspeaker team offered the PDF the "opportunity" to surrender, the Panamanian soldiers surrendered their arms and gave up with no casualties on either side.[51]

Special operators contributed to several operations in Panama City. Two AH-6 Little Bird helicopters and an AC-130 and their crews led the assault against Noriega and the PDF's headquarters, the Comandancia. After clearing snipers from the high rise within the compound, the lead helicopter was shot down. Both crew members survived and made their way to cover. The AH-6s were followed by Spectre gunships and Apache helicopters. The compound was taken by members of the 193rd Infantry Brigade, supported by Sheridan tanks of the only U.S. airborne armor unit, from the 82nd Airborne Division. Later that day, C Company from the 3rd Ranger Battalion, already exhausted from its assault on Torrijos-Tocumen airfields, cleared the Comandancia and Modelo Prison in search of PDF holdouts.

The final D-Day operation by special operations forces has never been admitted by the Department of Defense but is referred to in several sources on Operation Just Cause, particularly a June 1990 article by Neil C. Livingstone that appeared in *Washingtonian* magazine and was recommended by several special operators. The story tells of the dramatic and successful rescue of an American citizen, Kurt Muse, who had been arrested by the PDF after making illegal broadcasts designed to harass the Panamanian security forces and to provide mass communication for Noriega's opponents. Calling the broadcast Radio la Voz de la Libertad, Muse and his confederates kept the broadcasts going for more than a year before Muse was arrested on April 5, 1989, after he had returned to Panama from a brief trip to Miami.

Following interrogation by the Departamento Nacional de Investigacion (DENI), Panama's internal security investigators, Muse was placed first in a DENI facility, where he witnessed and heard the beating and torturing of several other prisoners. He was later moved to Modelo Prison, across the street from the Comandancia. Muse was allowed occasional visits by American embassy officials and physical examinations by a U.S. Air Force doctor. Following the coup in October, Muse was able to hear the interrogation and torturing of the rebellious officers.

In the days following the killing of the marine lieutenant by PDF soldiers, the security around Muse increased even further. On December 19, Muse's guard made it clear that if the United States invaded Panama, Kurt Muse would be the first to die. At 12:45 A.M. on December 20, Muse was awakened abruptly by sounds of machine-gun fire and people running down the hallway. Throwing himself to the floor, Muse heard the rockets and guns of an AC-130 Spectre gunship tearing into the Comandancia walls. The prison's lights were out and explosions in the hallway blew debris into Muse's cell. As told by Muse, "This apparition comes to my cell door. The guy looks like Darth Vader. He's wearing a funny-looking helmet, funny-looking goggles, funny-looking uniform, and has a funny-looking weapon."[52]

The apparition, according to the *Washingtonian* article, was a member of Special Forces Operational Detachment-D who, after blowing open the cell door, put a flak vest and helmet on Muse, took him down the corridor past several bodies, onto the roof and into a small Hughes D-500 helicopter with several other members of Delta. The helicopter was hit just as it lifted off the roof and the pilot was forced to "drive" it down the street, hoping to find a place to take off again. The helicopter was hit again, this time by fire from the Comandancia and crashed thirty feet to the ground. Muse and the soldiers from Delta escaped between the buildings until they were spotted by a Blackhawk helicopter and recovered by armored personnel carriers. Four of the Delta members were severely wounded, one with a critical chest wound, but all survived.

Most of the twenty-seven targets of the American invasion force were secure by the morning of December 20. Noriega surrendered from his refuge in the Papal Nunciature at Punta Paitilla soon after the combat ended. Within twenty-four hours after combat began, the American forces were faced with a new problem: rebuilding Panama as a nation. Although the importance of planning for operations in Panama once the fighting stopped had been anticipated by General Woerner, Generals Thurman and Stiner focused their attention on a quick and effective combat operation. The USSOUTHCOM staff was caught somewhat flatfooted when faced with the large-scale civil affairs and policing operations necessary at the conclusion of Just Cause. American forces had to shift from combat operations to civil-military operations, with some units becoming responsible for running major cities and towns, rebuilding local infrastructure, distributing food, and reestablishing law and order. Fires were burning throughout Panama City, believed by Carl Stiner to have been set by the PDF as it retreated, which added to a rapidly growing refugee problem. There still remained the problem of rounding up remnants of the PDF scattered throughout Panama City and the countryside. Fortunately, the American troops quickly made up lost ground, largely through the quick response and flexibility of special operations forces, particularly Special Forces, civil affairs, and psychological operations units. The civil affairs team translated, served as a liaison between American forces and local civil government, assisted commanders in taking care of refugees, and conducted assessments to determine where help was most urgently needed. Special Forces worked with U.S. Army units as liaisons with Panamanian military and civilians. PSYOP teams deployed loudspeaker teams and spread the word of American intentions and assistance. The importance of SOF in support of American combat operations and in the rebuilding effort that followed was even noted as a major lesson learned in an army study evaluating the conflict. This rebuilding operation was named Operation Promote Liberty on January 12, 1990.

Operation Promote Liberty

One of the most successful special operations in the days following the invasion demonstrated the ability of SOF to lower the level of violence in a conflict. After the success of the initial invasion, several large PDF garrisons remained throughout the country. An ad hoc Special Forces unit was organized to support a battalion from the 7th Infantry Division (Light), a Ranger unit, and an AC-130 gunship and their mission of rounding up PDF. The garrison towns were isolated and communications from PDF headquarters had been cut off. The soldiers inside were still armed and had to be convinced to surrender or taken by force. The question was how the American forces were going to get these PDF soldiers under control.

Members of the 3rd Battalion of the 7th Special Forces Group were assigned to the ad hoc unit. According to the command sergeant major for the unit, "The mission was for the Rangers and the 7th Infantry Division to go in and take these towns. Well, we volunteered to go ahead of them and prevent this from happening." The Special Forces soldiers came up with a plan referred to as the "Ma Bell Take Downs." A member of the Special Forces team would find a working telephone outside of the garrison and call the leader of the PDF unit inside while the AC-130 circled overhead. As described by the commander of the 7th SFG, "We'd call them on the phone and say, 'Look up. See the C-130? You can surrender to us, or they can blow you up. What would you like to have happen?'"[53] The Panamanian forces were given five minutes to decide, and every PDF unit in the six or seven towns visited by the Americans surrendered.[54]

Just Cause was declared complete on January 12, 1990. Operation Promote Liberty continued for the next year. The two most striking changes in the role of special operations forces in Just Cause compared with those in Operation Urgent Fury in Grenada were the joint command and control of SOF throughout and the Joint Task Force South's integration of SOF with the conventional forces. Overall the operational planners assigned special operations teams missions appropriate to their capabilities, with the possible exception of the SEAL operation at Paitilla airfield. At least partially as a result of increased coordination and integration, special operations forces had a substantial impact on the outcome of the conflict—particularly by reducing casualties on both sides. As described in a study conducted by the U.S. Army following Just Cause, "SOF/Conventional coordination and operations were common during *Just Cause*. Command relationships were not always precise, yet elements understood the intent and worked as a team to accomplish the mission."[55] In many instances, SOF units formed the nucleus of the operational element. Their specialty skills and ability to work with the local population were advantageous and were reinforced with conventional infantry acting in direct support or on standby as a quick reaction force. Civil affairs teams accompanied the lead elements of all initial combat assaults by army forces. The teams were usually attached to the maneuver battalions and served largely as advisers to the commanders in conducting civil–military operations. The teams had particular success acting as liaisons between the conventional unit and the local population.

Much of the impact of SOF in the outcome of the conflict in Panama came as part of a mission not initially considered by conventional planners: the rebuilding operations that were Promote Liberty. Special operations forces, particularly PSYOP and civil affairs units, were crucial in the reestablishment of the new Panamanian government. They were able to make the transition quickly from combat to rebuilding Panama by training the new Panamanian police force, restoring public facilities and services, and controlling and assisting refugees. As Just Cause ended and Promote Liberty gained momentum, conventional planners saw the need for planning for an American role in a conflict after the combat ended. Conventional planners and commanders also saw the critical role of SOF in carrying out these operations. After nearly a decade of attempting to reform and reorganize American special operations forces, progress had been made. Panama was proof that special operations forces were effective both as force multipliers and in reducing casualties on both sides. These lessons, even though imperfectly learned, would be applied in the next conflict faced by the U.S. military: the Persian Gulf.

9

Who's in Charge?

There is this continued undercurrent [in the Defense Department] with regard to resources that will destroy USSOCOM. [If the command has] to go [to Congress] every time and fight the resource problem . . . to reverse those resource decisions [taken by the Defense Department], the command will never succeed.

General Edward C. "Shy" Meyer, July 1988

As the U.S. Special Operations Command (USSOCOM) entered its second year of existence and the Office of the Assistant Secretary of Defense, Special Operations and Low-Intensity Conflict, welcomed its first confirmed assistant secretary in the summer of 1988, there was genuine fear in the SOF community, a belief that, despite the specificity of the law, the continued existence of these new special operations organizations and the rebuilding of the U.S. special operations capability were in no way guaranteed.

The Fight to Control Resources

The uncertainty over the future of SOF increased with the death of the oldest and most influential ally of special operations on Capitol Hill—Representative Dan Daniel. Daniel died of a heart attack in the spring of 1988. With his death, U.S. special operations forces and their supporters lost a man for whom a strong special operations capability was a central concern. A senior member of the House of Representatives, Daniel had had many friends, was widely respected, and could call in many IOUs. With Daniel's death, the feeling grew that what had been a very strong coalition was breaking up. Courting of the new administration and continued monitoring by Congress would be of great importance.[1]

This sense of unease among SOF advocates was palpable in interviews at the time. In July 1988 Sam Wilson warned, "I'm not sure, today, that they [Congress] understand the extent to which the whole business is being slow rolled within the Department of Defense. There are some very strong indications of increasing resistance—almost defiance—on the part of people in positions of considerable authority within Defense who have taken the position, as one of them is quoted, 'If we can hang out a couple of years, we'll get this legislation reversed.' "[2]

Wilson's concern in 1988 arose because of the absence of an assistant secretary of defense, special operations and low-intensity conflict (ASD [SOLIC]), and the inability of SOF to gain the control over its fiscal and manpower resources directed by Congress. General "Shy" Meyer continued the warning that introduced this chapter, "The next big battle is [Major Force] Program 11. . . . If you lose Program 11, you've lost the war. . . . I don't believe USSOCOM can ever be what it was intended to be if it loses Program 11. . . . [Senator] Sam Nunn is starting to fall off on that issue, and I've got to go back over and work on him. He says he's getting pressed by all the other people who say you really don't need to have special funding responsibility."[3]

Meyer and Wilson shared the fears of those members of the SOF community who understood that the key to power in the Defense Department, as is true in other government agencies, is in controlling resources. That is why Dan Daniel and Ted Lunger insisted on a "CINC with a checkbook" for special operations. Without this control, the needs of special operations forces would continue to slide "below the thin red line that separates those things approved for this year's list and those things simply carried forth into the future."[4] The legislation, perhaps because it was using the language of law rather than of Defense Department resource management, was far less clear on what it meant for SOF to control its own resources or what this checkbook entailed. Because of this ambiguity and the potential need for a substantial change in how the department managed its resources, this aspect of implementing SOF reorganization was the most critical and the most difficult element of rebuilding U.S. special operations forces.

Outsiders also made the point that USSOCOM and the Office of the Assistant Secretary of Defense needed to gain full control of SOF resource management and acquisition responsibilities if the rebuilding of an American special operations capability were to have staying power. An August 1988 Logistics Management Institute study (contracted by the Department of Defense), "The Next Step for Special Operations: Getting the Resources to

Do the Job," concluded that neither USSOCOM nor SOLIC had "sufficient authority to control the development of MFP-11 [Major Force Program 11] or the allocation of resources to special operations forces." The Office of the Assistant Secretary of Defense, Special Operations and Low-Intensity Conflict, said the study needed to develop policies and guidance that the secretary of defense would issue, giving USSOCOM the following authority:

— To plan all requirements necessary for a balanced, integrated special operations capability and prepare and justify to the Office of the Secretary of Defense (OSD) a Program Objective Memorandum (POM) for MFP-11;

— To prepare and control execution of a budget for research, development, and acquisition; [and]

—To create an acquisition organization within USSOCOM.[5]

The SOF community was facing a serious challenge in taking on the responsibilities legislated by Congress. The transition from an operational orientation to responsibility for running the new, servicelike organizations presented difficulties. The Office of the Assistant Secretary of Defense, Special Operations and Low-Intensity Conflict in the summer of 1988 was just welcoming its first confirmed assistant secretary, was understaffed, and had only begun to get organized. Furthermore, while the legislation gave the commander in chief of the U.S. Special Operations Command his own checkbook, USSOCOM's commander and staff were having difficulties viewing USSOCOM as something other than a "warfighting," or at least a "supporting," commander in chief (CINC). The command put most of its initial organizational efforts into building large operational (J-3) and intelligence (J-2) sections and paid much less attention to the organization's resource management functions. The command's operational orientation in its early years is understandable, given the background of General James Lindsay and his staff and the events in Panama during 1989 that ended with Operation Just Cause. Equally important, USSOCOM's tendency to think and act more like a "warfighting CINC" than a servicelike organization was encouraged by Department of Defense actions. The military services were slow in allowing USSOCOM to assume complete program and budget responsibilities, those responsibilities that characterize an independent military department or defense agency. The services were receiving support for their reluctance from much of the secretary of defense's staff, especially the offices responsible for managing Department of Defense financial resources: the Office of the Assistant Secretary of Defense (Program Analysis and Evaluation) and the Office of the Comptroller.

The Department of Defense

The debate over the who, and how, of the control of special operations resources was critical to the success and survival of the reorganization of U.S. special operations forces. To appreciate that debate, the resource decisionmaking process in the Department of Defense must be understood. If one does not understand how money is controlled and allocated, one can not understand how most major defense policy decisions are made. Basically, funding decisions determine which aircraft, tanks, and ships are purchased. Funding decisions determine which types of forces and equipment of which military service will be emphasized during the next ten to twenty years. Funding decisions affect the size and quality of each of the services, paying for soldiers, sailors, marines, and airmen (including special operators) and their training.

The importance to special operations of formal control over resources during the Defense Department allocation process is illustrated in the earlier discussion of SOF aviation and Initiative 17. Although Congress specifically authorized funding for the procurement and upgrade of SOF aircraft, because the U.S. Air Force had control of these resources it was able to declare support for the congressional action and then "reprogram" the funds into other programs the air force's leadership believed to be of higher priority than SOF.

Three hundred billion dollars, the approximate annual budget of the Department of Defense in the late 1980s, cannot be allocated by "shooting from the hip" as in smaller government agencies.[6] Resource decisions in the Department of Defense are nearly always made as a part of the planning, programming, and budgeting system (PPBS). This approach to decisionmaking was developed in the 1960s by Charles Hitch and Alain Enthoven, who worked for Secretary of Defense Robert McNamara, as part of a logical and rational "cost-benefit" method of allocating defense assets. The system was initially implemented by the "Whiz Kids" in systems analysis within the Office of the Secretary of Defense.[7] By the early 1970s, each military service had begun to develop its own cost-benefit analytic group to counter the strength of the OSD analysts. As it evolved, PPBS facilitated comparisons across common resource categories, but different measuring methods were used in each service. For example, the U.S. Army's "decision packages" allowed decisionmakers to see something closer to the true cost of a weapon system, including initial procurement, operation and maintenance, manning, and training costs. A similar process, with different terminology, occurs in the other services.

The fight for control over SOF resources centered on the programming and budgeting phases of PPBS. In these phases, the Defense Department's fiscal resources are allocated, and most of the department's major decisions about its future are made. In the several years following the passage of the first special operations reorganization legislation, Congress and informed members of the special operations community pushed to gain visibility for SOF funding through the creation of Major Force Program 11; give SOF the ability to make its own resource decisions through program and budget authority for USSOCOM; and gain membership for the assistant secretary of defense, special operations and low-intensity conflict, on the major decisionmaking body of the Office of the Secretary of Defense, the Defense Resources Board. Congress succeeded in the first two efforts but not the third.

The main decisionmaking document in the PPBS is the budget. The budget for each fiscal year is presented to Congress for approval by the president. The budget is derived from a process that begins with the planning phase of the PPBS. Seldom timely and frequently changed, planning is followed by the programming phase. Most of the programming phase is oriented toward the preparation every one or two years of program objective memorandums (POMs). The only organizations required by the Office of the Secretary of Defense to develop such memoranda are the military departments—the Departments of the Army, Air Force, and Navy[8]— and a handful of defense agencies such as the Defense Mapping Agency, Defense Intelligence Agency, and Defense Information Systems Agency. A little more than one year before the formal budget submission is made, the major components of the military departments begin to prepare their inputs to the POM of their respective military departments.[9] At the same time, the unified commands, and at one time the specified commands, prepare their recommendations for the resource allocation process, called integrated priority lists (IPLs), for the secretary of defense. Unified commanders, unlike the military departments or defense agencies, do not control their own resources and do not prepare POMs. USSOCOM, by arguing for programming and budgeting responsibility, was fighting to be more than a unified command and, in fact, to have responsibilities usually only found in the military departments or defense agencies.

In the late spring, each military department and defense agency submits its POM to the Office of the Secretary of Defense. The POMs are reviewed by the OSD and the Joint Staff. The OSD identifies any issues that are contrary to the secretary's Defense Guidance, other policy guidance from the secretary of defense, or anything that seems fiscally or operationally questionable. The highest-level body for resource decisionmaking is the Defense Resources Board. Membership on the DRB is limited to the most senior members of the OSD staff and the civilian secretaries of the military departments, and chaired by the secretary or deputy secretary of defense. The military chiefs (for example, the chief of staff of the air force) and the CINCs may be invited to make presentations or discuss issues at certain meetings, but they are not members and are not normally present at the final decisionmaking discussions. The final decisionmaking authority is the secretary of defense.

After one to six weeks of debate and discussion, the secretary of defense or the deputy secretary issues a program decision memorandum, listing each of his decisions on issues that arose during the review of the POMs. This memorandum is used along with the POMs to put together the Future-Years Defense Plan (formerly known as the Five-Year Defense Plan when it covered only five years), or FYDP. In the FYDP, funding is described in terms of eleven Major Force Programs including special operations. The budget, organized along the same Major Force Programs as the FYDP but looking only one year into the future, is submitted to Congress. Theoretically, no new resource allocation decisions are made during the conversion of the first year of the FYDP to a budget. However, as a result of new information or the delaying of difficult decisions, the secretary and deputy secretary may direct changes through program budget decisions (PBDs) at this time. Minor refinements are made by the OSD comptroller to ensure the budget submitted by the president to Congress is "executable."

Finally, the Defense Department submits its budget to the Office of Management and Budget in the executive office of the president. The OMB puts together the budget for the entire executive branch, and the president submits it to Congress in January or February, not quite eight months before the new fiscal year begins on October 1.

Controlling SOF Resources

The 1986 SOF reorganization legislation was somewhat unclear as to how much control over its own resources SOF should assume. The ensuing debate focused on the issues of who was responsible for programming and budgeting special operations resources and whether the commander in chief of U.S. Special Operations Command would participate in the resource decisionmaking process in the same manner as all other unified commanders or in some other manner.

According to the 1986 legislation the commander of USSOCOM would have the following responsibilities:

> Budget—In addition to the activities of a combatant command for which funding may be requested . . . the budget proposal of the special operations command shall include requests for funding for:
>
> (1) development and acquisition of special-operations-peculiar equipment; and
>
> (2) acquisition of other material, supplies, or services that are peculiar to special operations activities.[10]

The legislation established a new Major Force Program category of defense funding within the defense program, referred to as MFP 11, since it was the eleventh category in the FYDP.[11] Congress also eliminated the ability of the military departments to reallocate SOF funding once Congress has approved the president's budget:

> Program and Budget Execution—to the extent that there is authority to revise programs and budgets approved by Congress for special operations forces, such authority may be exercised only by the Secretary of Defense, after consulting with the commander of the special operations command.[12]

Contrary to later charges that the Office of the Secretary of Defense was deliberately delaying implementation of the legislation, Donald Latham, assistant secretary of defense for command, control, communications, and intelligence (ASD [C³I]) and the Office of the Assistant Secretary of Defense for International Security Affairs (OASD [ISA]), moved very quickly to give the yet-unformed command and office of the assistant secretary, special operations and low-intensity conflict, the programming and budgeting authority they believed to be the intent of Congress. By early January 1987, Latham's and Armitage's staffs were proposing guidance for the military services and the chairman of the Joint Chiefs of Staff to begin the implementation of the SOF reorganization legislation. Their draft guidance asked the military departments to identify those elements in their five-year programs that should be included in the new Major Force Program 11. The guidance also called for a POM to be developed and submitted by the commander of the new special operations command as early as the next program and budget cycle beginning in the late fall of 1987.[13]

Once the draft guidance was sent out by ISA and C³I for "coordination," the process in any bureaucracy that gives other offices the opportunity to offer approval, criticism, suggestions, or disapproval, the objections began to arise. The most controversial issues, according to ISA and C³I, were as follows: "the content of Program 11; whether USCINCSOC should have a budget, and if so, what will be included [in it]; and the procedures for preparing and reviewing Program 11 and the USCINCSOC budget, should there be one."[14]

There was also disagreement, discussed earlier, over which forces should be included under MFP 11, with the argument in its early stages including disagreement over Naval Special Warfare and U.S. Air Force special operations aircraft.

The legislation itself encouraged to some extent the debate in that the only direction that appeared clear was that the commander of the special operations command would have a budget. What was to be included in that budget, and whether or not having a budget implied having the authority to develop a separate SOF program, was less certain. Part of the confusion may have been because the directive was written by those outside of the internal Defense Department resource allocation process, although this explanation is rejected by many in the SOF community:

> The interpreters of the legislation mucked it up and made it difficult because . . . he [USCINCSOC] was the first CINC to be given direct checkbook authority. [The legislation] did not specify the authority in DoD PPBS language. Which was a mistake in the legislation but legislators should not have to write to our system . . . . [The legislation] was interpreted . . . vis à vis the PPBS system. It was crystal clear that the intent of the legislators was to give CINCSOC the same authority that was resident in any one of the Services in terms of controlling your destiny. The only stipulation . . . was that [the legislation] said 'SOF-peculiar' or 'SOF-unique.'[15]

Many in the Department of Defense did not believe, or refused to believe, it was "crystal clear" that Congress intended to give U.S. Special

Operations Command many of the same authorities as the military departments. Although it may not be reasonable to expect, nor even appropriate for, Congress to rewrite specific Defense Department resource decisionmaking procedures, ambiguity allowed debate and made it difficult for the SOF community to claim authority. The services did not want to give up control over SOF resources. Any funding for SOF given over to the new SOF organizations would come out of the military services' TOA or total obligation authority—their respective pieces of Defense Department funding. Even if special operations forces and procurement were removed entirely from service support, the services would lose the flexibility to reallocate the funding from SOF to those programs service leaders believed to be of higher priority. This "flexibility" was, of course, exactly what had been occurring over the past forty years and what Congress was trying to end by giving USCINCSOC a checkbook.

The military services, especially the U.S. Army and U.S. Navy, believed they should control SOF resources. The services agreed that the commander in chief of USSOCOM and the assistant secretary of defense, special operations and low-intensity conflict, could offer guidance. The services argued that the CINC and the assistant secretary could participate like any other assistant secretary of defense, through membership on the Defense Resources Board, or like any other unified commander, through the submission of an integrated priority list and guidance to the command's service components. Service objections were expressed early in the implementation process to the Office of the Secretary of Defense:

> The Army nonconcurs with the position you took on Program 11 (Special Operations Forces) in your cover brief and its attached draft memorandum. While we understand and fully support the continued revitalization of SOF, we believe that the Service must retain a significant role in the resourcing of SOF. Your proposal reduces our responsibilities for SOF to a dangerously low level where the Services may no longer accept advocacy for this priority force.[16]

Objections also came from the OSD, particularly from the Office of Program Analysis and Evaluation. Although the opposition of Program Analysis and Evaluation to draft guidance from the Office of International Security Affairs and C^3I was similar to that of the services—disagreement with a broad interpretation of legislative intent—the rationale and motivation were different. Under the direction of David S. C. Chu, Program Analysis and Evaluation, was, with the Office of the Comptroller, the office most responsible for directing and maintaining the Defense

Department's planning, programming, and budgeting system. Chu, who was already attempting to implement the Goldwater-Nichols Defense Reorganization Act and the new role for the unified and specified commanders (CINCs) in PPBS, worried about increasing "Balkanization" of the Defense Department program.[17]

As more elements in the Department of Defense were allowed to participate in resource decisionmaking, and as the Defense Department appropriations were further divided, referred to as the "fencing" of funds, Chu worried that the Defense Department would lose flexibility as it allocated its funding. He said he thought program and budget development for USSOCOM "was a poor idea." He did not want the department to be "splitting pots of money." By 1986, he said, the country would not want to "sustain . . . real increases," and he warned that difficult decisions loomed for "overall resource management in the department."[18]

David Chu's argument had little to do with whether or not the department should rebuild an American special operations capability. Instead, Chu argued, USCINCSOC should participate as any other CINC would in the PPBS. The assistant secretary of defense, special operations and low-intensity conflict (ASD [SOLIC]) could make full use of his membership on the Defense Resources Board to monitor service support for SOF and bring any shortfalls to the attention of the secretary and deputy secretary of defense. If more attention to SOF resourcing were required, an office within OSD, besides SOLIC, could be given responsibility to monitor and report.

The position that broad implementation of the legislation, beyond providing USSOCOM with its own budget, would weaken the integrity and flexibility of the department's resource allocation process, seemed to most SOF supporters to be directly contradicting the spirit of the legislation. David Chu and the Program Analysis and Evaluation office were identified by SOF supporters as key players in the department's "malicious implementation" of the legislation. To make matters worse in the eyes of the SOF reformers, Chu and his office argued long and hard, with a knowledge of PPBS and evident logic, making it difficult for Deputy Secretary of Defense William Taft to settle the issue with any speed. Each time Taft appeared to have made a decision, the services, the Office of the Comptroller, and especially the Office of Program Analysis and Evaluation found room for maneuver and reopened the question.

The first "resolution" on the control of SOF resources was in a March 27, 1987, memorandum from the deputy secretary of defense to the secretaries of the military departments and the chairman of the Joint Chiefs of Staff. Having received several memos protesting the guidance prepared by Donald Latham and Richard Armitage, Taft issued a memorandum chastising the services.

> The legal issues and directions from Congress are clear. . . .

> That CINCSOC have a budget is clearly directed by Congress and since airlift was the primary "peculiar item" Congress intended for that purpose, SOF aircraft must be included in the CINCSOC budget. In addition, funding for JSOC requires a discipline and support not now evident and these resources will be included in the CINCSOC budget. Navy Special Warfare Forces are and have been included in DoD descriptions of Special Operations Forces and their resources must be included under Program 11. . . .

> The principal changes proposed by the Services are not consistent with the obvious intent of the law. . . .

> We should proceed with deliberate speed to implement Program 11 in the spirit in which the guidance was provided.[19]

All three military departments did as requested and forwarded to the Office of the Secretary of Defense most of the information requested by the deputy secretary, but the final decision on who controlled SOF resources was not close to being made. There were still substantial disagreements over USSOCOM's budget authority and responsibility for planning, programming, and budgeting.[20] The services continued to argue for a narrow interpretation of the legislation, allowing USSOCOM to implement some of the SOF budget while maintaining "the Service's preeminent role in resourcing this essential force" subject to the oversight of the Defense Resources Board.[21] The Office of Program Analysis and Evaluation and the Office of the Comptroller continued to argue for SOF to monitor its resources through the participation of USSOCOM and the Office of the Assistant Secretary of Defense, Special Operations and Low-Intensity Conflict, in the PPBS process in the same way as any unified command or assistant secretary of defense.

The argument carried into the late summer of 1987. Both David Chu and Comptroller Robert Helm intended to fight this guidance until the secretary or deputy secretary issued specific guidance giving USSOCOM this authority.[22] Responding to the Program Analysis–Comptroller argument once again in August 1987, Acting Assistant Secretary Thomas Quinn and Assistant Secretary Armitage wrote in desperation to Deputy Secretary Taft. They pointed out that Taft had already resolved the issue of whether USSOCOM would develop and execute programs and budgets for SOF-peculiar items in his March memorandum. The other issues, they argued, were minor or had already been resolved:

> If we are to avoid further embarrassment and direction from Congress, you will want to reaffirm your decision on the first issue by approving the USCINCSOC program and budget authority for three areas: SOF-peculiar RD and A, SOF airlift, and JSOC. . . . Your previous decisions were correct and do not bear re-examination.[23]

As it turned out, Armitage and Quinn were correct. Congress would not let this issue go. The next year would see countless memos and meetings over the basic issue of whether or not the legislation required that USSOCOM have program and budget authority. Congressional frustration at the delay would increase. In fact Congress steadily escalated its response, first with several clarifications of congressional intent in the *Congressional Record*, then with modifications of the legislation, and, finally, with congressional threats to prevent confirmation hearings until the issue was resolved.

The View from USSOCOM

As it turned out, the services had little to fear from these new special operations organizations during the first year or more of their existence. Implementing a policy change as sweeping as the SOF legislation was complex and difficult. And neither USSOCOM nor OASD (SOLIC) was in any position to take on the broad, servicelike responsibilities described in the law for the first few years following the initial legislation. As already mentioned, John Marsh Jr., the first assistant secretary of defense, special operations and low-intensity conflict, was not in place until early 1988, and his initial task was to physically set up the SOLIC office. Ambassador Whitehouse was not confirmed until the summer of 1988. This was not an office that was in any shape to direct the military services or assume responsibility for resource allocation.

USSOCOM was further along than SOLIC but was certainly not ready to enter the debate in the year following passage of the legislation, much less take on full resource management responsibilities. Needless to say, USSOCOM was hampered because the initial debate over resource control first took place in early 1987 before there was a command or a commander. When the president established USSOCOM, General Lindsay reasonably focused his attention on the operational responsibilities of USSOCOM. Although in a May 1987 interview Lindsay recognized that there had long been a problem with money flowing away from SOF to the conventional forces and that it was important for SOF to have its own checkbook, his interest was in operational concerns rather than resource management.[24] In an interview reported on July 3, 1987, General Lindsay described the command's mission as providing "combat-ready special-operations forces for rapid deployment to support other unified commanders and to plan and conduct special operations if directed by the president or the secretary of defense." He also said, "Other responsibilities will include planning and developing joint special operations doctrine, tactics and procedures."[25] No mention was made by this long-time combat commander of the personnel development, training, acquisition, or resource responsibilities of this new command.

USSOCOM did not by any means entirely ignore the issue of SOF resources. But the command's initial foray into the resource allocation process was a tentative attempt to participate in the same way as the other unified commands. In July 1987 General Lindsay acted upon informal service invitations to participate in SOF-related 1990–1994 POM development, the programming phase that would lead to the 1990 Defense Department budget, much like any other CINC.[26]

Lindsay's "CINC-like" approach, as opposed to "servicelike" participation, was not surprising, given the newness of the command and the background of its commander and staff. The command had only been active a few months when the 1990–94 POM building began. Little emphasis was given to building a servicelike resource management staff. At best, USSOCOM's resource office was like that of a small unified command. Lindsay's staff structure was in part the result of building on the organization of the U.S. Readiness Command but also reflected the operational orientation of the professional careers of Lindsay and his senior staff. Intelligent and capable as they were, these were not men who had any significant experience with PPBS. Terms such as POM, PDM, and BES might have crossed the path of these men in the past but were largely the responsibility of bureaucrats and not operators, from the perspective of USSOCOM's leadership and the new members of its staff. When asked if there was a sense among the command's initial leadership that assuming full programming and budgeting responsibility was a critical responsibility of USSOCOM, an officer who was an early recruit to the command's resource directorate responded:

General Lindsay, the commander, and General Porter, who was the J-8 [Director for Resources], and General Lutz, who was the Chief of Staff, all said, "Yes, we've seen the law. We definitely want to control our own resource and budget per the feelings of Congress. We want to protect these resources from the service cuts that we [have historically taken.]" However, . . . being operators, they didn't have the slightest conception of what they were signing up to in terms of process, in terms of the cost of manpower, and how to accomplish it.[27]

The early operational focus of General Lindsay and his senior staff was re-emphasized in late 1987, when General Lindsay commissioned his staff to develop a U.S. Special Operations Command concept statement based on the roles, missions, and functions directed by Congress and other guidance including direction from the Joint Chiefs of Staff and the secretary of defense.[28] The draft mission concept was presented in the form of a tree with five branches. At the trunk of the tree is the USSOCOM mission statement, "to prepare assigned forces to carry out special operations, psychological operations, and civil affairs missions as required, and, if directed by the President or the Secretary of Defense, plan for and conduct special operations." The five major branches represent the major functional areas "which contribute to the success of the mission" as follows:

— Prepare SOCOM Headquarters to manage SOF within DoD;

— Prepare SOF to carry out assigned missions in low-intensity conflict environment;

— Prepare SOF to carry out assigned missions in mid-intensity conflict environment;

— Prepare SOF to carry out assigned missions in high-intensity conflict environment; and

— Prepare SOF to execute operations that are conducted in peacetime in pursuit of U.S. strategic objectives.[29]

USSOCOM's servicelike responsibilities, including training, acquisition, and the financial management responsibilities of programming and budgeting are all found within the first branch, "prepar[ing] SOCOM Headquarters to manage SOF within DoD." Most of these responsibilities are not specified until the fourth level of this branch. The remainder of this diagram, including one-fifth of the responsibilities under the "servicelike" responsibilities branch, is dedicated to "warfighting" responsibilities and operations.[30]

Nonetheless, as the command began to coalesce, it made increased efforts to learn about how SOF resources were managed, who controlled these resources, and the extent to which Congress intended USSOCOM to assume these responsibilities. In the winter of 1987–88 USSOCOM's small programming shop prepared the CINC's first integrated priority list and began to develop contacts in each of the military departments' programming and budgeting offices. USSOCOM's early participation was largely in watching and listening, with its program office under the direction of a U.S. Air Force special operations pilot who had no PPBS experience but who told fascinating tales of the *Mayaguez* incident. This initial group did, however, provide an important foundation for USSOCOM's more activist participation during the next few years. By the summer of 1988 General Lindsay, having become familiar with the planning, programming, and budgeting system, was working closely with Ambassador Whitehouse and the SOLIC staff to convince the secretary of defense to grant USSOCOM the full program and budget authority intended by Congress.

Congress Says "Enough!"

Congress refused to tolerate what it considered to be Defense Department foot-dragging. Time and time again during 1987 and 1988 Congress told the Defense Department that special operations forces were to be funded in a manner unique within the department and that the commander in chief of the U.S. Special Operations Command was like no other CINC. In the same act in late 1987 that put John O. Marsh Jr. in place as acting assistant secretary of defense, Congress attempted to put the argument over who controlled SOF resources to rest:

Resources for CINCSOF—The Secretary of Defense shall provide sufficient resources for the commander of the unified combatant command for special operations forces . . . to carry out his duties and responsibilities, including particularly his duties and responsibilities relating to the following functions:

(1) Developing and acquiring special-operations-peculiar equipment

and acquiring special-operations-peculiar material, supplies, and services.

(2) Providing advice and assistance to the Assistant Secretary of Defense for Special Operations and Low-Intensity Conflict in the Assistant Secretary's overall supervision of the preparation and justification of the program recommendations and budget proposals for special operations forces.

(3) Managing assigned resources from the major force program category for special operations forces of the Five-Year Defense Plan of the Department of Defense.[31]

The legislation also directed that the commander of the special operations command "shall have authority to exercise the functions of the head of an agency." This designation, although seemingly trivial, gave USCINCSOC unusual authority; authority not provided to any other unified commander in chief. Head of agency status gave USCINCSOC responsibility for the development and acquisition of equipment and material peculiar to special operations. USCINCSOC would also have the authority to establish a contracting organization and to make agreements with other agency heads to delegate procurement functions and assign procurement responsibilities. Following Secretary Carlucci's signing of the implementation memorandum in May 1988, USSOCOM began work on establishing its Special Operations Research, Development, and Acquisition Center (SORDAC).[32]

Following his confirmation in the summer of 1988, Ambassador Charles Whitehouse issued a series of memoranda, written with General Lindsay and USSOCOM between August and mid-December 1988, that joined SOLIC to the fight for control of SOF resources. In August Whitehouse began to challenge issues raised by David Chu and Comptroller Robert Helm. "It seems to me that a solution to this long-standing problem can be found which maintains the 'sanctity' of the PPBS process but which does not thwart the congressional intent to give USSOCOM the means to fulfill its unique responsibilities."[33] Whitehouse went on to say that USSOCOM could not even execute its legislated head of agency authority until the secretary of defense granted the accompanying budgetary and acquisition authority. "The problem," wrote Whitehouse, "might be resolved by a decision which basically gives USSOCOM responsibility for the preparation of program proposals in the same way other Defense agencies do (i.e., a POM)."[34]

In October 1988 Whitehouse prepared a paper for the secretary and deputy secretary of defense describing the options for implementing the resource control aspects of the legislation. By the fall of 1988, he offered the secretary five options that were being floated around the Pentagon:

— Option 1: Existing Procedures with Enhanced Execution Review. Services [continue to] program, budget, and execute SOF programs with oversight by ASD (SOLIC)/USSOCOM through the PPBS process.

— Option 2: USSOCOM/Services Submit Parallel POM/Budget Estimates. POM issue papers/PBD's [decisions by the Secretary and Deputy Secretary of Defense] resolve differences. Services execute SOF programs with ASD (SOLIC) and USSOCOM oversight as in Option 1.

— Option 3: USSOCOM Submits POM/Budget and Services Execute with ASD (SOLIC) and USSOCOM oversight as in Options 1 and 2.

— Option 4: USSOCOM Submits POM/Budget with Selected Execution. Using existing Defense Agency appropriations, SOF funding is allocated by OSD to USSOCOM which would suballocate to either services or USSOCOM component commands for execution.

—Option 5: Establish a New SOF Defense Agency. Establish new Defense Agency for SOF which would submit POM/budget and perform program execution. As an additional consideration, consolidate part or all of DSAA [Defense Security Assistance Agency—organization that advises on allocation of Foreign Military Assistance funds as well as managing most of these programs under the new Agency.] [35]

Option 1 is the proposal originally supported by the services and, to some extent, by David Chu and the Program Analysis and Evaluation office.[36] In his memo, Whitehouse warns the deputy secretary that Senators Cohen and Nunn, as well as Representative Hutto, had made statements for the record "affirming the intent of Congress, that USSOCOM be given the authority to prepare and execute a POM commencing no later than 1992."[37] In fact, the conference report on the fiscal 1989 legislation indicated that revisions to the SOF legislation were intended to "clarify that the commander of the special operations command would be responsible for executing budgets as well as for preparing and submitting to the Secretary of Defense program recommendations and budget proposals."[38] In his cover memo, Whitehouse went on to say that despite appearances, there was only one true option, to implement the legislation according to congressional intent, that is, Option 4, giving USSOCOM full program and budget authority.[39]

As the number of memorandums from every side in the debate increased during late 1988, Secretary Carlucci and Deputy Secretary Taft decided that, having postponed a decision several times because of congressional confirmation hearings, first for Ken Bergquist and then for Charles Whitehouse, they had another opportunity to postpone the decision—the arrival of a new administration. With a victory by George Bush in the election of November 1988, there would soon be a new secretary of defense in early 1989. Deputy Secretary Taft indicated his unwillingness to speak for the new administration in his letter to Representative Kasich in early November 1988. Kasich and Representative Hutto had written to Defense Department leadership in October, agreeing with Ambassador Whitehouse that there were no real options: Congress intended for USSOCOM to have full program and budget authority.[40] After assuring Representative Kasich that "the Department of Defense will comply with the law," Taft made it clear that there was little hope of compliance occurring on his watch:

> The next cycle of the Planning, Programming and Budgeting System (PPBS) currently calls for the preparation of Program Objectives Memoranda (POMs) to begin on August 1, 1989, with submission scheduled for April 1, 1990. If this schedule is adhered to, I would expect the Secretary of Defense in the next Administration to request CINCSOC to prepare a POM for Program 11 at that time. . . . I would be extremely reluctant, however, to prescribe to the next Administration the procedures it should use in preparing its budget proposals.[41]

In this same letter, Deputy Secretary Taft let slip his irritation at the high degree of congressional scrutiny and detailed direction:

> One more point should, I think, be kept in mind as you consider this subject. It is the *procedures* the Secretary of Defense follows in preparing budget proposals that we are talking about here. Of course, flawed procedures may generate flawed proposals. But even if the Secretary advances flawed proposals, *Congress can reject them*. At some point, prescribing procedures stops being cost-effective and becomes simply an obsession of perfectionist bureaucrats. . . .

I hope that in the case of special operations programs, in particular, if Congress again in the future feels that the budget proposals are inappropriate, you will consider this option before being drawn off yet further into procedural thickets.[42]

Taft's exchange with Representatives Kasich and Hutto is revealing in several ways. The first is the clear frustration of Defense Department leadership over persistent congressional direction and examination of an issue—how SOF resources were to be managed—that went deeply into the Defense Department resource decisionmaking process. This congressional scrutiny was unusual and intrusive. It struck at the heart of Defense Department autonomy.

At the same time, Kasich and Hutto's letter, when combined with Nunn's and Cohen's statements, declared that Congress was not going to let this issue go away. It had become a test of will and power and Congress was not going to allow the Defense Department to rework congressionally directed special operations reform. Jim Locher and the other authors of SOF-related legislation recognized that process is everything in an organization as large as the Department of Defense, and the most important process in the Department of Defense is the resource allocation process. Without formal participation in the process, in the manner of the military departments with programming and budgeting authority, special operations forces would never truly control their own resources and would forever be at the mercy of service decisions and OSD interests. Under the options that called for continuing the existing PPBS procedures, relying on OSD review through the Defense Resource Board, SOF would once again be at risk if the OSD stopped paying attention. If a strong special operations capability was to be built and maintained, the danger of "Balkanization" had to be accepted and USSOCOM had to be given the same resource authority as the military services.

Taft was not to get his wish of holding the decision for the next administration. Nor would Congress heed his chastising and stay out of internal Defense Department procedures.[43]

By January 1989, the transition team for the Bush administration's nominee for secretary of defense, Senator John Tower, was in the Pentagon. Assistant Secretary Whitehouse had provided Tower's team with the history of the special operations reorganization legislation and Defense Department actions since the passage of the legislation. Whitehouse also provided John Tower with a draft memorandum, for the secretary of defense's signature, providing USCINCSOC with program and budget development and execution authority.[44] Demonstrating once again the remarkable communication between SOF supporters in the Department of Defense and in Congress, Senators Nunn, Cohen, John Warner, and Edward Kennedy wrote to Secretary of Defense Frank Carlucci a few days after Whitehouse's memorandum about the draft directive:

> The [Armed Services Committees] conferees . . . intended that the Commander assume these budget responsibilities as soon as possible, but not later than for the budget for fiscal year 1992. . . . Therefore, it is essential that the internal DOD directive necessary for the Commander to implement his budget responsibilities be issued as soon as possible.

> We understand that this directive has been fully staffed within the Defense Department and only requires your final approval. We urge you to issue this directive quickly.[45]

As OSD staff were continuing to prepare option packages for Deputy Secretary Taft to present to John Tower, "Members of the Congress made clear that this nomination [Tower as secretary of defense] would have even further difficulties, to put it as politely as possible, if this matter was not resolved favorably to the special operations community."[46] Ultimately, John Tower asked Acting Defense Secretary Taft to end the debate and issue the directive. On January 24, 1989, what is commonly referred to as "the Taft memo" was signed:

> After considering the options presented in the Comptroller's memorandum of January 17, 1989, I have determined that program/budget development responsibilities for Special Operations Forces (MFP-11) are to be assigned to CINCSOC. He will exercise these responsibilities fully in connection with the FY92-97 PPB cycle.

> CINCSOC is also to assume budget execution responsibilities (1) for selected MFP-11 programs (as determined by CINCSOC) effective October 1, 1990; and (2) for all MFP-11 programs effective on October 1, 1991. . . .

> I direct all addressees to provide the US Special Operations Command the resources, support, information and assistance required to perform the above tasks.[47]

Once told to get on with it by Taft, the strongest opponents to giving USCINCSOC control over his own resources, the comptroller and the assistant secretary for program analysis and evaluation, worked to implement the directive. In fact, a handwritten note from David Chu's deputy to the staff member responsible for resource issues within SOLIC had the tone of congratulations after a battle well fought. The note is in a file labeled "SOC Surrender": "Dear John [Russ], You won. We were asked to prepare an implementation package, which is attached. Please give me a call if you have any problems."

Once he lost the battle, Chu believed that it was his job to implement the Defense Department leadership's and Congress's direction to the best of the department's capabilities. The Office of Program Analysis and Evaluation has continued that support ever since.[48]

Not surprisingly, Taft's direction did not end the debate. The issue in 1989 shifted from money to people as the services, OSD, USSOCOM, and SOLIC argued over how much control USSOCOM would have over its manpower. The command did not recruit personnel directly from the civilian population but instead recruited from the military services. The services recruited and trained new soldiers, airmen, marines, and sailors. Once through initial training, these men and women could volunteer for special operations assignments. The services were concerned that as the defense budget was cut, increasing SOF force structure would come from already decreasing service manpower. The services were, therefore, adamantly against giving up control over what they viewed as their personnel assigned to SOF units. The strongest proponent for USSOCOM having the authority to make force structure, investment, and operating cost choices and trade-offs was David Chu. USSOCOM itself appeared somewhat reluctant to accept responsibility for its own force structure. The debate over who controlled manpower within the SOF program lasted for most of the next year and further delayed USSOCOM's full program and budget responsibilities.

The resulting "peace treaty" was an agreement that allowed USSOCOM to move on with its program development but was unclear enough— requiring coordination with the military services over endstrength and their concurrence on any changes in the mix of active and reserve forces— that arguments still arise with some regularity over the extent to which USSOCOM can cut or increase both the size of its force and its active/ reserve balance.[49] The Atwood memo, signed by Deputy Secretary of Defense Donald Atwood on December 1, 1989, is the result of months of negotiation between the U.S. Army and USSOCOM and SOLIC.[50] This memo gave USSOCOM the go-ahead to begin building its own program, thus the ability to make its own resource decisions, as part of the fiscal 1992–97 PPBS cycle.[51] "As a general rule, starting with the FY 92–97 Program, USCINCSOC will program and budget for SOF. . . . Programs will be executed by the Military Departments, either directly, for Major Force Program 11 (MFP-11) and MFP-11-related programs contained in the appropriation accounts of the Military Departments, or by sub-allocation of funds from Defense Agency accounts to the Military Departments."[52]

The new commander in chief of USSOCOM, General Carl Stiner, was responsible for carrying out Taft's and Atwood's directions. Stiner assumed command in June 1990, and his career, like General Lindsay's, had been spent in operations, although Stiner had had a closer tie than Lindsay to special operations. General Stiner had served in a series of operational units oriented toward quick reaction contingencies and special operations. His special operations background included serving in the 1960s as a B-Detachment commander and being an operations officer for a C-Detachment. In Vietnam, he used his knowledge of special operations units when he served as an infantry brigade staff officer with responsibilities for overseeing the eight Special Forces camps in the brigade's area of operation. Following several operational assignments, including two with the 82nd Airborne Division, Carl Stiner took over the Joint Special Operations Command in 1984. After being in the middle of American responses to a series of crises including the hijacking of TWA Flight 847 and the *Achille Lauro*, Stiner left the JSOC in 1987 to assume command of the 82nd Airborne Division.[53] He was promoted to lieutenant general and assumed command of the XVIII Airborne Corps, including the 82nd Airborne and the 101st Airborne (Air Assault) Divisions, in October 1988.[54] As commander of the XVIII Airborne Corps, General Stiner was, as noted previously, the task force commander for Operation Just Cause.

General Stiner recognized the importance of USSOCOM's servicelike responsibilities, but his heart, like General Lindsay's, was with operations and he had little background in the intricacies of PPBS. Stiner's staff was composed largely of special operators who had an operational perspective rather than the viewpoint of a service staff.

In conversation, General Stiner makes clear that his greatest pride is in the staggering increase in the use of special operations forces by both conventional commanders in major conflicts such as Just Cause or Desert Shield and Desert Storm in Southwest Asia and in support of peacetime engagement. Under General Stiner's command, special operations forces increased their deployments supporting the regional CINCs by more than 30 percent between fiscal 1991 and fiscal 1992. During that same period SOF employment in support of the Defense Department's counterdrug mission increased by more than 100 percent. These same figures increased again in fiscal 1993 by approximately 30 percent.[55]

General Stiner grew into his role as the commander of an organization that was unlike any other unified command, and under his leadership USSOCOM made great strides in assuming its servicelike responsibilities. The resource management office successfully prepared SOF's first program objective memorandum (POM), USSOCOM's resource plan for 1992–97, and delivered it on time (unlike any of the military services and to the great surprise of all) to the Office of the Secretary of Defense in May 1990. A USSOCOM staff member who participated in the development of the first POM described the command's growing recognition by 1990 of the importance of controlling its own resources. His comments also reflect the bitterness that lingered in the command after the bruising bureaucratic battles:

> [USSOCOM] headquarters was galvanized in the POM effort. That was viewed as the high payoff because your first POM was your baseline, laid your foundation, needed to be done right. Everybody and his brother was going to be looking at it to shoot holes in it [and] to demonstrate that this fledgling organization was not capable of producing a quality product. There were an extraordinary number of people hoping for failure.[56]

Preparing the first POM, and later SOF's first budget, was a complicated and difficult task requiring transferring all SOF-related programs and some funding from the military services, developing a comprehensive data base and program tracking system, and linking up with current budget execution decisions and data.

Fortunately, USSOCOM often had invaluable assistance from some of its former opponents, particularly at the "working level"—those members of the service and OSD staffs who had to get the job done. The relationships among the USSOCOM, SOLIC, OSD, and military service staffs were rarely adversarial, aside from occasional disagreements over responsibility, after mid-1989. At first cooperation was informal and then grew through more formal channels, but most of the staff involved in the work took the approach, "We need to get this right so that whatever is produced makes the most sense for the force that we are fielding."[57]

One of the most difficult aspects of USSOCOM's program and budget development was meeting as a unified command with all the component commanders and making decisions about the midterm future of U.S. special operations forces. For nearly all involved, this step was an unprecedented occurrence. USSOCOM components from the U.S. Navy, U.S. Army, U.S. Air Force, and Joint Special Operations Command, most of whom had little experience in Department of Defense-level resource decisionmaking or even within their own service, had to make joint, cross-service resource decisions and not focus entirely on parochial interests. This was especially true in the development of the command's second and third programs. Dramatic cuts were planned for the Defense Department budget during the 1990s. The command could not afford all that it had hoped for and had to make trade-offs in acquisition programs and manpower across its components. Such cross-service decisions are still rarely accomplished in the Department of Defense. Nonetheless, the new servicelike Special Operations Command confronted the constraints in a thoughtful manner, making difficult trade-offs and developing a coherent and consistent resource plan for the next several years. Regardless of what the legislation intended or who was in charge, USSOCOM had produced its first POMs and budgets and defended them successfully. The struggles among the OSD, military services, SOLIC, and USSOCOM were all but over. The next step for USSOCOM was looking toward the future.

10

Desert Shield
and Desert Storm

We have to do things to make a difference. We're not going to do
things just to do things. . . . That's how we get guys killed. . . . It has
to contribute to what General Schwarzkopf's ultimate goals are. . . .
And we have to have the courage to say no if someone asks us to do
something that we're not capable of doing. . . . If we lose people, . . .
I will bear that burden because I will be responsible.

Rear Admiral Ray Smith, August 1990

Just past midnight on August 2, 1990, tanks from three Iraqi Republican Guard divisions rolled across the Kuwaiti frontier, quickly overrun-
ning Kuwait's armed forces. Minutes later, Iraqi special operations forces,
coming from helicopters and from the sea, assaulted Kuwait City, seizing
critical government facilities and the Amir's palace. Supporting armored
divisions moved south from Al-Jahra near the Iraq-Kuwait border and
blocked the main roads leading to the Saudi Arabian border. By that
evening, Kuwait City and Kuwaiti ports were under Iraqi control. By
August 4, Iraqi forces were taking up defensive positions and hundreds
of support vehicles were entering Kuwait, carrying massive amounts of
munitions and supplies for the occupying force. By August 6 elements of
at least eleven Iraqi divisions were in or entering Kuwait, for a total of
more than 200,000 soldiers and 2,000 tanks. On August 8 Saddam Hussein
proclaimed the annexation of Kuwait as the "19th Province—an eternal
part of Iraq."[1]

Surprised by the Iraqi assault, President George Bush declared after
consultation with American allies that the Iraqi invasion of Kuwait was
"naked aggression" and "shall not stand." Bush called for the "immediate,

complete, and unconditional withdrawal of all Iraqi forces from Kuwait; [and the] restoration of Kuwait's legitimate government." The president also expressed American concern with the security and stability of Saudi Arabia and the entire Persian Gulf, and the safety of American citizens in the region.[2] On August 5, Secretary of Defense Dick Cheney led a delegation to meet with King Fahd of Saudi Arabia. After hearing the American pledge of support for his kingdom and an intelligence briefing on the very real indications that Saddam Hussein's forces were able and willing to invade Saudi Arabia, thus gaining control of 40 percent of the world's oil reserves, King Fahd asked for American assistance. George Bush gave the order and the Department of Defense began mobilization and deployment of American military forces for Operation Desert Shield.[3]

Following the Iran-Iraq war, Iraq had become the dominant military power in the Persian Gulf region. The world's fourth largest military force, Iraqi forces were, compared with other non-Western forces, well equipped and had a decade of combat experience. The most capable units were the eight divisions of the Republican Guard Forces Command. These units were the elite of the Iraqi military and were equipped with Soviet-made T-72 tanks and BMP infantry fighting vehicles. There were fifty more divisions in the Iraqi regular army, although they were equipped with much older systems than the Republican Guard. Iraqi ground forces also included a large, though poorly trained and equipped, popular army, or militia. The Iraqi air force had MiG-29, Su-24, and F-1 aircraft, but the quality of the aircraft and air crews throughout the force was viewed as "uneven."[4] Iraq's air-defense network was highly capable, with the most formidable protection surrounding Baghdad. Iraq's navy included coastal patrol boats and antiship missiles. Finally, and most notoriously, Iraq had a short-range ballistic missile capability. Iraq owned Soviet-made Scud-B missiles as well as two variants produced in Iraq. These missiles could carry high-explosive warheads and were believed by the American government to be capable of carrying chemical and biological agents.

Four days after President Bush's announcement that American forces would deploy to the Persian Gulf, special operations forces and members of the 82nd Airborne Division's ready brigade were on the ground in Saudi Arabia. Eventually, more than 7,000 special operators would be part of the 540,000 members of the coalition led by the United States and Saudi Arabia. This was the largest deployment of SOF ever for the United States. Because of the lessons learned in Grenada, and in keeping with the special operations reform legislation, SOF came under joint command and control. Even more so than in Operation Just Cause, conventional and special operations unit commanders attempted to assign these forces missions that were appropriate to their size and skills. In an extension of the American experience in Panama, SOF's greatest impact came in reducing casualties, especially through liaison roles with coalition forces, a major deception operation off the Kuwaiti shoreline, and the creative and persistent use of psychological operations.

First in were Navy Special Warfare (NAVSPECWAR) units commanded by Captain Raymond Smith. Arriving with 100 men on August 12, NAVSPECWAR forces eventually numbered 260 people, the largest deployment for the community since Vietnam. Smith's force was also unusually diverse. "We had SEALs, Special Boat Units, we had our desert vehicles. We had SDVs (SEAL Delivery Vehicles). We had a little bit of everything we have [and were] heavy in boats. The first time we've ever deployed an SDV in a real war situation . . . since Vietnam."[5] The reason for this amalgam is that the Navy Special Warfare forces deployed without an assigned mission other than "just get there." By August 19 other special operators had yet to arrive, and so a twenty-man SEAL element and a U.S. Air Force Tactical Control team were sent into the desert to work with the Saudi army to teach them close air support, making the SEALs the first unit to operate in Desert Shield. After three weeks, the SEALs were replaced by a team from the 5th Special Forces Group. NAVSPECWAR forces worked throughout the conflict with the Saudi navy and U.S. Marines in a training, or foreign internal defense, mission. SEALs also joined with other forces, particularly special operations-capable troops from a marine expeditionary unit, to provide surveillance and early warning along the Kuwait and Iraq borders.[6]

Beginning in late August, coalition forces were authorized to use force in support of sanctions levied against Iraq by the UN Security Council. Forces from nineteen coalition navies conducted maritime interception operations. In the course of these operations, 7,500 merchant vessels were challenged and 964 were boarded. Authorized to disable any merchant ship that did not allow inspection of its cargo, coalition forces nevertheless made every effort to avoid resorting to disabling fire. If warning shots alone did not convince the ship's captain to allow inspection by the U.S. Coast Guard, coalition forces conducted "take down" operations, boarding by force teams from the U.S. Marine Corps, the British Royal Marines, and the U.S. Navy SEALs. Only eleven takedowns were ordered and all were successful. Coalition forces were never forced to resort to disabling fire.[7]

In October Captain Smith met with the exiled chief of naval operations of the Kuwaiti navy. For the next several months SPECWAR forces worked with the Kuwaiti navy, putting the three Kuwaiti ships in order and training the naval forces. Eventually, Smith and his units assisted the Kuwaitis in rebuilding their naval bases. Ray Smith, now rear admiral, still has the battle pennant given to him by the commander of the Kuwaiti navy in appreciation for the help given by the U.S. Navy special operators.

SOF Integration with Conventional Forces

Special operations as part of Desert Shield and Desert Storm were characterized by the tight control maintained by General Norman Schwarzkopf. Schwarzkopf was the commander in chief of Central Command, the unified command with responsibility for Southwest Asia. As such, he became the American commander of all non-Arab, non-Islamic forces within the coalition and the architect of the coalition strategy throughout Desert Shield and Desert Storm. All American special operations forces, except for civil affairs and psychological operations units, a few U.S. Navy SPECWAR forces deployed on navy ships as part of maritime interception operations, and a separate joint special operations task force came under the direct command of Colonel Jesse Johnson. Johnson was the commander of a subunified command within Central Command, Special Operations Command-Central, usually referred to as SOCCENT. SOCCENT was a joint command including components from the army, navy, and air force. For the most part, logistical support was provided by the military services, while operational command was the responsibility of Colonel Johnson. Civil affairs and psychological operations units had a more complex command relationship and were most often assigned in support of specific conventional commands.[8]

General Norman Schwarzkopf, an infantry officer, had a reputation for neither liking nor trusting special operations forces. U.S. Central Command (USCENTCOM) and U.S. Special Operations Command (USSOCOM) were both headquartered at MacDill Air Force Base in Tampa, Florida. Having two four-star generals on the same base is always a touchy situation, and the tension at MacDill was aggravated by the special operators believing USCENTCOM was a do-nothing command and the staff at USCENTCOM believing the special operators were out-of-control cowboys. As described by Douglas Waller, "No one nurtured the animosity [between the commands] more than CENTCOM's commander, General H. Norman Schwarzkopf III."[9] Rick Atkinson makes similar observations as he describes the "deep suspicion" of special operations forces held by

Schwarzkopf and many other military commanders participating in the Persian Gulf War.[10] The suspicion and distrust were not alleviated by tensions between Schwarzkopf and USSOCOM's new commander, General Carl Stiner. Stiner was fresh from his triumphs as the commander of American forces in Panama. He believed deeply in the capabilities of his special operations forces and argued forcefully for conducting unconventional operations in advance of a coalition offensive. Relations between the two generals reached a low in January 1991 when General Stiner arrived at Schwarzkopf's headquarters in Riyadh and offered an aggressive special operations campaign. According to several sources, Stiner indicated that he would be willing to move his own headquarters to Saudi Arabia to support coalition forces. His offer was not accepted.[11]

Schwarzkopf kept SOF on a short leash throughout Desert Shield and Desert Storm. He maintained control through his order that special operations across the border into Iraq or Kuwait could only be undertaken with his personal approval. Both he and the SOCCENT commander resisted most direct action operations, and a strong push by USSOCOM to work with the Kuwaiti resistance within Kuwait was resoundingly rejected. The need for Schwarzkopf's direct approval for each operation complicated planning for the SOF commanders and severely limited the number of cross-border operations that were conducted. Ray Smith (later to become rear admiral) described the effect of Schwarzkopf's order on SPECWAR operations, "You had to go to Riyadh and stand in front of him and brief him on what you were going to do, why you were going to do it, how it was going to work, and how it was going to help him. . . . a very onerous process. You had to send a mission concept to Riyadh and all the staffers would look at it and say, 'Yeah, it makes sense.' . . . He never turned down anything that I went and briefed. There were things that didn't get done only because I couldn't get on his calendar."[12]

One of the many proposed operations that did not happen was to have taken place within Saudi Arabia. Bedouins from Iraq had been crossing into the western region of the country in pickup trucks and shooting at coalition aircraft. They had hit a number of aircraft. Captain Smith and his staff proposed using the SEALs' fast attack vehicles (FAVs), highly capable dune buggies, to identify and capture the shooters. The mission was never approved because of the risk of precipitating an Iraqi invasion of Saudi Arabia.[13]

Certainly Schwarzkopf had good reason for caution. He had no interest in starting a war with Iraq before coalition forces were in place. The four-phased campaign strategy developed by Schwarzkopf and his staff had a precise timetable that he did not want to risk derailing with potential "provocations" in the form of Special Forces or SEAL operations or, worse, U.S. military prisoners being taken inside Iraq. Although it is very likely that Schwarzkopf, given his background with the most conventional of conventional forces, had misgivings about SOF, it is also true that by the end of the Persian Gulf War he seems to have developed respect for their capabilities. This was likely due to the many SOF successes, which significantly reduced coalition casualties during the conflict, and his relationship with the SOCCENT commander. In his autobiography, although General Schwarzkopf makes little mention of special operations, he does write of a conversation he had with Colonel Johnson shortly before coalition forces reclaimed Kuwait City: "Johnson was one of *Desert Storm*'s unsung heroes. Since his arrival in the gulf six months earlier he'd worked close to the front lines helping to hold the coalition together. I complimented him on the performance of his troops: they had run reconnaissance and made raids behind enemy lines, taught the Saudis, reorganized and equipped the Kuwaitis, and during the fighting, served as military advisors to Arab units."[14]

Perhaps SOF's greatest contribution to holding the coalition together was its mission of combining foreign internal defense operations, or training of foreign forces, with its newly expanded mission of coalition warfare. Besides U.S. Navy Special Warfare forces working with the Saudi and Kuwaiti navies as described above, SOCCENT provided specifically tailored Special Forces coordination and training teams (CTT) to work with the coalition forces. Initially, these teams were assigned to support Saudi ground forces, but as other nations joined the coalition and sent troops—Egypt, Syria, Oman, and Qatar among others—Special Forces teams were assigned to them as well. Within months, 109 teams were formed, assigned, and providing assistance to every level of the coalition forces, down to battalion level.[15]

Advice and assistance, especially in the initial stages of Desert Shield, included advising the coalition unit commanders on how to employ their forces most effectively in an integrated defense. Special Forces teams helped these commanders to move away from building sand berms to designing effective defensive systems, such as constructing minefields, digging antitank ditches, and covering them with artillery and air-launched fire. The CTTs advised the commanders on training best suited to operating with the coalition forces. They provided for the safety of the troops by working out contingency plans for passage through lines, if they had to withdraw, without killing other friendly forces. The CTTs also supplied General Schwarzkopf with regular updates on the status of the coalition units, linking the USCENTCOM planning staff with the Arab-Islamic units in particular.

One important role of the Special Forces teams was their liaison between non-U.S. units and American air support. Once the ground war began, this link became invaluable, preventing "blue-on-blue" casualties from friendly fire despite the similarities in structure and equipment of some of the Arab-Islamic forces with the Iraqi force. Sergeant First Class Alfred Sinclair, a member of the Special Forces team assigned to work with the 70th Egyptian Armored Battalion, described a time when he was forced to call in air support against Iraqi artillery:

> On 24 February the 70th battalion assaulted into Kuwait . . . The unit came to a defensive belt of barbed wire and mines. While we waited for engineers to clear the mine fields, the Egyptian tanks came under intense enemy artillery fire. I immediately contacted an airborne observation aircraft who directed two A-10s. . . . I contacted the A-10s, confirmed that they could see where the enemy artillery was impacting and told them that we were where the artillery was hitting. Once our position [was] confirmed, I directed the aircraft on a heading in the direction of the enemy . . . and we systematically eliminated four artillery positions in one hour.[16]

There were no Egyptian casualties from American air support.

Although many of the Special Forces spoke Arabic, a shortage of language-trained special operators prevailed throughout Desert Shield and Desert Storm. The widespread use and success of the teams demonstrated the need for Special Forces as trainers and liaisons with foreign forces. In this role, Special Forces must have a strong knowledge of conventional maneuver warfare doctrine and tactics. This requirement is becoming a critical issue since Special Forces is now a separate branch in the U.S. Army, and applicants for Special Forces training are no longer required to have an additional combat arms specialty. The Special Forces CTTs lived with the forces they were assigned to support and trained with them. They adapted their mission to reflect the needs of the forces they were advising and those of the coalition itself. Their coordination with teams assigned to adjacent coalition forces assisted in command and control between the units. The flexibility and unique skills of Special Forces, including language ability and cultural training, helped to integrate the forces from dozens of nations and cultures to fight together with few friendly fire casualties.

Special operations forces also worked to rebuild the Kuwaiti military units that escaped destruction during the Iraqi invasion. Owing to its small size, the Kuwaiti force's impact was minimal on the military capability of the coalition, but its political and psychological value was critical. Schwarzkopf's direction to SOCCENT was to get these forces ready to participate in the offensive campaign once it began and to get them involved as soon as possible.[17] As mentioned earlier, Naval Special Warfare units, particularly SEALs and members of the special boat units, worked to put the Kuwaiti navy back together, while members of 5th Special Forces Group assisted Kuwaiti ground forces.[18]

At first, the mission for the Special Forces was simply to assemble and train a special forces battalion and a commando brigade from remaining Kuwaiti forces. Training began in mid-September with sixty Kuwaiti soldiers. Soon, the 5th SFG's mission was expanded to include assembling and training four Kuwaiti infantry brigades. After initial delays because of a shortage of munitions and supplies, training for the infantry brigades began in late December. The 6,357 members of the special forces battalion, the commando brigade (renamed the Al-Tahrir Brigade), and the Al-Khulud, Al-Haq, Fatah, and Badr infantry brigades all participated in the ground war phase of Desert Storm.[19]

A "traditional" unconventional mission conducted by SOF during Desert Shield and during the air war portion of Desert Storm was special reconnaissance. From the beginning, SEALs and members of the special boat units ran security missions along the Kuwaiti coast. Beginning in October, SEAL platoons, along with marines, manned surveillance posts north of Ras Al-Khafji. When the Iraqis briefly overran the town in late January 1991, the SEALs coordinated close air support for the coalition forces before they were forced out.

Although they were not permitted to conduct long-range reconnaissance during Desert Shield, once the air war of Desert Storm began in January, Special Forces teams were sent into Iraq in search of Scud launchers and to conduct reconnaissance in support of the ground offensive.[20] Several teams flew into Iraq on SOF helicopters and took photos and soil samples to determine if the terrain or softness of the soil would hamper coalition forces as they moved through Iraq. Just prior to G-Day, the beginning of the ground war, Special Forces teams conducted twelve special reconnaissance missions deep into Iraq to watch for the repositioning of Iraqi forces and signs of an intended Iraqi counterattack.[21] These were A-teams of eight to ten men with weapons, communications, and medical specialties. They carried all their equipment, weapons, munitions, and supplies, enough to last for days or weeks, on their backs and were helicoptered into Iraq. Once in Iraq, the men constructed "hide sites." The hide sites were holes dug into the sand and reinforced with plastic pipe or wood brought in for this purpose. Constructing a hide site that cannot be seen even if one is standing on top of it is an art. Living inside these small holes shoulder-to-shoulder with your teammates for days on end requires the patience of Job.[22] Only two of the teams inserted just before the ground war were successful and undetected.[23] Several teams were extracted soon after landing because of the risk of being detected. One team had a harrowing experience that has become part of the lore of Desert Storm.

The team was buried in its hide sites north of the Euphrates River. The morning after the team had completed the construction of its sites, at least fifty people from the nearby village moved into the fields near the sites. Team members, hidden near a drainage canal, heard the voices of the children playing nearby suddenly become hushed, and they realized they had been detected. As the children ran away, several of the five snipers on the team came out of the holes ready to shoot. Their team leader, Chief Warrant Officer Chad Balwanz, "understanding that our fight was not with the children of Iraq," told them not to fire. Soon the team members were surrounded by the villagers, who fled when they saw the armed soldiers but soon returned with rifles. Moving from the hide sites and into a chest-deep canal, the team soon saw 150 Iraqi soldiers unloading from vehicles on the highway. Balwanz and his men destroyed their rucksacks and classified communications equipment after calling for close air support. They kept only their weapons and a single radio and moved into a new position. The Iraqis attacked and were initially repulsed, but because the Americans were outnumbered 15 to 1, they figured all was lost. Balwanz described the scene:

> When help arrived we were locked in heavy combat and had fought off repeated enemy assaults. For the remainder of the day sixteen sorties of F-16s provided close air support with a variety of munitions including cluster bombs and 2,000-pound bombs. Many were "danger close"—within 200 meters of our positions. At one point I led a counterattack down the canal and came face to face with the enemy point element. We eliminated the point element and the enemy withdrew down the canal. Expert marksmanship on the ground and F-16s in the air destroyed the enemy's will to pursue the fight.[24]

After six hours of combat, more than 150 Iraqis were dead. Balwanz and his team were pulled to safety by two Blackhawk helicopters from the 160th Special Operations Aviation Regiment. All of the team members survived.

Desert Storm

After months of gathering, organizing, and training, the coalition counteroffensive, Desert Storm, began January 17. At 3:30 p.m. on January 16, B-52 bombers were launched from Louisiana, carrying conventional cruise missiles toward the Persian Gulf. At 1:30 a.m. on January 17, American warships launched Tomahawk land attack missiles (TLAMs) toward Baghdad. Just after 2:00 A.M., Stealth fighters passed over the Iraqi border, also headed for Baghdad. At 2:38 a.m., two flights of helicopters, each led by two MH-53 Pave Low helicopters from the 20th Special Operations Squadron, made the first strike of the offensive.

The MH-53s led a total of eight AH-64 Apache attack helicopters from the 101st Airborne (Air Assault) Division. The Pave Lows added a long-range navigation capability and excellent combat survivability to the firepower of the Apaches. Their mission was to destroy two key Iraqi early warning radar sites in western Iraq, just over the Saudi-Iraqi border. Led by the Pave Lows to a point seven to ten miles from the radar sites, the Apaches destroyed the sites through the use of Hellfire missiles and 30mm cannons. The successful mission opened up an air corridor for the nearly 900 aircraft that flew into Iraq that day.[25]

In Desert Storm, special operations forces conducted many other direct action missions. MC-130E Combat Talon crews from the 8th Special Operations Squadron used 15,000-pound bombs to create overpressure and breach Iraqi minefields. In late January, special operations AC-130 Spectre gunships attacked Iraqi forces in southern Iraq, northeast Kuwait, and near Kuwait City. The Spectres also played an important role in the retaking of Khafji by coalition forces on January 29.

Naval SPECWAR units took the first enemy prisoners of war when they seized an armed offshore oil platform. In an operation on January 24, OH-58D helicopters operating from an American ship attempted to rescue twenty-two Iraqis from a minelayer sunk near Qarah Island. As the helicopters moved in to assist the survivors, Iraqi forces on the island opened fire. The USS *Curtis* returned fire with its 76mm guns, and SEALs from Naval Special Warfare Group 1 assaulted the island, carried by helicopters from the USS *Leftwich*. Resistance was light and the SEALs seized a large cache of weapons and sixty-seven prisoners. The Kuwaiti flag was raised above the island, the first Kuwaiti territory recaptured in the Persian Gulf War.[26]

The SEALs were an important part of coalition countermine warfare. There were SEALs in every helicopter that took off from U.S. Navy ships in the Persian Gulf looking for mines. If floating mines were spotted, the SEALs would drop from the hovering helicopters and swim to the mine. Once there, the SEALs attached a pretimed demolition charge to the mine and were picked up once again by the helicopters. The SEALs destroyed twenty-five mines in this manner.[27]

In one of the most spectacular and effective special operations of Desert Storm, Naval Special Warfare units played a major role in a coalition deception operation that held several Iraqi divisions near Kuwait City, preventing them from meeting the assault by coalition ground forces. There was much speculation that the coalition would conduct a marine amphibious landing as part of the ground offensive. As the coalition built up its forces in Southwest Asia, coalition commanders, including General Schwarzkopf, believed that an amphibious assault might be necessary to reclaim Kuwait. In preparation for such an assault, the U.S. Marine Corps deployed the 4th and 5th Marine Expeditionary Brigades and the 13th Marine Expeditionary Unit (Special Operations Capable). Iraqi leaders believed sufficiently in the likelihood of the assault and kept major elements of several divisions in Kuwait City to repulse any landing.

Reconnaissance by the SEALs, however, made it clear that Iraqi defenses and poor hydrographic conditions made such an assault highly risky. The coalition then began an elaborate deception campaign that convinced the Iraqis the amphibious landing was to occur. The campaign began after a member of a psychological operations unit came up with a way to increase Iraqi fears of an amphibious assault. The PSYOP unit created a leaflet called "the Wave." On one side is a picture of a gigantic wave in the shape of a marine coming ashore with a bayonet. In the background are Harrier aircraft and ships. The wave is about to crash on fleeing Iraqi forces. On the back of the leaflet are directions on how to surrender. The final instruction says, "If you do this you will not die." Command Sergeant Major John Meyer explained the thinking behind the leaflet, whose delivery was decided upon for maximum psychological effect: "Everybody in Saudi, of course, had to drink bottled water. There were millions of empty plastic water bottles just being thrown away every day. . . . [A sergeant thought] we [should] put the leaflets in some of the water bottles that we [would] just throw away anyhow: drop them off at sea and let the tides carry them ashore. Not only would . . . the leaflet [show] the marine coming out of the waves with the sword hacking up some Iraqis, but the fact that it actually came from the sea . . . indicate[d] that all these guys [were] out there waiting to come ashore."[28] The leaflets were stuffed into plastic water bottles and the bottles were dumped offshore. They began washing up on the beaches of Kuwait on January 14, the day before the coalition's deadline for Iraq to withdraw from Kuwait.[29]

In the culmination of the deception operation on February 23, the night before the ground offensive began, SEALs and special boat unit forces took off from their base at Ras Al Mishab in four high-speed boats. Seven miles out from Mina Saud on the Kuwaiti coast, Lieutenant Tom Dietz and his platoon of fifteen SEALs climbed into three Zodiac rubber boats and moved within 500 meters of the shore. Six of the men swam toward the shore, laying out a line of buoys used by the marines to mark amphibious landing zones. Once on shore, the SEALs placed six haversacks, each containing twenty pounds of C-4 plastic explosive and timers, on the beach. They set the timers to detonate at 1:00 A.M., three hours before the ground offensive was to start. The SEALs swam back to the rubber boats and then met up with two of the high-speed boats.

At 12:30 A.M., the crews of the other two high-speed boats opened fire on the beach from 300 meters offshore. Their sustained fire was followed by floating charges that exploded offshore for the next fifteen minutes. At 1:00 A.M., the haversack charges went off with tremendous explosions. The chaos was increased by air strikes directed at the beach and escape routes. The Iraqi divisions were fooled by this deception to such an extent that all of the Iraqi forces in place to defend against invasion from the sea remained fixed in place throughout the first day of the ground offensive. As a result, the Iraqis were unprepared to meet the coalition's "lefthook" as coalition forces swung around the Iraqi troops concentrated in Kuwait and enveloped them.[30]

Before the coalition offensive began in January, coalition commanders feared significant losses in its air forces. General Schwarzkopf originally designated the U.S. Air Force component commander (CENTAF) as the theater coordinator for combat search and rescue (CSAR), but because special operations aircraft were available and best suited to conduct long-range operations to recover downed air crews, CINCCENT designated Colonel Jesse Johnson as the commander of combat rescue forces. Throughout Desert Storm, SOF provided 24-hour, on-call CSAR for coalition air crews. U.S. Army SOF MH-60 helicopters, fleet-owned HH-60 and H-46 helicopters, and U.S. Air Force special operations MH-53J helicopters were all prepared for this mission.

Navy SEALs were on American and Kuwaiti ships in position in the northern Persian Gulf, air force and army special operators were just inside the Saudi border and in Turkey, waiting for the coalition's first strike on January 17. As it turned out, only thirty-eight coalition aircraft were downed during Desert Storm. Because of strict CSAR procedures requiring reasonable confirmation of the survivors' situation and location before a mission could be launched, and the loss of several aircraft over heavily fortified Iraqi positions, only seven search and rescue missions were launched, although one pilot was rescued by Kuwaiti partisan forces.[31] One of the missions was carried out by a SEAL element on January 23, rescuing the pilot within thirty minutes of his aircraft being shot down.[32]

The first successful rescue mission was carried out by U.S. Air Force Captain Thomas Trask and the crew of his MH-53J (Pave Low III) helicopter. At 7:30 in the morning on January 21, Trask and his crew were notified that a U.S. Navy F-14 had been shot down over northern Iraq and that the pilot had been spotted by his wing man. On its second attempt to pick its way through antiaircraft fire, a flight made all the more risky because it was broad daylight, and while maintaining contact with a pair of A-10s, the Pave Low crew made contact with the pilot, who had a hand-held survival radio. Just as the crew made contact, the A-10s spotted an Iraqi truck heading at full speed toward the navy lieutenant on the ground. Racing against the Iraqis, the helicopter dropped to the ground to pick up the pilot. As they rose back into the sky, Captain Trask saw the burning remains of the truck, destroyed by the A-10s.[33]

Of all the special operations that took place in Desert Shield and Desert Storm, perhaps that which most successfully opened the eyes of conventional military commanders and political leaders to the value of special operations in reducing the level of violence in a conflict and reducing the number of casualties on both sides were those missions carried out by the members of the 4th Psychological Operations Group. Psychological operations, or PSYOP, often carries the connotation of "brainwashing" or some other nefarious activity. In reality, as described by the commander of a company in the 9th PSYOP Battalion, these operations are about: "Communication. . . . We're not allowed to work on the black [covert] side. We can't do anything against Americans. . . . And everything we do must be the truth. . . . Normally, when you go into a place like Somalia or any of these troubled places throughout the world, the problem is information or if somebody's controlling the information. . . . What we try to do is take the truth . . . and get it down to the populace or whoever needs to hear it. And that's what we work at via radio, television, newspapers."[34]

The extensive use of psychological operations in the Persian Gulf is largely because of the success of PSYOP in Panama. Commanders learned in the course of Just Cause what the PSYOP units' capabilities were and recognized their great value in reducing casualties. From the beginning of the Gulf conflict, as the coalition forces were being pulled together, PSYOP teams were in demand.[35]

PSYOP teams conducted several missions as part of Desert Shield and Desert Storm, often working with other psychological operators from Saudi Arabia, Egypt, and Great Britain. The operations ranged from the mundane to the spectacular. Some of the communication was basic, for example, educating an Iraqi soldier that a Red Cross meant the same as a Red Crescent. At a more sophisticated level, coalition forces had to counter Saddam Hussein's attempt to exploit Islam. The coaliton worked to gain support from Hussein's Islamic neighbors. As described by a former commander of the 4th Psychological Operations Group, coalition psychological operators responded to Saddam's attempt to coopt Arab nations:

> We produced a film that had an Islamic theme to it. It started out with a quote from the Koran, something to the effect that brothers don't attack brothers and those who do shall suffer eternal shame. [There was] a man at the mosque as they were doing the evening prayers [who warned] 'now that you have violated the code as the Koran describes, this is what we have available to respond and we are justified in responding.' And then [the film showed] about ten minutes of [our forces] blowing up everything, [using] some of the biggest weapons we had. And then it closed out, once again back to the theme with the mosque and the evening prayers in the background: 'But he who shall recognize his transgressions . . . and mend his ways shall again be brothers.' And [the film] was shown around the world.[36]

The 4th Psychological Operations Group sent nearly one hundred loudspeaker teams to Saudi Arabia to work with the conventional combat units. Since the group had only six deployable Arabic speakers, it recruited Kuwaitis. The Kuwaitis did not speak English, so the British provided eight Arabic instructors from their school at Sandhurst. The instructors taught the recruited Kuwaitis enough basic English to understand the guidance from the American forces and gave the Americans a crash course in Arabic. The teams deployed with coalition combat units were successful in preventing many unnecessary casualties.

In one case, a PSYOP team supporting the British 7th Armoured Brigade was called forward by a British armor unit. The regiment had surrounded a reinforced Iraqi company that was occupying prepared defensive positions in a small Iraqi town. The PSYOP team moved between the British tanks and the town and, in Arabic, called for the Iraqis to surrender. The team warned the Iraqi troops that coalition forces controlled the sky and also had them surrounded with overwhelming ground force. If the Iraqis chose to resist, this force would be unleashed. Within fifteen minutes, more than 170 Iraqi soldiers poured from the town, waving anything white they could find. Not one shot had been fired.[37]

The most spectacular success of the psychological operations campaign was the result of the leaflet campaign. The PSYOP teams prepared and dropped the leaflets as part of preparing the battlefield. In battle, psychological operations "attacks the enemy's will to fight and deceives him, thereby forcing him to react to, rather than anticipate the actions of the attacker."[38] In the Persian Gulf War, psychological preparation of the battlefield began in December 1990. Part of this preparation was the work of the loudspeaker teams and the operation of a radio network, Voice of the Gulf, which provided war news to the Iraqi soldiers and citizens. The leaflet campaign, however, had the most dramatic success.

Beginning on December 30, the coalition began delivering 3-inch by 6-inch leaflets to Iraqi forces in Kuwait. Besides the coalition's use of water bottles as described earlier, the messages were dropped largely by MC-130 special operations aircraft but also by HC-130, A-6, F-16, and B-52 aircraft and artillery. As described in the 4th Psychological Operations Group account of the leaflet campaign:

> A PSYOP leaflet campaign is effective only if the message reaches the target audience in a timely manner. Leaflet disseminators use mathematical formulas to plot with reasonable accuracy the distance and direction that a leaflet travels before hitting the ground. Wind speed and direction are two important variables . . .Another important variable used in the dissemination formulas is the falling rate of the leaflet . . . based on the leaflet's size, weight and rotation pattern in the air.[39]

Twenty-nine million leaflets, with thirty-three different messages, were delivered into the Kuwaiti theater of operations.[40]

The leaflet operation used a building-block approach. The first phase emphasized peace and brotherhood between Iraq and its Arab and Islamic neighbors. Messages included a leaflet with a picture of two soldiers, one with the Iraqi flag and one with the Saudi Arabian flag, hand-in-hand in the desert with the caption "in Peace we will always remain hand in hand."[41] The next step, a more threatening approach, warned of the upcoming January 15 UN deadline for Iraq's withdrawal from Kuwait. One leaflet said, "This is only the beginning! This could have been a real bomb. We have no desire to harm innocent people, but Saddam is leading you to certain death and destruction. We want you to know the truth! Saddam is the cause. Yes, the Multi-National Forces have the ability to strike anywhere. . . and at anytime! Warning!"

Once the UN deadline passed and the air war began, leaflets encouraged Iraqi soldiers to abandon their equipment and surrender in order to save themselves. These leaflets continued the theme that coalition forces did not wish to kill the soldiers but were determined to end Saddam Hussein's ability to fight. One leaflet had two panels on the front. The first panel showed a burning tank and scorched skeleton while the second panel showed another burning tank with a soldier fleeing, but alive. The caption, in Arabic, stated, "Leave your equipment or defend it and die! The choice is yours!" Iraqi forces no longer felt protected by their armor since it was now a target.

The most terrifying and directly effective phase of the PSYOP campaign made use of B-52 bombers. Millions of leaflets printed on one side with a picture of the bomber, and referring to the specific unit being targeted, were dropped on dug-in Iraqi forces. The caption on the front read, "This is your first and last warning! Tomorrow, the 16th Infantry Division will be bombed!! Flee this location now!" On the back of these leaflets was printed the following: "The 16th Infantry Division will be bombed tomorrow. The bombing will be heavy. If you want to save yourselves leave your location and do not allow anyone to stop you. Save yourselves and head toward the Saudi border, where you will be welcomed as a brother."

The day after these first leaflets were dropped, as promised, monstrous B-52s would arrive and furiously bombard the Iraqi units. The next day, another leaflet was dropped. Again, the front of the leaflet pictured a B-52 while the back warned: "We have already informed you of our promise to bomb the 16th Infantry Division. We kept our promise and bombed them yesterday. Beware. We will repeat this bombing tomorrow . . . Either stay and face death or accept the invitation of the Joint Forces to protect your lives."

In another instance, soon after the Iraqi forces again were given a warning and told to flee, special operators flying MC-130s dropped 15,000-pound bombs on Iraqi positions. The following day, the surviving Iraqi troops received a leaflet: "You have just experienced the most powerful conventional bomb dropped in the war. It has more explosive power than 20 Scud missiles.You will be bombed again soon. Kuwait will be free from aggression. Flee south and you will be treated fairly. You cannot hide."

The combination of threats carried out, raw terror, and the promise of good and fair treatment for Iraqi prisoners had a tremendous effect. During the air war itself, according to the reports of several Iraqi officers, soldiers would become terrified when they heard B-52 bombers, even if the bombers were attacking another position. The result was abandonment of armor equipment and even desertions.[42]

The final phase of the campaign continued the threats, including that of the ground offensive, but also emphasized peaceful and safe surrender and eventual return home. A leaflet, again with two panels, showed soldiers in Saudi Arabia with plentiful food and water, while the second pamphlet pictured an Iraqi soldier surrendering in the proper manner: carrying the leaflet with his rifle over his left shoulder and pointing to the ground. The back of this leaflet had the emblem of the joint forces of the coalition with the words: "From HQ Joint Forces and Theater of Operations. You are invited to join the Joint Forces and enjoy full Arab hospitality, security, safety, and medical care. You will return to your homes as soon as the situation that Saddam has placed us in has ended. My brother Iraqi soldier . . .this invitation is open to you and your comrade soldiers."

During this last phase, many of the leaflets emphasized the overwhelming military superiority of the coalition forces and gave Iraqi forces directions on how to surrender: "Remove magazine from your weapon. Place weapon over your left shoulder with the muzzle down. Place your hands over your head and proceed slowly. Wave a white cloth to signal your peaceful intent or hold up this leaflet.

All armies of the Multi-National Forces understand that this pass shows your honorable commitment to peace."

The effect of this psychological preparation of the battlefield was beyond all expectations or hopes. When the ground war began, Iraqi soldiers surrendered in droves. There were reports of troops surrendering to any coalition personnel they could find, including a truckload of reporters. In the end, more than 85,000 Iraqi soldiers surrendered and more than 70 percent of them gave up as a result of the combined PSYOP and bomber campaign, many carrying the leaflets when they surrendered.[43] The PSYOP campaign saved not only the lives of Iraqi soldiers but the lives of conventional coalition forces who might have been killed had these troops chosen to fight.

The End of the War and Operation Provide Comfort

As in Just Cause in Panama, following the conclusion of Desert Storm's one-hundred-hour ground offensive, the focus of special operations shifted toward civil affairs. While civil affairs (CA) forces have been used in combat as liaisons between American forces and the host nation and its forces, in recent years CA forces have been at their busiest after a conflict ends, rebuilding countries where fighting has taken place and helping with refugees.

Civil affairs planners and forces, preparing for support of combat operations, were involved earlier in Desert Shield than in previous conflicts. Members of the 96th Civil Affairs Battalion, the only active duty civil affairs unit in USSOCOM, deployed in August. The 352nd Civil Affairs Command was called up in September. Civil affairs forces developed and conducted a program for all American personnel deploying to Saudi Arabia to prepare them for "the region's uniqueness and its history, customs, religion, law, and mores."[44] Once in Saudi Arabia, CA elements worked with the Saudi Arabian government to plan, coordinate, and implement "host nation support" for the forces pouring into the country. Early in Desert Shield, partially because of General Schwarzkopf's push to get combat units in the country as quickly as possible, the Saudis provided much of the water, fuel, and transportation until military support units arrived. Civil affairs personnel also worked with the Saudi government to develop a civil defense plan for the Saudis and organize emergency services.

Coalition planners recognized the risk to morale and to the coalition posed by potential damage to artifacts of Iraq's ancient cultural and religious heritage. Before the beginning of the air war, therefore, civil affairs and PSYOP personnel worked with U.S. Air Force planners to identify religious and cultural sites within Kuwait and Iraq that should be put on the "no-fire" target list. With their regional and cultural knowledge, these forces were able to identify mosques, religious shrines, and archaeological sites that were to be protected if at all possible. They also tried to identify primarily civilian facilities, such as schools and hospitals, and civilian residential and work areas. Once ground combat began, civil affairs units were assigned to coalition combat units, moving forward with these units into Kuwait and Iraq. Civil affairs personnel were responsible for minimizing civilian interference with combat operations and avoiding civilian casualties, often working with PSYOP loudspeaker teams to provide warning and direction. Civil affairs teams assigned to combat units also assisted displaced civilians and refugees and any enemy prisoners of war (EPWs) encountered on the battlefield.[45]

The number of refugees nearly overwhelmed coalition leaders. Coalition forces attempted to keep civilian refugees separate from prisoners of war, who were the responsibility of military police units. Civil affairs personnel assisted the military police in setting up temporary shelters and providing emergency food, water, and basic medical care. Any civilians caught up as the EPWs were rounded up became the responsibility of the civil affairs forces who worked to identify the refugees and repatriate them to Iraq.

As the refugees streamed out of the combat areas, two camps—referred to as "temporary refugee sites" in order to avoid responsibilities associated with establishing semipermanent camps—were established near the Saudi border in Iraq.[46] At the Safwan camp, run by the 404th Civil Affairs Battalion, the population rose from 1,300 to 13,000 people in four days. The camp at Rahfa initially had more than 12,000 refugees. Eventually, the Safwan refugees were moved to Rahfa for a total of more than 20,000 refugees. Running the camps was difficult. They had to be designed and constructed. Tents had to be put up and latrines dug. Everyone had to be fed. Everyone had to receive water. They had to be stopped from hurting one another in their desperation to receive food and water for themselves and their families. Medical care was provided, and a program to reunite families was put in place. Religious and ethnic differences had to be recognized and regional mores followed, such as separating the living area of single men from that of families or single women. The tension and potential chaos within such camps is severe.

One crisis that was averted by the dedication of the civil affairs personnel began when the cease-fire was in place. As U.S. Army forces began to withdraw from Iraq, civil affairs units were ordered to pull back. The civil affairs and other personnel at Safwan responsible for the welfare of 13,000 refugees, refused to withdraw. According to one of the civil affairs officers at the camp, the U.S. Army's 3rd Armored Division did not want to abandon the refugees or turn them over to the Iraqi government either. Negotiations began between Washington and Saudi Arabia and with the Kuwaitis, and eventually an agreement was reached that those refugees who wanted to could go to Iran. Several thousand chose this option. Those who wanted to stay were airlifted over a four-day period to the other large refugee camp in Rahfa.[47]

Throughout the conflict in the Persian Gulf, it was clear that, as one career military policeman and civil affairs officer said, "Many folks in the army still don't know the value [of] or how to use civil affairs units and assets. As the years have gone on, they're moving in the right direction. . . . If innocent civilians get involved, whether they get picked up as prisoners, whether they're injured because we're throwing shells back and forth at each other . . . there's something civil affairs can do to prevent that."[48]

The uncertainty of U.S. Army and other conventional forces about the use of civil affairs units often means that these units are called up late in the process. Although civil affairs personnel were included in the planning for Desert Shield and Desert Storm earlier than in any previous conflict, there were still problems of coordination. Some civil affairs units were called into action only at the last minute. For example, in several cases civil affairs forces did not arrive in Saudi Arabia to support coalition combat units until after these units had moved to preassault positions in preparation for the ground war.[49]

The greatest difficulty in civil affairs planning and operations is convincing military planners in the throes of preparing to fight a war to consider what will happen after the armed conflict is over. In October 1990, two months after the invasion of Kuwait by Iraq, the exiled government of Kuwait asked the American government for assistance in planning for the rebuilding of Kuwait. The State Department turned to the Department of Defense, but it took nearly two more months for the Kuwait Civil Affairs Task Force to be formed. According to the Defense Department report on the conduct of the Persian Gulf War:

> Despite notable CA successes discussed in this report, the civil implications of military operations did not receive as much early planning attention as would have been preferred. . . . The planning assistance to the Kuwait government, although requested in October, did not commence until December and it was done in isolation from the war plans prepared by CENTCOM.[50]

The Kuwait Civil Affairs Task Force was composed largely of members of the 352nd Civil Affairs Command. The sixty-three members of the 352nd were assisted by Kuwaitis who were attending school in the United States when Saddam Hussein invaded Kuwait.[51] The task force assumed that the Iraqis would destroy all Kuwaiti government institutions and severely damage Kuwaiti infrastructure during their occupation. The task force first developed a plan for reconstituting the Kuwaiti government and rebuilding the Kuwait physical plant. Once the plan was in place, task force members marshaled public and private resources to assist in implementing the plan once the Iraqis were chased out. Civil affairs personnel, nearly all of whom were in the U.S. Army Reserve, provided many of the experts needed to supervise implementation of the plan, including medical personnel, firefighters and police, veterinarians, an agronomist, city planners, government affairs specialists, and even economists. Other experts needed to help in the reconstruction were recruited from exiled Kuwaitis and American civilians.[52]

The day after Kuwait City was liberated, the Kuwaiti Civil Affairs Task Force moved in to put their plan into effect. They began by directing efforts to put out the more than five hundred oil well fires set by the Iraqis as a parting gesture to the Kuwaitis. The next stop was clearing the Kuwaiti ports, all of which were blocked with cars driven into the water by the Iraqis. The water system was repaired, followed quickly by the telephone system, emergency medical care, and transportation. Civil affairs personnel remained in Kuwait for more than two years after Desert Storm concluded.

The last special operation conducted as part of the Persian Gulf War was Operation Provide Comfort. Provide Comfort began as an effort to aid the Kurdish refugees from northern Iraq who were being threatened and killed by Iraqi forces, and the operation continues in a limited form today. Special operations forces established two task forces, one near the border in Turkey and the other near the border in Iraq. Their mission was to provide assistance to Kurdish refugees who were dying from dehydration and cholera and who needed food, clothing, shelter, and medical assistance. A noncommissioned Special Forces officer who served at a refugee camp with more than 65,000 Kurdish refugees near the Turkish-Iraqi border described his experience:

The refugees lived under every form of shelter, from plastic tarps to pieces of canvas left over from air dropped bundles. When we arrived there were fifty to a hundred people dying every day from disease, malnutrition, and land mines. We conducted a quick medical assessment to determine what we needed to do to lower the death rate and increase the overall health of the refugee[s]. The most critical need was for clean drinking water, as contaminated water was the primary cause of disease. Using our Special Forces engineers and a lot of hard work, we were able to open six major wells which provided enough clean water to supply most of the camp.

The initial re-supply effort was by parachute. This was dangerous because most open areas where the bundles were landing were mined. We changed this using CH-47 helicopters with sling loads. . . . Our SF medics treated everything from dysentery and cholera to gunshot wounds. On several occasions all of my personnel were involved providing some type of medical aid or emergency treatment. In Chuchurca, the next camp to ours, 250 kids with cholera were triaged and written off as "too far gone" by "Doctors without Frontiers." Our medics didn't buy that. For over 72 hours they hydrated, rehydrated, and treated those kids . . . only three of those kids died.[53]

Once the refugees were fit, many were returned to Iraq. American military forces maintained the two joint task forces on the border. Smaller way stations were spread throughout the mountainous region to provide food and water to Kurds as they moved through the area.[54] Occasionally, medical assistance would be provided if the situation was critical. What started as a two-week operation to air-drop food and act as UN observers continued for more than three years. In fact, the effects of the Persian Gulf War are still being felt, and special operations forces are still working to solve the problems as of this writing. PSYOP, Special Forces, and civil affairs personnel are still assisting the Kurds. Special operators are also deployed to assist in maintaining the no-fly zones in Iraq.[55] And civil affairs personnel are still deploying to Kuwait to assist in its rebuilding.

In Desert Shield and Desert Storm the professionalism and effectiveness of special operators demonstrated the ability of a strong and flexible American special operations capability, fully integrated with conventional forces, to assist the United States in reaching its political and military goals. As has been true in major conflicts since World War II, the value of SOF in the Persian Gulf should not be evaluated with measures of effectiveness—such as the number of enemy forces destroyed or the forward movement of the allied battle lines—used for conventional forces. SOF's greatest impact is felt in the successful completion of missions not easily taken on by conventional forces. This impact must be measured in less concrete terms, taking into account those things that did not happen. In Desert Shield and Desert Storm these terms may include numbers of enemy not available to fight because they surrendered after a psycho-logical operation or the number of coalition forces lives not lost as a result of the deception operation off the coast of Kuwait or through liaison work that prevented friendly fire losses among coalition forces. Finally, unlike most conventional forces, SOF played a major role after Desert Storm, rebuilding the war-torn nations, assisting in the reconstruction of Kuwait, and managing and supporting the nearly overwhelming surge of prisoners of war and refugees.

11

Moving Forward

With the conclusion of Desert Storm, U.S. special operations forces entered a new era. Although conventional commanders still had their suspicions about special operations forces, SOF's reliability and successes in the war did much to reduce this distrust. Certainly by the summer of 1991 it was clear to all that in the previous ten years the United States had successfully, though with some reluctance, created from the ashes of Desert One a broad, flexible, and strong special operations capability.

The Collapse of the Berlin Wall and the New World Disorder

Regional instability and lower-level conflict have increased in the years following Desert Storm, the collapse of the Soviet Union, and the subsequent release from the danger of a catastrophic global war. The American national security strategy of deterrence reduced the possibility of World War III, but it has much less effect in the new world. The crises faced by the United States and the international community are of a different type than the scenarios against which American military force structure was designed. Nor was Desert Storm, a conventional war on a smaller scale than had been anticipated during the previous forty-five years, the prototype for conflicts in the new world disorder. Instead, in the 1990s America has found itself facing crises resulting from ethnic conflicts and civil wars; crises in which the most demanding tasks for the United States appeared to be feeding the hungry and protecting civilians rather than facing off with professional military forces.

Since the collapse of the Berlin Wall, the military force that has been deployed most frequently by the president in response to international crises has been U.S. special operations forces. SOF has provided aircraft and crews to deliver food and medical supplies in Bosnia, had a civil affairs team operating in the former Yugoslavia as part of Operation Provide Promise, provided special operations advisers to peacekeepers in Macedonia, deployed observers for UN peacekeeping in the Western Sahara, and provided humanitarian and civic assistance throughout Africa, often through joint and combined exercises with host nation forces.

One of the most publicized special operations in recent years was in Somalia, as part of Operation Restore Hope. The Somalia operation demonstrated much of what is valuable in special operations. It also demonstrated the danger SOF faces in its future—the continued risk of misuse of its forces and the reality of high-risk, high-payoff operations.

The United States intervened in Somalia to put a stop to the devastation in a country where hundreds, and even thousands, were dying daily of hunger and disease. U.S. Navy SEALs were involved from the very beginning of the operation in December 1992. SEALs conducted hydrographic reconnaissance, laid out landing zones for U.S. forces, and guided the marines to the beaches of Mogadishu. Although American forces were sent to Somalia to protect the delivery of food to the destitute, particularly in the towns outside of Mogadishu, from the beginning there was a mismatch in expectations between the Somali people and their American saviors. The United States initially intended a brief humanitarian mission, but even before the troops arrived in December 1992, educated Somalis and clan leaders believed American forces would need to stay for at least a year to resolve the causes of starvation. One Somali official, quoted in a December 4, 1992, *New York Times* article, warned, "The Somalis think they [the Americans] will do a lot of things for them. And if they don't do these things—deliver the humanitarian food, then disarm the people and then bring people together for political reconciliation—it will revert to chaos."[1] As it turned out, the Somali official accurately predicted the not-so-far-away future.

The deployment of American-led forces to Somalia under UN auspices was the fourth major new military and humanitarian engagement accepted by the United Nations following the end of the cold war, following involvement in the Persian Gulf region and peacekeeping missions in Cambodia and the Balkans.[2] Within days of President George Bush's proposal to send troops to Somalia on a short-term mission, it became apparent even to those in the American government that the extent of the anarchy in Somalia was such that the UN commitment would have to be long term.

Eventually, the United States committed more than 20,000 troops to relief efforts in Somalia. The deployment included the U.S. Marines, the

U.S. Army's 10th Mountain Division, naval forces, aviation units, and many special operators. First into Somalia as part of Operation Restore Hope were the SEALs. Within days, civil affairs and psychological operations personnel arrived in the country. Civil affairs forces conducted MEDCAPs, medical capability exercises providing medical and dental care, in the rural regions of Somalia. The psychological operations (PSYOP) forces informed the people of Somalia of the mission and actions of the American and UN forces. Using loudspeaker teams, flyers, and a briefly published newspaper, the PSYOP unit publicized good work being done and countered misinformation coming from the clan leaders. According to one PSYOP commander deployed to Somalia:

> Every time I looked around there was some type of flyer or something coming down from one of the clans saying that [the U.N. forces were] trying to change [the Somali's] religion or trying to desecrate [Somali] culture. We were showing, . . . we would like to improve those living conditions, but we're not there to do a makeover of [the] country.[3]

Civil affairs and PSYOP teams worked together in programs to get local elders and governments together to assist them in regaining control over their provinces. With the assistance of the American teams, the local governments would sponsor the equivalent of town meetings and sporting events in an effort to counter the influence of the clans and gain the support of the people.[4] As in Desert Storm, leaflets were used to keep the Somalis informed and warn them not to interfere with the food convoys. The first leaflets were dropped on December 9, supporting the arrival of American forces and announcing the convoy operations. One leaflet, known as the "handshake" leaflet, depicted an American soldier shaking hands with a Somali man. Printed on the back was, "United Nations forces are here to assist in the international relief effort for the Somali people. We are prepared to use force to protect the relief operation and our soldiers. We will not allow interference with food distribution or with our activities. We are here to help you."[5]

These leaflets were dropped two or three days before the arrival of UN forces in each town. Just before the convoys moved through an area, another leaflet was dropped warning, "Our forces are here to protect relief convoys. Do not block roadways! Force will be used to protect the convoys." Loudspeaker teams preceded the convoys and made similar announcements.

Unfortunately, and not surprisingly, the special operation in Somalia that received the most attention was the October 3, 1993, raid to capture

General Mohamed Farah Aideed's lieutenants. This operation demonstrated the high-risk aspect of special operations, for which the cost of failure can be painful. This operation also demonstrated the risk of misuse of SOF in situations where the ad hoc, multinational nature of the operation results in degraded intelligence, weakened command and control, poor operational security, and unrealistic schedule constraints.

Rangers and Special Forces, supported by special operations aviation, were alerted on June 5, 1993, to begin preparation for deployment to Somalia immediately following an ambush of Pakistani soldiers by Somali militia in Mogadishu.[6] On June 17 the UN commanders in Somalia issued an arrest order for Somali militia leader Aideed. The 400-man Task Force Ranger, composed of Rangers, Special Forces, and special operations aviation units, was ordered to deploy on August 22, following the second of two incidents in which U.S. troops were killed or wounded by Somali forces using remote-controlled mines. In late August and September, Task Force Ranger conducted a half dozen raids, with mixed success, in an attempt to capture Aideed or his lieutenants.

On October 3, the task force received word from a Somali informant that a meeting of some of Aideed's lieutenants was to be held near the Olympic Hotel in Mogadishu that afternoon. Task Force Ranger launched a raid. After the force had successfully rounded up the militia leaders, tragedy struck the special operations force when one of the Blackhawk helicopters supporting the operation was shot down by a rocket-propelled grenade. Both pilots were killed. Subsequently, a second Blackhawk was downed, and several more helicopters were severely damaged. After more than fifteen hours of combat between Task Force Ranger and thousands of Somali militia and irregulars, one of several rescue attempts was successful. Eighteen Americans and one Malaysian (part of the rescuing Quick Reaction Force) were killed, and 84 Americans and 7 Malaysians were wounded. Somali casualties were more than 300 killed and 800 wounded.

The UN-ordered "arrest" of Aideed had the cast of police work about it, with the attendant implications of publicly acknowledged legal and civic authority. It was in fact a military mission to capture an enemy officer in hostile territory. The operation suffered because it straddled the fence between civic and military affairs. When members of the U.S. Special Operations Command (USSOCOM) were asked whether Task Force Ranger's mission was appropriate for a military force, not one questioned the mission or had doubts about whether the operation in Somalia was appropriate for special operations forces. General Wayne Downing, USSOCOM commander in chief during the operation, has stated, "The capture or recovery of personnel is a SOF mission and the forces assigned in Somalia were entirely appropriate to the mission."[7] Nonetheless, special operators carrying out the mission were placed at a great disadvantage as American and UN decisions took away many of the special attributes these forces bring to an operation. Most critical was the loss of secrecy. The alert to special operations forces in early June was quickly followed by a very public announcement of the UN arrest order for Aideed. Task Force Ranger's mission and its deployment were announced simultaneously with its arrival in Somalia. Compounding this loss of secrecy was the fact that intelligence resources available to the operation seemed to limit their information to daytime movements of Aideed and his men. The special operators therefore lost the advantage of their unique nighttime operations capability. This alone was likely to increase the risk of the mission. When multiplied by the complete loss of surprise entailed in the public announcements of UN intentions, it resulted in a loss of life that ultimately led to a public questioning of the wisdom of the entire U.S. mission in Somalia.

Despite the lessons of Just Cause and Desert Storm, a poor understanding of SOF's unique capabilities and requirements was demonstrated in the dismissal of Special Forces liaisons from non-U.S. United Nations forces in Somalia. As described earlier, Special Forces acted as liaison officers with Arab coalition forces in Desert Shield and Desert Storm. Special Forces operated in the same role during the initial UN deployment to Mogadishu in December 1992, but the teams were sent back by the conventional commanders after a few weeks. Had those teams been in place during the October raid, Malaysian and Pakistani support to the Quick Reaction Force would have been quicker and less chaotic. The same conventional commanders allowed the liaison teams back in Mogadishu in the weeks following the October 3 raid.[8]

Despite the loss in Somalia, U.S. special operations forces have continued to respond quickly and effectively to crises and instability throughout the world. Most of the deployments support civic or humanitarian operations. Typical of such operations is a recent medical exercise conducted in Botswana that assisted the Botswana military in providing vaccinations and health education to rural people.[9] Other deployments include the peacekeeping and humanitarian operations mentioned earlier and SOF support to refugees from Cuba and from Rwanda. Components of USSOCOM, including the Rangers and SEALs, were part of operations in Haiti in 1995. On any given day American special operators are deployed in more than fifty nations.[10]

Special Operations Forces Today

The third commander in chief of the U.S. Special Operations Command, General Wayne Downing, worked to complete the realization of the command's unique status. Downing continued the maturation process begun by Generals James Lindsay and Carl Stiner, enabling USSOCOM to grow from simply a unified combatant command to a servicelike organization. Downing also built on the efforts by the Office of the Assistant Secretary of Defense, Special Operations and Low-Intensity Conflict, and the command to "sell" SOF and its capabilities. He expanded SOCOM's early, narrow operational focus and pushed to solidify SOF's organizational status and the command's servicelike responsibilities.

Like Lindsay and Stiner, Downing has a long history of operational command. He has spent extensive time in the U.S. Army Rangers. Downing commanded the Ranger Regiment as well as the Joint Special Operations Command and U.S. Army Special Operations Command, the army component to USSOCOM. During Operation Just Cause in Panama, he commanded 4,400 special operations forces. Downing was the Joint Special Operations Task Force commander, reporting directly to General Norman Schwarzkopf, during and after the Gulf War in 1991 and 1992. Unlike Stiner and Lindsay, however, Downing had two tours in the Pentagon, including an assignment in Program Analysis and Evaluation in the Office of the Secretary of Defense. As a brigadier general, Downing was the first director of the USSOCOM Washington office. General Downing offered a combination of operational and bureaucratic experience that was invaluable in USSOCOM's development.

Not long after assuming command on May 20, 1993, General Downing talked about the shift in USSOCOM's view of its mission since its establishment in 1987.

> There was [initially] . . . real concern in the command about the corollary part of the mission . . . to conduct independent special operations. . . . In my estimation maybe even too much concern. . . . I don't think we put enough emphasis in those days on MFP-11. . . . And then the second thing was the RDA [research, development, and acquisition function]. So these are two areas that . . . traditionally we have not been strong in and that we are really working on. Those are my priorities.[11]

The shift in organizational concerns has been dramatic and is easily visible. If General Lindsay and his staff seemed to believe that the focus of the command should be on USSOCOM's operational mission, and General Stiner and his staff viewed USSOCOM as a combatant command with resource responsibilities, General Downing led a servicelike organization that, while not ignoring its operations responsibilities, emphasized long-range resource planning, financial management, and research, development, and acquisition. This change in focus has filtered down to a staff that is more frequently hiring functional experts in strategic planning, programming, budgeting, and acquisition.[12] According to a Special Forces officer who has served as a division chief at USSOCOM:

> Basically we are a force provider. The .0001 [probability] mission with this headquarters being a supported command hasn't occurred yet, may never occur. But basically we are a supporting command—supporting and providing forces to the other five warfighting CINCs.[13]

USSOCOM under the leadership of General Downing did not abandon its operational concerns. Instead, less emphasis was given to preparing operational plans for the rare instances when the commander in chief would wear his "warfighting" hat and more attention was, and continues to be, paid to a broadened definition of "preparing special operations forces." Plans are being made not only for today's operations but also for those ten to twenty years from now. General Downing recognized that the command was solidly established and that SOF had received the benefit of reorganization and increased funding under General Lindsay and General Stiner. On his watch he wanted USSOCOM to fully accept its servicelike responsibilities and continue to demonstrate SOF's ability to support the U.S. national security objectives. Building on Stiner's tremendous progress in gaining the confidence of the regional, unified commanders in chief and increasing the employment of SOF, General Downing worked to provide support for other government agencies, including the Drug Enforcement Agency, National Security Agency, and the Central Intelligence Agency. Downing believed that SOCOM could provide a valued capability to all these agencies, "reliable and, in most cases, low visibility support for their regional programs."[14] Both USSOCOM and the Office of the Assistant Secretary of Defense, Special Operations and Low-Intensity Conflict, pushed their organizations to participate in the Defense Department planning and resource allocation processes.

Guaranteeing a Future

More than fifteen years after the crash in the Iranian desert, the SOF community and its supporters have achieved their goal of a vital and capable U.S. special operations capability. The new organizations of USSOCOM and the Office of Assistant Secretary of Defense, Special Operations and Low-Intensity Conflict (OASD [SOLIC]) are now fully established, even if they do not fully match the vision of their creators. If the policy of a revitalized special operations capability is to be sustained, these organizations must now look toward the future, paying attention to three major areas. The first area of concern is a difficult one for all government agencies: moving beyond daily organizational concerns and developing a vision of the future of SOF. Second, SOF must reach a balance between the organizational requirements of a near-service and the operational effectiveness of its forces. Finally, based on the strengths of its organizational culture, members of the special operations community must protect and promote what is "special" about special operations forces.

A Road Map

Moving beyond the daily concerns of bureaucratic struggles and operational demands is difficult for any organization. It is especially difficult for SOF because the forces that make up the command have had long-range planning responsibilities only since USSOCOM was activated in 1987. The first years of USSOCOM and the Office of the Assistant Secretary of Defense, Special Operations and Low-Intensity Conflict, necessarily emphasized building the organizations rather than planning for the future. As established organizations, they now need to guarantee a continued strong special operations capability. They must look beyond the next major special operation or planning, programming, and budgeting cycle and develop a road map for the future. This road map has two components: an American policy toward conflict other than large-scale conventional wars and a "concept of operations" for special operations forces that includes an implementation plan.

As described in chapter 9, the SOF community has attempted to provide an overarching policy in the recent past. Assistant Secretary of Defense Jim Locher proposed a policy for "peacetime engagement" that addressed "national security policy for the arena outside of global or major regional war."[15] The Bush administration, however, was not yet ready to shift its attention away from the collapsing Soviet Union or the possibility of another war like Desert Storm. With the election of President Bill Clinton in 1992, Secretary of Defense Les Aspin attempted to organize the Office of the Secretary of Defense in such a way as to deemphasize cold war approaches to national security and place increased emphasis on low-intensity conflict. In doing so, however, Aspin did not call upon the assistant secretary of defense, special operations and low-intensity conflict. Instead, he created a plethora of assistant secretary positions, each responsible for a piece of what might have been SOLIC's pie. With Aspin's early vacancy of the office in January 1994, his successor, William Perry, backed away from Aspin's reorganization to some extent while continuing to hold a broader view of national security interests. Perry took the long overdue step of shifting responsibility for humanitarian assistance and counternarcotics policy to ASD (SOLIC). While these changes are promising, and reflect the reality of international security in the 1990s, a broad national security policy such as that offered by SOLIC's earlier peacetime engagement efforts has yet to be approved. The Office of the Assistant Secretary of Defense, Special Operations and Low-Intensity Conflict, should once again make an effort to develop such a policy by working with the unified, regional commanders, the National Security Council, and the Department of State to identify those contingencies other than major conventional war and possible American responses, military and nonmilitary, to these crises. Without this kind of umbrella policy, and a plan for its implementation that looks five to fifteen years ahead, economic and military resources available to the United States cannot be effectively employed.

Even if SOLIC does not have the influence to convince the Defense Department, along with the State Department, Central Intelligence Agency, Drug Enforcement Agency, and the National Security Council, to identify the linkage between political-military-economic forces in support of American national security interests, SOLIC and USSOCOM must at least work with their strongest supporters, the unified CINCs. Together they could provide the foundation for such a policy by defining low-intensity conflict and military operations other than war and then propose potential responses to these situations. Until such a policy is proposed and given at least tacit approval, there cannot be a comprehensive concept of operations for special operations forces that will provide a road map for decisions on resource allocation as SOF looks to the future.

Service Concerns versus Operational Needs

A second area of concern to SOF, especially for USSOCOM, is the need to balance the demands of running a near-service with the operational needs of SOF. Although this concern might appear ironic given the emphasis of this book on the importance of USSOCOM taking on its servicelike responsibilities and de-emphasizing its self-perception as a "warfighting CINC," the point here is not that USSOCOM should once again focus its attention on commanding actual operations but that USSOCOM and SOLIC must recognize that SOF is different from the four traditional military services. The new SOF organizations must fight against the temptation to become like the U.S. Army, U.S. Air Force, U.S. Navy, and U.S. Marine Corps and, instead, protect the strong, flexible, and innovative special operations capability that has taken ten years of struggle to rebuild.

SOF is better able to attend to its operational capability than the traditional services because of its size (that is, its lower requirement for logistical support), and the provision of general support—for infrastructure, common transportation vehicles, and health care—by the army, air force and navy. Special operations forces have a significantly higher "tooth-to-tail" ratio (operational versus support forces) than these services. It is, perhaps, for this reason that Congress was correct in creating USSOCOM as a unified command rather than a defense agency or separate service. As USSOCOM and SOLIC mature, they need to maintain this ratio and not fall victim to the same constraints, particularly the growth of headquarters organizations and tradition-bound basing policies, that afflict the traditional services.

Since 1987 the SOF community has seen rapid growth in its headquarters organizations. Much of this growth has been necessary as the forces from the army, navy, and air force became components of USSOCOM. The result was the establishment of U.S. Army Special Operations Command (USASOC), Naval Special Warfare Command (NAVSPECWARCOM), and Air Force Special Operations Command (AFSOC). Between each of these commands and the operational units, however, there is at least one other level of command. SEAL teams report to Naval Special Warfare Group 1 or 2. Special Forces or psychological operations groups report to Special Forces Command or Civil Affairs and Psychological Operations Command. U.S. Air Force special operations units report to a wing commander. These higher headquarters, including USSOCOM, place a tremendous burden on highly selective and small forces to contribute personnel to run the commands.

Evidence of the cost of this demand is visible in many operational units. For example, Special Forces A-Teams, the primary operational unit within Special Forces, are structured to be commanded by a captain whose deputy is a warrant officer drawn from the noncommissioned officer corps. There is a critical shortage of captains in Special Forces. Part of this shortage can be explained by the great expansion of Special Forces since 1986, combined with the difficult selection and assessment process. The necessary problem of selectivity is aggravated, however, by the manpower demands of each of the headquarters. A Special Forces captain should theoretically spend three years of his six to seven as a captain as an A-Team commander. In reality, many captains spend less than one year with the team. The result is discontinuity in the leadership of an organization that is operationally deployed six to nine months of every year and limited operational experience for the captain.[16]

A second traditional constraint limiting operational effectiveness is the structuring of SOF along the lines of American military service models. Although the military services from which SOF personnel are drawn are clearly distinct from one another, there is no reason these distinctions must be so clearly drawn within USSOCOM, especially for the basing and structure of special operations forces.

Despite the "joint" character of most special operations missions, special operations forces are stationed and structured in accordance with the tradition of their parent services. Special Forces, civil affairs, U.S. Army SOF aviation, and psychological operations units are largely stationed on army bases. SEALs and other Naval Special Warfare units are stationed on U.S. Navy bases. U.S. Air Force special operations aircraft units and the Special Tactics Group are stationed on U.S. Air Force bases. This type of basing is traditional and logical within the military services. But when it is combined with the command structure just described, it makes much less sense for special operations forces. Special operations forces need to be flexible, joint, and quick reacting. The best way to encourage these characteristics may be to undertake a new approach to operational command structure and basing.

Alternatives such as establishing joint, regionally oriented permanent task forces, making the most of SOF's regional orientation and organized the way these forces would operate, should be considered. SOF's combat command structures and basing were developed during the cold war, when special operators primarily supported conventional forces in a global war against the Soviet Union. SOF must reevaluate that force structure and develop an organizational and basing framework that supports the operational reality of SOF. For example, permanent SOF Regional Task Forces could be established, preferably located within the broader areas of responsibility (AORs) and composed of task units from all relevant components. The Navy Special Warfare component might include a certain number of SEALs, boats, and SEAL delivery vehicles working as one team. The U.S. Army component might have one or two A-Teams, civil affairs and PSYOP personnel, and, perhaps, a Ranger unit. U.S. Air Force special operations helicopters, perhaps with the addition of Special Tactics Group members, would make up the U.S. Air Force component. The task force commander's mission would be to train these forces together, deploy them together, and keep them together on a permanent basis. Members of the task force would become members of the same team rather than residing with the SEALs in Little Creek, Virginia, or the Rangers at Fort Benning, Georgia.[17]

The Risks to SOF Organizational Culture

The possibility of losing what's special about special operations forces is a risk that should be recognized by SOF and its supporters, but to protect against this risk is the responsibility of the commander in chief of these forces. The danger is largely internal. One threat to the specialness of SOF results from a command that has the bulk of its forces coming from one service, the U.S. Army. USSOCOM might be tempted to recreate the SOF world in the shape of its dominant element. Another threat, less amenable to the community's control, is the result of SOF's success in broadening its mission since 1986 and in demonstrating its effectiveness in the face of crises arising from new international instability.

The distinctiveness of SOF organizational culture has been discussed earlier. The strength of this culture laid the foundation for the rebuilding of U.S. special operations forces. There is much in this organizational culture that is common to all SOF elements: the values of independent and creative thinking combined with loyalty and trust in a small team. But the elements differ too, in ways that provide SOF with its breadth of capability and that are vital to the recruitment of special operators.

Volunteers for SEAL units go through basic underwater demolition and SEALs (BUD/S) training because they want to be SEALs, not because they want to become generic "special operators." Special Forces candidates want to become Green Berets, not SEALs, and U.S. Air Force special operators want to learn the skills of the air commandos. Similarly, each element of U.S. special operations forces appeals to individuals who are already looking for a challenge and a chance to do something different from a conventional military career. It is vital for the future of these forces that they not lose their uniqueness. It is tempting for USSOCOM, as it matures and assumes more servicelike responsibilities and works to promote special operations forces to government organizations outside of the Defense Department, to begin to treat each one of the units the same way. It is easier for officials to sell capabilities if they do not have to spend a great deal of time explaining the difference between a detachment, an element, a platoon, a squad, and a team. The temptation is to change the elements of the organization so that they are more alike and, perhaps eventually, not so special.

This temptation concerns those elements of USSOCOM that are not within the U.S. Army component. One SEAL officer described the pressure from USSOCOM to achieve conformity in unit organizations:

> It's the old Army three. You've got to have three battalions and each battalion has to have three companies and each company has to have three [platoons]. And you try to export that over to the SEAL business and [throws his hands up to indicate disaster]. . . . There have been pressures to make an [A-Team] look like a SEAL platoon. Because . . . they're not sure of the difference between a Ranger and a Green Beret.[18]

Rangers, Special Forces, and SEALs have skills and missions in common, yet each has its own special capabilities and competence. If one starts to curb the traits of SEALs or civil affairs or U.S. Air Force special operations helicopter units, if one tries to mold them into a traditional unit organization for ease of management, they will lose the appeal that draws unique people into unique organizations.

The second threat to SOF organizational culture comes from the once unimaginable broadening of the mission of U.S. special operations forces that has occurred since reorganization legislation was first passed in 1986. The special operations mission has expanded partially as a result of external influences. New instability at the end of the cold war has brought about many new conflicts. In most of these conflicts, special operations forces have had a significant role to play and have sometimes been the primary force. In each of these operations SOF has had a new or expanded role. The importance of civil affairs teams to rebuilding Panama had not been fully realized before Just Cause took place, but within hours of the conclusion of the conflict, units worked to house the homeless, provide police protection, and train a new police force and a reconstituted military. In Desert Shield and Desert Storm, civil affairs and psychological operations were enormously important, and liaison teams built the operational foundation for coalition warfare. The flexibility and ingenuity of SOF have allowed it to respond in ways that conventional forces cannot because of their size, doctrine, and political implications.

As USSOCOM searches out new ways to support U.S. national security objectives and new SOF supporters through the development of new "customers" outside the Defense Department, the risk to the special operations community increases. This risk has two parts. The first is an increased probability of failure as SOF is called upon to conduct operations outside its area of comparative advantage. Illustrations of this risk were provided by the use of SEALs to secure Paitilla airfield in Panama in 1989 and the constraints placed on special operators in Somalia in 1993.

A second category of risk to the successful future deployment of special operations forces is that SOF, in its search to be responsive to an increasingly large circle of customers, may lose what makes it special. As SOF has taken on new operational roles, the danger arises that these forces will lose their central focus, their unifying sense of mission. Part of this risk occurs because of the nature of special operators.

Special operators want to and are trained to "go into the most difficult combat situation . . . to face death and win."[19] Special operators will jump into the fight, whether or not it is appropriate to their capabilities. It is this cultural characteristic that Rear Admiral Ray Smith addressed when he told his navy SPECWAR commanders in Saudi Arabia, "We're not going to do things just to do things."[20]

The responsibility for managing this risk, however, lies with SOF's senior commanders as they continue to push SOF to be more responsive to, and gain greater acceptance by, the president, Defense Department leadership, the regional commanders, and non-Defense Department executive branch agencies. SOF's leadership must continue to "sell" SOF. At the same time, these leaders must protect and nurture the special capabilities, Philip Selznick's "distinctive competencies," that are at the core of the distinctive special operations forces organizational culture.

Protecting a Precarious Value

How did the successful rebuilding and protection of the American special operations capability come about? First as the result of SOF history and organizational culture, and then by the efforts of men who were tempered by this history and culture. The first perspective views the history of special operations forces and the strength of SOF organizational culture as the foundation upon which these forces could be rebuilt given the right combination of SOF advocates and current events. As described in chapters 2 and 3, much of what special operators do today has its roots in World War II when the first Office of Strategic Services (OSS) and underwater demolition team (UDT) units were deployed: psychological operations, training resistance forces, special reconnaissance, sabotage, and obstacle clearance. The history of U.S. special operations forces is in many ways separate from that of American conventional military forces and has resulted in an organizational culture—values, beliefs, and perspective—distinct within the American military. Special operators fight a different kind of war. A war that often involves more training of other forces than fighting. A war that frequently requires observation rather than attack. A war that pits a handful of special operators against large conventional forces. A war that is most likely to take place during "peacetime," before and after military conflict, in an attempt to prevent crises or put things back together if war is unavoidable.

Special operators know their history and see its effect on who they are today. The organizational culture that has developed as a result of this history has been maintained, in part, as a result of the connection with special operations in the past. Special Forces continue to emphasize foreign internal defense, training forces from other countries in civic as well as military skills. The SEALs still swim before they conduct many of their sabotage or reconnaissance missions. U.S. Air Force special operators are reminded of Terry Cochran and his air commandos when they insert special operators behind enemy lines or provide the only fire support for a Special Forces team.

SOF organizational culture has also been maintained though the inculcation of organizational values through selection, assessment, and training. Special operations training attempts to find and develop within individuals an extraordinary inner strength and an ability to think and innovate. At the same time, training emphasizes the sanctity and necessity of small teams, the unit that undertakes most operations. Only through belief in the team and trust among its members will special operators be successful.

The characteristics that have made SOF organizational culture and history distinctive within the primary American military culture have also been the same characteristics that have frequently placed special operators at odds with their conventional peers. American conventional military personnel have been, for most of the past fifty years, either unaware of SOF's unique capabilities or suspicious of them. Whether because of a lack of information, mistrust, or simply competing interests, the precarious value of an American special operations capability has, until the past few years, been consistently at risk of being overwhelmed by the primary organizational values of an American military organization that is, by necessity and tradition, a conventional military force.

Since 1980 the products of this distinctive history and organizational culture, the special operations community and its supporters, have battled to rebuild and protect these forces. Despite backlash against SOF during the 1970s, as the United States and its military attempted to shed the legacy of Vietnam, special operations forces did not go away. A core group of veterans from Vietnam remained in SOF assignments because they believed in the importance of special operations and in the values of SOF organizational culture. Those who stayed in risked their hopes for professional success as measured by promotions and longevity because they believed in what they did and could not find the same satisfaction in the conventional military or in civilian life. At the same time, the SOF community was able to attract recruits. Similar to the SOF veterans, these recruits were attracted by what they viewed as the ultimate physical and mental challenge and by the closeness of the teams, whether an A-Team, a SEAL platoon, or the crew of a gunship. Having survived the physical and mental rigors of training, recruits were not yet full members of the team. Instead, they joined a unit on probation. They learned about teamwork and the irrelevance of rank when each man had a job to do and was depending on his teammates to get their jobs done. The recruit learned to trust his teammates and to earn their trust. The recruit was taught what it meant to be a SEAL, in Special Forces, or an air commando.

A strong belief in the value of special operations led senior members of SOF to recognize in the late 1970s that if a special operations capability were to survive, it had to escape the legacy of Vietnam and prove its relevance to American national security interests. In the SEALs, men such as "Irish" Flynn and Ted Grabowsky focused on the needs and interests of their parent service—whose heart lies with the blue water conventional U.S. Navy. In Vietnam, the SEALs and UDTs had to a great extent separated from the fleets. After Vietnam, senior SEAL officers worked to prove their relevance to fleet commanders whose war plans were written in response to the risk of global conflict with the Soviet Union. By demonstrating their ability to support these plans, the SEALs did gain the support of the fleet, enabling the SEALs and Naval Special Warfare to survive, if not thrive.

Army special operators, particularly Special Forces, found relevance in the challenges of increasing tension and American interest in Central America. In El Salvador, Special Forces were deployed to Central America in small numbers to act as trainers and advisers to government forces. The rise of terrorism and the establishment of Delta within Special Forces provided a linkage between SOF and counterterrorism that remains to this day. The inability of Delta to quickly deploy in the late 1970s and early 1980s brought attention to the great deficiencies in SOF aviation. Eventually, this weakness became the focus of early efforts to reform and rebuild American special operations forces.

In truth, the successes of SOF in the late 1970s were meager at best. By 1980 little remained of the forces that had fought in Vietnam. Nonetheless, those that stayed and fought for the capability they believed in performed a critical service. Although special operations forces in 1980 were not capable of successfully completing the American attempt to rescue U.S. hostages in Iran, these "keepers of the flame," joined by a handful of supporters such as General Edward C. "Shy" Meyer and Lieutenant General Sam Wilson, had enabled SOF to survive the 1970s. In the 1980s, they provided the foundation on which SOF was eventually rebuilt and a critical element of the coalition of bureaucratic guerrillas that fought for SOF reform.

If SOF's past was preserved through the 1970s by a core of true believers, its future was won by the long and difficult process of making (and implementing) policy within the U.S. government. Policymaking, especially when the policy is directed by law, is complicated, sometimes chaotic, and never certain. Issues and policy solutions can take years to reach the floor of Congress. Even the most specific legislation, written by staff members with extensive experience in government agencies, may take years to implement owing to ambiguities in the legislation and the fact that government agencies are not homogeneous organizations but are instead composed of professionals with different interests and perspectives depending on the responsibilities of their immediate organizations.

In the reorganization and rebuilding of special operations, policymaking began with the formation of an initial coalition of SOF supporters soon after the attempted hostage rescue in Iran. This small and determined coalition cut across governmental lines to include active duty special operators, retired members of SOF, senators, representatives, and staff from Capitol Hill, civilians and the occasional senior officer in the Department of Defense, and the editor of a defense magazine who had perceived to his chagrin that many of the mistakes of the failed American rescue attempt at Son Tay in 1974 were repeated six years later in the Iranian desert. Few members of this coalition were to gain in any direct way from their participation in the fight for SOF reform. Representatives and senators received no votes because of their support. Civilian officials in the Pentagon received no raises. Some members of the coalition were penalized for their ardent support of SOF in the form of poor "officer efficiency reports" or short-circuited careers. All members of this informal group fought because they were convinced that a strong special operations capability was critical to the national security.

Although there were stirrings of SOF revitalization in the late 1970s, particularly with Naval Special Warfare's effort to reconnect with the fleet and the U.S. Army's establishment of a counterterrorist force, the beginnings of the campaign are usually traced to the aftermath of the Desert One tragedy. Despite the outcry and dismay over the deaths and "embarrassment" in the Iranian desert, it is likely—in fact certain—that an American special operations capability would not have been rebuilt during the 1980s were it not for a handful of people who believed deeply in the necessity of a broader American perspective on national security than preparing for an all-out war with the Soviet Union, and the crucial role of special operations forces in supporting U.S. national interests. Dismayed by the rapid decline of SOF during the previous decade, concerned by the rising threat of terrorism, saddened and angered by the loss at Desert One, this informal coalition negotiated and argued against indifference, suspicion, and a fear of change for nearly ten years.

Without Ted Lunger on Capitol Hill, the 1986 legislation reorganizing SOF would never have been written. Lunger's unremitting persistence was not, however, enough. His early alliance with Lynn Rylander in the Office of the Secretary of Defense, who himself was convinced by former Special Forces group commander Colonel George McGovern, was critical. The Rylander-Lunger alliance was strongly supported by a number of officers still on active duty, the "SOF Mafia," who provided the facts and figures to support the speeches and papers written by these men.

If Ted Lunger could not accomplish his mission on his own, neither Lunger nor Rylander had the clout to force SOF reform. The SOF campaign found the generals it needed in Representative Dan Daniel and in Noel Koch, the fiery principal deputy assistant secretary who was Rylander's boss. Koch had the access and the conviction to force the issue of SOF "revitalization" to the attention of the secretary and deputy secretary of defense. Dan Daniel brought to the battle a long and respected career in the House of Representatives. As a subcommittee chairman he could hold hearings. As a senior and well-liked member of Congress he could call in favors. Neither Koch nor Daniel would let the issue of SOF reform fade away.

This core group of SOF supporters found increasing support for their campaign. On Capitol Hill, they were joined by Representatives Hutto and Kasich. Senator William Cohen became an active supporter and eventually found allies in Senators Sam Nunn and Ted Kennedy. Although there was less support in the senior levels of the Department of Defense, Noel Koch, through his establishment of the Special Operations Policy Advisory Group, composed of retired senior military officers including Generals Shy Meyer and Sam Wilson, was able to increase pressure and maintain high-level visibility. The final piece of this informal coalition came from the press, notably Ben Schemmer and his relentless and unforgiving campaign for SOF reform in *Armed Forces Journal.* With monthly articles on special operations forces, written with the assistance of well-connected sources in the Pentagon, Schemmer was an unblinking watchdog over Defense Department special operations policy. His magazine provided a forum for supporters, and a few opponents, of SOF reform.

During the first half of the 1980s, SOF reform gained momentum on Capitol Hill, demonstrated in a buildup of speeches, letters, hearings, studies, and conference reports, all forcing upward a new American policy on special operations and low-intensity conflict. That policy found its voice when a well-informed and frustrated Congress provided the crusaders with a victory: it passed legislation establishing the U.S. Special Operations Command and the Office of the Assistant Secretary of Defense, Special Operations and Low-Intensity Conflict, and giving these new organizations control of SOF resources through the issuing of a "checkbook" to the commander of USSOCOM. As noted already, declaring policy—even when it has the force of law—does not ensure its successful or sustainable implementation. The campaign for SOF reform that culminated in the special operations forces reorganization legislation had not yet built the strong special operations capability for which the coalition was fighting. In fact, there was fear and hope on both sides of the issue that after initial gestures toward implementing the legislation, interest would be lost and SOF would remain last on the list of military service priorities with little permanent gain from a decade of effort. Passage of legislation was, once again, necessary but not sufficient for the protection and rebuilding of special operations forces. USSOCOM and the OASD (SOLIC) would take years to become mature and thriving organizations. Most important, it would take nearly four years of "peacetime engagement" within the Defense Department before the commander in chief of USSOCOM would have the checkbook that would give SOF the autonomy intended by Congress and necessary to secure its future.

Implementation of the 1986 and follow-on legislation, as with any complex establishing legislation, brought a new cast of key players. Part of this shift occurred simply because of the passage of time and attrition.

Colonel George McGovern died when the contest was just beginning. Dan Daniel died eighteen months after the first legislation was passed. Lynn Rylander died on the racquetball court before the first special operations program objectives memorandum (POM) was even begun. Noel Koch left in frustration and flames in the summer before the legislation was passed. Ted Lunger was forced from Capitol Hill, having burned many bridges, after Daniel's death.

Some of the reshuffling of the coalition was necessitated by the different requirements of implementing the legislation. General James Lindsay and General Carl Stiner were the first two commanders of U.S. Special Operations Command and were responsible for the growth of the command from a narrowly focused "warfighting CINC" to a near-military service. General Lindsay pressed for command of all special operations forces and laid the groundwork for USSOCOM to eventually assume its servicelike responsibilities. General Stiner executed those responsibilities to an extent never before seen in a unified command. General Stiner also made invaluable progress in gaining the trust of the conventional commanders, particularly the other unified, regional commanders, and broadening the mission and relevancy of special operations forces. Assistant Secretary of Defense Richard Armitage, because of his organizational responsibilities and beliefs, worked for the assumption by USSOCOM of its resource responsibilities and against the establishment of an effective ASD (SOLIC). Secretary of the Army John O. Marsh got SOLIC afloat and forced the nomination of a credible assistant secretary. Charles Whitehouse, although a "short-timer," had Secretary of Defense Frank Carlucci's ear and fought for SOF control of SOF resources. Jim Locher, having written the original and much of the follow-on legislation as a member of the Senate Armed Services staff, brought his vision of the SOLIC office to the Pentagon and worked to instill that vision in the new SOF organizations and the Department of Defense.

Those who joined the early skirmishes for the rebuilding of an American special operations capability did so because they believed this capability was critical to the protection and fulfillment of American national security interests. The U.S. government reinforces the correctness of their judgment with each call for special operations forces in response to a national emergency: in Panama; Saudi Arabia, Kuwait, and Iraq; Bosnia and Macedonia; Haiti; and, despite the tragedy of October 1993, the operation in Somalia. The informal coalition of supporters was composed of alliances that cut across organizational lines. Although in many cases the battle appeared to be between Congress and the Department of Defense, without the support of those associated with the Defense Department it is unlikely that Ted Lunger and Dan Daniel would have succeeded. Men such as General Shy Meyer and General Sam Wilson pushed the Defense Department and Congress to recognize that there was more to American national security than the risk of the Warsaw Pact forces coming across the German border. Noel Koch, Lynn Rylander, and George McGovern pushed SOF reform from within the Defense Department, and eventually allied with those pushing from the outside. Able to make some forward progress in "revitalizing" SOF, these men had their greatest success in keeping the issue of SOF reform visible throughout the entire defense community and gradually shifting the attention of national security decisionmakers to include crises and threats other than a third world war. Because of their willingness to persist in their fight, when the Soviet Union collapsed, the United States had a flexible and responsive force ready to participate in the new international security environment.

Notes

Chapter 1

1. David C. Martin and John Walcott, *Best Laid Plans: The Inside Story of America's War against Terrorism* (Harper and Row, 1988), pp. 21–23.

2. Martin and Walcott, *Best Laid Plans*, pp. 24–28.

3. International Institute for Strategic Studies, *The Military Balance 1993–1994* (London: Brassey's, 1993), pp. 39–40. According to the IISS, Canada's active duty force includes 20,000 in the army, 12,500 in the navy, and 20,600 in the air force.

4. General Wayne Downing, commander in chief, U.S. Special Operations Command, interview, October 1993.

5. James Wooten, *Special Operations Forces: Issues for Congress*, Report 84-227F (Congressional Research Service, December 1984), p. 4.

Chapter 2

1. Lieutenant Colonel Ian D.W. Sutherland, *Special Forces of the United States Army, 1952/1982* (San Jose: R. James Bender Publishing, 1990), p. 186.

2. Philip Selznick, *Leadership in Administration: A Sociological Interpretation* (University of California Press, 1957), p. 119.

3. One of the more public examples of a woman in U.S. Army special operations forces is SSG Renee Austin, who deployed to Ulaanbaatar, Mongolia, to support the U.S. country team as a Russian linguist and to work as a special assistant to the defense attaché. SSG Austin was the first American soldier authorized to wear Mongolian jump wings. As reported by Douglas C. Waller in *The Commandos: The Inside Story of America's Secret Soldiers* (Simon and Schuster, 1994), pp. 215–16, a handful of women serve as part of the Delta Special Forces detachment. All are assigned to the intelligence detachment. See chapter 5 for more on Delta.

4. Brigadier General William Kernan, director of Plans, Policy, Doctrine, Simulations, and Analysis (J-5), U.S. Special Operations Command (USSOCOM), interview, October 1993. Unless otherwise noted, ranks of those quoted in this book are as they were at the time of the interview; and unless otherwise noted, interviews were conducted by the author.

5. Eliot Cohen, *Commandos and Politicians: Elite Military Units in Modern De-*

mocracies (Harvard University Press, 1978), pp. 56–60.

6. When asked by the author to compare the identification a Special Forces member has with the army and with other special operators, General Wayne Downing, the current commander in chief of U.S. Special Operations Command, responded, "I would say without a doubt their strongest bonds are with the special operations forces . . . sometimes they [special operators] feel like the bastard stepchildren [in their military service]." Interview, October 1993. Nearly all special operators interviewed supported Downing's assertion.

7. Two case studies illustrate both Selznick's concept and how the primary value or mission of an organization tends to overwhelm the critical precarious value. Ashley Schiff demonstrates the precariousness of a value or capability that conflicts with the values of the primary organization in his examination of the U.S. Forest Service's thirty-year resistance to controlled burning as an element of forest management in his *Fire and Water*. Despite compelling evidence from academic and professional sources, the research organization within the Forest Service was unable to overcome the Forest Service's deeply held belief that all fire was catastrophic and should be prevented at all costs. This unifying belief was deeply inculcated in the service's strong and widely accepted sense of mission—a sense of mission that was one of the Forest Service's greatest strengths. The Forest Service's refusal to officially recognize the benefit, and perhaps necessity, of controlled fires did not end until the early 1940s, after twenty years of accumulated evidence in support of controlled fires and following several uncontrollable and disastrous fires. They were devastating infernos that could have been limited by the removal of underbrush and highly combustible "rough" with the controlled burning technique. See Ashley Schiff, *Fire and Water: Scientific Heresy in the Forest Service* (Harvard University Press, 1962); and Herbert Kaufman, *The Forest Ranger: A Study in Administrative Behavior* (Johns Hopkins University Press, 1981).

See also Pete Dawkins, "The Army and the 'Other' War in Vietnam," Ph.D. dissertation, Princeton University, 1979, in which Dawkins examines the attempt by army leadership to implement the army's declared new mission of nation building in Vietnam. Despite strong support from the top, including formal incentives, the program never achieved overall success, largely because it was outside the army's traditional missions of deterring and fighting wars.

8. This early history of U.S. Army Special Forces is drawn largely from Sutherland, *Special Forces;* and Leroy Thompson, *The Illustrated History of the U.S. Army Special Forces* (Secaucus: Citadel Press, 1988).

9. Quoted in James Adams, *Secret Armies: Inside the American, Soviet, and European Special Forces* (Atlantic Monthly Press, 1987), p. 22. This book is generally dismissed by special operators for its account of contemporary special operations. Its early history of American, Soviet, and European special operations forces, is, however, interesting and credible.

10. Thompson, *Illustrated History*, pp. 1–2. Jedburgh teams took their name from the area of Scotland where the Scots conducted guerrilla warfare against the

English during the twelfth century.

11. Lieutenant General William P. Yarborough, former commander of the army's special warfare center, in his foreword to Charles M. Simpson III, *Inside the Green Berets: The First Thirty Years, A History of the U.S. Army Special Forces* (Berkley Books, 1983), pp. xv–xvi.

12. Lieutenant Colonel Gary L. Bounds, *Notes on Military Elite Units*, report prepared for the Combat Studies Institute (Fort Leavenworth, Kans.: Army Command and General Staff College for the U.S. Army Training and Doctrine Command, March 1984).

13. Thompson, *Illustrated History*, p. 11.

14. Ibid., pp. 16–18.

15. Cohen, *Commandos and Politicians*, p. 26.

16. Colonel Bank is regarded as one of the fathers of Special Forces in the special operations community.

17. Thompson, *Illustrated History*, p. 21.

18. Simpson, *Inside the Green Berets,* p. 50.

19. In May 1960, the 77th SFG was renamed the 7th SFG.

20. Quotation from Orr Kelly, *Brave Men-Dark Waters: The Untold Story of the Navy SEALs* (Presidio, 1992), pp. 75–76.

21. May 25, 1961. Quotation from Andrew F. Krepinevich Jr., *The Army and Vietnam* (Johns Hopkins University Press, 1986), pp. 29–30.

22. Krepinevich, *The Army and Vietnam*, p. 31.

23. Ibid., pp. 32–33.

24. Colonel William G. Boykin, "Special Operations and Low-Intensity Conflict Legislation: Why Was It Passed and Have the Voids Been Filled?" individual study project (Carlisle Barracks, Pa.: U.S. Army War College, April 1991), pp. 5–6. Emphasis in original.

25. There is not the space in this chapter to adequately discuss Special Forces operations in Vietnam. Entire books could be, and have been, written on the subject. See particularly Krepinevich, *The Army and Vietnam*; and Simpson, *Inside the Green Berets*. See also Sutherland, *Special Forces*; and Thompson, *Illustrated History*. U.S. forces commander General Creighton Abrams's view of Special Forces is discussed in Lewis Sorley, *Thunderbolt: General Creighton Abrams and the Army of His Times* (Simon and Schuster, 1992), pp. 269–78. Sorley argues that contrary to the accusations of some members of the Special Forces, Abrams was not anti-Special Forces and, in fact, greatly respected the talents of several Special Forces commanders and noncommissioned officers.

26. Cohen, *Commandos and Politicians,* p. 72.

27. Colonel Eugene Bernhardt, interview, October 1993.

28. Colonel Corson L. "Corky" Hilton, interview, October 1993; and Bernhardt, interview. See also Simpson, *Inside the Green Berets,* pp. 169–72.

29. Simpson, *Inside the Green Berets* , p. 178.

30. See Henry G. Gole, "Shadow Wars and Secret Wars: Phoenix and MACVSOG," *Parameters, U.S. Army War College Quarterly*, vol. 21 (Winter 1991-92), pp. 95–105;

Thompson, *Illustrated History*; and Simpson, *Inside the Green Berets*.

31. Thompson, *Illustrated History*, p. 78.

32. Ibid., pp. 103–05; see also General Samuel Wilson, interview by John Partin, July 1988.

33. For a fascinating account of the Son Tay raid, see Benjamin C. Schemmer, *The Raid* (Harper and Row, 1976).

34. See, in particular, Dawkins, "The 'Other War' in Vietnam."

35. Wooten, "Special Operations Forces," p. 2.

36. Krepinevich, *The Army and Vietnam*, pp. 31–35.

37. Colonel Bernhardt, former A-Team commander, recounting his experiences in Vietnam, interview.

38. Thompson, *Illustrated History*, pp. 46–47.

39. Simpson, *Inside the Green Berets*, pp. 186–87.

40. Ibid., pp. 212–32.

41. Sorley, *Thunderbolt*, pp. 269–78.

42. One of the most outstanding histories of the U.S. Navy SEALs is Kelly, *Brave Men*. Much of this brief history is summarized from this book. John B. Dwyer, *Scouts and Raiders: The Navy's First Special Warfare Commandos* (Praeger Publishers, 1993), is an in-depth look at this earliest U.S. precursor to the SEALs.

43. Kenneth Macksey, *Commando: Hit-and-Run Combat in World War II* (Chelsea: Scarborough House, 1990), pp. 198–99.

44. Kelly, *Brave Men*, p. 41.

45. Macksey, *Commando*, p. 199.

46. Kelly, *Brave Men*. p. 37.

47. Ibid., pp. 47–48.

48. Captain Tom McGrath, interview, October 1993; and T. L. Bosiljevac, *SEALs: UDT/SEAL Operations in Vietnam* (Ivy Books, 1990). In the early 1980s, the navy converted all UDTs to SEAL teams.

49. Kelly, *Brave Men*, p. 77.

50. Ibid., pp. 97–99.

51. Bosiljevac, *SEALs*. One SEAL to receive the Medal of Honor was Lieutenant (j.g.) Joseph R. Kerrey, later to become governor (Bob Kerrey) of Nebraska and U.S. senator. This tradition of bringing home all dead and wounded, and the record of never having left one of their own behind, is frequently brought up by SEALs in interviews.

52. Kelly's book covers SEAL operations in Vietnam extensively. The most detailed accounting of SEAL and UDT operations in Vietnam is provided by Bosiljevac, *SEALs*. Bosiljevac is still on active duty as a SEAL, and he relied heavily on the "spot reports" and "barn dance cards" written by unit commanders at the end of every operation. A book quickly blackballed by SEALs is Richard Marcinko, *Rogue Warrior* (Pocket Books, 1992). Marcinko, regrettably according to the SEAL community, has been one of the most highly visible SEALs since his conviction on fraud charges in 1989 and the publication of his autobiography. The book is reminiscent of the writings of the tabloid press, but it provides examples of both

SEAL operations in Vietnam and what happens when "rogue warriors" are allowed into the small, independent, nearly autonomous units that often typify special warfare.

53. Cathal L. "Irish" Flynn, then a lieutenant (j.g.) and later rear admiral. Quoted in Kelly, *Brave Men*, p. 105.

54. Bosiljevac, *SEALs*, pp. 27–28; and Kelly, *Brave Men*, pp. 110–11.

55. Bosiljevac, *SEALs*, pp. 48–60.

56. Ibid., p. 181.

57. Rear Admiral Ray Smith, interview, Coronado, Calif., December 1993; Captain Ron Yeaw, interview, February 1994; and Bosiljevac, *SEALs*, pp. 180–81, 183.

58. Little has been written on the history of air force special operations, although work is currently under way in the office of the historian of Air Force Special Operations Command (AFSOC). The best account of air force special operations in France comes from Bernard Victor Moore II, "The Secret Air War over France: USAAF Special Operations Units in the French Campaign of 1944," study prepared for the Air University Press (Maxwell Air Force Base, Ala., November 1993). Information in this section comes from Moore and a pamphlet prepared by the historian's office at AFSOC, "Heritage of the Quiet Professionals."

59. Moore, "Secret Air War."

60. Major R. D. Van Wagner, *1st Air Commando Group: Any Place, Any Time, Anywhere*, Military History Series 86-1 (Montgomery: Air Command and Staff College, 1986), p. 23. Little has been written on the 1st Air Commando Group. Wagner's book provides a concise history of both 1st Air Commando Group operations in Burma and the British operations that preceded them. Unless otherwise noted, this history is derived from Van Wagner's book.

61. Van Wagner, *1st Air Commando Group*, p. 27.

62. Ibid., p. 34.

63. Colonel Billy B. "Rusty" Napier, interview, October 1993; and Van Wagner, *1st Air Commando Group*, p. 30.

64. Van Wagner, *1st Air Commando Group*, pp. 52–53.

65. Ibid., p. 47.

66. As noted above, little has been written on air force special operations. Unless otherwise noted, information on post–World War II air force special operations comes from Air Force Special Operations Command, "Heritage of the Quiet Professionals."

67. Simpson, *Inside the Green Berets*, p. 183.

68. Krepinevich, *The Army and Vietnam*, pp. 3–6.

69. Ibid., pp. 270–71.

70. Brigadier General William Kernan, U.S. Army, former commander, 75th Ranger Regiment, interview, October 1993.

71. McGrath, interview; and Captain John Gantley, interview, March 1993.

72. For example, Gantley, interview.

73. Smith, interview.

74. Gantley, interview.

75. The SEAL insignia, which was also worn by UDT members before the two types of units were merged, is referred to as "the Budweiser," in recognition of its resemblance to the beer logo. The insignia was designed almost as a joke because of frustration about the refusal of naval aviators to approve any insignia that remotely resembled their wings. The insignia features wings, an anchor, and a pistol to represent the sea, air, and land element of the special warfare-SEAL mission. McGrath, interview.

76. Commander Bert Calland, interview, December 1993.

77. Smith, interview.

78. Special operations were, of course, only a part of the *Mayaguez* incident. There was a general breakdown in command, control, communications, and intelligence across the board during the crisis. The history of the incident is found in Roy Rowan, *The Four Days of Mayaguez* (W.W. Norton and Co., 1975), and *Seizure of the Mayaguez,* Hearings before the Subcommittee on International Political and Military Affairs of the House Committee on International Relations, 3 vols., 94 Cong. 1 sess. (Government Printing Office, 1975), pt. 4, pp. 116–27. See also Richard G. Head, Frisco W. Short, and Robert W. McFarlane, *Crisis Resolution: Presidential Decision Making in the Mayaguez and Korean Confrontations* (Westview Press, 1978).

79. National command authority refers to the chain of command from the president to the secretary of defense.

80. Conversation with Colonel Robert Undorf, USSOCOM, January 1987.

81. Bosiljevac, *SEALs*, pp. 178–79.

82. Bosiljevac, *SEALs,* pp. 178–79; and Kelly, *Brave Men,* pp. 175–79.

83. Commander Thomas Campbell, interview, December 1993.

84. Rear Admiral Irve LeMoyne, interview, March 1993. In the spring of 1994, Rear Admiral LeMoyne was made the deputy commander in chief, U.S. Special Operations Command, and the senior SEAL admiral on active duty; and Bosiljevac, *SEALs*, p. 184.

85. LeMoyne, interview; and Captain Ron Yeaw, interview.

86. William J. Flavin, "Concept for the Strategic Use of Special Operations Forces in the 1990's and Beyond," individual study project (Washington: Center for Strategic and International Studies, 1991), p. 44.

87. Sutherland, *Special Forces*, p. 240; and Simpson, *Inside the Green Berets*, p. 236.

88. Sutherland, *Special Forces*, pp. 246–316; Lieutenant Colonel Corson L. Hilton, "United States Army Special Forces: From a Decade of Development to a Sustained Future," individual study project (Carlisle Barracks, Pa.: U.S. Army War College, 1991).

89. Hilton, "United States Army Special Forces," p. 4.

90. Hilton, interview.

91. Ibid.

92. Bernhardt, interview; and Campbell, interview.

93. Hilton, interview.

94. Flavin, "Concept for the Strategic Use," p. 38.

95. Hilton, interview.

96. Kernan, interview.

97. Wilson, interview by Partin.

Chapter 3

1. Herbert A. Simon, *Administrative Behavior: A Study of Decision-Making Processes in Administrative Organizations*, 3d ed. (Free Press, 1976), p. 198.

2. Philip Selznick, *Leadership in Administration: A Sociological Interpretation* (University of California Press, 1957), pp. 40–41.

3. Ibid., pp. 41–50, 57–58. Herbert Kaufman provides the case that illustrates Selznick's theory. See Herbert Kaufman, *The Forest Ranger: A Study in Administrative Behavior* (Johns Hopkins University Press, 1960), especially pp. 161–98. Kaufman demonstrates how "the Forest Service has enjoyed a substantial degree of success in producing field behavior consistent with headquarters directives and suggestions," partially through an elaborate system of directing and reporting but largely because of the nurturing of a strong and distinct organizational culture.

4. James Q. Wilson, *Bureaucracy: What Government Agencies Do and Why They Do It* (Basic Books, 1989). See especially pp. 93, 95–98, 101–05.

5. Samuel Huntington, *The Soldier and the State: The Theory and Politics of Civil-Military Relations* (Belknap Press of Harvard University Press, 1957). Morton Halperin, *Bureaucratic Politics and Foreign Policy* (Brookings, 1974); Arthur T. Hadley, *The Straw Giant* (Random House, 1986). Some of the most interesting innovation literature includes Barry Posen, *The Sources of Military Doctrine: France, Britain, and Germany between the World Wars* (Cornell University Press, 1984); Eliot Cohen and John Gooch, *Military Misfortune: The Anatomy of Failure in War* (Vintage Books, 1990); Stephen Peter Rosen, *Winning the Next War* (Cornell University Press, 1991); and Chris C. Demchak, *Military Organizations, Complex Machines* (Cornell University Press, 1991).

Huntington writes of a "military ethic" that emphasizes "the permanence, irrationality, weakness and evil in human nature. It stresses the supremacy of society over the individual and the importance of order, hierarchy, and division of functions. It stresses the continuity and value of history." Others have provided descriptions of identifiable "subcultures" within the military forces.

6. Eliot Cohen, *Commandos and Politicians: Elite Military Units in Modern Democracies* (Harvard University Press, 1978), p. 17.

7. Ibid., p. 17.

8. John M. Collins, *Green Berets, SEALs, and Spetsnaz: U.S. and Soviet Special Military Operations* (Pergamon-Brassey's, 1987), p. 82.

9. Captain Tom McGrath, interview, October 1993.

10. Wilson, *Bureaucracy*, p. 93.

11. Admiral Ray Smith, commander of the Naval Special Warfare Center, Coronado, Calif., interview, December 1993.

12. General Wayne Downing, interview, October 1993.

13. Brendan Rogers, interview, Naval Special Warfare Center, December 1993.

14. Rogers, interview.

15. Interview, Naval Special Warfare Center, December 1993; and letter, Captain R. L. McKay, assistant chief of staff, Naval Special Warfare Command, June 1995.

16. Rogers, interview.

17. Ibid.

18. Most of the description of BUD/S training comes from a briefing and tour provided by the Naval Special Warfare Center and from discussions with several SEALs. The description of fire control comes from Orr Kelly, *Brave Men, Dark Waters: The Untold Story of the Navy SEALs* (Presidio, 1992), pp. 87–88.

19. A SEAL commander of a special boat unit described the purpose of the probationary period as follows, "They have to prove that they are not out of bounds in . . . terms of their behavior. . . . They have to show that they are able to fit into an organization, into this culture, into this fraternity. . . . And if they can't do that, if they're evaluated by their peers as being someone who can't fit into this organization, then they're booted out." Commander Thomas Campbell, interview, December 1993.

20. Downing, interview.

21. Description of the Special Forces Assessment and Selection program was provided by a noncommissioned officer trainer and Colonel Kevin Getty, Camp MacKall, May 1994.

22. Colonel Kevin Getty, interview, May 1994.

23. Descriptions of the Special Forces Qualification Course were provided by Major Greg Phillips, F-Company commander, Camp MacKall, May 1994. Some details of the course structure are found in a briefing by the 1st Special Warfare Training Group.

24. As described in chapter 2, an A-Detachment, or A-Team, is the primary operational element for Special Forces.

25. A version of Robin Sage has been taking place for over forty years, and the Special Forces instructors have worked closely with those who live where the exercise takes place to gain their support and warn them about military action at night.

26. According to the company commander responsible for running the Q-course and Robin Sage, "We have our own Pineland auxiliary. . . .We have third generations . . . the grandfathers, the father, and the sons have come and they drive trucks for us, they play intelligence officers in the sector command." Major Greg Phillips, interview, Fort Bragg, May 1994.

27. When asked if Robin Sage still contained the large hazing element common in the past, the major in charge of this phase of training responded, "It used to be you would come into a sector command meeting and it was a tongue-lashing. It

was verbal abuse. It was, "you Americans, you're worthless." Well, where does America fight today? Ninety-nine percent of the time, we've had some kind of coalition operation with [the host nation]. We're brothers in arms. We've trained together. . . So we don't go through this hazing anymore. We go through a much more mature process of the training to see that the young man can think." Phillips, interview.

28. Major J. J. Elliot, interview, October 1993.

29. Colonel Billy B. Napier, interview, October 1993.

30. Ibid. Napier also described the difference between conventional and special operations air force pilots with the following illustration from Operation Just Cause in Panama in 1989, "The two airplanes that [covered the] Ranger drops at Tocumen airfield and Rio Hato had [army] Rangers inside the gunships. And these guys could talk on the radios and hear everything my crew was hearing and saying and doing with the guy on the ground. And [the Ranger] could say, "Now look for this guy [the Ranger commander] to do that, or when [the Ranger commander] would go into a formation [the Ranger in the AC-130] would say, that's typical. What he's thinking is, he's taking fire from this direction. Go look for your target up there. So we'd already be moving in that direction with our sensors. . . we'd be ahead of the game. And there are no Rangers in the back seats of F-15s. That's special operations versus conventional."

31. Lieutenant Colonel Bob Hudson, Office of the Assistant Secretary of Defense, Special Operations and Low-Intensity Conflict, interview, February 1994.

32. Their indignation was expressed by a special operations pilot, "In effect what he did in special operations was take us away from our roots. We don't want to be identified with a bomber unit, no matter how glorious. . . . We'll put up our medals and what Cochran won and what we did in the special operations units in Vietnam, we'll put our medals side by side with any unit in the United States Air Force. We would like to have that heraldry [the 1st SOW]. So what if it didn't start until World War II, we don't care, we're damn proud of it. But General McPeak didn't see it the same way." Napier, interview.

33. Simpson, *Inside the Green Berets*, pp. xxi–xxii.

34. Ted Lunger, interview by John Partin, memorandum for the record, Washington, 1988; and Colonel Scott Stephens, interview, March 1993.

35. Kelly, *Brave Men*, p. 53.

36. Colonel William G. Boykin, "Special Operations and Low-Intensity Conflict Legislation: Why Was It Passed and Have the Voids Been Filled?" study project (Carlisle Barracks, Pa.: U.S. Army War College, April 1991), p. 6.

Chapter 4

1. Lieutenant General (ret.) Sam Wilson, interview, April 1994; Charlton Ogburn, *The Marauders* (Quill, 1982). Interestingly, Wilson is now president of Hampden-Sydney College (founded with Patrick Henry by Wilson's great-great-great-great grandfather), a professor of political science, speaks several foreign languages,

yet does not hold any college degrees. See also General Sam Wilson, interview by John Partin, July 1988.

2. General Edward Charles "Shy" Meyer, interview by John Partin, July 1988.

3. Ibid.

4. David Martin and John Walcott, *Best Laid Plans: The Inside Story of America's War against Terrorism* (Harper and Row, 1988), pp. 35–36; and Meyer, interview by Partin.

5. Meyer, interview by Partin.

6. The U.S. Army does not officially confirm or deny the existence of Delta. It is, however, referred to in many open-source publications, including Martin and Walcott, *Best Laid Plans;* Adams, *Secret Armies: Inside the American, Soviet, and European Special Forces* (Atlantic Monthly Press, 1987); and Steven Emerson, *Secret Warriors: Inside the Covert Military Operations of the Reagan Era* (Putnam, 1988). The establishment of Delta, including President Carter's request for assurance from his military leadership, is also discussed in Colonel William Boykin, "Special Operations and Low-Intensity Conflict Legislation: Why Was It Passed and Have the Voids Been Filled?" study project (Carlisle Barracks, Pa.: U.S. Army War College, 1991). Surprisingly, the unclassified Infantry Branch newsletter contains a job announcement entitled "Assignment Opportunities in Delta." The announcement explains that "assignments with the 1st SFOD-D provide realistic training and experience that are both personally and professionally rewarding." Officer applicants must be captains or majors, college graduates, and have a minimum of twelve months' successful command as a captain. The unit was Delta simply because Special Forces already had A, B, and C teams or elements.

7. Martin and Walcott, *Best Laid Plans,* pp. 36–38.

8. Meyer, interview by Partin.

9. Ibid.

10. Quoted in Martin and Walcott, *Best Laid Plans*, p. 39.

11. Boykin, "U.S. Special Operations Forces," p. 4.

12. Meyer, interview; and Boykin, "Special Operations Forces," p. 6.

13. The disorientation and isolation of the SEALs after Vietnam is revealed by the only member of SEAL Team 2 who served three tours in Vietnam, "The SEALs were really grasping for something to do. . . . We came back from Vietnam. . . . All of a sudden our reason for being [was gone]. . . . After about six months [in the United States], you were ready to go do something again. And there wasn't anything available. There was nothing playing. What [were] we going to train for? . . . The only thinking had been—get ready for Vietnam. [Now] no mission." Captain Ron Yeaw, interview, February 1994.

14. Yeaw, interview.

15. Commander Robert W. Looney, interview, December 1993.

16. Most of the information in this section came from interviews conducted in March and December 1993 with several senior SEAL officers including Rear Admiral Irve C. LeMoyne, Rear Admiral Ray Smith, Captain Jack Gantley, Commander Tom Campbell, and Commander Looney.

17. Yeaw, interview.

18. Interviews with Commander Looney, Captain Yeaw, and Commander Campbell.

19. Interviews with Commander Looney, Commander Campbell, Captain Yeaw; and Orr Kelly, *Brave Men, Dark Waters: The Untold Story of the Navy SEALs* (Presidio, 1992), provides a good description of the revamping of the SEAL mission. See pp. 213–14.

20. Lynn Rylander, interview by John Partin, 1989; and interviews at USSOCOM, October 1993.

21. *Defense Department Special Operations Forces*, statement by Noel Koch before the Subcommittee on Readiness, Special Operations Panel, of the House Armed Services Committee, 98 Cong. 2d sess. (Government Printing Office, 1984).

22. The story of Desert One has been told many times. One of the best accounts is found in a book on the history of America's response to terrorism from 1979–89, *Best Laid Plans*, written by two journalists, David Martin and John Walcott. It is recommended by many members of the SOF community. Other books about the Iranian hostage rescue attempt are interesting but have clear agendas, particularly the ones by Colonel James H. Kyle, *The Guts to Try* (Orion Books, 1990), and Colonel Charlie Beckwith and Donald Knox, *Delta Force* (Harcourt Brace Jovanovich, 1983). Kyle and Beckwith were the commanders of the air component and the U.S. Army's Delta Force respectively. Kyle's book is extraordinarily detailed. Adams, *Secret Armies*, and Emerson, *Secret Warriors*, also discuss Desert One.

23. Martin and Walcott, *Best Laid Plans*; and Wilson, interview.

24. Martin and Walcott, *Best Laid Plans*, pp. 14–15.

25. The site had been prepared in advance on April 1, 1980, by a combat control team led by Air Force Major John Carney. Carney was covertly infiltrated to the site in order to mark out a landing zone. Colonel John Carney, U.S. Special Operations Command (USSOCOM) briefing, March 31, 1993.

26. Martin and Walcott, *Best Laid Plans*, pp. 12–13.

27. Colonel John Carney, USSOCOM briefing, March 31, 1993; and Martin and Walcott, *Best Laid Plans*.

28. Martin and Walcott, *Best Laid Plans*, pp. 21–23.

29. Ibid., pp. 24–28; and Master Sergeant Michael Vining, briefing, March 1993.

30. General Carl Stiner, briefing, March 1993.

31. Special Operations Review Group, *Rescue Mission Report*, unclassified version, Washington, the Pentagon, August 1980, pp. 1–2.

32. Boykin, "Special Operations and Low-Intensity Conflict," pp. 6–7.

33. Office of the Chief of Staff Army, "STRATSERCOM/JSOA Chronology," Working Paper, USSOCOM archives, Tampa, Fla., undated, but it includes the establishment of the Joint Special Operations Agency in 1984. See also papers prepared by Lieutenant Colonel Bruce Mauldin in 1982 and 1983 on his experience in, and observations of, U.S. Army special operations. Mauldin served on Joint Task Force

1-79 and in the army's special operations office (ODSO).

34. Meyer, interview by Partin.

35. Ibid.

36. John Partin, memorandum for the record, interview with Ted Lunger, July 1988.

37. Hilton, interview, October 1993; and Bernhardt, interview.

38. CSA, "STRATSERCOM/JSOA Chronology."

39. Hilton, interview, March 1993; Sutherland, *Special Forces*, pp. 60, 245; and Boykin, "Special Operations and Low-Intensity Conflict," pp. 6–7.

40. Martin and Walcott, *Best Laid Plans*.

41. Hugh Cox, "The 1980's: A Decade of Evolution for Air Force Special Operations," *Air Commando Newsletter*, December 1992, pp. 11, 21–27.

42. This senior officer who flew AC-130s commented on the effect that serving in the 1st SOW could have on an officer's career, illustrating the precariousness of SOF's position in the air force, "What was happening was that it was not considered a mainline mission of the United States Air Force. . . . They were not mainline airplanes, most of them . . . were holdovers from Vietnam. They had dumped [into the unit] a lot of people that were beyond the system's ability to promote for marginal records [or] a lack of desire. They were intermingled with the good guys. So promotion rates in . . . the late seventies and early eighties were not very good. [This] made it feel like we were being prejudiced against on promotion boards and things like that. In reality, I don't think we were. In reality what we were doing was not promoting all those guys. . . . I will say that the young people that we got in, including me, in those days, . . . had no trouble competing. I could rise to the top because there weren't that many across the board that were that good." Colonel Billy B. "Rusty" Napier, interview, October 1993.

43. Colonel Scott Stephens, interview, March 1993.

44. Cox, "The 1980's," p. 21.

45. Ibid.

46. Ibid., pp. 21–22.

47. Stephens, interview.

48. Lieutenant Colonel Bob Hudson, interview, February 1994; and Cox, "The 1980's," p. 21.

49. Cox, "The 1980's," p. 24.

50. Interview, October 1993.

51. Cox, "The 1980's," p. 24

52. Hudson, interview.

53. Noel Koch, interview, April 1994.

54. Ibid.

55. Noel Koch, interview by John Partin, January 1989; and Lynn Rylander, interview by John Partin, January 1989.

56. Koch, interview; and Greg Nelson, interviews, spring and summer 1993; and Rylander, interview by Partin.

57. Rylander, interview by Partin.

58. Ibid.

59. Koch, interview.

60. Ibid.

61. Ibid.

62. Koch, interview by Partin.

63. *Defense Department Special Operations Forces*, statement by Noel Koch.

64. Simpson, *Inside the Green Berets*, pp. 34, 146.

65. Wilson, interview.

66. Koch, interview.

67. Koch, interview by Partin.

68. Rylander, interview by Partin.

69. Koch, interview by Partin.

70. Ibid.

71. Koch, interview.

72. Memorandum by Deputy Secretary of Defense Paul Thayer, October 3, 1983. Thayer also stated that the memo should be widely disseminated to ensure that the priority attached to the program was clearly understood; and Koch, interview.

73. CSA, "STRATSERCOM/JSOA Chronology."

74. Meyer, interview by Partin; and CSA," STRATSERCOM/JSOA Chronology."

75. Rylander, interview by Partin; and Partin, memorandum for the record, interview with Lunger..

76. Partin, memorandum for the record, interview with Lunger.

77. Ibid.

78. CSA, "STRATSERCOM/JSOA Chronology." Kelly's sponsorship by Lieutenant General Wilson was mentioned by Lunger, interview by Parin.

79. Rylander, interview by Partin.

80. Lunger, interview by Partin; and Koch, interview by Partin.

81. Koch, interview by Partin.

82. This same issue will arise once again after the reorganization of SOF. Rylander, interview by Partin.

83. Wilson, interview.

84. Lieutenant General Fred K. Mahaffey (U.S. Army) and Lieutenant General David L. Nichols (U.S. Air Force), memorandum, August 23, 1984.

85. Stephens, interview, March 1993.

86. Koch, interview.

87. Quote from Rylander, interview by Partin. Remaining material from Rylander, interview by Partin; and Koch, interview by Partin.

88. Rylander, interview by Partin.

89. Partin, memorandum for the record, interview with Lunger; Koch, interview by Partin; and Rylander, interview by Partin.

90. Koch, interview; and Stephens, interview.

91. Stephens, interview; Koch, interview; and interviews, USSOCOM, October 1993.

92. Rylander, interview by Partin; and Koch, interviews by author and by Partin.

93. The establishment of JSOC, in fact, created within the SOF community what could have become SOF's own precarious value—the formal assignment of the army's Rangers to the new command. Although Rangers in many way seem the antithesis of special operations forces, they have had a long informal relationship with SOF, including supporting the attempt to rescue the hostages in Iran. Like Special Forces, Rangers travel light, fighting with nothing heavier than 60mm mortars and light, hand-held antitank weapons; and primarily with their own rifles and machine guns. Unlike Special Forces, Rangers are truly an assault force, a highly trained, light infantry force of "door-kickers." They are an airborne unit, parachute trained, and capable of night operations with or without night vision devices. Because they travel light and fast, they have little sustainability and generally move in quickly, complete their mission, and are reinforced by heavier, more sustainable, units.

As noted earlier, the army does not confirm or deny the existence of Delta, and the navy does not confirm or deny SEAL Team 6. Both units are, however, referred to frequently throughout Mark Adkin, *Urgent Fury: The Battle for Grenada* (London: Lexington Books, 1989); Kelly, *Brave Men*; and Time-Life, *Commando Operations: The New Face of War* (Alexandria, Va.: Time-Life Books).

94. *Defense Department Special Operations Forces*, statement by Noel Koch.

Chapter 5

1. By far, the best source of information on Urgent Fury is a book written by Mark Adkin, a British military officer who served as the Barbados Defense Force Caribbean Operations staff officer before, during, and after the U.S. invasion of Grenada. *Urgent Fury: The Battle for Grenada* (London: Lexington Books, 1989) is interesting and remarkable in its detail of the history of Grenada, events preceding the invasion, and the invasion itself. The book is especially noteworthy because Urgent Fury has always been handled with great secrecy by the U.S. government. All after-action reports and testimony have remained classified. For the role of special operations forces, Adkin's book is the most complete, but Orr Kelly's *Brave Men, Dark Waters: The Untold Story of the Navy SEALs* (Presidio, 1992), adds detail about SEAL operations (Kelly also relied heavily on Adkin's book in his account). The Time-Life book *Commando Operations, The New Face of War* (Alexandria, Va.: Time-Life Books) provides an interesting summary of special operations in Grenada although it is somewhat at odds with Adkin and Kelly in accounting for the early loss of SEALs.

2. Adkin, *Urgent Fury*, pp. 109–10.

3. Ibid., p. 110.

4. Ibid., pp. 27–42; and Time-Life, *Commando Operations*, pp. 65–66.

5. Adkin, *Urgent Fury*, pp. 48–76.

6. Ibid., pp. 97–98.

7. Kelly, *Brave Men*, p. 206; and Adkin, *Urgent Fury*, pp. 107–10, 118–19.

8. Adkin, *Urgent Fury,* pp. 128, 132.

9. Ibid., pp. 138–40.

10. See note 93 in chapter 4.

11. Adkin, *Urgent Fury*, pp. 136–38.

12. Kelly, *Brave Men*, p. 208.

13. Adkin, *Urgent Fury*, pp. 140–42; Time-Life, *Commando Operations*, p. 68; and Kelly, *Brave Men*, pp. 206–10.

14. The lower weight and the limit is found in Time-Life, *Commando Operations*. The higher weight estimate is in Kelly, *Brave Men*.

15. Time-Life, *Commando Operations*.

16. Kelly, *Brave Men*, pp. 210–11.

17. It was clear that strategic surprise had been lost by Sunday, October 23. The Revolutionary Military Council was making desperate attempts to convince the United States not to invade, and it was calling for Great Britain to stop the coming attack. Adkin, *Urgent Fury*, p. 158.

18. Kelly, *Brave Men*, p. 211; and Time-Life, *Commando Operations*, pp. 69–71.

19. Adkin, *Urgent Fury*, pp. 174–75.

20. Kelly, *Brave Men*, p. 208.

21. Ibid., p. 206.

22. Time-Life, *Commando Operations*, pp. 76–78.

23. Kelly, *Brave Men*, pp. 205–07.

24. Adkin, *Urgent Fury,* p. 256; and Kelly, *Brave Men,* p. 208.

25. The story of the assault on Richmond Hill Prison is told in Adkin, *Urgent Fury;* and Time-Life, *Commando Operations*.

26. Adkin, *Urgent Fury*, pp. 174–75. Adkin suggests that a better mission might have been protecting the students at the True Blue campus adjacent to Point Salines.

27. Adkin, *Urgent Fury*, p. 236.

28. Ibid., pp. 194–96.

29. Ibid., p. 203.

30. Ibid., pp. 338–40.

31. Ibid., p. 309.

Chapter 6

1. R. Lynn Rylander, interview by John Partin, January 1989.

2. Major General Wesley Rice, director, JSOA: "Statement before the House Appropriations Committee, Subcommittee on Defense Appropriations," 98 Cong. 2 sess. (Government Printing Office, April 1984); and Rylander, interview by Partin.

3. *Congressional Record*, April 3, 1984, p. S3660. Interestingly, despite this opening shot, Senator Thurmond's name does not arise again in the story of SOF reform.

4. *Congressional Record*, speech to the 23rd Air Force, delivered by Noel C.

Koch, principal deputy assistant secretary of defense, International Security Affairs, April 3, 1984, pp. S3660–62.

5. *Congressional Record*, April 3, 1984, p. S3661.

6. Ibid.

7. Rylander, interview by Partin.

8. Transcript of a statement by Noel C. Koch before the Special Operations Panel, Subcommittee on Readiness, House Committee on Armed Services, September 6, 1984.

9. Ibid.

10. Rylander, interview by Partin; and Noel Koch, interview, April 1994.

11. Koch, interview by Partin.

12. Ibid.

13. Deborah G. Meyer and Benjamin F. Schemmer, "Air Force Leaders Do a 180 Degree Turn on Special Ops, Will Beef Up Forces," *Armed Forces Journal International* (June 1985), pp. 34–36.

14. Rylander, interview by Partin.

15. Koch, interview; and Rylander, interview by Partin. This story was also reported in Meyer and Schemmer, "Air Force Leaders," pp. 34–36.

16. Memorandum cited in Noel Koch, "Is There A Role for Air Power in Low Intensity Conflict," *Armed Forces Journal International* (May 1985), pp. 32, 36, 38, 42.

17. Colonel Scott Stephens, interview, March 1993.

18. In 1968 Schemmer purchased *Armed Forces Journal. AFJ* was then, according to Schemmer, editorially bankrupt and nearly financially so. The magazine was being kept alive by several wealthy owners who loved the magazine, first published in 1863, but were aging and uncertain what to do with it. They sold *AFJ* to Schemmer for $1,000. Schemmer turned the magazine around and built it into the major defense magazine in the United States. Benjamin F. Schemmer, interview, March 1994.

19. Schemmer published a book on the operation, expressing his outrage that the wealthiest nation in the world could not respond quickly and effectively to a call for help from its captured soldiers See Benjamin F. Schemmer, *The Raid* (Harper and Row, 1976).

20. This campaign for SOF reform was not Schemmer and *Armed Forces Journal's* only crusade during 1985. During this same period he took on the more narrow cause of getting a new bayonet for the army. Today Ben Schemmer has one of the first new bayonets mounted on the wall of his home.

21. "Book Review—Desert One, 1980—and 'Delta Force'" *Armed Forces Journal* (November 1983), p. 109, and (December 1983), pp. 4, 6.

22. When told of the number of articles and letters that appeared during this period, Ben Schemmer replied, "Forty-five? I wish I had published more!" Interview.

23. See, especially, Noel Koch, "Two Cases against a Sixth Service," and J. Michael Kelly (deputy assistant secretary of the air force, manpower, reserve

affairs, and installations), "For Special Ops," both in *Armed Forces Journal* (October 1985), pp. 102ff.; and Colonel Alan L. Gropman, USAF, "Air Power and Low-Intensity Conflict: An Airman's Perspective," *Armed Forces Journal* (May 1985), pp. 34ff.

24. Evidence of insider sources includes the printing of internal Defense Department memoranda and tidbits like the story of Noel Koch and his 33-foot rope. Although the magazine makes clear at several points that Noel Koch is not the unidentified source, one could guess that at least one source was in Koch's office, most likely Lynn Rylander.

25. Some of these articles included "SecDef Wants Aviation Review," "Without an SOF [airlift] Plan, No $, Say Conferees," a "dart" (a negative award given monthly by *AFJ*, in contrast to a "laurel") given to the Military Airlift Command for its "really dumb ideas" for replacing the AC-130 Spectre gunship, and "December Was Not a Good Month for USAF Special Operations." *Armed Forces Journal* (May 1985), p. 42 (September 1985), p.114; and (January 1986), p. 26.

26. Editor's note, *Armed Forces Journal* (May 1985), pp. 32–33.

27. Noel C. Koch, "Is There a Role for Air Power in Low-Intensity Conflict," *Armed Forces Journal* (May 1985), p. 36.

28. Gropman, "Air Power and Low-Intensity Conflict," pp. 38–39. Emphasis in original.

29. Deborah G. Meyer and Benjamin F. Schemmer, "An Exclusive *Armed Forces Journal* interview with: Noel C. Koch," *Armed Forces Journal* (March 1985), pp. 36–52.

30. Ibid.

31. Meyer and Schemmer, "Exclusive *Armed Forces Journal* Interview with: Noel C. Koch," p. 40.

32. Ibid., p. 42.

33. Letters by Colonel Ray E. Stratton, USAF; Major General R.V. Secord, USAF (ret.).; and Colonel R. C. Dutton, USAF, *Armed Forces Journal* (May 1985), p. 6. General Secord does not mention in his letter that he was a member of the Special Operations Policy Advisory Group.

34. Letter by Lieutenant Colonel (ret.) George T. Talbot Jr., U.S. Army, *Armed Forces Journal* (May 1985), p. 8.

35. Ted Lunger, interview, July 1988; and Colonel William G. Boykin, "Special Operations and Low-Intensity Conflict Legislation: Why It Was Passed and Have the Voids Been Filled" (Carlisle, Pa.: U.S. Army War College, 1991), pp. 22–23.

36. Representative Dan Daniel, "U.S. Special Operations: The Case for a Sixth Service," *Armed Forces Journal* (August 1985), pp. 70–74.

37. Ibid., p. 72.

38. Ibid.

39. Some advocates, such as Representative Daniel, refer to the establishment of a "sixth military service." In this case, Daniel is including the Coast Guard with the U.S. Army, U.S. Navy, Marine Corps, and U.S. Air Force as military services. Others who discuss the establishment of a new special operations military service

as the "fifth service" are referring to the Department of Defense military services (minus the Coast Guard).

40. Daniel, "U.S. Special Operations," pp. 72, 74.

41. Koch, "Two Cases against a Sixth Service," pp. 102–09.

42. Lunger, interview by Partin; and Boykin, "Special Operations," pp. 22–23. Koch did most of his own writing but did receive "talking points" from Rylander. Noel Koch, interview, April 1994.

43. Kelly, "For Special Ops," pp. 102–03.

44. Ibid., p. 103.

45. Ibid., p. 105.

46. Koch, "Two Cases against a Sixth Service," pp. 102–09.

47. Ibid., p. 105.

48. Senate Committee on Armed Services, *Defense Reorganization: The Need for Change*, Staff Report, 99 Cong. 1 sess. (Government Printing Office, October 1985).

49. Lunger's visit to Mellon is described in Boykin, "Special Operations," p. 23; Senate Armed Services Committee, *Defense Reorganization;* Jim Locher, interview, March 1993; Locher, interview by John Partin, July 1988; and William S. Cohen, "Fix for an SOF Capability That Is Most Assuredly Broken," *Armed Forces Journal* (January 1986), pp. 38–45.

50. Locher, interview by Partin; and Locher, interviews, March 1993 and March 1994.

51. Cohen, "Fix for an SOF Capability," p. 39.

52. Ibid., p.42.

53. Ibid.

54. Ibid., p. 43.

55. Ibid., p. 45.

56. Ibid., p. 39.

57. Rylander, interview by Partin; and Lunger, interview by Partin.

58. Meyer and Schemmer, "Air Force Leaders."

59. According to a report in the *Armed Forces Journal*, the tests, run by Boeing Vertol, were successful, but they were run under ideal conditions (not the nighttime, adverse weather conditions common in a special operation). As cited in *AFJ*, Representative Daniel subsequently wrote a letter to Deputy Secretary Taft criticizing the tests, "What we have to show for a year -long effort to equip a CH-47 helicopter for aerial refueling is one clear weather broad daylight movie." Deborah Meyer, "Taft Makes 'Solomonic' Decision on SOF Transfer by Splitting Mission," *Armed Forces Journal* (October 1985), p. 28.

60. Ibid.

61. According to Noel Koch, the army was "just shipping parts and crap all over the country with Federal Express and the UPS." Interview by Partin; also reported in *Armed Forces Journal*, January 1986.

62. *Department of Defense Authorization Act, 1986*, H. R. 1872, 99 Cong. 1 sess. (GPO, May 1985), pp. 89–90, 93.

63. *Congressional Record*, May 23, 1985, p. S6974.

64. "New Agency, Service for Special Ops?" *Armed Forces Journal*, August 1985, p. 28.

65. "October 2 Remarks by Senator Sam Nunn," reprinted in *Armed Forces Journal* (October 1985), pp.14–15.

66. Benjamin Schemmer, "Congress Directs DoD to Look Hard at Special Operations Agency," *Armed Forces Journal* (February 1986), p. 24.

67. Deborah Meyer and Benjamin Schemmer, "Congressional Pressure May Force Far More DoD Dollars for Special Ops," *Armed Forces Journal* (April 1986), p. 20.

68. Secretary of Defense, *Annual Report*, February 1986.

69. "Special Operations Funding in FY 87," *Armed Forces Journal* (March 1986), p. 50.

70. David Chu, interview, April 1994.

71. *Armed Forces Journal* also reported that the report was sent out of the Office of Program Analysis and Evaluation for coordination on Friday, March 21, with responses due the following Monday. *Armed Forces Journal* (April 1986).

72. Letters to the Honorable Barry M. Goldwater, chairman, Senate Armed Services Committee, and the Honorable Les Aspin, chairman, House Armed Services Committee, signed by William H. Taft IV, April 1, 1986.

73. Office of the Assistant Secretary for Program Analysis and Evaluation, *Historical Narrative on SOF Congressional Legislation*, 1988–89 (Department of Defense, 1989).

74. Noel Koch, letter to Senator William Cohen, summer 1986.

75. Rylander, interview by Partin.

76. Koch, interview by Partin.

77. Copy of September 15, 1986, Noel Koch letter to Senator William Cohen, provided by Noel Koch, April 1994.

78. Ibid.

79. Wilson, interview by Partin.

80. After leaving the government in 1986, Koch established a consulting firm specializing in threat assessments, travel security, and high-end, technology-aided security consultation. The appreciation of special operators for Koch's earlier efforts was evident in the memorabilia in his office (a collection that included an unusual selection of counterterrorist "souvenirs"). On one wall was a letter from a commander of the 20th Special Operations Squadron. In his letter the lieutenant colonel wrote that the 20th SOS owed its existence to Noel Koch's work.

81. Locher, interview by Partin.

82. S. 2453, "Enhancement of Capabilities to Combat Terrorism," offered by Senator Cohen on May 15, 1986, to the 99 Cong. 2 sess.

83. Ibid.

84. John Partin, memorandum for the record, interview with Chris Mellon, July 1988.

85. Locher, interview by Partin.

86. Andrew Krepinevich, *The Army and Vietnam* (Johns Hopkins University Press, 1986).

87. Locher, interview.

88. Locher, interview by author and interview by Partin.

89. Locher, interview.

90. Vuono responded, "I agree. We discussed in T [tank] this morning." Major General Moore, memorandum to Lieutenant General Vuono, May 16, 1986.

91. Lunger, interview by Partin.

92. Letter from Secretary of Defense Caspar Weinberger to the Honorable Dan Daniel, June 26, 1986.

93. Letter from John A. Wickham, Jr., General, U.S. Army chief of staff and John O. Marsh, Jr., secretary of the army, to Honorable Dan Daniel, House of Representatives, June 23, 1986.

94. See interviews with Ted Lunger, Jim Locher, and Sam Wilson.

95. Rylander, interview by Partin.

96. See Rylander, Mellon, and Locher, interviews by Partin.

97. R. Lynn Rylander, deputy director special planning, memorandum to Mr. [Richard] Armitage, assistant secretary of defense (international security affairs), July 29, 1986.

98. Ibid.

99. Locher, interview. Chris Mellon agrees with Locher's assessment. Mellon stated in a January 1988 speech at the National Defense University, "In part, the different prescriptions offered by House and Senate members may have resulted from the fact that the House Armed Services Committee had one panel looking at special operations matters and another panel looking at the broader issues of defense reform. In the Senate, the same members worked on both issues."

100. Lunger, interview by Partin; and Locher, interview.

101. Andrew J. Harris, "Executive and Congressional Efforts to Reorganize Special Operations Forces," paper presented to the annual conference, International Studies Association, April 1, 1988.

102. Subcommittee on Readiness of the House Armed Services Committee, *Comparing a National 'Special Operations Force Command' (SOFC) and Proposed 'National Special Operations Agency' (NSOA)*, Congressional Hearing Resume, 99 Cong. 2 sess. (1986); Witnesses: Admiral William J. Crowe Jr., CJCS, Honorable Richard L. Armitage, ASD (ISA), Lieutenant General (ret.) Sam Wilson.

103. Locher, interview by author and interview by Partin; and Schemmer, interview.

104. Locher, interview by Partin.

105. There is some indication that Representative Daniel brought in Major General Scholtes to testify before the Senate Armed Services Committee. Lunger, interview by Partin.

106. Locher, interview; see also Locher, interview by Partin; and Schemmer, interview.

107. Locher, interview.

108. Partin, memorandum for the record, interview with Mellon.

109. Wilson, interview by Partin.

110. *National Defense Authorization Act for Fiscal Year 1987*, Conference Re-

port 99-1001 to accompany S. 2638, 99 Cong. 2 sess. (GPO, 1986); and Public Law 99-661, I0 4. S. C. part B, section 1311, subparagraph A, November 14, 1986.

111. Public Law 99-661.

112. This legislation is discussed later in this book.

113. Locher, interview. Jim Locher had the unusual opportunity of writing most of the SOF legislation as the head of the Senate Armed Services Committee staff and serving as the second confirmed assistant secretary of defense, special operations and low-intensity conflict.

Chapter 7

1. Jim Locher, interview, March 1993.

2. Public Law 99-661.

3. FORSCOM and, for example, STRATCOM, were the last single-service specified commands, and they were deactivated between 1990 and 1993.

4. Public Law 99-661.

5. William H. Taft IV, deputy secretary of defense, memorandum, October 31, 1986.

6. Ibid.

7. Kelly would later gain national attention as the spokesman for the Joint Chiefs of Staff during Operation Desert Shield/Desert Storm.

8. Congressional reaction to later Defense Department decisions on the location of the new command were indicative of their initial assumption that the new special operations command would be located in the greater Washington, D.C., area.

9. Remarks by Admiral William Crowe at the USSOCOM activation ceremony, June 1, 1987.

10. U.S. Readiness Command, Office of the Command Historian, *Report on Mission and Deactivation of the United States Readiness Command* (MacDill Air Force Base, Florida, 1987), pp. 34–35. This report is classified secret, but an edited, unclassified version was obtained by the author.

11. Ibid., pp. 35–36.

12. Ibid., pp. 1–2.

13. Ibid., p. 40.

14. Admiral Crowe's remarks at the USSOCOM activation ceremony, MacDill Air Force Base, Florida, June 1, 1987.

15. Lieutenant General (ret.) Sam Wilson, interview, April 1994. Quote from Wilson, interview by John Partin. Kelly's meeting with Wilson is also discussed by Major General Thomas W. Kelly, interview by John Partin, June 1987.

16. Wilson, interview by Partin.

17. Wilson, interview by Partin; and John Partin, memorandum for the record, USREDCOM, January 13, 1987. USREDCOM documents are available from Office of the Command Historian, MacDill Air Force Base, Florida.

18. The 'tank' is a special conference room used by the Joint Chiefs of Staff.

19. U.S. Readiness Command, memorandum for the record, January 13, 1987; Joint Special Operations Agency, *Report by the JSOA to the Joint Chiefs of Staff on Establishment of the US Special Operations Command*, finalized January 8, 1987 (Department of Defense, 1987), includes Kelly's summary of the options under consideration; and U.S. Readiness Command, *Report on Mission and Deactivation*, p. 55.

20. In his interview in June 1987, Major General Kelly indicates that it was at a tank meeting on January 23 that the Joint Chiefs decided to locate the command in Tampa. Nonetheless, a January 16 memorandum from Colonel William Lucas, secretary to the Joint Chiefs of Staff, notifies the director of the Joint Staff that "on 9 January 1987, the Joint Chiefs of Staff approved the recommended actions in paragraph 3 of JCS 2542/175." This paragraph states Option One quoted in the text. See "Report by the JSOA to the Joint Chiefs of Staff on Establishment of the U.S. Special Operations Command, 9 January 1987."

21. U.S. Readiness Command, *Report on Mission and Deactivation*, p. 55.

22. John Partin, memorandum for the record, USREDCOM, January 30, 1987, reporting on a staff meeting led by General Lindsay on January 24, 1987.

23. Kelly, interview by Partin.

24. General James Lindsay, interview by John Partin, May 1987.

25. Representatives Earl Hutto, Dan Daniel, John Kasich, letter to Secretary Weinberger, March 11, 1987.

26. Vice Admiral P. F. Carter, director of the Joint Staff, memorandum to the secretary of defense, March 18, 1987.

27. *Making Continuing Appropriations for Fiscal Year 1987*, Conference Report to accompany H.J. Res. 738, 99 Cong. 2 sess. Report 99-1005 (Government Printing Office, October 1986).

28. U.S. Readiness Command, *Report on Mission and Deactivation*, p. 58

29. Fred C. Ikle, under secretary of defense (policy) for the director, Joint Staff, memorandum, February 10, 1987; and U.S. Readiness Command, *Report on Mission and Deactivation*, pp. 43–44.

30. U.S. Readiness Command, *Report on Mission and Deactivation*, pp. 43–44.

31. Letter from General James J. Lindsay to Admiral William J. Crowe Jr., June 25, 1987.

32. Message from Joint Chiefs of Staff, Washington, D.C., May 6, 1987.

33. Major General Leon W. Babcock Jr., USAF, USSOCOM J-5, "Assignment of Army PSYOP Units to USSOCOM," issue paper (Fla.: MacDill Air Force Base, 1987).

34. Colonel William A. Depalo Jr., Commander 4th Psychological Operations Group, Fort Bragg, memorandum, May 29, 1987.

35. Ibid.

36. Position of Fred Ikle, under secretary of defense, General Richard Stilwell, and the Marine Corps.

37. The U.S. Army and 1st SOCOM argued that these forces should remain assigned to 1st SOCOM, reporting through the army command to USSOCOM. See

Babcock, "Assignment of Army PSYOP."

38. Richard Armitage, assistant secretary of defense for international security affairs, memorandum to the secretary of defense, May 20, 1987.

39. Admiral William J. Crowe Jr., memorandum to the secretary of defense, June 16, 1987.

40. Lieutenant Colonel Andrew G. Gembara, memorandum to director, Special Operations Command, Washington office, June 15, 1987; and Major General Leroy N. Suddath, memorandum for General J. J. Lindsay, June 16, 1987.

41. Letter from James J. Lindsay to William H. Taft IV, June 25, 1987.

42. *USSOC Implementation Task Force Working Paper,* March 20, 1987.

43. Letter from General James J. Lindsay to Caspar W. Weinberger, June 30, 1987.

44. Letter from Caspar Weinberger to General James J. Lindsay, July 23, 1987.

45. Vice Admiral P.F. Carter Jr., director, Joint Staff, memorandum to the secretary of defense, July 28, 1987.

46. Special Operations Division, J-3, *Information Briefing on the OPCOM Assignment of Naval Special Warfare Groups* (Department of Defense, September 24, 1987). This paper was originally classified secret. An unclassified version of the paper was provided to the author.

47. Special Operations Division, J-3, *Information Briefing.*

48. Lieutenant David Eichenberger, executive officer to USINCSOC, "SECDEF's Performance Review (SPR) and Tank Session, 29 Sep 87," memorandum for the record, September 30, 1987. The implementation message was sent from Admiral Crowe to General Lindsay on October 1, 1987.

49. Ibid.

50. Interview with Rear Admiral Raymond Smith, December 1993; see also Gantley, interview.

51. USREDCOM, "Discussion of USSOCOM Issues," memorandum for the record, January 13, 1987.

52. Secretary of Defense, *Report on the Reorganization of DoD Special Operations by the Secretary of Defense to the United States Congress* (Department of Defense, February 1987).

53. Lindsay, interview by Partin; and U.S. Readiness Command, *Report on Mission and Deactivation,* p. 95.

54. President Ronald Reagan, memorandum for Caspar W. Weinberger, "Establishment of Combatant Commands," April 13, 1987. Just before Reagan's approval there was a flurry of memorandums in the Joint Staff and the Office of the Secretary of Defense. The subject of the correspondence was the disestablishment of REDCOM and the establishment of FORSCOM. Assistant Secretary of Defense for Program Analysis and Evaluation David S. C. Chu believed that the JCS plan lacked detail "concerning the disposition of USREDCOM's non-special operations forces (SOF) missions, responsibilities, organizations, and personnel among the other combatant commands"; and that there was an "asymmetry between Army and Air Force non-USSOC organizations in the post-USREDCOM environ-

ment." (David S. C. Chu, assistant secretary of defense, director of the Office of Program Analysis and Evaluation, "Comments on the JCS Proposal Establishing the U.S. Special Operations Command," memorandum for the secretary of defense, March 31, 1987.) Chu continued his protest even after Assistant Secretary of Defense for International Security Affairs Richard Armitage wrote the secretary that "the JCS recommendations are generally satisfactory" with some minor revisions. Armitage did recommend the establishment of a Washington office for the new command, a recommendation that was approved by Secretary Weinberger. (Richard Armitage, assistant secretary of defense, Office of International Security Affairs, "U.S. Special Operations Command," memorandum for the secretary of defense, April 2, 1987.) Armitage recognized the validity of Chu's concerns but argued that if the JCS plan were not accepted, the secretary could not forward the Unified Command Plan changes to the White House, thereby affecting General Lindsay's nomination for USCINCSOC. The White House had informed the Department of Defense that it would not process Lindsay's nomination until "the recommendation on the establishment of the USSOC is received because, in effect, there is no command for Gen. Lindsay to assume." (see Armitage's memorandum). Chu finally recommended the disestablishment of REDCOM, thus delaying the activation of FORSCOM. (David S. C. Chu, memorandum to the secretary of defense, April 3, 1987.)

55. Caspar Weinberger, memorandum for the chairman, Joint Chiefs of Staff, May 5, 1987.

56. Colonel Edwin P. Wasinger, staff judge advocate, memorandum, March 6, 1987.

57. Lindsay, interview by Partin.

58. National Defense Authorization Act for FY 88 and FY 89, H. Rept. 100-446, Conference Report to Accompany H. R. 1748, 100 Cong. 1 sess. (Government Printing Office, November 1987).

59. Remarks by Deputy Secretary Taft to the Activation Ceremony of United States Special Operations Command, MacDill Air Force Base, Fla., June 1, 1987.

60. Ibid.

61. Remarks by Deputy Secretary Taft, MacDill Air Force Base.

62. There is some debate over whether SOF is nearly the fifth or the sixth military service. Although Senator Cohen and Representative Daniel referred to a "sixth service," military personnel are more likely to use "fifth" in recognition of the Coast Guards' distinctive mission.

63. James Q.Wilson, *Bureaucracy: What Government Agencies Do and Why They Do It* (Basic Books, 1989), pp. 101–05.

64. Colonel Corson L. Hilton, interview, October 1993.

65. A military "component" is a higher-level headquarters that reports to a unified or specified four-star commander. A component commander is usually a two-star general or flag officer. An example of a component command in the conventional forces is Third Army, which is a component of Forces Command, or the Second Fleet, which reports to Pacific Command. Since the reorganization of

SOF, the three components are U.S. Army Special Operations Command (USASOC), U. S. Air Force Special Operations Command (AFSOC), and the U.S. Naval Special Warfare Command (NAVSPECWARCOM).

66. As mentioned earlier, relatively few women are associated with special operations forces. Women generally serve in special operations support roles including medical and communications personnel. There are also women in the civil affairs and psychological operations units.

67. Hilton, interview.

68. Ibid.

69. Lou Baxter, interview, March 1993.

Chapter 8

1. Secretary of Defense, *Secretary of Defense Report to Congress on Special Operations Reorganization*, February 20, 1987, p. 2.

2. P. J. Budahn, "Special Operations Command Will Be Activated April 16," *Army Times*, March 9, 1987, p. 6.

3. Letter from Representatives Earl Hutto and Dan Daniel, cochairmen of Special Operations Panel, Subcommittee on Readiness, and Representative John R. Kasich, ranking minority member, Special Operations Panel, Subcommittee on Readiness, to Caspar W. Weinberger, secretary of defense, March 11, 1987.

4. Letter from Senators William S. Cohen and Edward M. Kennedy to Secretary of Defense Caspar Weinberger, May 19, 1987.

5. Colonel Scott Stephens, interview, USSOCOM, March 1993.

6. R. Lynn Rylander, interview by John Partin, January 1989.

7. Lou Baxter, interview, March 1993.

8. This phrase comes up frequently in discussion on the early implementation of the SOF reorganization legislation. See interviews with Colonel Scott Stephens (March 1993), Lynn Rylander (January 1989), Noel Koch (1988 and 1994), and Lieutenant General Sam Wilson. Although these words were not actually used by Representatives Hutto, Kasich, and Daniel in their March 11, 1987, letter to Secretary Weinberger, "malicious implementation" is certainly what they were accusing the Defense Department of, if not accusing the secretary himself.

9. *Secretary of Defense Report to Congress*. The Defense Department's update to Congress on implementation of the SOF reorganization legislation was less than three and a half pages long; not any longer than the legislation itself.

10. David B. Ottaway, "Delay on Guerrilla Command Irks Hill; Weinberger Wants 12th Assistant Secretary's Post Created," *Washington Post*, March 10, 1987; and Rylander, interview by Partin.

11. Ottaway, "Delay on Guerrilla Command."

12. Vernon A. Guidry Jr., "3 Key Congressmen Assail Delay on Special Forces," *Baltimore Sun*, March 12, 1987, p. 3.

13. Rylander, interview by Partin.

14. Ibid.

15. Letter from Representatives Earl Hutto, Dan Daniel, and John R. Kasich to the secretary of defense, March 11, 1987.

16. Letter from Senators William S. Cohen and Edward M. Kennedy to the secretary of defense, May 19, 1987.

17. Rick Maze, "Congress Gets Special Operations Candidate," *Army Times*, June 22, 1987.

18. Jim Locher, interview, March 1993.

19. Ibid.

20. General Edward C. "Shy"Meyer, interview by John Partin, July 1988.

21. National Defense Authorization Act for FY 88 and FY 89, H. Rept. 100-46, Conference Report to Accompany H.R. 1748, 100 Cong. 1 sess. (Government Printing Office, November 1987), sec. 1211.

22. Locher, interview.

23. Lieutenant General (ret.) Sam Wilson, interview, April 1994.

24. Ibid.

25. Ibid.

26. Wilson, interview by Partin, July 1988.

27. Public Law 100-456, 101 Stat., 10USC, September 25, 1988.

28. Locher, interview.

29. Low-intensity conflict has been defined as "political-military confrontation between contending states or groups below conventional war and above the routine, peaceful competition among states. It frequently involves protracted struggles of competing principles and ideologies. Low-intensity conflict ranges from subversion to the use of armed force. It is waged with political, economic, informational, and military instruments. Low-intensity conflicts are often localized, generally in the Third World, but may have regional and global security implications."
See John M. Collins, "Special Operations Forces: An Assessment, 1986-1993," Washington, Congressional Research Service, July 1993.

30. Office of the Assistant Secretary of Defense (SOLIC), *Peacetime Engagement*, Working Paper, Draft 4.0 (Department of Defense, November 1991).

31. SOLIC, *Peacetime Engagement*, p.15.

32. Christopher Jehn, assistant secretary of defense (force management and personnel), memorandum for assistant secretary of defense (SOLIC), draft memo and executive summary, December 6, 1991. Force management and personnel proposed moving more of the civil affairs units, nearly all of which are in the reserve force, into the active force and also expressed concern about the United States responding unilaterally; and Michael Parmentier, Force Management and Personnel, interview, March 1993.

33. Locher, interview.

34. Ibid.

35. Statement by Chris Dye, briefing, Fort Bragg, N.C., March 31, 1993.

36. General Maxwell Thurman, commander in chief, U.S. Southern Command, during Operation Just Cause, in the foreword to Thomas Donnelly, Margaret

Roth, and Caleb Baker, *Operation Just Cause: The Storming of Panama* (Lexington Books, 1991). Operation Just Cause is the most well-researched and well-told book on the U.S. invasion of Panama. Unless otherwise noted, much of the description of the operation is from this book.

37. General Carl Stiner, briefing, Fort Bragg, N.C., March 31, 1993.

38. The most compelling book written on the building of the Panama Canal and Panama's history is David McCullough's *The Path between the Seas: The Creation of the Panama Canal* (Simon and Schuster, 1977).

39. Donnelly, Roth, and Baker, *Operation Just Cause*, pp. 3–5.

40. Ibid., pp. 7–8.

41. Ibid., pp. 35–46.

42. General Carl Stiner, interview, March 1993.

43. Donnelly, Roth, and Baker, *Operation Just Cause*, provide the most detailed force list for Just Cause, pp. 81–83.

44. Ibid., p. 72.

45. Center for Army Lessons Learned, *Operation Just Cause Lessons Learned, Volume II; Operations,* Bulletin 90-9 (Kansas: Fort Leavenworth, October 1990), pp. II-4-5.

46. Napier, interview. Colonel Rusty Napier took two of the gunships forward into Panama in preparation for the invasion.

47. Center for Army Lessons Learned, *Operation Just Cause Lessons Learned, Volume II*, p. II-19–20.

48. Notes from telephone conversation with General Carl Stiner, March 1995.

49. The story of the Paitilla airfield operation is told in Donnelly, Roth, and Baker, *Operation Just Cause,* pp. 114–20; and Orr Kelly, *Brave Men, Dark Waters: The Untold Story of the Navy SEALs* (Presidio, 1992), pp. 220–23, 226–34. Some information in this section is from an interview conducted at Special Operations Command, October 1993, and a telephone conversation with General Carl Stiner, March 1995.

50. The lower figure is in Center for Army Lessons Learned, *Operation Just Cause Lessons Learned, Volume I: Soldiers and Leadership*, Bulletin 90-9 (Kansas: Fort Leavenworth, October 1990), p. I-11. The higher figure comes from Donnelly, Roth, and Baker, *Operation Just Cause*, p. 349.

51. Center for Army Lessons Learned, *Lessons Learned, Volume II*, pp. II-21, 22.

52. Neil C. Livingstone, "Danger in the Air," *Washingtonian*, June 1990, p. 205.

53. Colonel "Ranger" Roach, Commander, 7th Special Forces Group, interview, May 1994.

54. In telling the same story, a former company commander in the 3rd Battalion explains the different approaches of Special Forces and conventional units: "There were cases where they'd [members of the 3rd Battalion, 7th SFG] go into the [Panamanian] town—ten guys—they'd get all the weapons, they'd secure the weapons, talk to the people [gather up the PDF], and make friends with everybody in town. Everybody's having a fiesta, they're glad there's no problems. And here comes the 7th ID with . . . mop-top camo [camouflage]. I mean, their eye-

balls are camouflaged, they've got bayonets hanging all over them. The [Panamanian] people are terrified. . . . And here's the 7th ID rolling in ready to kill people. And it's not the [American] soldiers' fault. They're pumped up—you're in a combat zone—close with and destroy the enemy. And the [Panamanian] people are going, 'What did we do? What did we do? The avenging angels are coming.' [By the end of the operation] they're saying, 'You guys are great, just hang around. But the other people [the conventional infantry unit] are weird.' " Interview with Command Sergeant Major, 7th Special Forces Group, May 1994.

55. Center for Army Lessons Learned, *Lessons Learned, Volume II,* pp. II-3, II-4.

Chapter 9

1. Lieutenant General (ret.) Sam Wilson, interview by John Partin, July 1988; and General Edward C. "Shy" Meyer, former chief of staff, U.S. Army, interview by Partin, July 1988.

2. Wilson, interview by Partin. The transcript of the interview indicates that Wilson was asked if the official he referred to was the chief of staff of the U.S. Air Force, and he nodded in agreement.

3. Meyer, interview by Partin.

4. Wilson, interview by Partin.

5. James E. Giles and others, *The Next Step for Special Operations: Getting the Resources to Do the Job,* Report SO801R1 (Bethesda, Md.: Logistics Management Institute, August 1988), pp. iii–iv.

6. This was the approximate Defense Department budget at the time the debate over the control over SOF resources was occurring. As of June 1996, the Defense Department budget for fiscal 1997 is approximately $260 billion.

7. Two interesting books on the development of PPBS and the Whiz Kids are Charles Hitch, *Decision-Making for Defense* (University of California Press, 1965); and Alain Enthoven and K. Wayne Smith, *How Much Is Enough? Shaping the Defense Program, 1961-1969* (Harper and Row, 1971). Systems analysis became the Office of Program Analysis and Evaluation in the early 1970s.

8. The U.S. Marine Corps is a component of the Department of the Navy and does not submit its own POM to the Office of the Secretary of Defense.

9. These components played a significant role in program development during the 1980s when defense budgets were increasing or declining only slightly. Less component input has been requested by the military departments since about 1990, when the budget began to decline dramatically. The military departments have had to make large cuts in recent years, and the components always want more.

10. P.L. 99-661. 100 Stat. 3984-85.

11. The other Major Force Programs in the defense budget include Reserve and National Guard forces, Military Pay, and Strategic Forces.

12. *Making Continuing Appropriations for Fiscal Year 1987,* Conference Report

to Accompany H. J. Res. 738, 99 Cong. 2 sess. (Government Printing Office, October 1986), pp. 128–31.

13. Director, Special Operations Technology, OASD (C³I), memorandum, January 20, 1987. Package includes draft guidance, draft memorandum to secretaries of the army, navy, air force, chairman of the Joint Chiefs of Staff. Comments included in this package indicate that the first draft of this guidance was circulated during the first week of January.

14. Assistant Secretaries Donald Latham and Richard Armitage, memorandum, February 3, 1987, package prepared by the director, Special Operations for ASD (C³I) and ASD (ISA).

15. Colonel Dave Merriam, deputy director for logistics and former deputy chief of programs, J-8, interview, March 1993.

16. Major General S. R. Woods Jr., director, Office of Program Analysis and Evaluation, Department of the Army, memorandum, January 8, 1987.

17. David S.C. Chu, interview, April 1994.

18. Ibid.

19. William H. Taft IV, deputy secretary of defense, memorandum, March 27, 1987.

20. Director, Special Operations, memorandum, June 2, 1987.

21. Major General S. R. Woods Jr., memorandum for Mr. Peter Bahnsen, director, Special Operations, ASD (C³I), April 23, 1987; also director, Special Operations, memorandum, June 2, 1987.

22. David S.C. Chu, director, Office of Program Analysis and Evaluation, and Robert W. Helm, assistant secretary of defense (comptroller), memorandum, August 21, 1987.

23. Nathaniel M. Cavallini, memorandum for Thomas P. Quinn, acting ASD (C³I) and Richard L. Armitage, ASD (ISA), August 26, 1987.

24. General James J. Lindsay, USCINCSOC, interview by John Partin, May 1987.

25. Roger A. Gribble, "Anti-Terror Force Touted," *Wisconsin State Journal,* July 3, 1987.

26. General James Lindsay, chairman of the Joint Chiefs of Staff for the deputy secretary of defense, memorandum through chairman JCS," unsigned draft, July 15, 1987.

27. Lou Baxter, interview, March 1993.

28. Guidance from the Secretary of Defense and the Joint Chiefs of Staff is found in the Unified Command Plan, the Joint Strategic Capabilities Plan, and Robert T. Herres, vice chairman, Joint Chiefs of Staff, memorandum, May 29, 1987.

29. One-fifth of the responsibilities under the branch entitled "prepare SOCOM headquarters to manage SOF within DoD" are in support of "prepar[ing] SOCOM headquarters to execute select special operations missions as a command at direction of NCA" (National Command Authorities). The SOCOM concept statement, diagramming the roles, missions, and functions of USSOCOM, prepared by

Sage Analytics International, is enclosed in a letter dated May 6, 1988, from General James J. Lindsay to the director of program analysis and evaluation in the Office of the Secretary of Defense.

30. Ibid.

31. "National Defense Authorization Act for Fiscal Years 1988 and 1989," conference report to accompany H.R. 1748 "Implementation of Special Operations Forces Reorganization," 100 Cong. 1 sess. (Government Printing Office, November 1987), p. 144, sec. 1211.

32. Joint Staff, internal staff paper, May 25, 1989.

33. Charles S. Whitehouse, assistant secretary of defense, special operations and low-intensity conflict, memorandum for the deputy secretary of defense to Major General Gordon E. Fornell, August 19, 1988.

34. Ibid.

35. Whitehouse, memorandum, October 13, 1988.

36. As indication of his concern for the PPBS process, Chu had also offered Option 5, believing that the Defense Department already knew how to work with defense agencies in the existing planning, programming, and budgeting system. Establishing a SOF defense agency created an organization that had all of the resource decisionmaking authority SOF supporters were demanding. The Special Operations Command did not see the issue in the same way as David Chu. According to USSOCOM's programming office, Option 5 was "a DoD bureaucratic ruse to get around legislation because of the fear of setting a dangerous precedent by giving a CINC [program], budget and execution authority." Chu, interview; and SOJ8-P, USSOCOM, information paper, Programming Office, December 20, 1988.

37. Whitehouse, memorandum, October 13, 1988.

38. Charles Whitehouse, assistant secretary of defense, memorandum, attachment 1, "History of CINCSOC Program and Budget Proposals (Section 167, 10 U.S.C.)," January 5, 1989, quoting from conference report 100-753, 100 Cong. 1 sess. (GPO, July 1988). On September 28, 1988, Senator Sam Nunn and Representative Earl Hutto made clear their views on the intent of existing legislation. Emphasis was placed on USSOCOM having the only POM for SOF programs and full budget execution authority. "The conferees fully intend that the commander of the Special Operations Command would have sole responsibility for preparation of the Program Objectives Memorandum for all Special Operations Forces and for other forces assigned to his command." *Congressional Record*, September 28, 1988, p. S13468.

39. Whitehouse, memorandum, January 5, 1989.

40. Letter from Representatives Earl Hutto and John R. Kasich to the Honorable William H. Taft IV, deputy secretary of defense, October 5, 1988.

41. Letter from Deputy Secretary William H. Taft IV to Representatives John R. Kasich and Earl Hutto, November 1, 1988.

42. Ibid. Emphasis in original.

43. William H. Taft IV, memorandum, December 12, 1988.

44. Whitehouse, memorandum, January 1989.

45. Letter from Senators Nunn, Cohen, Warner, and Kennedy to the Honorable Frank C. Carlucci, secretary of defense, January 9, 1989.

46. Chu, interview.

47. William H. Taft IV, memorandum, January 24, 1989.

48. Chu, interview.

49. Chu, interview; and Michael Parmentier, director for readiness and training, interview, February 1993.

50. David S. C. Chu, memorandum, draft, June 22, 1989. (All in package prepared by OSD, staff of the Office of Program Analysis and Evaluation, October 13, 1989.)

51. "This memorandum provides policy and procedures for the Military Departments and USCINCSOC to use in developing the FY1992–1997 Program Objectives Memorandum (POM), the Budget Estimate Submit (BES), and budget execution procedures for Major Force Program 11 (MFP-11) and other programs that support SOF.

52. Donald Atwood, deputy secretary of defense, memorandum, December 1, 1989.

53. Carl Stiner's role in these crises is discussed in David C. Martin and John Walcott, *Best Laid Plans: The Inside Story of America's War against Terrorism* (Harper and Row, 1988), pp. 161–202, 235–57.

54. With the exception of any discussion involving the two hijacking incidents, this biographical material comes from conversations with General Carl Stiner in March and October 1993.

55. General Carl Stiner, interview, March 1993.

56. Merriam, interview.

57. Ibid.

Chapter 10

1. Unless otherwise noted, information on Iraqi actions and forces before and during the Persian Gulf War of 1990-91 comes from Department of Defense, *Conduct of the Persian Gulf War, Final Report to Congress* (April 1992). There are three volumes, for a total of more than 1,000 pages. This report is particularly valuable for providing facts and figures on American, coalition, and Iraqi forces, giving an account of the campaign plan and actual operations, and a chronology of Desert Shield and Desert Storm. Rick Atkinson's *Crusade: The Untold Story of the Persian Gulf War* (Houghton Mifflin Company, 1993), is a well-told and detailed account of Desert Shield and Desert Storm, providing more information on individuals and relationships during the conflict. Atkinson's book is sometimes promoted as the answer to General Norman Schwarzkopf's autobiography, *It Doesn't Take a Hero* (Bantam Books, 1993) (clothbound, 1992). Schwarzkopf's book is a very readable account of his life and career with an insider's (to say the least) account of the Persian Gulf War. In *The Commandos: The Inside Story of*

America's Secret Soldiers (Simon and Schuster, 1994), Douglas Waller focuses on the participation of special operations forces in the crisis and describes SOF training in detail from first-hand experience. The Defense Department report, the above-mentioned books, and many interviews are the sources for this brief account of SOF in Desert Shield and Desert Storm.

2. Department of Defense, *Conduct of the Persian Gulf War*, p. 22.

3. Desert Shield refers to the mobilization, deployment, and buildup phase of the Southwest Asian conflict. Desert Storm begins with the initiation of the allied counteroffensive in January 1991.

4. Department of Defense, *Conduct of the Persian Gulf War*, pp. 11–14.

5. Rear Admiral Ray Smith, interview, December 1993.

6. Department of Defense, *Conduct of the Persian Gulf War*, p. J-8.

7. Ibid., pp. 62–80.

8. A more detailed discussion of command relationships and organization is provided ibid., pp. J-2–J-5.

9. Waller, *The Commandos*, p. 229.

10. Atkinson, *Crusade*, p. 142.

11. General (ret.) Carl Stiner, phone conversation with author, March 1995.

12. Smith, interview.

13. Ibid.

14. Schwarzkopf, *It Doesn't Take a Hero*, p. 538.

15. Department of Defense, *Conduct of the Persian Gulf War*, pp. J-8, J-9.

16. Sergeant First Class Alfred Sinclair, briefing, Fort Bragg, N.C., March 1993.

17. Smith, interview.

18. Smith, interview; and Department of Defense, *Conduct of the Persian Gulf War*, p. J-8.

19. Department of Defense, *Conduct of the Persian Gulf War*, pp. J-7, J-8; and General (ret.) Carl Stiner, interview, March 1993.

20. "Scud-hunting" receives detailed attention in Waller, *The Commandos,* and Atkinson, *Crusade.* Although militarily insignificant, the Iraqi Scud attacks, especially those directed at Israel, were a major political problem. These attacks caused great concern to the United States because they greatly increased the likelihood that Israel would override American arguments and enter the war. The probable result would then be the dissolution of the coalition. Eventually, more than one-third of coalition air combat and support missions were diverted to hunting Scuds (Schwarzkopf, *Hero*, p. 486). According to Waller and Atkinson (Waller, *Commandos*, pp. 335–51; and Atkinson, *Crusade*, pp. 140–142, 174, 179), at the recommendation of General Wayne Downing, teams from Delta supported by U.S. Air Force special operations air crews and members of the 160th Special Operations Aviation Regiment went deep into Iraq in search of Scud launchers. The British Special Air Service lost two of its members when they froze to death in a similar operation.

21. Department of Defense, *Conduct of the Persian Gulf War*, p. J-11; and Atkinson, *Crusade*, pp. 369–70.

22. Atkinson, *Crusade*, pp. 370–71, provides a detailed description of special reconnaissance skills and operations. Information on hide sites comes from interviews at Fort Bragg, May 1994. Special thanks to the sergeant who acted as my spotter and gave me the tour of hide sites.

23. John Partin, USSOCOM historian, discussion with author, January 1995.

24. Ibid.

25. Department of Defense, *Conduct of the Persian Gulf War*, pp. J-12,13; and Major Corby Martin, briefing, Fort Bragg, March 1993.

26. Department of Defense, *Conduct of the Persian Gulf War*, pp. 264, J-12, 13, 14; and Smith, interview.

27. Smith, interview; and Department of Defense, *Conduct of the Persian Gulf War*, p. J-13.

28. Command Sergeant Major John Meyer, 4th Psychological Operations Group, interview, May 1994.

29. 4th Psychological Operations Group (Airborne), *Leaflets of the Persian Gulf War*, booklet, Fort Bragg, N.C.

30. Much of the description of the deception operation is drawn from an account provided by Lieutenant Tom Dietz at a briefing at Fort Bragg, N.C., March 1993, and an interview with General Stiner by the author. The deception operation is also covered in Department of Defense, *Conduct of the Persian Gulf War*, pp. xxi, 294, J-14; and Atkinson, *Crusade*, pp. 369–70.

31. Department of Defense, *Conduct of the Persian Gulf War*, p. J-16; and Lieutenant Colonel Robert Hudson, interview, February 1994.

32. Smith, interview.

33. Captain Thomas Trask, briefing, Fort Bragg, March 1993.

34. Major Kevin L. Tompkins, interview, May 1994.

35. Master Sergeant Boltman, interview, May 1994.

36. Colonel Anthony Normand, chief of staff, U.S. Army Special Operations Command, interview, May 1994.

37. Story told by Sergeant Jack Webb, briefing, Fort Bragg, March 1993.

38. Department of Defense, *Conduct of the Persian Gulf War*, p. 343.

39. 4th Psychological Operations Group, *Leaflets of the Persian Gulf War*, p. 5.

40. Department of Defense, *Conduct of the Persian Gulf War*, pp. J-20, J-21.

41. Nearly all leaflets are found in the booklet by the 4th Psychological Operations Group. The author received some leaflets and explanations of their meaning and use from members of the group while at Fort Bragg, May 1994.

42. Stiner, interview; interview with members of the 4th Psychological Operations Group, May 1994; and 4th Psychological Operations Group booklet, p. 9.

43. Stiner, interview.

44 Department of Defense, *Conduct of the Persian Gulf War*, p. J-24.

45. Ibid.; and interviews with members of the 304th Civil Affairs Brigade, March 1994.

46. Interviews with members of the 304th Civil Affairs Brigade, March 1994.

47. Ibid.

48. Colonel Wendell Rich, 304th Civil Affairs Brigade (USAR), March 1994.

49. Interviews with members of the 304th Civil Affairs Brigade, March 1994; and Department of Defense, *Conduct of the Persian Gulf War*, p. J-26.

50. Department of Defense, *Conduct of the Persian Gulf War*, p. J-26.

51. Stiner, interview.

52. Colonel Randy Elliott, briefing, Fort Bragg, March 1993; and Stiner, interview.

53. Sergeant Major Bernard Bragdon, briefing, Fort Bragg, March 1993.

54. Sergeant First Class Lynch, interview, May 1994

55. One of the twenty-six people killed in a friendly fire shoot-down by aircraft enforcing the no-fly zone of an American helicopter in Iraq was a Special Forces colonel.

Chapter 11

1. Jane Perlez, "Expectations in Somalia," *New York Times*, December 4, 1992, p. A1.

2. Paul Lewis, "First U.N. Goal is Security; Political Outlook Is Murky," *New York Times*, December 4, 1992, p. A14.

3. Major Kevin L. Tompkins, interview, May 1994.

4. Tompkins, interview.

5. United Task Force Somalia, *Psychological Operations in Support of Operation Restore Hope*, booklet, May 1993.

6. There are two detailed and outstanding newspaper accounts of the October 3, 1993, raid in Somalia. The first is a two-part series written by Rick Atkinson for the *Washington Post* ("The Raid That Went Wrong; How an Elite U.S. Force Failed in Somalia," January 30–31, 1994). The second is a four-part series by Patrick J. Sloyan for *Newsday* (December 5–8, 1993). The general description of the operation comes from these sources unless otherwise noted.

7. Letter from General Wayne Downing to the author, March 24, 1994.

8. The dismissal of Special Forces liaison officers was discussed by General Wayne Downing, interview, October 1993.

9. Captain Beverly Revell, 304th Civil Affairs Brigade, interview, March 1994.

10. General Carl Stiner, interview, March 1993

11. General Wayne Downing, interview, October 1993.

12. Ibid. It should be noted, however, that the director for resources (J-8) under General Downing was a U.S. Air Force C-141 pilot and the head of the programming office is a SEAL. Both have outstanding service records and neither has any experience with the program and budget system at the military service or four-star, regional-commander level. However, analysts in the Office of Program Analysis and Evaluation in the Office of the Secretary of Defense hailed USSOCOM's six-year program, submitted December 1993, as the best of all the military services.

13. Colonel Eugene Bernhardt, Special Operations Command, interview, October 1993. Emphasis added.

14. Downing, interview.

15. James R. Locher, ASD (SOLIC), memorandum for assistant secretary of defense (force management and personnel), November 19, 1991.

16. Mark Lumpkin, a warrant officer who, because of the shortage of captains, commands a team in the 7th Special Forces Group, explained, "I'm commanding right now. . . . There's only two . . . company grade officers out of six teams. . . . these officers end up [serving] a maximum one year to 18 months on an A-Team. They have all these staff jobs [that higher-level commands] pull them up for. . . . We are doing their [officers'] jobs for them so they can fill staff jobs." Interview, Fort Bragg, May 1994. The warrant officer's observation was confirmed by a captain serving in the same Special Forces group as the commander of another A-Team. The warrant officer pointed out that one Special Forces team trapped in Iraq (see chapter 10) was commanded by a warrant officer.

17. Particularly helpful in suggesting alternative approaches to organizing SOF operational units were Captain Ron Yeaw, U.S. Navy; Colonel Scott Stephens, U.S. Air Force; and Jim Crawford, recently retired from the U.S. Army.

18. Captain Ron Yeaw, interview, February 1994.

19. As a SEAL officer explained, "One of the things that is not obvious at first glance is . . . what makes a special operator. And that is an absolute internal mandate to go into the most difficult combat situations you can, to face death, and to win. That's what it takes to get through training. That's what most of the guys want when they start training and then training reinforces that. . . . To go into very risky, very personally risky situations, where it's one on one, and go duke it out with the bad guy. That's what SOF guys want." Ibid.

20. Admiral Raymond Smith, interview, December 1993.

Index

Abrams, Creighton, 20, 62
Adams, Tom, 93
A-Detachments/Teams. *See* Special
  Forces Groups
Adkin, Mark, 95, 98, 100, 105
Administrative Behavior (Simon), 44
Aerospace Rescue and Recovery
  Service, 78
AFJ. See *Armed Forces Journal
  International*
Africa, 251
Ahmann, Jim, 82
Aideed, Mohamed Farah, 253–54. *See
  also* Operation Restore Hope
Air Commando Newsletter, 75
Air commandos: disbanding of, 35;
  reorganization of SOF and, 76;
  training, 55–57; in Vietnam, 33; in
  World War II, 4, 28, 29, 30, 31–32
Air commandos, groups: Air Com-
  mando Group, 1st (Project 9), 7,
  28, 29, 30, 31–32
Aircraft: bombers, 28–29, 197–98,
  235, 236; combat, 77; fighters,
  236; gunships, 33, 55–56, 77, 78,
  103, 128, 193, 194, 199, 236;
  special operations, 33, 55–56, 87–
  88, 98, 100, 102–03; transports,
  31, 32, 33, 69, 70, 71–72, 75, 77,
  79, 98, 102, 114, 196. *See also*
  Helicopters; Initiative *17*; Operation Rice Bowl

Air Force, U.S.: culture of, 45; Iranian
  hostage rescue, 1, 69, 75; in
  Operation Desert Shield and
  Desert Storm, 229, 238–39; special
  operations forces, 35, 55–56, 75–
  79, 87–89, 115–16, 118–20, 130–
  31; Vietnam, 32–33; wings, 33;
  World War II, 32. *See also* Aircraft;
  Combat Crew Training Squadron;
  Helicopters; Initiative *17*
Air Force, U.S. Army (USAAF):
  composite/mixed wings, 30, 32;
  Korean
War, 32; World War II, 28–32
Air Force, groups: Air Division, 2nd,
  75, 78, 79; Air Force, 9th, 76;
Air Force, 23rd, 78, 163–64; Bom-
  bardment, 5th, 28; Bombardment
  (Carpetbaggers), 801st, 28–29;
  Combat Search and Rescue, 76,
  114, 238–39; Fighter, 23rd, 30;
  Provisional Unit (Air) 5318th, 31;
  Special Operations Wings (SOW),
  56–57, 75, 76, 77, 79, 95, 103;
  Project *9*, 30; Tactical Control
  Team, 229; Tactical Fighter Wing,
  1st, 56
Air Force Special Air Warfare Center,
  U.S., 32
Air Force Special Operations Force
  (USAFSOF), 33, 75, 117
Alison, John R., 30, 32

Allen, Jim, 77
Allen, Terry, 91
Anderson, George, 25
Arias, Arnulfo, 188–89
Armed Forces Journal International (AFJ), 116, 117–27, 128, 130, 131, 136, 268
Armitage, Richard, 140, 142–43, 144, 157, 177, 184, 212–214, 269
Army and Vietnam, The (Krepinevich), 136
Army, Department of, 62–63. *See also* Department of Defense
Army Times, 178
Army, U.S.: culture of, 45; decisionmaking in, 207; in Grenada, 97–106; in Operation Desert Shield and Desert Storm, 228, 235–37, 239–48; in Panama, 196–97; resource and budget management, 211; in Somalia, 251–52, 253; special operations forces, 73, 74–75, 87–89, 115–16; USSOCOM, 155; in Vietnam, 34. *See also* Department of Defense; Initiative *17*
Army, U.S., divisions/groups: Airborne, XVIII, 64, 151, 190, 191, 224;
Airborne, 82nd, 61, 94, 95, 96, 105, 151, 190, 192, 196, 197, 199, 224, 228; Airborne, 101st, 224, 236; Armored Division, 3rd, 245–46; Aviation Battalion, 160th, 97, 101; Battalion, 1st, 102, 196, 198; Battalion, 2nd, 197; Battalion, 3rd, 196, 197; Cavalry, 1st, 61; Civil Affairs, 155, 156–58, 160–61, 174, 192, 197, 200, 202, 244–48, 252, 262; Infantry Brigade, 193rd, 190, 192, 199; Infantry Division, 7th, 190, 192, 201; Mountain Division, 10th, 251–52; Psychological operations, 155, 156–58, 160–61,

174, 192, 198, 200–01, 237, 239–45, 248, 252, 262; Rangers, 11, 91, 94, 95, 96, 97, 100–01, 102–05, 115, 123, 192, 196 197, 253, 254; Special Operations Aviation Regiment, 160th, 235–36; Special Operations Command, 1st (SOCOM), 75, 156, 158, 163, 196; Special Operations Squadrons, 236
Arnold, Henry H. "Hap," 29–30, 31, 32
ASD (SOLIC) (Assistant secretary of defense, special operations and low-intensity conflict). *See* Department of Defense
Aspin, Les, 131, 258
Assistant secretary of defense, special operations and low-intensity conflict (ASD[SOLIC]). *See* Department of Defense
Atkinson, Rick, 230–31
Atwood, Donald, 223–24
Austin, Hudson, 93, 105

Baltimore Sun, 172, 176–77
Balwanz, Chad, 235–36
Bank, Aaron, 11, 12, 58
Barletta, Nicolas Ardito, 189
Basic Underwater Demolition/SEAL (BUD/S) training, 48–52, 261. *See also* SEALs; Underwater Demolition Teams
Beckwith, Charlie, 2, 62, 63–64, 70, 72
Beirut, 133
Bergquist, Kenneth S., 178, 220
Bishop, Maurice, 92, 93
Blackburn, Donald, 16, 82
Blue Spoon plans (Panama), 190
Bosnia, 187, 250, 251, 269
Botswana, 254
Brady, Nicholas, 182
Brown, Harold, 64, 71
Brzezinski, Zbigniew, 64, 71

Bucklew, Phil H., 21
Budget management, 203–26
BUD/S. *See* Basic Underwater
Demolition/SEAL
Burke, Arleigh, 25
Burma. *See* World War II
Bush, George, 94, 181–82, 186, 190,
191, 194, 251, 257–58. *See also*
Operation Desert Shield and
Desert Storm

CA. *See* Civil Affairs
Calderon, Ricardo Arias, 190–91
Cambodia, 37–38, 61–62, 251
Carlucci, Frank, 180, 218, 220, 222,
269
Carter, Jimmy, 2, 64, 71, 81
Carter, P.F., 159
CCRAK. *See* Covert Clandestine
Reconnaissance Activities, Korea
CCTs. *See* Combat control teams
CCTS. *See* Combat Crew Training
Squadron
Central Intelligence Agency (CIA): in
Grenada, 94; in Iran, 69; OSS and,
9; SOF and, 17, 20, 26, 32, 42
Cheney, Dick, 182, 228
Chindits, 29, 30, 31
Chu, David S.C.: Initiative *17*, 128,
131; resource and budget
management, 211–12, 213, 218,
219, 223
Churchill, Winston, 29
CIA. *See* Central Intelligence Agency
CIDG. *See* Civilian Irregular Defense
Group
CINCs. *See* Commanders in chief
Cisneros, Marc, 190
Civil Affairs (CA). *See* Army, U.S.,
divisions/groups
Civilian Irregular Defense Group
(CIDG), 14, 15, 18–19, 33
Clark, Bruce, 12
Clinton, Bill, 82, 258

Coard, Bernard, 93, 105
Cohen, Eliot, 45
Cohen, William: Department of
Defense, 129, 130, 134–37, 141,
143, 170, 173; letter from Koch,
Noel, 132–34; OASD (SOLIC),
178, 182; resource and budget
management, 154, 219; SOF
reorganization, 116, 125–26, 144,
153, 154, 268
Colby, William, 27
Cold war: Bush administration, 181–
82, 186, 257–58; conventional
military, 111; Grenada, 92;
peacetime engagement and, 185;
priorities of, 119; SEALs, 65, 66–
67; Special Forces Groups, 12;
special operations forces, 35, 42,
68, 79
Collins, John M., 46–47
Combat control teams (CCTs), 1, 95
Combat Crew Training Squadron
(CCTS), 32
Combat Search and Rescue (CSAR),
238. *See also* Air Force groups
Combined Operations Pilotage
Parties (COPP; Britain), 21
Command, control, communications
and intelligence (C³I), 132
Commanders in chief (CINCs), 74,
218
Commands: combatant, 94, 95, 149–
50, 158, 160, 188, 190, 191; Joint
Special Operations, 95, 106, 131,
155, 156, 163, 213, 224, 255; Joint
Strategic Services, 156–57; Naval
Special Warfare, 162, 163;
resource management, 207; SOF
reorganization and, 130, 135, 137,
138, 139–40, 141–42, 154; special
operations, 259; Special Operations Command-Central, 230;
specified, 149, 154, 163; U.S.
Central, 230; USSOCOM and, 160.

Commands: combatant *(continued)*
  See also Military Airlift Command;
  U.S. Special Operations Command
Conflict. *See* Low-intensity conflict
Congress: Department of Defense
  and, 220–22; failure of Iranian
  hostage rescue, 3, 5; low-intensity
  conflict, 184–85; OASD (SOLIC),
  3, 178, 179; resource and budget
  management, 213, 214, 216–26;
  SOF reorganization, 86–89, 107–
  12, 127–49, 266–68; USSOCOM,
  172–73, 176, 207, 217–26
Conventional military: air force, 76,
  87–88; distrust of SOF, 4, 6, 7–8,
  11, 12, 14, 16–17, 20, 35, 42–43,
  73, 230–31, 239–40, 264–65; cold
  war and, 111; low-intensity
  conflict, 34; naval, 25, 37; reform
  of SOF and, 108, 110–11, 122–23,
  128, 141–42; SOF integration with,
  230–36, 246, 248–49, 254; Special
  Forces Operational Detachment-
  Delta, 63; U.S. military weakness,
  61, 125–26. *See also* Defense
  Department
Coogan, R.T., 38
Coordination and training teams
  (CTTs), 232–33
COPP. *See* Combined Operations
  Pilotage Parties
Coulter, D.T., 38
Counterterrorism. *See* Terrorism
Counterterrorist Joint Task Force, 73
Covert Clandestine Reconnaissance
  Activities, Korea (CCRAK), 11
Cowan, William V., 144–45, 176
Cox, Hugh, 75–76, 77, 78, 168
Crowe, William, 142–44, 151, 152,
  153, 155–56, 157, 162, 164
CSAR (Combat Search and Rescue).
  See Air Force groups
CTTs. *See* Coordination and training
  teams
Cuba, 92, 254

Daniel, Dan: ASD (SOLIC), 178, 179;
  death of, 203, 269; Department of
  Defense, 170–72, 174; Joint
  Special Operations Agency, 86,
  108; JSOA and, 111; SOF reorgani-
  zation and, 86, 88, 107–08, 116,
  121–23, 126, 129, 137, 139, 141–
  42, 143, 267; Wilson, Samuel and,
  60
Davidson, Tim, 113, 134
DeBobes, William, 140
Defense appropriations bill. *See* U.S.
  Special Operations Command
Defense Guidance, 77, 82, 208
Defense Intelligence Agency, 61
Defense Resources Board, 111, 139,
  143, 160, 207, 208, 211
Defense Special Operations Agency
  (DSOA), 126–27, 130, 137
Delta force. *See* Special Forces
  Operational Detachment-Delta
  (SFOD-D)
Depalo, William, 157
Department of Defense: Congress
  and, 220–21; failures according to
  Koch, Noel, 133; OASD (SOLIC),
  3, 135, 146, 166, 175–84, 204–05,
  212, 213, 223, 255, 256, 257, 258,
  268, 269; report on Persian Gulf
  War, 246; resource and budget
  management, 127, 203–14, 217–
  26; SOF reorganization and, 124,
  127–49, 150; USSOCOM and, 154,
  161, 170–87, 204, 205–06, 209,
  217–26, 258. *See also* Conven-
  tional military; Koch, Noel; U.S.
  Special Operations Command;
  Weinberger, Caspar
Department of Defense Authorization
  Act of *1986*, 129, 131
Department of Defense Reorganization Act of *1986* (Goldwater-
  Nichols; Nunn-Cohen), 125, 136,
  140–48, 191, 208–09
Desert One. *See* Operation Rice Bowl

Desert Shield. *See* Operation Desert Shield and Desert Storm
Desert Storm. *See* Operation Desert Shield and Desert Storm
Dietz, Tom, 238
Donovan, William "Wild Bill," 8–9
Downing, Wayne, 47–48, 164, 192, 254, 255–56
Drug trafficking, 189, 190, 225
DSOA. *See* Defense Special Operations Agency
Dye, Chris, 187

Eifler, Carl, 10
El Salvador, 80–81, 265–66
Endara, Guillermo, 188, 190–91
Enthoven, Alain, 206
Erskine, Donald, 98–99

Fane, Francis Douglas, 58
Five-Year Defense Plans (FYDPs), 131, 218. *See also* Future-Years Defense Plan
Flying Tigers, 30
Flynn, Cathal "Irish," 27, 66, 265
Forces Command (FORSCOM; U.S. Army), 63
Ford, Guillermo "Billy," 190–91
FORSCOM. *See* Forces Command
Fort Bragg (NC), 11, 41, 64, 74–75
Fort Lewis (WA), 75
Future-Years Defense Plan (FYDP), 208
FYDPs. *See* Five-Year Defense Plan; Future-Years Defense Plan

Gabriel, Charles, 77, 117, 130–31
Gairy, Eric, 92
Geopolitical issues, 61–62
German, Link, 85
Goldwater, Barry, 125, 129, 130, 131, 137
Grabowsky, Ted, 66, 265
Green Berets. *See* Special Forces
Grenada, 91–106, 133, 135, 143, 144

Gropman, Alan L., 118

Hagler, Ralph, 102
Haiti, 187, 254–55
HALO. *See* High-altitude/low-opening jump training
Hamilton, Bill, 25
Helicopters: in Grenada, 96, 100, 102; in Iran, 1–2, 69, 70–72, 75, 114; in Operation Desert Shield and Desert Storm, 234–35, 236, 238–39; in Panama, 198–99, 200; Pave Low helicopters, 76, 87, 88–89, 107, 114, 128, 130, 236, 239; in Somalia, 253; special operations, 56, 76, 77, 78, 87–89. *See also* Initiative *17*
Helm, Robert, 213, 218
Herrara, Roberto Diaz, 189
Herres, Robert, 161, 163
Higgins, Kevin, 194–95
High-altitude/low-opening (HALO) jump training, 55
Hilton, Corson L. "Corky," 40, 148, 167
Hitch, Charles, 206
Holloway Commission, 72–73, 89, 117
Holloway, James, 72, 82
Hussein, Saddam, 227. *See also* Operation Desert Shield and Desert Storm
Hutto, Earl: Department of Defense, 170–72, 178; resource and budget management, 174, 219, 220; SOF reorganization, 110, 117, 268; USSOCOM, 219, 220

Ikle, Fred, 155, 156
Initiative *17*, 87–89, 112–15, 118–20, 128, 129, 131, 143
Inside the Green Berets (Simpson), 57
Institute for Military Assistance, 61
Integrated priority lists (IPLs), 207
IPLs. *See* Integrated priority lists
Iran, 1–2, 3, 5, 33, 69–73, 79, 135
Iraq, 244, 269. *See also* Operation Desert Shield and Desert Storm

Jamaica, 93–94
Jedburgh teams, 9, 10, 11, 29. *See also* Office of Strategic Services
John F. Kennedy Center for Military Assistance, 75
Johnson, Jesse, 230, 232, 238
Johnson, Ken, 125, 140, 144–45
Johnson, U. Alexis, 14
Joint Chiefs of Staff: role of, 138–39; STRATSERCOM and, 74; SOF reorganization, 84–85, 137–38, 140, 149; USSOCOM and, 159–60
Joint Endeavor for Welfare, Education, and Liberation Movement (Grenada), 92
Joint Special Operations Agency (JSOA), 84, 85–86, 89, 108, 109, 111, 124, 164, 177. *See also* Commands
Joint Special Operations Command. *See* Commands
JSOA. *See* Joint Special Operations Agency

Kasich, John, 143, 170–72, 174, 178, 220, 268
Kauffman, Draper L., 21–22, 24
Kelly, J. Michael, 123
Kelly, Orr, 24, 95, 96, 97, 98, 99–100
Kelly, Tom, 85, 151, 152, 153
Kennedy, Edward, 173, 178, 222, 268
Kennedy, John F., 4, 13–14, 16–17, 65
Kennedy, Robert, 14
Kernan, William, 42, 198
Khomeni, Imam Ayatollah, 1, 69
King, Ernest J., 21
Kingston, Robert, 62, 63, 64
Koch, Noel: as advocate for special operations, 80–86, 87, 107, 108–13, 116, 118–19, 120–21, 123–24, 267; Department of Defense, 173; Initiative *17*, 88, 89, 112–13, 131; resignation, 132–34, 269; "thirty-foot-rope trick," 113–14
Koenig, John, 99

Korean War, 11, 12–13, 25, 32
Krepinevich, Andrew, 34, 136
Kupperman, Robert, 62, 63
Kurds, 247–48
Kuwait, 229–30, 234, 244, 246–47, 269. *See* Operation Desert Shield and Desert Storm

Lambertsen Amphibious Respiratory Unit (LARU), 24
Lambertsen, Christian, 24
Language training, 233
LARU. *See* Lambertsen Amphibious Respiratory Unit
Latham, Donald, 132, 209, 212–13
Leadership in Administration (Selznick), 7, 44–45
Lemnitzer, Lyman, 14
LeMoyne, Irve "Chuck," 39
Lewis, Rudy, 100
LIC. *See* Low-intensity conflict
Lindsay, James: as commander of USSOCOM, 162–63; Panama, 190; USSOCOM, 151–52, 174, 215–16, 217, 218, 256, 269; special operations forces, 156, 157, 159, 160, 161–62
Livingstone, Neil C., 199
LLDB. *See* Luc Uong Dac Biet
Locher, Jim: ASD (SOLIC), 136–37, 182–84, 185, 269; SOF reorganization, 125, 136–37, 140, 141, 144–45; Tower, John and, 182
Low-intensity conflict (LIC); in the *1990*s, 250, 258; ASD (SOLIC), 179; need for SOF in, 111–12; "peacetime engagement," 185–87, 257; political issues of, 180, 184–85; as a priority, 119, 121, 124, 136, 137, 164–65, 184–85, 270; SOF reorganization and, 135
Lucas, Keith, 101
Luc Uong Dac Biet (LLDB; Vietnam), 14–16
Lunger, Ted: Congress and, 86–87,

108, 110, 121, 123, 125; departure from Capitol Hill, 269; Initiative *17*, 88; JSOA, 85; SOF reorganization, 128, 137, 139, 141–42, 143, 144–45, 267; STRATSERCOM and, 74

MAC. *See* Military Airlift Command
MacArthur, Douglas, 24–25
MacDill Air Force Base (FL), 152–54, 230
Macedonia, 251, 269
MACV/SOG. *See* Military Assistance Command Vietnam/Studies and Observations Group
Mahaffey, Fred, 115, 119
Major Force Programs (MFPs): program implementation and, 203, 210, 255; resource and budget management, 142, 145, 158, 171–72, 174, 208, 222, 224; SOF reorganization, 140–41, 204–05, 207, 209
Manor, Leroy, 82
Marine Corps: in Grenada, 94, 95–96, 100–01; Iranian hostage rescue, 1, 69, 70–71; in Somalia, 251–52; USSOCOM and, 155
Marine Corps, groups: Amphibious, 22nd, 94, 95–96, 101; Expedition-ary Brigades and Units, 190, 237; Task Force Semper Fi, 192
Marsh, John O., Jr., 138, 179–81, 214, 217, 269
Mayaguez incident, 37, 68, 135
McCain, John, 191
McCone, John, 14
McFarlane, Robert, 39, 109
McGovern, George, 80, 81, 113, 134, 267, 269
McGrath, Tom, 47
McPeak, Merrill, 56–57
Meadows, Dick, 69
MEDCAPS, 252
Mellon, Chris, 125, 136, 140, 141, 144–45

Metcalf, Joseph, 94, 97, 102
Meyer, Deborah G., 120
Meyer, Edward Charles "Shy": 7th Special Forces Group, 68; ASD (SOLIC), 178–79; Department of Defense, 203; Major Force Program 11, 204; retirement of, 111; SOF reorganization, 73–75, 84, 85, 108, 134, 266; terrorism and, 61–64
Meyer, John, 237–38
MFPs. *See* Major Force Programs
Mike forces, 19, 33
Military Airlift Command (MAC): Air Force Special Operations Forces and, 77–79; Grenada and, 95; Initiative *17* and, 88; USSOCOM and, 155, 160, 163–64
Military Assistance Command Vietnam/Studies and Observations Group (MACV/SOG), 16, 18
Missiles, 236
Mobile training teams (MTTs), 13, 42
Moellering, John, 152
Montgomery, Sonny, 108
Moore, William, 137
Murrow, Edward R., 14
Muse, Kurt, 199–200

National Command Authorities, 155, 156
National Defense Authorization Act of *1987*, 145, 179
National Security Council, 135
National Special Operations Agency, 137, 138–39, 140
Naval Special Warfare Center, 48, 155, 158, 163
Navy, U.S.: culture of, 45; Iranian hostage rescue, 1, 69, 70; in Operation Desert Shield and Desert Storm, 229–30, 234, 236, 237; post-Vietnam, 36–39; resource and budget manage-ment, 211; special operations in,

Navy, U.S.: culture of *(continued)* 35–39, 115–16; spending on SEALs, 68, 158; SPECWAR, 20, 36, 37, 159–61, 213, 231; USSOCOM and, 155, 156, 158–62. *See also* SEALs; UDTs

Navy, U.S., groups: Naval Special Warfare Units, 155, 156, 192, 229–30, 234, 236, 237

New Jewel Movement (Grenada), 92

New York Times, 251

Nichols, Bill, 108

Nichols, David, 115, 119

Night Stalkers, 97, 101, 196

Nix, John, 104

Noriega, Manuel, 187, 188, 189, 190–91, 193, 200

Nunn, Sam: Department of Defense, 129, 130, 134, 143; resource and budget management, 204, 219, 221, 222; SOF reorganization, 125, 137, 144, 153, 268

Oakley, Robert, 180

OECS. *See* Organization of Eastern Caribbean States

Office of Management and Budget (OMB), 208

Office of the Secretary of Defense. *See* Department of Defense; Weinberger, Caspar

Office of Strategic Services (OSS), 4, 7, 8–10, 24–25, 264. *See also* Jedburgh teams

Office of the Special Assistant for Counterinsurgency and Special Activities, 86

Officers: in Air Force Special Operations Forces, 76, 79; in SEALs and UDTs, 25, 35–36, 48; in Special Forces, 41, 48–49, 259–60; special operations forces, 146, 167–68, 265, 266; USSOCOM, 164, 167–68

Olympics (*1972*), 63

OMB. *See* Office of Management and Budget

Operation Desert Shield and Desert Storm (Iraq, Kuwait, Saudi Arabia), 227–250, 262

Operation Farmgate (Vietnam), 32

Operation Just Cause (Panama), 187–201, 224, 255, 262, 263, 269

Operation Nimrod Dancer (Panama), 191

Operation Promote Liberty (Panama), 201–202

Operation Provide Comfort (Iraq, Kuwait), 244–49

Operation Provide Promise (Yugoslavia), 250–51

Operation Restore Hope (Somalia), 251–54

Operation Rice Bowl (Iran), 1–2, 3, 5, 33, 69–73, 79, 81, 117, 135, 267

Operation Thursday (WW II), 31

Operation Torch (WW II), 21

Operation Urgent Fury (Grenada), 91–106, 117, 143, 144, 192

Operation Waterpump (Laos, Thailand), 33

Organizational culture, 44–48. *See also* Special operations forces

Organization of Eastern Caribbean States (OECS), 93–94

OSS. *See* Office of Strategic Services

Panama, 42. *See also* Operation Just Cause; Operation Nimrod Dancer; Operation Promote Liberty

Panamanian Defense Forces (PDF), 189–91, 192, 193, 195, 197, 201

Peacetime Engagement (SOLIC), 185–86. *See also* Low-intensity conflict

People's Revolutionary Army (PRA; Grenada), 92, 93, 98–99,

Perry, William, 258

Persian Gulf War. *See* Operation Desert Shield and Desert Storm

Phillips, Greg, 44
Planes. *See* Aircraft
Planning, programming, and
    budgeting system (PPBS), 206–07,
    211–12, 213, 215, 218, 220
POMs. *See* Program objective
    memorandums
Powell, Colin, 186, 187
PPBS. *See* Planning, programming,
    and budgeting system
PRA. *See* People's Revolutionary
    Army
Prayer Book plans (Panama), 190, 192
Precarious values, 7
Price, Mel, 108
Prisoners of war: in Operation Desert
    Storm, 236, 242–43, 245, 249;
    SEALs and, 28
Program objective memorandums
    (POMs), 207–08, 210, 215, 220, 225
Project 9. *See* Air commandos,
    groups
Psychological operations (PSYOP).
    See Army, U.S., divisions/groups

Quadrant Plan, 29, 31
Quinn, Thomas, 213–14

Radio Free Grenada, 98
Radio la Voz de la Libertad, 199
Rangers. *See* Army, U.S., divisions/
    groups
Reagan, Ronald, 79, 111, 163, 189,
    190. *See also* Cold war; Grenada
REDCOM. *See* U.S. Readiness
    Command
Refugees, 245–46, 247–48, 249
Rheault, Robert, 20
Rice, Douglas, 85
Rodriguez, Francisco, 193
Rogers, Bernard, 64, 74
Ropka, Lawrence, Jr., 140, 177, 178,
    179–80
Rwanda, 254

Rylander, Lynn: *AFJ* articles, 128; as
    advocate for special operations,
    80, 81, 83, 84, 85, 87, 108, 110,
    164; death of, 269; Initiative *17*,
    89, 112–13; resignation of Koch,
    Noel, 132; SOF reorganization,
    121, 123, 134, 139–41, 175, 177,
    267

SAC. *See* Strategic Air Command
St. George's Medical School. *See*
    Grenada
SAS. *See* Special Air Services
Saudi Arabia, 240, 244, 269. *See also*
    Operation Desert Shield and
    Desert Storm
Schemmer, Benjamin F., 116, 117–18,
    120, 127, 268. *See also Armed
    Forces Journal International*
Scholtes, Richard, 89, 95–96, 97, 104,
    105, 143
Schwarzkopf, Norman: Operation
    Desert Shield and Desert Storm,
    230, 234, 237, 244, 255; use of
    SOF, 8, 230–32
Scoon, Paul, 95, 97, 99–100
Scouts and Raiders, 4, 20–21
Secure Enroute Communications
    System (SECOMPS), 194
SEALs (Sea, Air, and Land): character-
    istics of, 46–47; conventional
    Navy and, 65–67, 158, 265;
    creation and organization, 25–26;
    forerunners of, 20–25; in Grenada,
    91, 94, 95–97, 98; in Haiti, 254–55;
    mission of, 160; in Operation
    Desert Shield and Desert Storm,
    229, 234, 236–37, 238, 239; in
    Panama, 187, 195–96; post-
    Vietnam, 28, 35–39, 65–67;
    secrecy and, 24; in Somalia, 251,
    252; support of, 27–28, 68, 116;
    training of, 22, 26, 27, 37, 41, 48–
    52, 65–66, 67, 261; USSOCOM

SEALs *(continued)*
and, 155, 158–62, 174; in Vietnam, 26–28. *See also* Officers; Underwater Demolition Teams
SEAL Teams: No. *1*, 27, 37–38; No. *2*, 27, 192; No. *3*, 115; No. *4*, 91, 95–96, 101, 192; No. *6*, 96, 97, 98, 106; Special Boat Unit *26*, 187, 192
Secord, Richard, 82, 121
Seiffert, Ed, 71
Selznick, Philip, 7, 44–45, 263
SF. *See* Special Forces
SFGs. *See* Special Forces Groups
SFOD-D. *See* Special Forces Operational Detachment-Delta
SGCI. *See* Special Group, Counterinsurgency
Shultz, George, 184
Shultz, Richard, 144
Simon, Herbert, 44
Simons, Arthur "Bull," 16, 116–17
Simpson, Charles, 12, 57
Sinclair, Alfred, 233
Singlaub, John, 16
Smith, Raymond, 36, 47, 50, 162, 227, 229–30, 231, 263
SOE. *See* Special Operations Executive
SOG. *See* Military Assistance Command Vietnam/Studies and Observations Group
Somalia, 187, 251, 263, 269
Son Tay Raid (Vietnam), 16–17, 69, 116–17
SOPAG. *See* Special Operations Policy Advisory Group
Soviet Union, 228. *See also* Cold war
SOW (Special Operations Wing). *See* Air Force groups
Spadafora, Hugo, 189
Special Air Services (SAS; Britain), 62, 63
Special Forces (SF): in Central America, 265–66; in Grenada, 94, 101; group structure, 11, 14–15; increases in, 115; mission of, 11, 15; in Operation Desert Shield and Desert Storm, 232–33, 234, 247–48, 254; in Panama, 194–95, 201–202; postwar reductions, 4–5, 13, 20, 39–41; in Somalia, 253, 254; support of, 68, 116, 128–129; training, 40–41, 51, 52–55; Vietnam War and, 14–20, 35, 39, 42; volunteers for, 41. *See also* Office of Strategic Services; Officers
Special Forces Groups (SFGs): A-Detachments/Teams, 11, 14–15, 40–41, 234–35, 259–60; 1st, 13, 40, 75; 3rd, 40; 5th, 14, 20, 40–41, 64, 80, 229, 234; 6th, 40, 61; 7th, 14, 40–41, 65, 78, 192, 194–95, 201; 8th, 40; 10th, 11–13, 40–41, 75, 110; 14th Operational Detachment, 13; 77th, 13, 151
Special Forces Operational Detachment-Delta: air force and, 68; criticism of, 117; establishment of, 63–65; in Grenada, 95, 96, 97, 100; Iranian hostage rescue, 1, 69; in Panama, 192, 199–200; support of, 68; terrorism, 266; training and style of operations, 63–64
Special Group, Counterinsurgency (SGCI), 13–14
Special Operations Command (SOCOM). *See* Army, U.S., divisions/groups
Special Operations Executive (SOE; Britain), 9
Special operations forces (SOF): in the *1970s*, 68, 265, 266; in the *1980s*, 89–90, 110, 114–15, 117, 187, 188, 201–202, 250, 257, 266, 268; in the *1990s*, 250–51, 254–63; aircraft for, 87–88, 115–16; Congress and, 86–89, 107–12, 127–47, 266–67; culture of, 44, 45–46, 57–

59, 147, 165–68, 169, 261–63, 264–65; development of, 2–5, 7, 8, 11–13, 34, 259, 266; as an elite force, 45–48, 63, 73, 78, 121–22, 259, 263, 265; forces included in, 154–62; Grenada landing and, 91–106; Iranian hostage rescue and, 69–73; "Liberation Front" and "Mafia," 57–58, 74, 87, 267; as a military service, 122–24, 261–63; in Operation Desert Storm and Desert Shield, 228–29, 232–44; post-Vietnam, 4, 11, 34–35, 58, 60; public pressures for reform, 116–27; as a precarious value, 7, 8, 259, 263–70; reform of, 79–90, 105–06, 107–12, 127–47, 267; resource management, 203–26; in Somalia, 253; style of operation, 6, 7, 10–11, 46, 146; support and funding for, 68, 79, 87, 90, 111, 127, 130, 131–32, 139, 143, 145, 146, 154, 204; training, 4, 46, 47, 63, 72–73, 156, 168, 264. See also Air commandos; Conventional military; Initiative 17; SEALs; Special Forces; Vietnam; individual military services

Special Operations Policy Advisory Group (SOPAG), 73, 82, 86, 176–77, 180, 184

Special Operations Review Group. See Holloway Commission

Special Operations Wing (SOW). See Air Force groups

Special Planning Directorate, 81

Special Services Force, 1st (U.S.-Canada), 4, 10–11

Special Tactics Group (STG; U.S. Air Force), 55

Special Warfare Center (U.S. Army), 20

Special warfare. See Navy, U.S.

SPECWAR. See Navy. U.S.

STG. See Special Tactics Group

Stilwell, Richard, 156, 158

Stiner, Carl: Operation Desert Shield and Desert Storm, 231; Operation Just Cause, 188, 191, 192, 200; special operations forces and, 231, 224–25; USSOCOM and, 72, 256, 269

Strategic Air Command (SAC), 78

Strategic Services Command (STRATSERCOM), 73–74, 85, 136

STRATSERCOM. See Strategic Services Command

Sutherland, Ian, 6

Tactical Air Command (TAC), 76, 77, 78

Tactical Satellite Communications (TACSAT), 194

Taft, William: Initiative 17, 114, 128, 131; resource and budget management, 212, 220–21; SOF reorganization, 150, 178; USSOCOM, 158, 164–65

Taylor, Maxwell, 14

Taylor, Wesley, 102, 103

Terrorism: Beckwith, Charlie and, 63–64; Cohen, William and, 134–35; Delta force and, 266; hijacked Lufthansa in Somalia, 64; Koch, Noel and, 133; Meyer, Edward Charles and, 61–63, 73–75; U.S. national security and, 62–63. See also Low-intensity conflict; Special Forces Operational Detachment-Delta

Thayer, Paul, 83, 108

Thurman, Maxwell, 191, 192–93, 200

Thurmond, Strom, 109

Tixier, Edward L., 176

Torrijos, Omar, 189

Tower, John, 182, 221–22

Training and Doctrine Command (TRADOC; U.S. Army), 62, 63, 64

Trask, Thomas, 239
Trost, Carlisle, 161–62
Turner, Richmond Kelly, 23

Underwater Demolition Teams
(UDTs): establishment of, 20–21;
need for, 58, 65; post-Vietnam, 36–
37, 39; SEALs and, 27–28, 67–68;
Vietnam, 27–28; World War II and,
20–21, 23–25, 264. *See also* SEALs
United Nations, 229, 251, 252, 253.
See also Operation Desert Shield
and Desert Storm; Operation
Restore Hope
USAAF. *See* Air Force, U.S. Army
USAFSOF. *See* Air Force Special
Operations Force
U.S. Naval Combat Demolition Train-
ing and Experimental Base, 23
U.S. Readiness Command
(REDCOM), 85, 151–54, 163, 168–
69, 174–75 *See also* U.S. Special
Operations Command
USS *Caron*, 99
USS *Clifton Sprague*, 96, 97
USS *Curtis*, 236
USS *Fort Snelling*, 102
USS *Grayback*, 28
USS *Guam*, 94, 99
USS *Leftwich*, 236
USS *Maddox*, 27
USS *Nimitz*, 70, 71
U.S. Special Operations Command
(USSOCOM): activation and
bureaucracy, 162–69, 170–87, 255,
257, 261–62; commander in chief,
218, 219–20, 222–23, 268, 269;
Congress and, 3, 172–73; Cox,
Hugh and, 75; forces included in,
154–62; Iranian hostage rescue
and, 72; legislation, 3, 144–47,
268; location and size, 151–54,
164, 174–75, 177–78, 180, 230;
mission and taskings, 165–66,

184–85, 215, 216–18, 226, 255–61,
262–63; Operation Desert Shield
and Desert Storm, 231; Panama,
190; OASD (SOLIC), 183–84, 218;
REDCOM and, 151–54, 163, 164,
168–69, 174–75; resource and
budget management, 203–06, 207,
208–26, 256, 268; SOF reorganization and, 109, 149–50, 260–61;
Somalia, 253–54; Special Operations Research, Development, and
Acquisition Center, 218; Stiner,
Carl and, 224–25. *See also*
Department of Defense; Special
operations forces
USS *Perch*, 28
USS *Tunny*, 28
USS *Turner Joy*, 27

Van Wagner, R.D., 29
Vaught, James, 2, 69, 71
Vessey, John, 85, 94, 95
Vietnam: Golf of Tonkin incident, 27;
postwar era, 33–43; special
operations forces and, 4–5, 11, 14,
17–20, 26–28, 168
Vogt, 83
Voice of the Gulf, 241
Volckmann, Russ, 11
Vuono, Carl, 137, 191

Waller, Douglas, 230
Warner, John, 144, 222
Warner, Volney, 64
Washingtonian magazine, 199, 200
Washington Post, 172, 176
Wasinger, Edwin, 164
Webster, William, 184
Weinberger, Caspar: Initiative *17*, 89,
128; JSOA and, 111; SOF reorgani-
zation, 77, 81, 82, 130, 137–38;
SOLIC office, 176, 177; SOPAG
and, 86; USSOCOM, 156, 159–62.
See also Department of Defense

Welch, Larry, 76
Whitehouse, Charles, 181, 214, 217, 218–20, 221–22, 269
Wickham, John, 111, 138, 153
Wilson, James Q., 45, 165–66
Wilson, Samuel: conventional military and SOF, 6, 43; Koch, Noel, 134; ASD (SOLIC), 179, 180; resource and budget management, 145; SOF reorganization, 60–61, 72, 82, 153, 266; USSOCOM, 168
Wingate, Orde C., 29, 30, 31, 32
Woerner, Frederick, 189–90, 191, 200
Wolfowitz, Paul, 187

World War II: air commandos, 4, 28, 29, 30, 31–32; Air Force, 28–31; OSS, 4, 7, 8–10, 24–25, 264; operations, 21, 31; special operations forces, 4, 7, 20–25, 28–32; UDTs, 20–21, 23–25, 264
Worthington, George, 66

Yarborough, William P., 14
Yeaw, Ron, 60, 67
Yosich, George, 12
Yugoslavia, 251

Zumwalt, Elmo, 39

CPSIA information can be obtained at www.ICGtesting.com
Printed in the USA
BVOW07s0019300913

332345BV00002B/3/A